THE
STRATEGY OF
VICTORY
1914-1918

'I would rather Bury you than see you in a red coat . . .'

Ann Robertson to her son, Will: 1877

Field-Marshal Sir William Robertson, Bart.

THE
STRATEGY OF
VICTORY
1914-1918

*The Life and Times of
the Master Strategist of World War I:
Field-Marshal Sir William Robertson*

BY VICTOR BONHAM-CARTER

HOLT, RINEHART AND WINSTON

NEW YORK · CHICAGO · SAN FRANCISCO

To

Derek Boyd

Contents

Illustrations

Illustrations in the Text

Preface

IT would not have been possible to write this book without the generous and expert assistance of others. I wish in particular to record my gratitude to the following:

Lord Robertson of Oakridge, son of the Field-Marshal, who loaned me his father's papers and talked to me freely about his father's life, character, and career. At no time, however, have I felt under any irksome restriction as to the use of this material or the portrayal of the man I was writing about. Lord Robertson himself—more widely known as General Sir Brian Robertson —has of course had a notable career in the Army, and so I was able to profit by his professional advice on a number of purely military problems as well. I am also grateful to him and to the respective publishers for permission to quote liberally from his father's two books—*From Private to Field-Marshal* (Constable, 1921) and *Soldiers and Statesmen, 1914–1918* (Cassell, 1926).

Earl Haig and Mr Robert Blake, the Haig Trustees, for allowing me full access to the Haig Papers, and to reproduce extracts from letters, diary entries, and other original material. I am also obliged to Mr Blake for historical advice, and to him and the publisher for allowing me to make numerous quotations from his book—*The Private Papers of Douglas Haig, 1914–1919* (Eyre & Spottiswoode, 1952).

Brigadier Sir Edward Beddington for allowing me to read and quote from his Unpublished Memoir, and to draw upon his first-hand reminiscences of the Field-Marshal.

Mrs Sandison for allowing me to read and quote from the private papers of her father, the late Brigadier-General Sir James E. Edmonds, Official Military Historian.

Captain Alastair Murray, RM, for allowing me to read and quote from the private papers of his grandfather, the late General Sir Archibald Murray.

I am also grateful for the gracious permission of Her Majesty the Queen in publishing extracts from certain letters written by Lord Wigram, when (as Major Clive Wigram) he was equerry and assistant private secretary to her grandfather, the late King George V.

I wish also to thank the following: Professor J. R. M. Butler, Mrs Cooper, Colonel Lord Malise Graham, Lt-Col. W. R. V. Isaac, Major-General Sir John Kennedy, Miss Nancy Maurice, Councillor Hugh Peck, Mr John Terraine, Mr W. E. Vickers, Miss Coombs of the Library of the Imperial War Museum, Mr William Park of the National Library of Scotland, Lt-Col. F. W. Young of the Library of the Staff College, and particularly Mr D. W. King of the Library of the War Office, without whose constant help and profound scholarship I would have been quite unable to complete my task.

Quotations taken from books and all other printed sources are duly acknowledged in the Notes.

As to illustrations, I wish to thank the following:

Lord Robertson for Plates 1–12, 14, 16–19, 21, 22.

Earl Kitchener for the letter on pages 140–1.

Mr John Connell, William Collins & Co. Ltd, and the Commandant of the Staff College for the essay extract and comments on pages 334–7.

The *Daily Telegraph* and the British Museum Newspaper Library for the letter on page 367.

The Imperial War Museum for Plate 15.

The *Radio Times Hulton Picture Library* for Plates 13, 20, 23.

VICTOR BONHAM-CARTER
East Anstey, North Devon

September 1962

Introduction

1914–18 was such a holocaust that it is hard even now to avoid all emotional judgments. So strong is the sense of horror that the war is still regarded not only as a ghastly experience—which it was—but as one which could largely have been avoided, had the British generals been less stupid. The French generals are blamed far less, the Germans—who lost the war—hardly at all.

This is not history, but humbug.

Part of the difficulty arises, I suggest, from assuming that you should arrive at a final judgment on *all* aspects of the war. But that is not possible; it is not even possible about more distant convulsions in history. Too little may still be known about an event or its causes, or the effects of it may be too speculative for positive assessment. Certainly no single historian can give the whole story. All he can do is to tell the tale as truthfully as the evidence will allow, and try to throw new light on controversial points. He must leave his theories to the judgment of the reader. This is the rule I have tried to follow in this book about Sir William Robertson—or Wully, as he was generally and affectionately known.

As one of the principals, Wully incurred much of the odium poured on those who directed the war from the British side: mainly because, with Haig, he was chief proponent of the Western school of strategy. In short, he believed in winning the war in France and nowhere else. In my view he was right. With the possible exception of Gallipoli, a great imaginative conception with real strategic possibilities thrown away by a lack of planning, all the other fronts outside France involving the Western Allies were peripheral, geographically and strategically: Palestine, Mesopotamia, the Balkans, Italy. Considerations of terrain and distance put them out of court as decisive fronts, while the Germans could always reinforce them with comparative ease. It was the old controversy between interior and exterior lines, as Wully never tired of telling Lloyd George, and as Lloyd George soon sickened of hearing.

But there was another important point. Strategically correct or not, the British could not avoid exerting their main effort in

France, since from the very start of the war the British Expeditionary Force was subservient to French demands. On land the French bore the brunt for the first two years, incurring fearful casualties without loosening the German hold upon occupied territory, and then looked to the British to play a comparable part. By that time the BEF had expanded to over fifty divisions, a great national army, mostly volunteers. Even so it was insufficiently trained, and hardly had enough ammunition to sustain a big offensive, yet it had to fight. Thus it was launched on the Somme in 1916 before it was really ready, and on a front chosen by Joffre, a choice not prompted by any strategic advantage. Likewise, in the spring of 1917, it was compelled to fight Arras and ancillary battles, not because they offered decisive opportunities in their own right, but to support the abortive French effort on the Aisne. Hitherto, therefore, the BEF—now a factor of real force in land operations—had been committed to campaigns forced upon it by circumstances or political necessity.

Then came Passchendaele or, more properly, Third Ypres—the first major British offensive in the west, conceived and controlled by a British commander (Haig), with the French in a secondary role. The origin, development, and dénouement of Third Ypres is still shrouded in controversy, and certainly no final judgment can be pronounced as yet—if ever. But, all else apart, I hold the view that in the summer of 1917 the British had to launch an offensive *somewhere* in Europe. By then, it will be remembered, Russia was virtually out of the war, and it was only a question of time before Germany regained the initiative in the west by transferring large numbers of divisions across from the eastern front. The only question was whether the British should attack in Flanders, as Haig wanted, or in Italy, as Lloyd George wanted. Haig supported his case with contradictory arguments about the state of the French and German Armies, but advanced cogent reasons for attacking in Flanders, where a break-through would cut vital communications and endanger the entire German flank. Wully had his doubts, but he supported Haig in the end because he regarded the alternative in Italy as a blind alley and a trap (as was proved by Caporetto), and because he deeply distrusted Lloyd George's amateur strategy. Ultimately Third Ypres went off at the end of July, made some progress at high cost, and then stuck in the autumn mud. It is generally considered the most terrible of all the battles in the west, though casualties were less than on the Somme. In my view, it is impossible to come to any hard and fast conclusion about its effect upon the course of the war, although its impact upon the attitude of the British Government to strategy was quite definite, and it was indirectly one of the reasons why Wully left the War Office in February 1918.

By that time he had been Chief of the Imperial General Staff for just over two years, since December 1915: responsible not only for the shape, efficiency, and deployment of the Army, but chief military adviser to the Government and right-hand man of the Secretary of State for War. In those two years he had achieved a position of unique authority for the CIGS, welded the General Staff into a homogeneous body of highly trained officers at work under the conditions of war, and gained for it proper recognition as the instrument of direction of a great Army. As to himself—everyone acknowledged his professional excellence, organising ability, and massive character. He had a phenomenal memory and eye for significant detail. Supremely practical, he went to the heart of every matter, and made himself felt by his thoroughness, knowledge, and will-power. Yet the sheer force of the man was permeated with humour and humanity. As one of his subordinates said: 'We were all frightened to death of him, yet admired him greatly and were very fond of him.' Undoubtedly Wully was a great soldier and a great man. Of course he had his shortcomings. He was short of—but not devoid of—imagination; indeed on occasions (such as the retreat from Mons) he had shown truly marvellous prescience and resource. He was cautious, but not exaggeratedly so; here again his strictly practical approach to a problem was often mistaken for a lack of broad understanding, whereas he had seen only too well that a bold proposition would founder because it had not been thought out in detail. 'I've 'eard different', was his crushing and conclusive comment on one occasion. He never really liked foreigners, and he found most of his civilian colleagues a trial. If they were ignorant of military matters, as they usually were, he had no patience with them. He was thus rigid in debate, speaking out bluntly and straight as he always did to everyone; but he wrote excellent appreciations, full of wisdom and sensibility, which have stood up well to the scrutiny of posterity.

As a strategist he has been accused of narrowness. Certainly his strategic advice never varied. Namely that, not only was France the nearest and logistically the most favourable front, but also strategically correct for the greatest concentration of force. In his view the formula was perfectly simple. If we were beaten in France, we lost the war. If we beat the Germans in France, we won the war. All other fronts were determined by what happened there. If, as I believe, he was right, why did the war last so long and why was it so costly? Much of the answer may be found in the difference between strategy and tactics.

Briefly, by early 1915, thanks to the machine gun, trench systems, and barbed wire, defence had mastered offence and continued to do so for the next three years or so. The process was only reversed in 1918 after protracted experiments and bitter experience in warfare, leading to the development of the tank, the aeroplane, and new artillery techniques. Their application was largely a matter of tactics, the business of commanders in the field; and it was application (rather than organisation or production) which proved such a difficulty. Of course many mistakes were made in the field, at all levels of command, and there was a ghastly toll of lives; but that the problems took so long to solve does not necessarily call for sweeping criticism of British generalship. It is true that military thought and training had stagnated in England until the late 19th century, when the old Duke of Cambridge was Commander-in-Chief, but it had been jolted into life even before the Boer War, and after that event vastly stimulated by a succession of reforms and able reformers and thinkers, both officers and civilians. The problems of trench warfare were both complex and costly and confronted both sides. But, just as doctors may be nonplussed for a time by some new epidemic, so too were the generals: that they were not able to find an immediate solution does not mean that they were merely stupid and callous.

Be that as it may, Wully did not conceive it as part of his job as CIGS to advise Haig or any other field commander on how to conduct their battles. Strategy and the general organisation of men and resources were his business, tactics and the handling of a specific front were theirs. 'Stick to your own piece of carpet, boy', he used to say to his staff officers. That was orthodox and correct, and no one would quarrel with it as a general rule of conduct. But, like all general rules, there are times when it is better relaxed. It should never, for example, exclude the right of the strategist to discuss, or disagree over, tactics with the tactician, or vice versa. As it was, an over-strict adherence to the rule landed Wully in difficulties over Third Ypres. Although he had aired his doubts to Haig beforehand, he suppressed them later when the battle was going on longer and proving far more expensive than he had anticipated. True, Haig was a reserved man, possessed of great moral and military authority as commander of the BEF, and he was convinced by the rightness of his own plans to defeat the German Army in the west; yet Wully as good as admitted afterwards that he wished he had overcome his professional and personal reluctance to question Haig's methods, and insist that the battle be closed down far earlier than it was.

The demarcation between strategy and tactics had a bearing, likewise, upon Wully's relations with the Prime Minister and the War Cabinet. The apparent inability of tactics to fulfil strategic planning induced Lloyd George to doubt the strategy itself. Sickened by the casualty lists, he became convinced that the Western policy was at fault, and sought thereafter to switch the main effort on land to other fronts—the Balkans, Italy, and Palestine—but without success. Frustrated and unable to unseat Wully, he then proceeded to mount all kinds of pressures against him, and eventually succeeded in by-passing him by sending Henry Wilson as Permanent Military Representative to the Supreme War Council at Versailles at the end of 1917, a move that finally brought about Wully's dismissal early in 1918.

Such a situation need never have arisen, had there been adequate machinery for the direction of the war. Once the Committee of Imperial Defence had been allowed to lapse, there was no inter-departmental or inter-Service organisation for the formulation of strategy, and no inter-Allied planning staff until late in 1917. And so Ministers had to choose between the experts as best they might, or play at strategy themselves—

a game which many of them were only too pleased to play, at any rate (as Wully remarked wryly) as regards *military* operations. Anyone could lay down the law about that! A remark which reflected the wide gulf between civilians and soldiers, 'frocks' and 'brass-hats', and owed its origin perhaps to the reaction against the Army after the Civil War in the 17th century. It was only after the First World War—in the peace years and during the Second World War—that the solution was evolved: a joint planning organisation, integrated with a hierarchy of committees, where representatives of the Services, departments and the Government could arrive at agreed decisions based on comprehensive information.

However, without the experience and errors of the First World War, many of the successes of the Second would never have come about. It is therefore only right to gear an account such as this to the progress and limitations of the period. Nothing is easier, sitting in comfort with all the facts at your command, than to write with hindsight: to pick on a man's mistakes, isolate his words and actions, and make him look a fool. Whereas, in truth, beset with anxiety and imperfectly aware of what was going on, he was labouring heroically to master a novel and often a superhuman situation.

And so, in order fully to appreciate the stature and achievement of Wully Robertson, it is essential to read his life within the context of the times, and to look through his eyes: to know that he was of humble origin, educated only at a village school, began life as a servant, and rose from private soldier to field-marshal—a record never equalled in the British Army before or since: that he did it by determination, ability, and force of character; and that in the doing of it he never lost his simplicity, his homely ways and speech, and his strong faith. Those were the foundations of the man. It was the irony of his life that, though a natural leader—a true soldier's general—he never had a command; but spent most of his service as a staff officer, organiser, and planner. Such is the shape and purpose of this book: not a strict biography with every detail preserved and every anecdote reproduced, either of his private life or public career: but the story of a remarkable man told against the background of the British Army which he served, loved, and helped to create.

Postscript

Since writing this Introduction, there has occurred the publication of John Terraine's fine study of Haig in *Douglas Haig, The Educated Soldier* (Hutchinson). Inevitably, certain passages have caused controversy, particularly with regard to casualties in the First World War. So far as this book is concerned, the actual total of casualties is not of prime importance, although there is no dispute about the vast number of men demanded and used up by the Army, especially by the British Expeditionary Force in France. Manpower, however, was of overriding importance to Wully Robertson. Quite apart from the horror of it all, it proved, perhaps, the severest and the most relentless of all his problems. Moreover, he had to wrestle with it in the most invidious position: standing, as he did, between Haig (and the commanders on the other fronts) who called continually for men, and the Prime Minister of the day who, for various reasons, was unwilling to release them. First, it was Asquith who was reluctant on principle to bring in conscription or apply it wholeheartedly. Then it was Lloyd George, who rightly diverted many men to other employments as the war developed and new demands arose from agriculture, industry, and the expansion of the Services themselves, but who also at a critical time in early 1918 withheld men from France, as a means of controlling strategy and putting a brake upon the Westerners. With regard to casualty statistics, I cannot see how those published in the Official History in their revised form can be effectively contradicted, and I subscribe to the general sense of Mr Terraine's remarks on pages 235–6 of his book.

V. B-C.

Summer, 1963

Lincolnshire Lad

IN THE DAYS when grandmothers wore lace caps, and the parlour maid refused to walk out with Tommy Atkins, young William Robertson had no thoughts of the Army. No one in the 1860s, and not many in the 1870s, took the Queen's Shilling unless he had to. At William's home at Welbourn, prospects were better than that. Country boys went on the farm or the railway, or tramped a dozen miles to Lincoln to find work in a factory. Some, like William, of a serious and disciplined disposition, attracted the attention of the gentry and disappeared into domestic service. It was a natural progression.

William, it seemed, was destined to be a servant. Born on January 29th 1860, his upbringing was exemplary. His mother, Ann Dexter Beet, was a woman of strong character and passionate religious principle, who influenced him deeply. He gave her complete devotion. For him, as for her, religion was a reality which sustained him all through his life, while the Church of England was as necessary to the British Empire as the Queen herself. His father, Thomas Charles Robertson, whom he also loved and respected, made perhaps less impression. From him he inherited that natural classless dignity of distant Scottish forebears, who had migrated south a century or two before. But there was nothing noticeably Scottish about William, for the Robertsons had long since been absorbed into the vein and substance of Lincolnshire. Small farmers and tradesmen, most of them, modest people but well founded. Thomas Robertson was no exception, as village tailor and postmaster, with an unpretentious shop opposite the green. Every morning, after the arrival of the mail cart, he would sort the letters and make the rounds in company with his big collie. The dog suited him somehow, for Thomas was well built and well turned out, and always wore a flower in his buttonhole. Clearly a man of standing, with a touch of *panache*.

Welbourn lies in a strip of limestone country, west of the

fenland, just off the road from Leadenham to Lincoln: a long languid village, stocked with mellow buildings, till lately more stone than brick, and liberally sandwiched with white chestnuts and other flowering trees. The church, St Chad's, is large and unremarkable, with a Victorianised chancel and a 14th-century crocketted spire sticking up at the end of the street. Nowadays it seems rather large for the congregation. Not so when the incumbent was the Reverend Frederick Leslie-Melville, Canon of Lincoln, who lived in the plain rectory nearby. Leslie-Melville was a stalwart Anglican, who habitually referred to the Dissenting chapel as 'that hole in the wall', and he virtually owned the village school. This was a church foundation, and remained so long after the Act of 1870, which introduced compulsory education to all children between the ages of 5 and 13, and set up Board schools where denominational schools were either absent or inadequate. All the Robertsons were taught there—William and his two elder brothers and four sisters, seven in all. They called him Will in those days.

Will liked school. He was an avid reader, showed much interest in geography and maps, and had a certain aptitude for drawing. He wrote well too, and the school treasured one of his early essays for many years. In fact he was one of Miss Wilson's best pupils, and ended up as a monitor, earning 6d. a week for teaching some of the younger ones. Although a stickler for social conventions, Leslie-Melville was a man of discernment, who liked to encourage a promising boy. He soon picked out Will, and had him up to the rectory for extra lessons with his daughters, then learning French from a *Mademoiselle*. After leaving school Will went to the rectory as garden boy and so managed to continue his education.

He did not stay long, however, either with the Canon or his next employer, Parson King, the eccentric squarson of Ashby-de-la-Launde. The story goes that when ordered to carry the housekeeper's Bible and prayer-book to and from church on Sundays, Will was so irked that he finally ran away. A story only, though not an impossible one. We next hear of him about the year 1875 as a footman in the service of the Cardigan family at Deene Park, Northamptonshire. Deene was, and remains today, one of the great country houses of England, and the Brudenells (who had been created Earls of Cardigan in 1661 by Charles II) were one of the most remarkable of noble families. At Deene, William—a very proper name for a footman —may well have acquired his first liking for the Army.

In 1868, only seven years earlier, had died James Thomas Brudenell, 7th Earl of Cardigan, lately Colonel of the 11th Hussars, Inspector-General of Cavalry, and hero of the Charge of the Light Brigade at the battle of Balaclava in October 1854. Cardigan had had a tempestuous life. In the Army—though undoubtedly brave—he was notorious for his ungovernable temper and tyrannical treatment of his officers. In private life, he was equally known for his impossible arrogance and immoral behaviour. With a handsome face, proud bearing, and elegant figure, he had no difficulty in attracting women, and his mistresses were legion. In 1858 his wife, from whom he had long been estranged, died. Cardigan, then aged 60, was living in London with a Miss Adeline de Horsey, a fashionable lady of beauty and temperament and nearly thirty years his junior; the *affaire* was common gossip. Their marriage therefore caused no surprise, and they spent the last ten years of Cardigan's life at Deene in apparent amity and undoubted splendour.

Deene was already filled with fine paintings, but recently Cardigan had added an extraordinary collection of heroic pictures and statuettes of himself, and many relics of Balaclava. To please his wife he then had built a magnificent ballroom, 70 feet long by 40 feet high, for which Lady Cardigan designed heraldic stained glass windows, representing the family's forebears of royal descent. This room also contained a musicians' gallery, where played a private band composed of local people, who practised twice weekly in the village school. The band kept going until 1876, and was entirely in keeping with the regal state sustained at Deene, even after Cardigan's death. Will Robertson cannot fail to have been impressed, but there were other flamboyancies with which he was more closely concerned.

For example, Lady Cardigan's carriage-and-four was driven by

'. . . two postilions on the near-side horses, dressed in red jackets, white breeches and top boots. Two footmen used to stand on the back of the older carriages. (Though she did not die until 1915, Lady Cardigan was never known to get into a motor car). Her footmen (all six-foot high) wore black tail-coats liberally sprinkled with crested silver buttons, scarlet breeches, white stockings with buckled shoes, and of course had their hair powdered.'[1]

It can thus be hazarded that Will did service as one of these flunkeys, decked and powdered as described; he was just under six foot in height. In 1915, incidentally, he was a Major-General and Chief of Staff to the British Army in France. Lady Cardigan's death must have aroused some curious memories.

All the servants, women as well as men, who could be spared from duty, were expected (if not actually commanded) to attend Sunday morning service at Deene church. They made up a large and imposing congregation, seated by precedence down the nave, with Lady Cardigan and her friends in the family pew in front. As a sincere churchman, Will needed no persuasion to attend. He had a pleasing baritone voice and sang in the choir, and was on good terms with the Reverend Edward Sylvester, curate of Deene 1865–73, and rector 1873–95. It was during the latter's curacy that the church was vulgarly restored in spurious Gothic by G. F. Bodley, and a tomb of imposing dimensions erected in the south aisle. It is no less impressive today, bearing two life-size effigies of Lord and Lady Cardigan, a memorial entirely characteristic of them both.

How long Will Robertson stayed at Deene is not known, or why he left for his last situation with the Vernon family at Hanbury Hall, near Droitwich, in Worcestershire. No doubt it was simply to better himself. Apart from one or two letters home and a few personal recollections left by acquaintances, there is no detailed record either of this new employment, or indeed of any of his four years in domestic service between leaving Welbourn School in 1873 and joining the Army in 1877. Many years later he is said to have remarked gruffly in a reminiscent vein to one of his staff officers: 'Boy—I was a damn bad footman,' and left it at that. But why the Army? It is reasonable to suppose that he had been impressed by the martial atmosphere and mementos of the Cardigans—the Earl had indeed been a cavalry officer of the most exaggerated kind— and that this had prompted Will not only to volunteer, but to choose the cavalry in preference to any other arm. His action horrified his family, who subscribed to the popular view that all soldiers were lewd and licentious. His mother, particularly, was distraught. She wrote:

'My very Dear Boy
   you never could Mean what you put in your Letter on Sunday . . . do you think I could bear to hear My Boy's name with Topham Bracknell and Jackson . . . and what cause have you for such a Low Life . . . you have as Good Home as any one else in our Station . . . you have kind and Loving Sisters . . . you know you are the Great Hope of the Family . . . if you do not like Service you can do something else . . . there are plenty of things Steady Young Men can do when they can write and read as you can . . . [the Army] is a refuge for all Idle people . . . I shall name it to no one for I am ashamed to think of it . . . I would rather Bury you than see you in a red coat. . .'[2]

Will was not to be dissuaded, however. He had made up his mind, and that was that.

'I was seventeen and three-quarters years old when . . . I took the Queen's Shilling from a recruiting sergeant in the city of Worcester on the 13th of November 1877. The minimum age for enlistment was eighteen, but as I was tall for my years the sergeant said that the deficient three months would involve no difficulty, and he promptly wrote me down as eighteen years and two months—so as to be on the safe side. I was detained at Worcester for four days, receiving in the meantime two shillings and a halfpenny per diem for board and lodgings. The recruiting sergeant, a kindly disposed individual, took possession of the whole sum, giving me in return excellent, if homely, accommodation and food at his own house.'[3]

From Worcester Will was posted to G Troop, 16th Lancers, then stationed at Aldershot where, as he wrote home, he was advised to deposit his watch with the sergeant-major, since it was unsafe to leave it lying about. He also said that his Troop commander, Captain Graham, was a kind-hearted man; but that the subaltern, Lieutenant Freddy Blair, was 'somewhat of a terror'. Forty-one years later, in 1918, when the former recruit had become General Sir William Robertson, GOC Eastern Command, lately Chief of the Imperial General Staff, the former lieutenant was his military secretary. If anyone was a terror then, it was not Freddy Blair. But that is anticipating.

The British Army As He Found It

FOR whatever reason young William Robertson joined the Army, the fact remains that in 1877 a trooper's prospects were hardly encouraging. None the less they must have seemed to William far more exciting than a career as a servant. It was true, too, that the recent reforms associated with the name of Edward Cardwell, Secretary of State for War in the Gladstone ministry of 1868–74, promised and did in the end achieve great things, introducing an entirely new system of regimental organisation and recruitment, and opening the way for promotion by merit—even from the ranks. In that and other respects they laid the foundations of the modern British Army, and Cardwell is rightly remembered as one of our few great military reformers. By 1877, however, the new measures had only just begun to take effect, and had made but small impression upon the conditions of barrack life and the atmosphere of military service.

Robertson wrote:

'Regiments were still composed mainly of old soldiers who were, in many cases, addicted to rough behaviour, heavy drinking, and hard swearing. . . They could hardly be blamed for this. Year in and year out they went through the same routine, were treated like machines—of an inferior kind—and having little prospect of finding decent employment on the expiration of their twenty-one years' engagement, they lived only for the present, the single bright spot in their existence being the receipt of a few shillings—perhaps not more than one—on the weekly pay-day.'[1]

What then was the Army really like when he enlisted at Worcester in November 1877?

The short answer is that it still had many of the characteristics of the Army of the Peninsular War and of Waterloo. In 1815 this had been a remarkably large and efficient organisation, the creation, partly of administrators such as the Duke of York when Commander-in-Chief at the Horse Guards, partly of fighting generals such as Sir John Moore and the Duke of

Wellington. Unfortunately Wellington kept such a tight hold upon military affairs, for some thirty-seven years after Waterloo had been won, that the Army became atrophied. Thus the period 1815–52 was a bleak one for soldiers, and the consequences were duly harvested in the blunders and bunglings of the Crimean War 1854–5. For these, however, the Duke cannot be held solely responsible. Successive governments, and behind them the nation at large, were just as guilty; for there was no real desire to face up to realities, or even to admit the necessity for an army at all.

Soon after 1815 the Army was reduced from a peak of nearly 700,000 men to a standing strength of just over 100,000, a tiny force with which to fight petty wars and to garrison an empire scattered over the whole world. It only meant that duty had to be done at the expense of efficiency, and to the extreme detriment of the men who served. Since the Army was virtually without reserves, and since only the Guards were regularly stationed at home, four-fifths of the line battalions spent whole decades abroad without relief.[2] Even when a battalion did return for a spell of home duty, it was posted abroad again all too soon for a further long period of absence. In most foreign stations, moreover, conditions were disgraceful. Cholera and tropical fevers, bad diet and insufficient food, and the habit of drinking cheap spirits out of hunger and sheer boredom, resulted in an appalling mortality. It was common for units to lose 50% of their strength through sickness alone, not to mention desertion and crime.

Nor was home service invariably pleasant. Quite apart from primitive conditions, the Army was frequently called upon to maintain public order, especially in the 1820s and 1830s when there was much social unrest, and before the police forces had been properly organised. It was not therefore popular with the working class. Nor was the middle class much better disposed, owing to the heavy burden of taxation and the growing conviction—as the years of peace passed—that an armed force was an unnecessary luxury. The Navy, it was argued, was quite sufficient to keep any future enemy at bay. The need for troops overseas was but grudgingly accepted. How the units were to be kept up to strength, without drafts and a proper reserve organisation at home, was a subject simply not faced.

Foreign garrisons had at any rate one advantage. So hostile were the public and Parliament that 'out of sight, out of mind' seemed the most prudent policy for the Army. Absence was the key to survival.

But there was another reason for this hostility. In the eyes of democratic Englishmen, nurtured by the Reform Act of 1832 and the new conceptions of *laissez-faire* and personal liberty, the Army was above all a *social* anachronism—a relic of feudalism and aristocratic privilege and graft. For this the system of purchase was largely responsible. An intending officer had to *buy* his commission and, except for vacancies created by casualties in battle, his promotion as well. The rates of purchase were officially fixed, yet competition among officers was so keen that the price of each commissioned rank was invariably exceeded. In the 1850s the regulation price of a captaincy ranged between £1500 and £5000, of a lieutenant-colonelcy between £5000 and £9000. The market or over-regulation price was about twice this amount. The exact figure depended upon the individual bargain and the regiment, the Foot Guards generally commanding the highest price.[3] In addition a private income was considered essential in order to meet the expenses of mess and regimental life. In some units, notably the Guards and the Cavalry, such income had to be substantial. In any event a private income was one of the marks of a gentleman, regarded as the only person fit to become an officer. There were very few exceptions to this rule. The result was that in peace-time promotion from the ranks was a rarity, and the great majority of officers were men of means and favoured birth, who belonged to a closed order of society. Even within this caste, abuses were encouraged by the system of purchase. It was common for the younger sons of the aristocracy not only to buy their way into fashionable regiments, but by means of money to rise rapidly over the heads of older, more experienced, but poorer officers, and indulge in expensive uniforms and entertainments. By careful exchanges and reversions to half-pay, they were able to accelerate the rate of promotion and reduce the time spent on foreign duty, or even avoid it altogether.

A flagrant case of this kind was that of the 7th Earl of Cardigan, whose widow William Robertson served at Deene in the 1870s. Cardigan bought the command of two regiments:

of the 15th Hussars in 1832, from which he was removed two years later; and of the 11th Hussars in 1838. In each case he paid the astonishing sum of £40,000 or thereabouts. As already described, though brave, he made outrageous use of his acquisitions and indulged his talents for tyranny, violence, and personal splendour. He was in fact one of the worst advertisements for the purchase system, although—to be fair—it must be said that many officers were the reverse, not least the Duke of Wellington himself.

Yet, with all this, purchase had a respectable background, and was resolutely defended on moral grounds until its abolition by Royal Warrant in 1871. Its origin is obscure, and may have dated back to the Middle Ages, when officers of the Free Companies of mercenaries enjoyed rights of booty and ransom. However that may be, the system was not officially recognised until after the Restoration, and then—it has been suggested—with a different, more edifying, purpose.[4] In this case the aim was to ensure that officers should be men of substance and respectability, and *not* mercenaries with an interest in loot.

Purchase money was a guarantee of motive and conduct, and was thus bound up with the desire for social stability rather than military proficiency. And although officers were regularly paid by the Government in the ordinary way, scales of pay were not high, while half-pay was regarded as a retaining-fee for a man of means, not as a minimum income upon which he might live when out of military employment.

Obviously high purchase and low pay were bound to invite abuse. For example, when a new regiment was raised, most of the expense was defrayed by the Colonel—usually a local dignitary and landowner—who recruited the men and nominated the officers. In order to recoup himself, the Colonel would invite intending officers to contribute. In other words he sold them their commissions, and they in turn sold to their successors—hence the continuity of the practice and the great difficulty in bringing it to an end; hence too the opportunity for profit. Upon the Colonel also rested both the responsibilities of ordinary welfare and discipline in the regiment, and of clothing and feeding the men through the medium of block grants from the Government. Here was another source of abuse. Since the commanding officer had to make good deficiencies out of his own pocket, he naturally made sure that the margin lay in his favour. In this way it became customary to make a profit on rations and uniforms, as well as on the sale of commissions.

In the 18th century corruption spread all the way down the line, in the Army as in other public institutions.[5] When Sergeant-Major William Cobbett, in his priggish innocence, tried to show up the Quartermaster of the 54th Regiment in 1791, for taking a cut on the men's provisions, he was thwarted by authority, and compelled to flee the country. Such practices did not end until the second half of the 19th century, when public opinion had been so aroused as to push through the necessary reforms—including the abolition of purchase and the payment of £7 million in compensation to serving officers. Even then the social restrictions, placed upon obtaining and holding a commission, died hard; as young William Robertson was soon to find out.

As for the conditions of Army life for the men after 1815, they were not inviting. Even so they were often better than those encountered in civil life, especially by the Irish peasants who provided the majority of the rank and file. Take any young fellow picked up by the recruiting sergeant in a market town. After being well plied with liquor at Government expense, he was slipped the Sovereign's Shilling and enlisted for 21 years.[6] He may or may not have been fully aware of what he was doing, certainly not what he was in for. Motives for enlistment were engagingly set out in a book of the period as follows[7]:

TABLE

Showing the probable proportion to each other of the causes which induce men at present to enter the Army

1 Indigent—embracing labourers and mechanics out of employ, who merely seek for support	80 in 120
2 Indigent—respectable persons induced by misfortune or imprudence	2 in 120
3 Idle—who consider a soldier's life an easy one	16 in 120
4 Bad characters—who fall back upon the army as a last resource	8 in 120
5 Criminals—who seek to escape from the consequence of their offences	1 in 120
6 Perverse sons—who seek to grieve their parents	2 in 120

7	Discontented and restless	8 in 120
8	Ambitious	1 in 120
9	Others	2 in 120

Whatever his motive, henceforward his home was the tent or the barrack-room, and his employment the niceties of drill, discipline, and guard. Barracks had been introduced as recently as 1792, and replaced the billeting of troops in ale-houses, a most unpopular practice with inn-keepers who protested that they were underpaid and that the presence of troops scared away trade. Many of the early barracks were constructed in the shape of a square, designed—it has been said—to stop enemies from getting in and soldiers from getting out. At all events they were austere, prison-like places, which served less to provide shelter in a reasonable manner than to prevent the inmates from becoming soft when the time came for active service.

The barrack-room itself was a long draughty dormitory, with windows high up in the walls, and the floor covered with cots on either side of a central gangway: an improvement upon the time when palliasses had to be laid directly on the boards. Sanitation was primitive. Tubs did duty in the corridors, and fresh water had to be drawn from tanks and wells outside. Separate married quarters were not officially recognised, although some wives were permitted to live in barracks. Senior NCOs were comparatively well off in this matter, but private soldiers were rationed on the basis of one wife per eight cavalrymen or per twelve infantrymen—a curious differentiation. In most barrack-rooms, therefore, would be found one or two sections for married men and their families, perhaps a corner screened off by blankets or canvas sheets, which made for privacy of a sort. In fact it was the children who suffered most, for they were taught to drink and got into other bad habits. Lessons had gone entirely by the board until the Duke of York founded his Royal Military School for soldiers' sons at Chelsea; but even this was a pioneer and lonely effort, a long way ahead of its time. Nevertheless, the presence of women did something to raise the standards of behaviour and ordinary everyday comfort. A wife might cook extras for some of the men, and wash and mend their clothes in return for a pittance stopped from their pay.

Of course food, as always, was one of the chief subjects of interest to the private soldier, and one in which he was worst treated by the authorities. Until 1840 there were only two official meals a day—breakfast at 7.30 am, and dinner at 12.30 pm—after that he was assumed to go for nineteen hours without eating. What happened of course was that he paid for extra food himself, either by going outside the barracks or by buying from visiting tradesmen. Until the 1870s he even had to pay for his official meals, the daily ration being 1 lb of bread and ¾ lb of meat, for which he was charged 6d. All groceries, vegetables, and other essential extras had to be bought on top of this, so that more than half his pay went on food.[8] Nor was that the end of his commitments. There was the weekly washing to pay for, cleaning materials, and the occasional replacement of clothing, once the original free issue had worn out.

Robertson wrote:

'A beneficent regulation . . . laid down that in no case should he [a private soldier] receive less than a penny a day! In my regiment the custom was never to give less than a shilling a week, but even this sum did not go far to supplement the allowance of food, to say nothing of beer and tobacco.'[9]

For cooking, two coppers were issued to each company, one for potatoes, and one for meat,

'which was always beef and always boiled, for there were no means of roasting or baking it. . . Since he lost appetite for the eternal beef-broth and boiled beef, he was naturally hungry and weak in the evening, and took refuge in drink.'[10]

And since liquor was cheap, it was the obvious substitute for both food and amenities; but its effects were disastrous and merely confirmed the bad reputation of the Army. Yet it was the civilians, through Parliament, who held the cure in their hands, but no Government took any initiative in the matter.

Nearly every improvement of the soldier's lot sprang from within the Army itself, thanks mainly to the efforts of regimental officers, who shamed the Government into action. Good conduct badges and pay; libraries and reading-rooms; gardens; savings schemes; cheap suppers and coffee, from which was evolved the regimental canteen, with profits going to the welfare of the men; separate barrack-rooms and even lodging houses for married soldiers and their families; many more regimental schools; and so forth. The barracks, like the hospitals and the medical services, were not really taken in hand until after the Crimea, and then only at the stern insistence of Florence Nightingale. Here the chief improvements included dining-rooms (in place of mobs of soldiers at the cookhouse); washing places and latrines; recreation rooms and grounds; and, perhaps most important of all, the acceptance of the idea that cooks should be taught how to cook and provided with equipment that worked, notably the Soyer stove. This made possible a balanced diet, and so improved the variety and bulk of the three official meals (tea had been introduced in 1840) that much of the soldier's reliance upon liquor was removed.

*   *   *

The Crimean disasters also exploded a whole range of organisational changes, which culminated in the Cardwell reforms of the 1870s. The tragedy was that it needed an unnecessary war, only won at a fearful cost of human life and suffering, in order to set the explosion off. Individual officers had already sounded the alarm in the 1840s, but no one had listened.

It was discovered, first of all, that the British Army was controlled, not by one authority but by seven, all largely independent of each other. They were:

The Secretary of State for War and the Colonies, who was responsible for the total strength of the Army, the selection of senior officers for commands in war-time, and the overall conduct of war. He also allotted garrisons to colonial stations.

The Commander-in-Chief, who exercised command of military forces at home, though not abroad. In the latter case the commanding officer on the spot reported directly to the Secretary of State. The C-in-C was also responsible for the discipline and efficiency of the Infantry and the Cavalry, though not of the Artillery and the Engineers. He had charge of the enlistment of private soldiers, and of the commissioning and promotion of officers. In appointing senior officers to commands, however, he had to refer to the Home Secretary or to the Secretary of State, according to circumstances. He had no control over fortifications, or over arms, equipment or supplies.

The Chancellor of the Exchequer, who controlled at source all finance affecting the Army. He also directed the Commissariat, a department of the Treasury, which issued certain stores, arranged transport, and checked the spending powers of commanding officers at home and abroad.

The Secretary at War, an independent Minister, who was specifically in charge of Army finance and administration, though with certain important exceptions. He also saw to the passing of the Mutiny Act every year.

The Master-General of Ordnance, a military officer of high rank (first instituted in the reign of Richard III), who was in charge of the discipline and efficiency of the Artillery and the Engineers, the issue of war-like equipment and stores, and the construction and armament of fortresses. He was assisted by a Board of Ordnance, part-military, part-civilian, and practically commanded an army of his own.

The Home Secretary, who was responsible for various military matters affecting the United Kingdom, including the Militia and the Yeomanry.

The Board of General Officers, which had been set up by George I in 1714 to do the work of a Headquarters Staff, and of some of the other authorities mentioned. By 1854 this Board was concerned with little else than the clothing of the Infantry and the Cavalry.

There is no need to dwell upon the stupidity of this system, or upon the appalling muddles which inevitably ensued. As Florence Nightingale never tired of pointing out, the dead, dying, and diseased soldiers of the Crimea were ample proof of that. The public outcry which followed her disclosures and the reports of William Howard Russell, correspondent of *The Times*, directly influenced the panic measures of 1855, by which control of the Army was 'consolidated'. This meant that finance and most of the supporting services were transferred to the Secretary of State for War, who, however, gave up the Colonies. The combatant corps all passed to the Commander-in-Chief, who remained virtually independent of the Minister. The two sat in separate offices—the S of S in Pall Mall, the C-in-C at the Horse Guards—and communicated by letter. They were often in opposition, and were known at times to loathe each other. Thus, although the multiplicity of duties was much reduced, the essential fault remained—of divided control, as between civil and military. It ran like a fissure through the entire system and had already done so for some two hundred years—though originally for good constitutional reasons.

When the Army was recruited after the Restoration—in broad terms from Cavalier officers and Roundhead rank and file—great care was taken to prevent it becoming ever again the instrument of dictatorship, as had happened under both Charles I and Oliver Cromwell. Ultimate power must always remain in the hands of Parliament, although the King was allowed to *command* the troops, as part of the privilege known as the Royal Prerogative. Parliament retained control partly through finance, by which all credits for the armed forces had to be agreed by annual legislation (the Mutiny Act); and partly by denying the Army a transport service of its own.

It was shrewdly foreseen that an army without waggons (and so without supplies) could not fight. Thus whenever stores and ordnance were moved about the country, application had first to be made to the civil power. At home this was done by the local impressment of horses and vehicles, as authorised by justices of the peace and the constables; abroad it was done by hiring civil contractors. Although the regulations were modified in detail, this principle held good all through the 18th century, surviving with success the stresses of the Jacobite risings of 1715 and 1745. It was only at the very end of the century, when dynastic dangers had disappeared and the French wars begun, that the principle was broken; and even then not finally. In 1794 was raised a body known as the Royal Waggoners (first entitled a Corps, then a Train), which survived until 1833. The Royal Waggon Train was the Duke of Wellington's main transport service in the Peninsular, although the provision of supplies remained the business of civilian commissaries as before. After 1833 no new units were raised until the hurried formation of the Land Transport Corps in 1855 which, after many years and changes, evolved into the Royal Army Service Corps, responsible for both supplies and transport.

In effect, once the railways had supplanted horse-drawn waggons as the chief means of transport, this form of check upon the Army lost its force. But finance remained, and for years the civil servants concerned regarded themselves as inquisitors whose job it was to question every move by staff officers: hence the frustration, actual and inherent, at every level of the administration.

The War Office Act of 1870, and the others that followed it, known collectively as the Cardwell Reforms, were radical and revolutionary. They changed the whole face of the British Army. Yet it had required fifteen years and much public disquiet to bring them about. It was realised soon after the Crimean War that the 'consolidation' of 1855 had been too hurried to last. The scheme had never been properly thought out, while the habits and suspicions of the past went far too deep to be eradicated all at once. Minor shifts and alterations to the organisation of control started almost immediately, and continued against a background of foreign wars and colonial unrest: the Indian Mutiny of 1857–8, the Chinese War which ended in 1860, the Ambeyla and Abyssinia Expeditions of 1863 and 1867. There was also the American Civil War of 1861–4, although hardly anyone thought it had a bearing upon military thinking in Europe. Much more notice was taken of Napoleon III, whose troops had restored French military reputation in the Crimea, beaten the Austrians in Italy, and seemed at times to be threatening England. The Volunteer movement, one of the predecessors of the Territorial Army, was born in 1859 entirely out of patriotic fervour and fear of France. Even more significant was the rise of Prussia by her victories over Denmark in 1864, Austria in 1866, and finally France in 1870–1. It was this latter campaign, and the concern it aroused, that gave Edward Cardwell the opportunity for which he had been preparing since first appointed to the War Office in 1868.

Cardwell had no real military knowledge, but he was an experienced politician, with a clear legal mind. He was also immensely persistent, and was fortunate to be well advised, among others, by Colonel Garnet Wolseley, an officer of force and vision, and a future Commander-in-Chief. In two years Cardwell launched four main schemes of reform, as follows:

(1) *War Office Act, 1870*

This ended the anomaly of dual control, and gave the Secretary of State for War supreme authority over all military affairs. Under him were placed three principal officers:

The Commander-in-Chief, who controlled all combatant troops, both regular and auxiliary (the Military Department).

The Surveyor-General of Ordnance, who was responsible for most stores and munitions (the Control or Supply Department).

The Financial Secretary, who saw to finance and administration (the Financial Department).

All these officers and departments were transferred to Pall Mall, which had the effect of reducing much unnecessary correspondence. We are told that the number of letters reaching the registry at the War Office fell from 1500 to 900 daily! It was not, however, a universally popular move. The Duke of Cambridge, an explosive character, who held the post of Commander-in-Chief from 1856–95, signified his displeasure by continuing to have the 'Horse Guards' printed on his notepaper, although in fact he was now sitting in Pall Mall.

(2) *Short Service Act, 1870*

This abolished long service of 21 years, and substituted short service of 12 years (6 with the Colours, 6 with the Reserve, later 7 and 5 respectively). The purpose was to create a reserve, on the Prussian model, of trained men who could be called out in time of war, while permitting a small standing army in time of peace. It was also hoped to attract more recruits of a higher quality, better able to profit from the improved conditions of Army life, now promised or coming forward. The results were encouraging. Enlistment rose steeply, the active strength of the Army was increased, and the time spent on foreign service reduced. The numbers posted abroad also fell, owing to the new arrangement whereby self-governing colonies provided their own garrisons, and to the possibilities of quick reinforcement from home through the Suez Canal, opened in 1869. In fact about 90,000 men were on service abroad, including India, and a similar number at home, not counting the reserves who would soon become available under the new system. There were, however, also some 280,000 auxiliaries for home defence, made up of militia, yeomanry and volunteers. Since the Act was designed partly to counter the dangerous international situation of 1870, there was no doubt that Cardwell gained both an immediate as well as a long-term success in introducing it.

(3) *Abolition of Purchase, 1871*

Cardwell was determined to end this vicious practice once and for all, but without alienating the officers who had a vested interest in it, and before the compensation bill had risen too high. He therefore offered to settle at full over-regulation rates, and laid the matter before Parliament. The Bill was passed by the House of Commons but rejected by the House of Lords, on the grounds that purchase was an indispensable part of the social structure of the Army. But Cardwell had his way none the less. He was advised that since purchase had originally been introduced under the Royal Prerogative, all that was needed was a new Royal Warrant to cancel the old one. This was duly done, without of course further reference to Parliament, but in the knowledge that the matter had been properly aired in public. There was no doubt whatever that informed opinion was generally in favour of abolition, civil as well as military, and the £7 million compensation was not grudged. It was clearly a step of the utmost importance. For one thing, it at last made possible the award of commissions and promotions on grounds of merit. For another, it freed the machinery of postings. Officers could now be sent to jobs and units which needed them, whether at home or abroad; and the whole crooked business of buying vacancies or avoiding duty by bribed exchanges or calculated reversions to half-pay was swept away.

Military Forces Localisation Act, 1872

Before this date, all infantry regiments had been distinguished by numerals, according to precedence in line of battle (hence 'line regiments'), and not by county or regional titles. Cardwell introduced the system whereby the country was divided into regimental districts, mostly on a county basis, each with a central depot. Here barracks and parade ground were constructed, and an administrative headquarters set up, where recruits from the surrounding locality could be received and trained. Since the majority of regiments consisted hitherto of single battalions, it was decided henceforward to link them together in pairs and give them territorial titles corresponding to the districts. For example, the 49th and 66th Foot became the 1st and 2nd Battalions of the Berkshire (later Royal) Regiment, with their depot at Brock Barracks, Reading. In general, the practice was for one of the two regular battalions to be stationed abroad, usually in India where there was a possibility of active service, the other at home—the latter providing drafts for the former. In addition one or more militia battalions were brought into the scheme, later renumbered 3 and 4 (as the case might be), and treated in the main as a source of recruits for the regulars.

The building of the depots and the process of reorganisation took several years, but were virtually completed in 1881 when Hugh Childers was Secretary of State for War in Gladstone's second ministry. It was Childers who made sure that Cardwell's conceptions were fully implemented, despite the opposition of the die-hards led by the Duke of Cambridge himself. By then, localisation was clearly proving its worth. It worked in with short service, helped keep the balance of home and foreign service, enabled recruits to be better and quicker trained, and encouraged local loyalties and *esprit de corps*. In this it did much to break down the traditional barriers between soldiers and civilians. The process was taken a step farther when the Volunteers were gathered in and associated with the other battalions.

*　　　*　　　*

Such was the background of events when William Robertson enlisted in the 16th Lancers at Aldershot at the end of 1877. Aldershot, by the way, was not one of the new depots—for the cavalry had not been reorganised on a district basis like the infantry—but simply one of the main camps where cavalry regiments were stationed. Obviously all these high-level reforms were above William's head, but he was soon to find out lower down what drill and tactics were like; and these had hardly been touched since the Crimea. In the 1870s the British Army was still a collection of independent corps, often jealous of one another, and imperfectly trained even in their own branches of the profession. Training was mostly confined to individuals and small units; formations were rarely exercised. The cavalry, for instance, concentrated on troops and squadrons. The weapons used were the lance for the charge, the sabre for cutting and slashing at close quarters, and the muzzle-

loading horse pistol. The carbine was carried only by those few
men in each troop who acted as scouts and skirmishers.

'They had a very sketchy knowledge of the use of this weapon
and, like everyone else, but a hazy idea of either scouting or skir-
mishing. Later carbines were issued to all men, and the horse
pistols were withdrawn; but for some years musketry was universally hated and deemed to be a degradation and a bore. In no case
could it have been of much value, since the annual allowance of
ammunition was fixed at 40 rounds a man, and 30 rounds of these
were fired at distances between 500 and 800 yards.

'Pipe-clay, antiquated and useless forms of drill, blind obedience
to orders, ramrod-like rigidity on parade, and similar time-honoured
practices were the chief qualifications by which a regiment was
judged. Very few officers had any ambition beyond regimental
promotion. "Squadron leader" was a name and not a reality, for
beyond commanding it on parade this officer had no responsibility
of any kind connected with the squadron as such. In all other respects each of the two troops which then formed a squadron was a
separate and independent unit, the troop commander being subordinate only to the regimental commanding officer. Once a week or
so, the latter held his "field-day", when the regiment as a whole
attended parade and spent the greater part of two or three hours in
carrying out a series of complicated drill-book movements. . . For
the remainder of the week training, as understood in those days, was
the preserve of the adjutant, whose parades were attended only by
those officers who were junior to him in rank, and by a comparatively small proportion of the men.'[11]

Occasionally a 'battle' took place, when the cavalry was
given its head—in this instance on ground at the back of the
Staff College, Camberley.

'My squadron was ordered to charge a battalion of the opposing
infantry. Down came our lances to the "engage", the "charge" was
sounded, and off we went at full speed, regardless of everything
except the desire to make a brave show worthy of our regimental
predecessors, who had delivered the immortal charge at Aliwal
some thirty-odd years before. The enemy received us in square,
with fixed bayonets, front rank kneeling and rear rank standing,
the orthodox method of dealing with a cavalry charge. Finding our
opponents too strong—or for some other reason—the order was
given, "troop right-about wheel", and so near were we that, in
wheeling, the outer flank was carried on to the infantry and one of

the horses received a bayonet in his chest. Being too seriously injured to live he was shot, but in other respects we were congratulated on having accomplished a fine performance.'[12]

The infantry was in no more advanced state than the cavalry. Tremendous importance was attached to guard duties and parade ground gyrations—'barrack-square ballets' was the contemptuous name given them by Wolseley—while battle order still depended on the line and the square, as in the 18th century. Field craft and the intelligent use of ground by each individual soldier, part of the pattern of fire and movement, were not fully grasped until the Boer War, when they had to be learned the hard way. Only then was scarlet finally discarded as regulation uniform, though some clung to pipe-clay for the whitening of belts and gloves, and virtually all were committed to the interminable polishing of brass buttons and badges. On the other hand, the infantryman was not ill armed. Since 1860 the Government small arms factory at Enfield had been manufacturing an improved rifle of French pattern, which fired with reasonable accuracy up to 600 yards. The breech-loader arrived with the Snider in 1864, and the Martini-Henry hammerless in 1871. Within a few years this was replaced by the Lee Metford .303, the first magazine rifle, which gave way in 1895 to an improved version, the Lee Enfield—an excellent weapon, of long range and accuracy, which did successful service in the Boer and the two world wars. The machine gun, however, was still at a primitive stage. The Maxim—the first model which harnessed the action of the gun to the loading and ejection mechanism—did not appear until 1883, and was not widely adopted by any army until the early 1900s.

Similarly, the artillery had been making fair progress since the 1860s, with the appearance of breech-loading field pieces, having rifled barrels, and firing cylindrical shells. These gradually ousted the smooth-bore muzzle-loaders, constructed of bronze or cast iron, discharging shell or round shot. In the 1880s steel finally replaced the other metals; and there were comparable improvements in the manufacture of fuses, propellants, shell fillings, and the design of range finders and gun parts.

Much of this technical progress, however, was discounted by the fact that, with a very few exceptions, senior commanders and staffs were incapable of handling large bodies of troops. Hardly any real combined training was ever done. Brigade manœuvres had taken place at Chobham in 1852—the first of their kind for very many years—and were considered an extraordinary venture. 'Sham fight' was the popular description, with all the overtones of unreality that that implied. Then came the Crimea, where divisional control of a kind was exercised, though with very little benefit to the troops, and battles had to be won in spite of the command. Afterwards no peace-time exercises on any scale took place until 1871–2–3, and then only prompted by the emergency of the Franco–Prussian war, as authorised by Act of Parliament. Those held at Cannock Chase in August–September 1873 are of some interest. They lasted a month, and consisted of a division on either side, each of two brigades of infantry, one of cavalry, three battalions of artillery, and various supporting troops. Regulars and auxiliaries both took part, and the event was well reported in the Press. Public relations were good. The *Staffordshire Advertiser* reported that residents seemed pleasantly surprised at the civility met from soldiers of all ranks. Militarily, however, many defects came to light, not least the bad umpiring due to sheer lack of experience on the part of the directing staff. An interesting innovation was a demonstration at which infantry advanced by short rushes under covering fire from the flank—a presage of modern infantry tactics, which does not seem, however, to have been developed.

One of the chief handicaps to formation training was the difficulty of obtaining land. Private landowners were reluctant to lease property for the purpose, and deeply resented coercion. The Government, on the other hand, was not yet prepared to purchase large tracts, as it did on Salisbury Plain later in the century. Meanwhile, combined exercises were confined to the more important camps, at Aldershot, Colchester, and the Curragh. Aldershot had been started in 1855, and it soon became the principal training centre of the British Army. It had several advantages. It was close to London. It was large enough to accommodate a considerable number of troops of all arms—a division, at least—and there was some scope for field exercises in the country round. Above all, it concentrated in one place many of the aids and institutions needed to teach the soldier his profession—schools, workshops, ranges, etc—and to keep him in good heart. By the standards of the day, it fed and housed him well, certainly better than elsewhere. Food was bought in bulk, and the camp had its own butchery, bakery and stores; it even had a school of cookery. And there were other facilities for recreation and civilised living which, not long previously, had been regarded as totally unnecessary, if not actually detrimental to the soldier's morale.

Although life in the cavalry was no picnic, it is clear that young William Robertson was fortunate to have enlisted no earlier than he did—in 1877. The bad old days were only just round the corner.

The Ranker

SINCE Aldershot was the best camp in England, William Robertson was fortunate to be sent there. However, life in the barracks turned out so rough that he actually thought of deserting in the very first week. The fault lay with his companions, many of them old sweats from long service days, with all the habits and hiccups of the pre-Cardwell age. He described them long afterwards with dry humour and understanding, and even with affection.

'These rugged veterans exacted full deference from the recruit, who was assigned the worst bed in the room, given the smallest amount of food and the least palatable, had to "lend" them articles of kit which they had lost or sold, "fag" for them in a variety of ways, and, finally, was expected to share with them at the regimental canteen such cash as he might have in the purchase of beer sold at 3d a quart.

'It so happened that I joined the regiment on pay-day, and accordingly the greater number of my newly-found companions spent the evening at the canteen—then a mere drinking saloon—or at public houses in the town. On return to quarters, if not before, old quarrels were revived or new ones started, and some of them had to be settled by an appeal to fists. One of these encounters took place on and near the bed in which I was vainly trying to sleep, and which was itself of an unattractive and uncomfortable nature. Argument and turmoil continued far into the night, and I began to wonder whether I had made a wise decision after all. I continued to wonder for several nights afterwards, and would lie awake for hours meditating whether to see the matter through, or get out of bed, put on my plain clothes (which I still had), and "desert". Fortunately for me another occupant of the room removed the temptation these clothes afforded, for, having none of his own, he one night appropriated mine, went off in them, and never came back.'[1]

It is not difficult to imagine the scene—the slim young recruit, with his dark hair and keen eyes, putting up silently and solidly with the milling drunks. William was neither a prig nor a prude. He had been born and reared in a humble home, still spoke his native Lincolnshire, while his formal education had begun and ended in a village. He knew all about the seamy side of life. But he had also been accustomed to decency everywhere he had lived, in his own home and in the big houses where he had worked. Above all he was a religious man: not pietistic, but in the straight simple sense that he read the Bible regularly, drew strength and comfort from it, and went to church twice on a Sunday as a matter of course. In short, he was an honest uncomplicated Christian, with strong evangelical convictions and a firm respect for the discipline of the Church. And so he remained all his life. Religion and a deep devotion to his family, especially to his mother—an intensely devout woman, who filled her letters with Biblical quotations—were his two main supports. They helped him develop qualities which began modestly enough as the shy deference and determination of a recruit. Later they turned, less comfortably, into dogged drive and forceful bearing, which made him such a formidable personality when senior staff officer of the British Army; but his humanity was never far away.

His sense of family was constantly expressed in his letters, in plain yet moving language; likewise everyone at Welbourn was eager and anxious to hear from him. At the start, except for one short message, they had to wait nearly six weeks, and then at last a long letter came in January 1878: four pages of detailed news in a fluent and sophisticated handwriting.[2] He had, he wrote, been fearfully busy settling in, and latterly had been sick with a sore throat, hence his silence. But he was well aware of their anxieties and was deeply apologetic, beginning 'Undoubtedly you will think me the most unloving and ungracious of sons . . .' and ending 'please do not think me unloving, hoping you are well, I am your very loving son, W. R. Robertson.'

These were not empty phrases, but straight from the heart. Between them he sandwiched a vivid and accurate description of life as a recruit, packed with facts and figures, such as village people delight in. How he had arrived at Aldershot, and was now living in a barrack-room, 'where there are about 16 of us'. He listed his bedding carefully—iron bedstead, mattress, pillow, 4 blankets and 2 sheets. He remarked later that the blankets were seldom if ever washed, clean sheets issued only once a month, and clean straw for the mattress once every three months. The remaining furniture—apart from racks and hooks for equipment and a shelf for belongings—consisted of four benches and two deal tables, ranged down the central gangway. These served every purpose from eating and drinking to writing letters and cleaning kit; likewise the few bits of crockery; the same mug, for instance, might be used for tea, shaving water and as a receptacle for pipe clay.

The quantity of kit appalled him, and he wrote down almost every item in his letter.

'1 Valise, 1 Stable Bag, 1 Hold All, 1 Knife and Fork, 1 Spoon, 1 Razor, 1 Lather Brush, 3 Baggage Straps, 1 Comb and Brush, 1 Lace Brush, 1 Button Do, 1 Clothes Do, 2 Boots Do, 1 Tin Blacking, 1 Tin of Oil, 1 Tin Brass Paste, 1 Lance, 1 Sword, 1 Carbine, 1 Pistol, 1 Lance Helmet, 2 Caps, 1 Tunic, 1 Jacket, 1 pr Trousers, 1 pr White Ducks (Stables), 1 pr Riding Breeches, 1 pr Jack Boots, 1 pr Wellington Do, 1 pr Highlows Do (Stables), 2 pr Drawers, 1 pr Braces, 3 Flannel Shirts, 3 pr Socks, 2 Towels, 1 piece Soap, 2 pr Spurs, Cartridge Case, Cap Case and numerous belts.'

The uniform was smart but unpractical, not least the round 'pill-box' cap, which he described as 'about the size of a breakfast saucer, and kept in its place immediately above the right ear by a narrow chin-strap worn under the lower lip (never under the chin in the cavalry, except on mounted parades).'[3]

He was kept busy, too.

'Rise at 6.30. Make up Bed, go to Stables, clean your own horse out, saddle it ready for riding school at 7. About 30 or 40 in riding school till 8. Come in, water, feed, and tie up horse, get breakfast, 8.15. Go fetch a bundle of hay from Stores 9. Foot Drill until 10. 10.45 go to Stables. Groom horse and clean things used at riding school etc until 1. 1 Dine. 2.30 Foot Drill until 3.30. 3.45 Tea. 4 School until 5. 5.30 go to Stables until 6.15 grooming horse etc and then done for the day.'

William did recruit training for nine months, a long strenuous period, of which only some three weeks were allotted to the art of firing a rifle. Most of the time was spent on foot drill (including the 'goose-step' and 'drawing swords by numbers'), physical exercises, and riding drill. He described the riding instructor as one 'whose aim was not to give his pupil confidence but as many falls as possible. . . He seldom possessed a decent pair of hands, and his system of training a horse was of the break-down rather than the break-in type.'[4] Otherwise the days were spent in a round of fatigues and stable work and endless polishing.

To William's distress, Sunday was the worst day of all. First, he had to turn out in full dress for church parade, which was of course compulsory. Then there was the general rush before the CO's inspection of stables and quarters. Indeed, there were more chores on that day, supposedly a holiday, than on any other. And why? Simply, he said, because the weekdays were sacred to the officers for hunting and hacking and the social round. This was not just an old sweat's grumble, but the caustic comment of a serious soldier on the way cavalry officers took their duties. The fact was that only a few officers looked after their men or tried to learn their profession. Most of the regimental responsibilities were borne by the NCOs.

Once his recruit training was over, William was introduced to the mysteries and *mystique* of guard. The day guard consisted of a corporal, trumpeter, and five men. Their job was to provide certain orderlies, the sentry at the gate, and the ceremonial reception of important visitors. Ceremony, in fact, was their chief concern, and it served principally to build and maintain morale. The men were paraded before the RSM, who demanded an abnormally high standard of turn-out and a proud bearing. They were on show, as it were, both to the civilians who passed by and to their own comrades, representing the camp, the regiment, and the whole British Army. All this was stimulating and significant. Together with battle honours, regimental customs, and privileges of dress—which every soldier knew by heart—it contributed to that fugitive quality, *esprit de corps*, which was the foundation of discipline and the hallmark of every unit worthy of the name. William delighted in it.

He took no pleasure, however, in that other aspect of guard duty—the custody of prisoners. Men might be confined to the guard-room for the most trivial reasons (such as returning late to camp) or for the most serious (such as desertion). There they had to stay in the most miserable circumstances until brought before the CO. Not unnaturally, many tried to escape, either from the guard-room itself (which was difficult), or while under escort (which often was not). In either case the consequences were extremely serious for the guard, who in their turn suffered arrest and probably imprisonment. William once had the bad luck to lose a prisoner, and he never forgot it. The man broke away near Waterloo Station, and made good his escape with the aid of friends. When William and his party got back to Aldershot they were immediately placed under arrest, awaiting court-martial. With heads shaved, they were pushed into the guard-room—a bare place of boards, without furniture or mattresses, badly lit and ill-ventilated—and had to stay there three weeks. Fortunately they were then released, without coming to trial, by an act of clemency on the part of the GOC. On the next occasion, when a sergeant in Ireland, William took no risks. He handcuffed his eleven prisoners to the four members of the escort, and kept them all harshly bound together most of the way from Belfast to Limerick, a railway journey of twelve hours!

As to operational training, some account has already been given. William related how some of the old soldiers used to talk big about the 'battle' of Cannock Chase several years earlier, otherwise the subject was covered by parade ground exercises, field days, and individual contests with sword and lance, much like a medieval tourney. It was in fact a repetition *ad nauseam* of most of what he had had to do as a recruit. The rifle hardly counted at all. There was very little idea of preparing for war.

*　　*　　*

William spent ten and a half years in the ranks, during which time he gained quick and regular promotion. Lance-Corporal in February 1879 (18 months after joining), Corporal in April 1879, Lance-Sergeant in May 1881, Sergeant in January 1882, and Troop Sergeant-Major in March 1885 at the age of 25. His was by no means a unique record, but it was a very good one. He had got on by hard work, keen intelligence, and dogged determination. He had become proficient in everything a trooper had to do, and he commanded natural respect as a NCO. At the same time he was a highly disciplined soldier. He had committed only three so-called crimes, all in his first two years, the record of which was happily lost when the regimental defaulters' book providentially disappeared; otherwise he had a clean sheet. Unfortunately his further prospects were far less encouraging. Only one higher non-commissioned rank, that of Regimental Sergeant-Major, remained open to him in the ordinary way, and that was a question of waiting for dead man's shoes. True, he might easily have become a Riding-master or a Quartermaster, which carried commissioned rank, but these were specialised dead-end jobs. It was inconceivable that a young man of William's calibre should end up in this way.

The obvious course was to take a commission in order to continue his career, and that is what he would have done today. Indeed, nowadays he would have been given officer training at a far earlier stage. In the 1880s, however, matters were not so simple. Despite the prospects opened up by Cardwell, there were still less than half a dozen promotions a year from the ranks. Some of these, moreover, included the occasional gentle-man ranker, whose progress was deliberately accelerated so that he might regain his social status with the least possible delay.[5] For the true ranker, such as William Robertson, there were formidable difficulties—educational, financial, and social.

Education, perhaps, was the least of the three. The average regimental officer was not a highly educated person, even though he may have been to a public school. Promotion exams were not hard, and generally it was considered bad form to study. As a NCO William had probably acquired more tech-nical knowledge than most junior officers, and he was already a regimental instructor in musketry, signalling, and elementary intelligence duties. Otherwise all that was required was a First Class Certificate of Education, which he duly obtained. It included Reading, Writing to Dictation, Arithmetic, Official Letter and Précis Writing, and one Extra Subject.[6]

Finance was more serious, but at least it was tangible. William told his father that a cavalry officer needed a private income of not less than £300 a year, and this according to other sources was a conservative figure. A Second-Lieutenant was paid just over £100 a year, a Captain less than £200, so that a round figure of £500 a year was about the minimum needed to meet living and mess expenses, and all those regimental extras (such as the upkeep of the band) towards which an officer was expected to subscribe. On these grounds alone William had to refuse the chance of a commission more than once.

Social barriers, however, were the real crux, because they were intangible and spiritually overwhelming. A true ranker could never disguise his origin. He was continually being given away by his accent, tastes, habits, jokes, relations, friends (or lack of them), enforced parsimony, or whatever. Such things were considered embarrassing in the 1880s, if not disgraceful, and in the most snobbish units a ranker officer was practically unknown. A social misfit was got rid of at once, by violence if necessary. For example, a former subaltern in the 18th Hussars left this illuminating record.

'Well, supposing, as was sometimes the case, a new man was gazetted to a regiment, and was found to be a wrong 'un, or even only quite out of touch with the other officers, being short of class, or socially unfit, or for other reasons, of which they only could be best judges, one had no remedy with the authorities, and if one didn't want to be burdened with the chap for ever, one had to take the law into one's own hands, and get rid of him by any means in one's power. . .

'But if he took no notice, life in the regiment was made so hot for him that he was glad to clear out to save his skin. He was never allowed to go to sleep, except in a wet bed; everything he possessed was broken up; and he sometimes found himself in the horse-trough to cool his brain. I remember one chap who wouldn't go, and was shut up in a room full of hay, which got alight, and he was then put in a horse-trough to put the fire out. He was a very bad case, a shocking cad, who joined with a wife off the streets, and with whom it would have been impossible to live. He had every hint, and the last, before the hay episode, was that he found all his luggage packed, and at the station; but no! We had to apply the "ordeal by fire", and then he *did* go!'[7]

William, of course, was perfectly aware of what lay ahead, although it would have been extraordinarily bad luck to run into such extreme injustice as this. Nevertheless he expected ostracism and a good deal of loneliness, and admitted to his father that 'the true ranker is often miserable in himself and a nuisance to his brother officers'. He was making things harder too by wishing to stay in the cavalry, which was a socially exclusive arm. Had he decided to apply for a commission in a county infantry unit, such as the South Staffordshire Regiment, where mess expenses were kept low and rankers allowed in now and then without fuss, his path would have been easier. Another difficulty was the fact that his CO, Whigham, never liked him personally, and disapproved of promotion from the ranks on principle. Nothing could be done while *he* remained. On the other hand he received constant encouragement from other officers in the regiment, and from Canon Leslie-Melville at Welbourn, from whom the idea of a commission originally came. And so, after the regiment was transferred to Ireland in 1882 and he had risen to sergeant, William quietly set about his preparations. In 1883 he took the First Class Certificate of Education as noted, and set himself to read all the books on tactics, strategy, and military history that he could find. They were not many. Then Whigham left, and the two COs who followed him each encouraged William in turn. For two years he held back, mainly for lack of money. But in 1886 he finally accepted the proposal to take a commission in India, where the pay was much higher than at home, and expenses proportionately less. As a subaltern he would earn about £400 a year, and this with care would just enable him to make ends meet. The die was cast. Further vexatious delays, however, followed, and it was not until June 1888 that he was gazetted Second-Lieutenant in the 3rd Dragoon Guards, then stationed at Muttra.

From Dublin he was given a generous and affectionate send-off by his old regiment, and travelled to the depot at Canterbury to wait for a passage to Bombay. He filled in the intervening time with leave and a refresher musketry course at Hythe, where the new Maxim machine gun was being demonstrated. In a revealing letter to his mother, he laid bare all his hopes and fears for the future. He was deeply sensitive of his new position.

Hythe
Sunday

'My dear Mother

I must now write and tell you that I am in pretty good spirits and very good health. I had a long weary journey on Tuesday, arriving here as you know a day too soon. Well I could not pluck up sufficient courage to go to the Officers' Mess that night, so took up my abode in the town until the next night when I had to go. Well I got on middling but wished myself home a good many times, indeed I never remember leaving home more depressed than this time. You see its all amongst strangers—strangers in more ways than one.The next day I got on better and am now very fairly settled and comfortable. The officers who now know me are very nice, but its a difficult business because you see I feel that I am acting under a false flag if they do not know my previous life. However I always out with it if the occasion demands, so it will soon be known throughout the school, and then I shall be all right because of knowing to whom they are talking. . . I have just been asked by a very nice officer to go over to Folkstone with him this afternoon, on the impulse I assented. Well that was wrong. If I go there money will be spent and a Sunday spent wrong, so I have made escape and do not intend going. . . Amongst other things we have to give 4 lectures on the science of musketry which will be given before 69 other officers— all critics, and several of whom are noblemen. This will require a good deal of nerve and study, but I hope to go up with a good heart and come off all right. . . I find that the clothes Father made me compare very favourably with any others here and feel very thankful for the trouble he has taken and hope to repay him one day. . . Have not quite got into eating about a dozen courses after 8 at night. Still I frame pretty well and I find myself quite ready after going from 1 o'clock to 8. . . Now you know how I go on and I really am comfortable. Of course I should like a bit more companionship during my walks but that will come in time, anyway, it does not much matter as I do not care much about it at any time, only one is liable to despondency with too much of one's own company.

Give my best love to all . . .

I am

Your very affectionate son

W. R. Robertson.'[8]

His mother understood his fears and feelings only too well, and gave him all the comfort she could. Long reconciled to his choice of career, indeed deeply proud of his progress, she wrote regularly and concluded a later letter in words that never varied in their message, expressing as they did all her love and simple faith:

'My Dear William Good bye and May God Bless you and Keep you is the constant Prayer of your Loving Mother Ann Robertson. 'Deuteronomy Ch 4 Verse 9.'[9]

Her death in 1893—when William was on the way home,

hoping to enjoy his first spell of long leave after four years in India—came as a bitter blow. He drew strength from the memory of her until the very end of his life.

*   *   *

William reached India in December 1888, and soon settled down with his new regiment. He was kindly received by his brother officers, and the work was essentially familiar to him; in fact it was neither difficult nor strenuous. He needed all his self-denial, however, to keep his end up in the mess.

'Water was the only drink I could afford, while for smoking I had to be content with a fixed amount of tobacco and cheroots at two shillings a hundred. It was not altogether agreeable to be seen drinking water at mess when others were drinking champagne, or to defer smoking till leaving the mess because pipes were not allowed, but it had to be done.'[10]

He also had to exert will power in adapting himself to the Indian climate, in order to maintain the momentum of his career. Instead of resting in the heat of the day, like everyone else, he spent his afternoons learning Hindustani, much to the disgust of his *munshi* or teacher, a stout person of lethargic disposition.

'To keep awake when teaching after his mid-day meal was entirely beyond his powers, and he could not understand why I should wish to work while other Sahibs either took their lessons in the evening or not at all. By degrees I caused him to see that this was not my method of doing business. . .'[11]

Such was the start of a strenuous two years. By the end he had succeeded in qualifying as an interpreter in five Indian languages, adding a sixth (Gurkhali) a year or two later. It was sheer application, for he did not find the work easy, and all did not go well at the first attempt. Once, for example, he had the bad luck to be examined *viva voce* in Pushtu by a Mohmand, who insisted on discussing the Christian belief in the Trinity—a hard subject at the best of times. Naturally enough, this part of the exam had to be taken again! This remarkable sustained effort bore fruit, not only in the extra income earned, but in his subsequent advancement as a staff officer.

The other way in which he got on was simply to make himself indispensable in the regimental office. He took on any job that was offered him, standing in for the adjutant when ill (which provided some useful experience in administration and military law), acting as secretary of the district assault-at-arms committee, and negotiating with contractors—besides playing a full part in training and regimental duties. He was prominent, too, in horsemanship and in the handling of arms, and found some time for sport. In short he kept himself fit and free, physically and mentally. But it was a long hard row and a lonely one, and he felt the strain at times. He wrote to his father:

'Let me hear soon how you all are, it is so miserable out here—*you dont know*—to be wondering how you all are. I'd much rather be sure of hearing the bad news as well as the good as not to know whether you are all right or not. . . I'm afraid I do not remember how often I *must* feel cut off from *all* friendship. So far as I know, not *once* has any one in my present sphere taken offence at being in my company, but there is much difference between this and sincere mutual interest; this cannot naturally be between a born gentleman and one who is only now beginning to *try* to become one. In the midst of the highest society one's thoughts fly back to far off Welbourn and its well remembered little bits of domestic life of my early days. There I see real love, whilst here amid all the gaiety and apparent friendship I feel that were I not an officer tomorrow, there would be perhaps none to recognise me. Poor human nature is so very weak, it must have somewhere to look for support and sympathy and it *does* require some sign to reassure it.'[12]

This was not just an isolated moment of depression, but the revelation of something far more permanent and profound. It was the cry of a man who was emotionally alone, and who *had* to keep his feelings to himself. The very exertion of raising himself from a raw village boy, less than twenty years before, appeared at times to exhaust him. The burden of class was always there, and it needed all his resources of faith and determination to keep going. The worst, however, was almost over. Within a very few years he was to gain immensely in self-confidence and contentment, through marriage, promotion, and official recognition of his abilities.

In 1891 William had his first experience of active service. A large body of tribesmen were raiding the frontier near Kohat, and a mixed force of infantry and artillery had to be sent quickly to deal with them. It was the sort and size of expedition that British and Indian troops frequently had to mount, and which acquainted them with the conditions of war in a way in which no exercise in peace-time could ever do. India was in fact the active training area of the British Army and William was fortunate to have been sent there. On this occasion his organising ability was tested, for he was posted as Railway Transport Officer, first to Hassan Abdal, then to Kushalgarh, to supervise the entire movement of the Kohat force. He was notably successful, overcoming all the urgent problems of supply, animal (mostly mules) and troop transport, and generally imposing order upon a situation which at one moment showed every sign of slipping into chaos. He showed plenty of resolution, too, in dealing with extravagant claims from quartermasters and paymasters, once the emergency was over. It was thanks to this and his previous record, and his knowledge of languages, that he received orders in the following year to report to Army HQ at Simla.

*   *   *

As so often happens, William suddenly found that, as well as reaping the rewards of merit and hard work, luck was beginning to come his way. His new job, for example, was closely connected with the recent arrival of General Sir Henry Brackenbury, the new Military Member of the Viceroy's Council, a post equivalent to that of the Secretary of State for War in Britain. Brackenbury was a remarkable man who was to influence William at several points in his career, a highly educated officer of great drive and vision, with a breadth of military and diplomatic experience behind him. As the first Director of Military Intelligence, he had already reanimated the Intelligence Branch at the War Office, and introduced a Mobilisation section, which was in some sense the forerunner of Operations. In India he saw at once that the Intelligence organisation at Army HQ was hopelessly inadequate, and he determined to expand and improve it, appointing officers only of proved professional ability in preference to the social stars who populated Simla at that time. Had it not been for Brackenbury, William would not have got near Simla, nor perhaps would he have wanted to.

William was fortunate in his immediate superiors, too: in Colonel Elles, who directed the Intelligence Branch; and in Lieut-Colonel Mason, RE, who was in charge of the North-West Frontier Section, in which William worked. This section was responsible for all the territories adjoining northern India, from Tibet in the east to the borders of Persia in the west: an immense, wild and largely undetermined tract, where fighting was the principal tribal occupation. This fact alone demanded the attention and sometimes the intervention of the Indian Government, not to mention the larger potential threat of Russian expansion in the background. So small was the sum of accurate information about this whole area—culled in the main from passing travellers and past punitive expeditions—that immediate steps were taken to start reconnaissances, and scientifically to record the information so gained. William was concerned in all this, and spent a whole year compiling a handbook, *The Gazetteer and Military Report on Afghanistan*, a work of immense detail and length. Its value was very great. Moreover, as a method and standard of recording facts it set the pattern for his later Intelligence work in the War Office. It also imprinted on his mind the absolute need for accuracy and meticulous detail, which is the basis of staff duties.

He also played a notable part in the active business of securing information. In June 1894 he started on a three months' journey to the Pamirs, by way of Gilgit and the mountainous north of Kashmir. He travelled with a small escort by pony, mule, and on foot, and was enthralled by the staggering splendour of the scenery and the sheer geographical adventure, all glowingly described in his book. After reaching the snow line, he crossed the Darkot Pass at over 15,000 feet, and finally reached his destination—the cold and arid plateaux of the Pamirs at the foot of the Himalayas. He returned to India in August, by a more westerly route via Chilas and Khagan. Before the expedition dispersed, however, he took a characteristic step. By conversing assiduously with a Gurkha member of the party, he made himself sufficiently proficient in Gurkhali to pass the prescribed examination, thus bringing his bag of Indian languages up to six.

In the following year he had his first experience of warfare, and gained his first decoration. Following a feud among members of the reigning family of Chitral, a border state lying to the west of Kashmir, disorders had broken out in the capital, where the British Political Agent and a small force of Indian troops were besieged in the fort under the command of Captain Townshend, known to students of the First World War as Townshend of Kut. A rescue operation was immediately organised: a division from Peshawar in the south and a small column from Gilgit in the east. William was posted to the former as a Brigade Intelligence Officer, and accompanied the advance northward through the Malakand Pass, across the Swat River, and on via Dir to Chitral itself, where the siege had just been raised by the arrival of the Gilgit column from the east. Sharp fighting was encountered in the first few days, and several actions fought, after which serious resistance collapsed. Eventually the troops were engaged in pacification and reconnaissance duties about the country.

It was on one of these that William fought a contest on his own, as a result of which he was severely wounded and fortunate to escape with his life. His task was to report on a road running south from Dir, for which he was given an escort of Gurkhas and the services of two local guides. The latter were said to be trustworthy, one of them being known as the 'Kazi'. At the start all went well, the guides proving knowledgeable and helpful.

'I was suffering from dysentery at the time, and on the third day's march gave my sword to the "Kazi" to carry, as I was unable to bear its weight round my waist. Being mounted, I gradually forged ahead of the escort, and was followed by the two guides only. Suddenly, and to my utter amazement, I was twice fired at from behind, and could not imagine what had happened. Looking round I saw the "Kazi" rising from his knee, and in the act of throwing aside the smoking 12-bore breech-loader which he had been carrying since we left Dir, preparatory to achieving with his sword—or rather *my* sword—what he had failed to accomplish with his gun, for although he could not have been more than ten yards away when he fired, he had missed me with both barrels. He was yelling with the fury of a madman, and I realised that he had become "ghazi"—a religious fanatic—not an uncommon occurrence on the frontier. The goat-track on the steep hillside along which I was riding would not permit me to move right or left, or to turn the pony round so as to face my man, and the only alternative was to dismount. In doing this I stumbled and fell, the result being that I was in a half-sitting position when the "Kazi" arrived at close quarters and proceeded to slash wildly at me. As there was neither time nor opportunity to draw my revolver while this vigorous sword practice was taking place, I could only scramble to my feet and floor the fellow with my fist. Just as I did this I observed that the other so-called guide, kneeling on one knee a few yards away, was waiting his opportunity to fire the moment he could do so without hitting his companion. Whilst my attention was distracted in this way, the "Kazi" jumped up and the pair of them made off. Pulling out the revolver at last, I brought down the "Kazi" as he was in the act of flying up the hill-side, and then I remembered no more till the Gurkhas arrived, they having hastened to the spot on hearing the sound of firing. They picked up the "Kazi", who had been hard hit but not killed, and a native hospital orderly did his best temporarily to patch up my wounds.'[13]

Later the 'Kazi' was executed by shooting and his body burned, and William awarded the DSO, which he described wryly as 'then a rather rare decoration'! He also came in for some teasing for having been cut about with his own sword! The incident was reported in the *Daily Graphic* of July 15th, and illustrated with a good deal of artist's licence.

By the end of the summer of 1895, William had sufficiently recovered from his wounds to rejoin the Intelligence staff at Simla. By this time he had been promoted Captain—only seven years after being commissioned—and had his feet securely planted on the lower rungs of his career. Even so, he might have remained an undistinguished though conscientious officer but for two things: his marriage in late 1894, after his return from the Pamirs, and his decision to sit for the Staff College.

His bride was Mildred, daughter of Lieut-General T. C. Palin of the Indian Army, and their marriage—which only ended with William's death in 1933—was an outstanding success. At the outset, however, it caused a considerable shock —in the context of those days, an understandable one. By his wife's sister and by other members of the Palin family, William was considered socially inferior, 'not good enough for Min', and they made snobbish and hurtful criticisms in the way that relatives are known to do. It took time and patience to bring them all round, and William was marvellously forebearing. In due course all were pacified, indeed the severest critics were only too happy to bask in the warmth and glory of his later successes, and to come to him for help. He never held it against them. Meanwhile tragedy followed trouble, for the first baby— a boy, Hugh—died in infancy, despite the ministrations of the Commander-in-Chief's own doctor. The death of their first-born, combined with the family displeasure over their marriage, hit William and Mildred very hard. In time their grief was assuaged by the birth in 1896 of a second son, Brian, who accompanied them as a five-month-old baby when they returned to England at the end of that year. All the while Mildred gave her husband that companionship and confidence in society that he so badly needed; and she helped him devotedly to overcome the next obstacle in his professional career, the all-important entrance examination to the Staff College.

This exam, William noted, was not particularly difficult, but it was highly competitive. Most candidates put in time at crammers in London, and took leave for the purpose. William could afford neither to take leave nor to give up his job at Simla; and so, as on previous occasions, he did all his studying in his spare time.

'By rising regularly every morning between four and five o'clock, in winter and summer, I was able to get through a large amount of spade work, crude and ill-directed though it might be, before going to the office for the day.'[14]

The curriculum was varied and included two foreign languages, of which one had to be French or German. William knew no German and only a very little French. Fortunately he discovered a French teacher in Simla, and chose Hindustani, in which he was proficient, as his second language. In other subjects he enlisted the help of a local schoolmaster and of colleagues on the staff, while his wife always heard his lessons whenever he chose to recite them. In this persevering and painful way he passed ten months in preparation, oppressed always by the thought that if he failed there would be no second chance, for by then he would be too old for admission.

Eventually he sat for the examination and qualified in every subject, but just missed one of the open vacancies. He was given a special nomination, however, on the recommendation of the C-in-C, Sir George White, and so became the first ranker officer ever to enter the Staff College. In December 1896 he left for England.

'The voyage was very unpleasant, rough weather prevailing almost continuously. The nurse was the worst sailor of the party, next to myself, and succumbed as soon as we started, and in our cabin! Fortunately the man-servant of the officer occupying the adjoining cabin was an obliging person, and undertook to look after the child during my wife's absence at meals. He had once been a prize-fighter!'[15]

William had spent eight and a half years in India, nineteen in all in the Army. Although he did not know it at the time, he had also left regimental life behind him for ever.

4

On the Staff

WHEN William arrived at Camberley in January 1897, the Staff College had been in existence for nearly a century. Its progress, however, had been painfully slow and uncertain, and its survival at times largely a matter of luck. The need to train officers in military administration, the handling of formations, and the theory of warfare was simply not recognised until disasters like the Crimea caused a public outcry. This was entirely in keeping with the British distrust of professionalism, especially in the Army, where staff duties were long regarded as a casual accomplishment, which any regimental officer could pick up if he wanted to. The majority did not want to, and boasted about it. It was thanks to the example of Prussia in 1870–1, and the foresight of a few brilliant men such as Wolseley, that steps were taken to reanimate the Staff College, and work out an effective staff system for the Army. However, the old Duke of Cambridge in his later years as Commander-in-Chief put up such a dogged defence that it took a second Crimea—the Boer War of 1899–1902—to lay bare the deficiencies, and to force through the final reforms. Only then was a General Staff, in the accepted sense of the term, created.

A staff officer is—by basic definition—one who assists the commander, and issues orders under his authority. In the British Army today he operates at various levels: at the War Office, at an area or command headquarters, or with a formation in the field. The lower categories of staff duties are performed by regimental officers, usually without special training; the higher by officers who have generally, though not invariably, passed the Staff College (p.s.c.). The latter may either be regimental officers (up to the rank of Lieutenant-Colonel) or officers (of the rank of Colonel upwards) too senior for regimental duty. In most cases they are known as General Staff Officers, and are distinguished by grades of duty as well as by rank.

In the early days staff officers operated *only* in the field.

Appointments were temporary, made by the commander chosen to lead the campaign. It was not until 1795, when the Duke of York became head of the Army, that a permanent headquarters staff was first established at the Horse Guards. During the Napoleonic wars the organisation grew, and district commands and staffs were set up for home defence. In most cases officers who filled these posts owed their appointments to nepotism or private pressure, backed where necessary by bribery—a fascinating and profitable occupation in which Mrs Clarke, the Duke's mistress, played a powerful part. Ability therefore had to take its chance, although in fact many able officers found themselves in the right places.

Such was the state of affairs when the Royal Military College was founded in 1799. In that year the Senior Department (forerunner of the Staff College) opened its doors to 26 young officers at High Wycombe, while the Junior Department (forerunner of Sandhurst) did likewise to cadets at Great Marlow. Both owed their birth to Colonel Gaspard le Marchant, a Channel Islander and a cavalry officer of distinction, who had been deeply shocked by the lack of education in the Army.[1] The Senior Department promised well. Le Marchant recruited an able staff, under a remarkable chief instructor, General Jarry, a French royalist *émigré*, who had served under Frederick the Great and commanded the latter's famous *Kriegsschule*. The course lasted two years and was a strenuous one. It included Surveying, Mathematics, Fortification, Castramentation (siting and construction of camps), Tactics (mostly out-of-date Prussian stuff), and a little Administration. No practice was given in written orders. Operations were still regarded as the business of the commander in the field, who used aides to carry his orders by word of mouth. The system worked tolerably well, since battles were still conducted within eyeshot and amenable to close personal control. None the less, Wellington was pleased enough to have skilled staff officers about him, and towards the end of his campaigns the majority of such men had passed through the Senior Department.

After Waterloo a general reaction set in against the Army, and the axe descended on the Royal Military College. In 1832 all public funds were withdrawn, so that fees remained the sole source of income. It is amazing that the College survived at all. That it did so was largely due to the heroic efforts of the senior professor, John Narrien, a mathematician and man of humble birth. With a handful of colleagues he wrestled with tactics and other unfamiliar military subjects, and with the indifference and indiscipline of the few students who bothered to attend. The best that could be done was to teach a little elementary engineering. Even then, standards were lenient, and the tests artfully cooked when the inspectors came round.

Meanwhile staff duties and appointments had almost disappeared within the Army itself. District commands lapsed, except in Ireland, and no campaigns of note were fought outside India, which was a very long way off. Initiative was stifled by long spells of garrison duty abroad, and by the deadening hand of the Duke of Wellington, who hated the idea of education and thought it subversive. He was fully supported by senior officers and colonels of regiments, who shared his views almost to a man. Occasionally an innovation slipped through, but nothing radical was attempted until after the Duke's death in 1852. By that time it was too late to put through any serious reforms before the Crimea revealed the full extent of the rot. The disasters and sheer ineptitude of that campaign impelled the Secretary of State for War to say:

'The system by which an army should be provisioned, moved, brought to act in the field and the trenches, taught to attack and defend, is non-existent. . . We have no means of making general officers or of forming an efficient staff.'[2]

There was no such thing even as a contemporary manual of staff duties, and Murray's *Peninsular Instructions* of 1810 had to be hurriedly reprinted *as it stood* for issue in the Crimea. Nothing was done about staff training, however, until the campaign was over, when the young Duke of Cambridge, the new Commander-in-Chief—surprisingly a keen reformer in those days—bestirred himself about the whole question. A new body was set up, the Council of Military Education, to control most questions affecting admission to the Army, promotion, and officer training. Regulations issued in 1857 outlined the professional qualifications expected of staff officers—an admirable range of accomplishments, including legible handwriting—and transformed the Senior Department into the Staff College.

Thirty vacancies were offered for a two-year course, open to all branches of the Service by means of examination. There were no fees. So far, so good. But all was lost when it came to the curriculum, still heavily weighted in favour of engineering subjects. Prince Albert saw the danger at once, and asked:

'What is to be gained by making officers of the Army, and the Staff in particular, abstract *mathematicians* instead of scientific soldiers?'

True, Languages and Riding (under the fearsome Captain Brooke, who let off pistols under slow mounts) made their appearance, but a student was really judged by his skill in sketching, or demonstrating Euclid, or seeking clues to the conundrums of the Reverend J. F. Twisden, MA, professor of mathematics and astronomy. There was little attempt to work out schemes on the ground and reproduce the conditions of war.[3]

All this fed the fires of the next crisis. Staff jobs were not being given to Staff College graduates, as had been promised, and the public was becoming uneasy. Shortly before Cardwell took office a new enquiry was launched which showed the way things were going at Camberley and also revealed the Duke of Cambridge in his true colours. Despite his initiative in setting up the new Staff College, the Duke had been increasingly perplexed by all that went on there. So he now roundly declared that the Staff was best recruited from the regiments, *without benefit of training*, and thus gave his approval to the state of affairs which he had formerly condemned!

Fortunately wiser counsels prevailed and Cardwell gave them his support. The reforms that arose out of the enquiry were generally expressed in the principle: 'obtain the best regimental officers procurable, train them practically, give them a reasonable assurance of the staff employment for which they have been trained, and place them in the appointments for which they appear best fitted.'[4] Under Colonel Hamley, the new commandant, and his successors, definite though slow progress was made towards making the Staff College an effective instrument of military education. Less attention was paid to the niceties of surveying and more to military history, organisation, and techniques, and to a better knowledge of languages.

Hamley was the first to take his students out into the country-side, and encouraged riding—not as a parade but as a useful means of studying ground and a pleasant exercise. He also instituted termly confidential reports, and weeded out the duds at an early stage. But all this was not done quickly. It took a generation to achieve real standards and open the doors to a wider range of candidates, some from the Indian Army, capable of staff work and high command in war.

*   *   *

The state of the Staff College was, of course, closely linked to the staff structure of the Army itself. The reorganisation of the former coincided with the Cardwell Reforms, and after that progress both at Camberley and the War Office marched to-gether, though always in the face of opposition. At first it boiled down to a personal struggle between Garnet Wolseley and the Duke of Cambridge.

Wolseley was a brilliant, thrusting officer, who fast made his name as a thinker, organiser, and field commander. As author of *The Soldier's Pocket-Book*, he provided at an early date an astonishingly full and compact guide to military practice. In the late 1860s he rendered excellent service in Canada, and he was one of Cardwell's chief advisers as Assistant Adjutant-General. In the next twelve years he conducted campaigns in Africa with outstanding success, including the daring night attack which overwhelmed Arabi Pasha at Tel-el-Kebir in Egypt in 1882: a manœuvre which depended on meticulous planning, accurate intelligence, and iron nerve: in short, staff work and generalship of the highest order. He gathered round him a group of trusted subordinates, nearly all graduates of the Staff College, who came to be dubbed the Garnet Ring. They were an élite, adored by the public, but resented by the die-hards formed up behind the old Duke, who feared the worst when Wolseley was appointed Adjutant-General in 1881.

For his part, Wolseley was determined to press ahead with staff reforms, but—although he and the Duke saw eye to eye about very little—they were substantially in agreement about one important matter: the transfer of control from civilian to military hands of supplies and transport. Wolseley made this demand with all the authority of a commander who had suffered from the old system in the field. Again he had his way. In 1888 the office of Surveyor-General was abolished and the bulk of his duties (the Supply Department set up by Cardwell) handed over to the Quartermaster-General. Since the latter was subordinate to the Commander-in-Chief, this move had the effect of strengthening the position of the Duke, who now enjoyed virtual control over all military affairs except finance. On the face of it this was a surprising manœuvre on Wolseley's part, in view of the antagonism between the two men; in reality, it was no surprise at all. Wolseley hoped one day to succeed the Duke; indeed he was the obvious choice. He therefore looked forward to inheriting sufficient powers to enable him not to resist Army reforms—as the Duke had been doing for decades—but to accelerate them. In this Wolseley must be credited with acting from patriotic, and not merely from personal, motives. He had devoted his whole life to the Army, and was easily the most able and educated soldier of his generation.

Alas, he was reckoning without two things, and these were to shroud the end of his magnificent career in an atmosphere of failure and frustration. One was the sheer complexity of Army administration, now in a state which no man could be expected to direct single-handed. The other was the opposition of Parliament. No Secretary of State would tolerate for long the depletion of his own powers, following the events of 1888, while the appalling bottle-neck created at the Duke's office merely emphasised the need for some new action. In short, centralisation had gone too far.

Such were the origins of the Hartington Commission, set up in 1889 to enquire once again into the workings of the War Office. Its recommendations were blunt: abolition of the post of Commander-in-Chief and his replacement by a Chief of Staff, who would co-ordinate the work of heads of departments, formulate military policy, and advise the Secretary of State— in short, a General Staff system on continental lines, and the forerunner of the Army Council which only finally came into being in 1904, after the unhappy experiences of the Boer War. But the Commission was before its time. The Duke was indignant, and so was the Queen, if only because the last vestiges of the Royal Prerogative were under fire. Wolseley, too, was deeply displeased, for he saw in this the shattering of the instrument of reform which he had so carefully prepared. In the event opposition proved too strong, but when the Duke finally did retire in 1895 (after 39 years at the head of the Army), the Commission's recommendations were adopted in compromise form—and a most unsatisfactory compromise it was. Wolseley became Commander-in-Chief at last, only to find himself 'the fifth wheel on the coach'. Although he remained 'principal adviser of the Secretary of State on all military questions, and charged with the general supervision of the Military Departments at the War Office', yet the heads of these departments were now given direct access to the S of S, without any need to consult the C-in-C. Thus Wolseley had to shoulder responsibility without power, merely acting, as he said, as 'vice-chairman of a debating society'. He had no hesitation in making his complaints public.

Such was the unhappy situation when Britain went to war with the Boers in 1899: a war which revealed to a stunned and horrified nation the full extent of the Army's deficiencies, and not only those deriving from faulty machinery at the top. Since 1895 Wolseley had striven hard to wipe out the locust years of the old Duke's regime, and he did at least succeed in sending out to South Africa some seven divisions within the first few months. This was a large effort by comparison with the usual run of colonial wars, and would have been quite impossible had not Wolseley made his own plans and set up a small mobilisation staff. But of course it was nothing like enough. In the end it required almost half a million men and two and a half years to beat the Boers to a standstill. By that time much else had been shown up—inadequacy of training (of both officers and men), shortage of supplies (almost from the outset), a lack of skilled staff officers, and the fact that very few senior commanders had ever attended the Staff College or even led so much as a division in the field.

The Army came out of the war with a pricked reputation, but it was a providential pricking in view of the far greater war which followed twelve years later. By then a transformation had occurred, beginning with the War Office and the Staff. After three further enquiries,[5] an Army Council was finally set up in 1904 composed of four military and three civil members under the chairmanship of the Secretary of State. The Commander-in-Chief was replaced by a Chief of Staff (the senior military member), and a command system installed for the country at large. Behind this, a General Staff organisation was worked out, as applied to the whole field of administration, personnel and operational planning, and manned by a new generation of educated and experienced men. The way was now open for the re-building of the Army as a fighting force, capable of engaging in a European war: a task that was to take up most of the following six or more years in which Richard Burdon Haldane held office as Secretary of State for War, 1905–12. Fortunately for the Army, Haldane was of the calibre of Cardwell, a very great reformer.

* * *

William Robertson joined the Staff College in January 1897 and graduated at the end of December 1898. He could hardly have timed it better, for he emerged at the very moment when there was an urgent need for trained staff officers, ready to ride the tide of war and reform. Provided he seized his opportunities, he was bound to advance, and advance he did far and fast. It was the turning-point of his career. Within a very few years he had risen from a diffident ranker captain to a full colonel of high professional ability, confident of his powers, bothered no longer about social origins. He was fortunate, too, in that the Staff College had passed the point at which it was regarded as a 'haven for shirkers'. Since the appointment of Colonel Hildyard as commandant in 1893, the College had been attracting some of the best young brains of the Army: men like Haig and Allenby, who—with William and others—were to rise to high positions in the First World War. Hildyard hated cramming, and would have abolished all written examinations by outside examiners if he could. Students were assessed on their all-round abilities, a yardstick which suited William particularly well.

For, naturally, he was nervous about how he would get on at Camberley. Nervous about his lack of education, and still shy about his position in society. He was also worried probably about money, having nothing to live on but his pay. It was said that in those days £3000 was needed to see a student through his time at the College, and that in fact William was given £2000 by some kind friend. Neither statement has been substantiated. But it is certainly true that most officers had money of their own, or were helped out by their fathers. Not so William, who must have lived very frugally, as he had done before and would do so again. All these fears were to disappear. Hildyard was a sympathetic and understanding man, who soon reassured William as to his supposed shortcomings. As to lack of knowledge, this was overcome partly by hard work, partly by the goodwill of brother officers, notably J. E. Edmonds (later the Official Military Historian), who helped him with some of his written work, as he also helped Haig. In the end William justified all expectation, being classed second in his year, and—characteristically—spent part of his leave with a family in France in order to strengthen his qualifications as an interpreter.

The value of the Staff College derived not only from teaching and learning, but also from the common approach to problems which characterised all students, and from their comradeship. When you *know* how a man is likely to react in any situation, by reason of his training, then you have a tradition of behaviour upon which you can rely, *whoever* fills the post. And that is important in war. It is also human to add that there is a bond between Staff College graduates—anyone who has been to school or university recognises this—a professional and personal association which counts for a great deal in a man's career afterwards.

Two of William's contacts at Camberley were of immediate importance to him. One was Colonel G. F. R. Henderson, instructor in military history, author of the classic *Stonewall Jackson*, a born teacher, immensely conscientious, and a most lovable man. Henderson thought well of William's work, and when he became Director of Intelligence to Lord Roberts in South Africa, he sent for William to join his staff. The other was General Brackenbury, whom William had already known in Simla, and whom he now met again at the manœuvres on Salisbury Plain in the autumn of 1898. Brackenbury was chief umpire on one side, having the assistance of a group of students from the Staff College. William was one of these, and managed by forceful measures to procure some information from the cavalry which Brackenbury urgently needed. Brackenbury did not forget this, and it was probably he who indirectly had a hand in William's appointment in the new Intelligence organisation at the War Office after the Boer War.

*   *   *

On leaving Camberley, William was given a provisional attachment as Staff Captain in the Intelligence Division at the War Office, then located in Queen Anne's Gate, at some distance from the main offices in Pall Mall. At that date Intelligence was the only branch of the General Staff primarily concerned with operational planning,[6] having reached that position—as so often happened—largely by empirical means. In origin it stemmed from the Crimea, when the expeditionary force found itself characteristically without any maps. This led to the hurried formation in 1855 of the Topographical and Statistical Department 'to procure maps and statistical information of the seat of war'. Sixteen years later it was transferred to Queen Anne's Gate under the direction of Captain Charles Wilson, RE, who was briefed by Cardwell to reconsider its duties on the Prussian model, following the important part played by Intelligence in the campaigns of 1866 and 1870–1. As a result a Intelligence Division was set up in 1873 under the Quartermaster-General, but with direct access to the Commander-in-Chief and Secretary of State. Wilson, however, declared himself dissatisfied, not so much with the organisation as with the fact that no one in high places really understood what Intelligence was for or what it could do. None the less, he must be considered the true founder of this branch of staff duties.

Nothing further happened until the appointment of Major-General Sir Henry Brackenbury in 1886, the first to be styled Director of Military Intelligence, and a name already familiar to readers of this book. Brackenbury was a man of force and ideas, a close associate of Wolseley, and thus highly suspect to the old Duke of Cambridge. This was well illustrated by Lord Edward Gleichen who was serving in the Intelligence Division at the time:

'I remember at some dinner-party in those days finding myself next to the Duke of Cambridge after the ladies had withdrawn. He very kindly asked me what I was doing, but when I had broken to him that I was working in the Intelligence Department [*sic*] he looked grave; and, leaning over and putting his hand on my knee, he said, "So you are under Brackenbury? A dangerous man, my dear Gleichen, a very dangerous man!" A curious thing to say to a junior subaltern about his Chief.'[7]

Gleichen described Brackenbury as having a 'pasty-yellow, black-moustached face and an almost uncanny power of getting at the root of a complicated matter in a word or question or two.'[8] He was all that and more, and became in effect the second founder of Intelligence by widening its scope and functions, making contact with other Government departments, and securing funds from the Treasury. With Wolseley's backing he created a Mobilisation sub-division, and promoted the idea that Intelligence should concern itself with all operational questions at home and abroad—the precursor, in fact, of General Staff work in its widest sense as strategical planning.

By 1899 the impetus imparted by Brackenbury had petered out. In William's words Intelligence and Mobilisation were 'more or less under the Commander-in-Chief, Lord Wolseley'. The fact that they were located on the opposite sides of St James's Park did not make for efficiency. With an absurdly small establishment of some twenty officers, the two Divisions constituted 'the only semblance of a General Staff then in existence'. The then DMI was Sir John Ardagh, a protégé of Brackenbury and former head of Mobilisation, and whom Gleichen described as:

'. . . silent, monocled, skinny-necked (he always reminded me of a marabou stork, I fear), the writer of beautifully expressed farseeing memoranda on the most abstruse questions. . . He never spoke, and when he sent for us to give him information on certain subjects, there was dead silence on his part whilst we talked. I once gave him a full account of Morocco matters during the space of something like half-an-hour. He leant back in his chair, never interrupted once nor took a note, and at the end he slowly screwed his eyeglass in and said in a hollow, faded voice, "Thank you".'[9]

Yet Ardagh and his officers did remarkably well, and despite fierce criticism during the Boer War, theirs was one of the few organisations to survive the scrutiny of the Elgin Commission, appointed to enquire into the conduct of that war. It was the machinery, not the men, who were at fault. With less than twenty officers it was hardly possible to provide an infallible Intelligence service over the whole world, nor was this really attempted. Most attention was paid to Africa and the Near East, the natural outcome of colonial expansion, while European countries were comparatively neglected. On the basis of his Indian experience, William was attached to the sub-division dealing with Asia and Russia in Europe; and since his boss and only colleague, Captain Waters, was a Russian linguist, Asia became his province. Waters left this interesting note:

'Looking over confidential reports on officers who had recently passed out of the Staff College, one on Captain W. R. Robertson arrested my attention. He had started life by enlisting . . . had worked very hard to improve his natural gifts, and after obtaining a commission, was employed for a time in the Intelligence Division at Army Headquarters in India.

'The report on him by the Commandant of the Staff College was very favourable, and I resolved at once to get Robertson, if this could be managed: there was no lack of suitable candidates. It all worked, for once, according to plan, and he joined the War Office staff as a temporary measure. I soon found that he was the very man required, a great worker, and absolutely reliable.

'Not long after he had taken up his duties I happened to be on leave, but was in London. One night, after dinner, he came to see me in, naturally, a great state of mind, and said he was to be transferred to Dublin in the capacity of a Garrison Instructor, an appointment which, as he had no influence, would lead nowhere; he might possibly have attained the rank, in years to come, of Lt-Colonel, and then have been placed on retired pay. His post was to be taken by a very capable and pleasant officer, but having got Robertson I wanted to keep him on account of his sterling qualities. The horizon, however, was black, the change having been practically settled during my absence. I went to the War Office on the following morning, and, using all the artifices of which I was capable, I got the decision rescinded. I was told that I had apparently made up my mind not to get on with anybody else!'[10]

Such is the first-hand account of William's near-escape from oblivion at a critical stage of his career, although in fact it is unlikely he would have been overlooked in the war days that followed. Nevertheless, Waters did him a good turn, and he was able to repay the debt some years later when, as Chief of the Imperial General Staff, he sent Waters on a mission to Russia.

Soon afterwards, in April 1899, William was given a permanent posting to the Colonial sub-division or section under Captain Altham, one of the best Intelligence officers the British Army has ever had, a man of keen brain with immense capacity for work, who taught William a great deal. The Colonial section dealt *inter alia* with South Africa, which was Altham's personal concern. Portents of war with the two Boer republics were on every hand, and it is amazing now to think that Altham managed somehow single-handed to keep abreast of all the reports and demands that poured in every day. Naturally he had to throw all the remaining colonies at William. So things continued until October, when war was finally declared and Altham disappeared on active service to Natal, leaving William to act in his place.

So here he was, acting head of the key Colonial section, less than a year after arrival at the War Office, dealing as a Captain with operational matters that nowadays would be handled by a group of officers from more than one Directorate. If anything, the work intensified as the news from South Africa steadily deteriorated—Mafeking, Kimberley, and Ladysmith besieged, and a series of defeats in the field, culminating in Stormberg, Magersfontein, and Colenso, all in one 'black week'. Nostrums for winning the war poured into the office from every source, in addition to the legitimate demands of superiors, and the preparation of a daily Intelligence summary for the Cabinet, showing the dispositions of the troops and the latest information about the enemy. All this was the business of William and one assistant, who was continually being replaced, as one man after another left for the front.

Obviously the burden was unnecessary, but the solution did not simply lie in a larger establishment. While given too much to do, Intelligence also lacked recognition, with the result that many of the vital reports and appreciations were never read by the men directing the campaign. All this provoked bitter comment. Intelligence was specifically accused of failing to warn the Government of enemy strength and intentions, and to provide our troops with proper maps. These accusations were squarely refuted by Altham and William before the Elgin Commission in 1903. They were able to show, for example, that the number of Boer troops had been slightly *over-estimated*, likewise of guns (107 instead of 99), while ammunition was calculated almost exactly (33 million rounds). They had also given warning of the advance on Ladysmith. But no strategic appreciation before the war would have counted for much, since for political reasons the Government had decided against reinforcing the tiny British force in South Africa until too late. As for maps, virtually none were ready since no funds had been allocated. The best that could be done was to reprint a farm survey map and a school atlas or two. These awkward answers had powerful repercussions, as will be shown.

But all this lay in the future. Meanwhile William persevered with his job, fearful lest he be left in London until the war was over. He need not have worried. On December 30th he embarked for Cape Town, with orders to join his old Staff College instructor, Colonel Henderson, lately appointed Director of Intelligence on the staff of Lord Roberts.

*   *   *

William spent nine months in South Africa, much of it on Roberts' campaign which turned the whole course of the early part of the war. Soon after arrival an army corps was assembled, transport and artillery re-formed, and a deception scheme put into operation, preparatory to launching the main force across the Modder River into the western part of the Orange Free State. Whether Henderson contributed any part of the tactics is not known, but he was responsible for working out the deception scheme, by which the Boer commander, Cronje, was cut off and forced to surrender. As Henderson's assistant, William was active collecting and studying reports (some from agents) regarding the enemy strength and position. In the end the deception was brilliantly done, and even William was unaware of all that was afoot until the last moment. But it was a dangerous and arduous move, involving marching a large body of troops and animals in the heat of February, the hottest month on the veld, round the flank of a normally mobile enemy. It succeeded. But bold as the conception was, and forcefully executed, the operation was by no means without fault. Staff work was still a weakness, as William carefully noted. Although the plan was good, too many details were left to chance, start-times and march-tables were not worked out, and subordinate commanders remained unaware of the precise movements and intentions of their colleagues. This looked like the negation of Staff College training. The trouble was that some of the senior officers, including Roberts himself, had never passed through the Staff College (at any rate in its better days). They were inclined to keep their ideas to themselves and work by rule of thumb, which was totally inadequate in the face of a resourceful and well-armed opponent.

Fortunately the Boers were themselves unskilled in the handling of large formations, and by now were in full retreat. By early June, Pretoria—capital of the Transvaal—had surrendered, and the end of the war seemed in sight. In fact it continued until May 1902, through the Boers' resort to guerrilla warfare, and their skill in evading pitched battles. The manner in which they were worn down, by the construction of 4000 miles of blockhouses linked with barbed wire and by a campaign of attrition, need not be described here. Long before this William had returned home to his old job in the Colonial section of the War Office, remaining there from October 1900 till September 1901, when the whole of the Intelligence Division was reorganised. Although mentioned in despatches, he was disappointed at being left out of the long list of honours and awards. The reason, it seemed, was that he had done sufficiently well in the past. He was told that had he not already been awarded the DSO (there was no bar in 1900), it would have been awarded to him now; and that had he not been promoted to major, after only twelve years commissioned service, he would have been given a brevet majority. This was poor comfort. William considered that he had been harshly treated, and that had he not been a 'ranker' he would have received something. He persisted, and in the end he was given a brevet lieutenant-colonelcy in a supplementary Gazette.

*   *   *

Between 1901 and 1907, when William left the War Office, Intelligence underwent two major reorganisations, as part of the creation of a General Staff proper. In 1901 it was combined with Mobilisation into a single Directorate, which included a Foreign section with William at its head, bearing (as noted) the rank of Brevet Lt-Colonel. He then had four sub-sections and nine officers under him. The appointment was a surprise. True, his record was excellent, but so was that of several other candidates, some of whom were his seniors. However, nobody grudged him his advancement. It is thought that Brackenbury had a hand in picking him out, and recommended him to Roberts, successor to Wolseley as Commander-in-Chief. However that may be, William certainly enjoyed an element of luck in addition to exerting ability. Luck is a commodity that no man, however distinguished and deserving, can afford to do without; and William was no exception. He had come a long, hard way, and he lost no time in justifying both his good fortune and his enlarged responsibilities. Moreover, the brevet meant that after three years, all being well, he would automatically move up to full Colonel.

'This happened, and from being one of the oldest Lieutenants in the Army in 1895, I became in less than nine years one of the youngest Colonels.'[11]

To complete the record. In 1904 Mobilisation was transferred to Military Training, and Intelligence retitled Operations with extended duties and establishment. The Foreign section (already enlarged) was raised to eight sub-sections to cover all the first- and second-class military powers of the world. William was not only confirmed in his appointment as head of the section, but a year later his term of office was specially prolonged so that he did not leave the War Office until early in 1907. By that date—in a little over five years—he had transformed Foreign Military Intelligence, and had left his own personal impression upon it.

What were his methods? Clearly, there was nothing haphazard about them, no strokes of genius or of lightning analysis. Quite the contrary. They derived logically from a shrewd mind and elephantine memory, fanatical attention to detail, and common sense that never faltered. William never hurried. He spent the autumn of 1901 and most of 1902 taking stock, and found hardly a single worth-while record or appreciation of the resources of a foreign power in the files of the section.

'There were some small non-confidential hand-books, largely compiled from newspapers . . . and various memoranda which dealt with certain operations that we might have to undertake in the event of war, but these . . . did not give a complete survey of the enemy's resources, or anything like it.'[12]

The first thing needed was more money for securing information and the appointment of better military attachés. The latter were mostly ill paid, all at the same rate—whether stationed in Paris or Caracas—regardless of the cost of living or the necessity to entertain, in order to pick up the barest facts. Hitherto the difficulty had been side-stepped by selecting rich amateurs, some of them remarkably simple.

'I remember a military attaché who . . . sent us a map, under every precaution of secrecy in the way of sealing-wax, red-tape, and extra envelopes, showing the peace distribution of the armed forces of a certain country, which he stated had been confidentially given to him by a friendly colleague. Incredible as it may seem, the price of the map and the name of its continental publisher were printed at the bottom!'[13]

All this was quickly improved. More money was extracted from a reluctant Treasury, and new blood introduced both to his own staff—all but one of the heads of the sub-sections had been changed by January 1903—and to the Intelligence service as a whole. There was great need to know more facts, and pass this knowledge on to the average serving officer. So the translation fund was doubled, and a wide circulation given to foreign military and technical journals, backed up by lectures from members of the Foreign section itself. Grants were obtained so that section officers might visit the countries they were studying and get to know them at first hand. William also travelled widely himself—to America, North Africa, and many parts of Europe, notably France, Belgium, and the Balkans, all past or potential battlefields. In the autumn of 1903 he drew up a *Conduct of Work*, a directive that laid down objectives and methods, and stressed the production of hand-books, comprehensive and up to date, for each foreign power—more or less along the lines on which he had himself worked at Simla eleven years previously. These hand-books—issued as General Staff publications—represented a basic element of strategic planning. Without them it would have been impossible to draw up realistic plans about the composition of the new British Army or its role in a European war—a task executed between 1904 and 1914, involving the formation of the British Expeditionary Force and the establishment of the Territorial Army.

1904 was the critical year, both militarily and politically. From then dated the real beginnings of the Committee of Imperial Defence (to advise the Cabinet on Defence policy as a whole), the reorganisation of the War Office and the creation of the General Staff (with Directorates of Operations, Training, and Staff Duties), and the new alignment with France (the *Entente Cordiale*) which led three years later to the understanding with Russia. Before then—so far as strategic studies were concerned—William had been working in the dark, although he had had his own private convictions about the real enemy, almost since his return from South Africa in the autumn of 1900. At that time Britain was still regarded—and still regarded herself—primarily as a colonial power, with but little interest in Europe. France and Russia were the traditional opponents, since both had large colonial possessions. Russia threatened India and our interests in Persia and the Near East, a fact that so influenced Roberts and Kitchener—both colonial soldiers and both in high places—that William was kept busy well into the 1900s on 'Russian' plans of little reality. France likewise took up a lot of attention. The Fashoda incident of 1898 was still raw, and a series of 'forts' against French invasion were being constructed round London as late as 1896.[14] In 1901 William composed a paper on 'The Military Resources of France and probable method of their employment in a war between France and England.' Revised up to 1903, it was a factual study of the strength and intentions of a then potential enemy, although in his own mind it was but a purely academic exercise.

Germany, he felt sure, was the real enemy, and he tried hard —and at first unsuccessfully—to communicate his conviction to others. At that time, before the *Entente*, it was certainly difficult to see how the two countries could wage war against each other effectively. A sea and colonial contest would not have been decisive, while a German invasion of Britain (even via

Belgium and the Straits of Dover) was hardly more practicable than a British invasion of Germany via the Baltic (despite Admiral Fisher's enthusiasm for the idea). But some hard facts remained, and William set them out with great force and clarity —and extraordinary prescience—in a discussion about a possible *alliance* between the two countries to the detriment of Russia. The date was November 1902.

'It is not an exaggeration to say that in no other European country is hatred of England so general or so deep-rooted as in Germany. Historically viewed, there exists no ground either for Germany to hate England or for England to hate Germany. We have only once been at war with her—in 1805—at a time when she was subservient to Napoleon; while we have often fought with her and even for her. . . A multitude of Germans live happily in England, and many Englishmen find themselves at home in Germany. Intermarriages between the inhabitants of the two countries are common; and, generally, there would seem to be abundant reasons why Germany and England should be in the closest accord.

'That this is *not* the case is due to several causes, one of which is that Germany in her dealings with the other Great Powers is always doubtful whether we can be relied upon to help her, and she is embarrassed accordingly. . . Another, and the most potent, cause is the rivalry in trade and colonial enterprise, and in this respect Germany is the aggressor. Indeed, the hope of superseding us in the commercial and naval supremacy is the governing idea of the national imagination. It may be argued that this is a perfectly laudable ambition, but it should be remembered that the fact of one nation being engaged, with every right and remarkable efficiency, in undermining the foundations of another is not in itself an aid to good relations between them, and certainly not to a reliable alliance. Moreover, it must not be supposed that the anti-English feeling was a product of the Boer war, and that it sprang only from an uncontrollable Press and from the lower orders. On the contrary it has existed in every grade of society for many years past, and it has come to stay.

'Nor can we reckon on the good offices in our behalf of the Kaiser. . . Those who believe that sentimental considerations of a purely personal[15] kind will be allowed to stand in the way of the Kaiser's political ambitions, can hardly be aware of the diplomatic steps he is said to have undertaken against England when he despatched the telegram to Kruger.

'It is, perhaps, just as difficult to reconcile the interests of England with those of Russia as it is with those of Germany. At the same time, once Russia is convinced that we have no intention of taking sides with Germany, or of encouraging those German projects which are hurtful to her, she will probably be far more amenable in her dealings with us than she has been in the past; and the same may be said with respect to France. Both countries, much as they may dislike us, would prefer our supremacy to that of Germany.

'It has also been urged at different times that unless we combine with one or other of the Great Powers, the latter may combine against us; but this argument ignores the fact that we are indispensable to Europe. Our function has long been to help to maintain the balance between continental Powers, which have always been divided by their interests and sympathies into opposing groups. At one time the centre of gravity has been in Vienna, at another in Madrid, at another in Paris, at another in St Petersbourg. We have thwarted, or helped to thwart, each and every Power in turn which has aspired to continental predominance; and concurrently, and as a consequence, we have enlarged our own sphere of Imperial ascendancy. This preservation of the balance of power would still seem to be our true role, and in playing it at the present time we should recollect that a new preponderance is now growing, of which the centre of gravity is Berlin. If this growth is really as great as Germany proclaims, it is high time that we abandoned all notions of effecting an alliance with her.'[16]

He concluded:

'that the alliance is not practicable;
'that even if it were, it would not be worth the price we should have to pay for it;
'that instead of regarding Germany as a possible ally we should recognise her as our most persistent, deliberate, and formidable, rival.'[17]

And this was written nearly two years before the *Entente* by a former village boy, who had finished schooling at the age of 13.

* * *

In 1904 the outlook at the War Office quickly changed, and William soon established excellent relations with the Director of Military Operations, Major-General J. M. Grierson, whom he now served. Grierson was a brilliant officer with a firm grasp of the potentialities of his new job, and he fully appreciated

William's efforts to promote sound strategic studies on the basis
of worthwhile Intelligence. Together they so furthered the work
that by the end of 1906, when Grierson left the War Office,
followed shortly after by William himself, they had reached
reasoned conclusions about most foreign commitments involving British troops.

Germany, however, remained the prime concern. Grierson
had been Military Attaché in Berlin 1896–1900, and was well
aware of her resources and intentions. He began at once to
work on schemes for common action with the French and
Belgians. A War Game was played early in 1905 to study the
employment of British, Belgian, and German troops (William
acting as German commander), in the event of a German
attack on France through Belgium. This was followed by visits
to the Franco-Belgian frontier, and an inspection of the area
where much of the fighting in 1914 actually took place, and by
staff conversations in 1906 with Huguet, French Military
Attaché in London, and with the Belgian authorities as well, it
being clearly understood that for political reasons no actual
military commitment could be made. Although these first
approaches lapsed after Grierson's departure, he and William
must be given credit for their energy and foresight. No further
action was taken until 1909, when Henry Wilson (as Commandant of the Staff College) decided to visit his opposite number,
General Foch, Commandant of the Ecole Supérieure de Guerre
in Paris. Wilson's charm, ability, and command of the French
language soon thawed out Foch, and it was their collaboration
that eventually produced the plans governing the role of the
BEF at the outbreak of the war.[18] Grierson died tragically on
August 17th 1914 on the way to take up command of II Corps
in northern France.

William left the War Office in January 1907, after a long and
momentous tour of duty. He had established a department
and made the system work so well that the structure has survived to this day. Only his will and vast capacity for work
could have created and kept such a job under one hand.
Here he made his reputation and prepared the way for high
appointments.

According to a subordinate his manner—though truly unaffected as it had always been—yet marked the change that

came over his career. He was reserved, always seemed deep in thought, and walked with a slow measured tread. There is a strong impression that he spoke with a Cockney accent, and a multitude of stories are attributed to him, in which he exhibited a pithy down-to-earth Cockney type of humour. It may be so. Yet some who knew him well said he had no recognisable accent, only a roughish intonation which probably derived from his country origin. Perhaps like Jimmy Thomas, the Socialist minister, he dropped his aitches designedly and played up to the role expected of him as a self-made man, and thereby gave birth to a legend. Most agree he could be gruff, rarely wasted a word, and grunted disconcertingly. Certainly he knew far more than he said, and was apt to surprise people when he chose. On one occasion when dictating a letter to a shorthand writer, he suddenly put his finger on a line with the remark, 'I never said that', and then repeated the correct version. The clerk, who had worked for him for years, never realised that William had any knowledge of shorthand. Again, it was never quite certain how much German he knew. He always insisted on full translations, yet sometimes looked at German documents in a way that suggested he had an idea of their contents. When he took leave of the German sub-section in 1907, he turned on his heel at the door and offered to take on any translation work they cared to send him. The request was acceded to, although he complained bitterly of the rates of pay, which incidentally he himself had been instrumental in fixing! His memory was phenomenal. One day he wanted a paper in a hurry. The officer who appeared said: 'Very good, sir, I will see if we have it.' William looked up quickly and replied: 'I know quite well you have it', and proceeded to quote the name and number of the file, in which it was to be found. He had filed it personally as a junior officer five years previously![19]

Gruff, formidable character that he became, squarely and solidly built, he never lost his humanity. All bore witness to this, and spoke of him with that mixture of respect and affection which betoken great and lovable men. The name by which he came to be known in the Army, though rarely spoken out loud even by equals, was 'Wully'. It suited him somehow.

5

Preparing for War

FOR the first time in his life Wully found himself unemployed.
It was an unpalatable experience. Half-pay, so-called, was
more like one-third pay in reality, and his income as a substantive Colonel fell from £800 to £300 a year. As he had no
money of his own, this was an extremely serious matter. With
three young children—Brian (born 1896), Rosamund (born
1901), and Helen (born 1905)[1]—and all the usual commitments of a family man, the strictest economies had to be made
and survival became a struggle.

Since his return from South Africa Wully had taken a house
at Woking, travelling daily to the War Office by train. He had
no carriage or car, walked to and from the station for good
exercise, and otherwise relied on a bicycle. Brian, then a young
schoolboy, remembers the expeditions they used to make together: a family picnic at Wisley, or cycling about the then
unspoiled countryside of Surrey, with stops at inns to munch
their sandwiches and drink an occasional glass of beer or ginger
pop. Calling was *de rigueur*. There was no box for visiting cards
at the gate, as in Simla, and it was considered a social come-
down to have to do the round on foot or by bike. But the
Robertsons did it just the same. Likewise, church on Sundays.
The family normally attended Woodham Church where they
had a reserved pew; otherwise, in the holidays, Wully would
sometimes take his son round other churches in the district,
where the sermon was said to be good, or the parson could be
relied upon for a sound Broad Church service. Theirs was a
happy unaffected existence without luxuries, other than an
annual holiday at Bognor or in North Wales. When electricity
came to Woking, they were content to forgo the expense and
continue with their oil lamps. It meant, nevertheless, that on
half-pay alone there was very little margin for further scraping
and saving.

Characteristically Wully refused to be idle, and with the
active help of his wife set about translating the German manuals

sent him by the War Office. They brought in a little much needed money, but it was grinding work. Mildred did the literal translation, while Wully converted her 'construing' into technical terminology, for German was one of the few languages he had not attempted to learn seriously. But at least it gave him an insight into German Army policy, especially the development of heavy artillery and machine guns, yet one more pointer to the war which he felt positive was coming.

Half-pay, fortunately, lasted less than four months, but when it did come to an end, Wully had to face another disappointment. He knew that for his own good, and for the advancement of his professional career, he ought now to have command of troops. In fact he had not done any regimental soldiering since India, and even his active service in South Africa had been on the staff. As things turned out, he not only failed to get a command now, but had to wait until 1918—after holding the highest staff post in the Army, Chief of the Imperial General Staff—when he went to Eastern Command, and after that commanded Home Forces and the British Army of the Rhine: all three in the nature of consolation prizes at the end of a distinguished career.

His was by no means a unique experience. Henry Wilson was another who captured some of the best posts as a staff officer—he succeeded Wully as CIGS in 1918 and, like him, became a Field-Marshal—but, with one exception,[2] held no command after the Boer War. On a lower plane Frederick Maurice, Wully's right-hand man in France and at the War Office—of whom more later—was a staff officer for most of his Army life. The fact was that good staff officers in the higher grades were at a premium, and men like Wully had to pay the penalty of quality. In Wully's case it was particularly ironical, for of all men he was a born commander—shrewd, tough, immensely practical, a man of decision and strong will, at his best under pressure, and who inspired trust. But fate decided otherwise. For most of his life he had to be a teacher, planner and adviser, tied for long stretches to a desk and an office.

In May 1907, instead of the brigade he had hoped for, Wully was offered the comparatively junior post of Assistant Quartermaster-General in the Aldershot Command, and this he accepted on the private understanding that it would soon lead to something better. It did. At the end of the year he succeeded Archibald Murray—the first of several successions—as Chief of Staff with the rank of Brigadier-General. At the same time Sir John French was followed by Sir Horace Smith-Dorrien as GOC. Meanwhile, as AQMG, Wully had been gaining invaluable experience in the whole field of supply and administration of a large body of troops; and this was to stand him in good stead in the fierce days ahead, when QMG to the BEF in France from the retreat to the Marne to the advance to the Aisne.

At that time Aldershot was still the principal training command of the Army, with two infantry divisions (Grierson had one), one cavalry brigade, and a number of ancillary units. Facilities were only fair, but much hard and imaginative training was done, thanks to Wully's efficiency and to the drive and foresight of the GOC. Smith-Dorrien was not always easy to get on with. He suffered from attacks of gout in the head, when he was liable to give vent to fearful explosions of temper. Not long after arrival, Wully experienced one of these rages. He stood straight up to his chief, survived, and thereafter had no further trouble. Indeed, the two men became the best of friends. But these were minor afflictions, for in truth Smith-Dorrien was an excellent commander. He cared deeply for the well-being of the private soldier, abolished a whole lot of pettifogging restrictions on the men's free time, improved the comfort of barracks and made real provision for recreation. He treated everyone, whatever his rank, as an individual capable of thinking for himself. In training he insisted on self-reliance and intelligent discipline, no less than on proficiency in field craft and the ability to handle a rifle. He encouraged realism— as in the sudden mobilisation of troops and the improvisation of battle situations, and enterprise—as in the development of new signals techniques and of the infant air arm. He found much to criticise, however.

Both he and Wully, for example, were horrified at the conservatism of the cavalry, still wedded to the charge, the lance and the sword. One of the lessons of the Boer War had been the value of mobility—using the horse as a means of movement only—for reconnaissance, and for the ability to bring fire to bear quickly from some new quarter by *dismounted* troops. This demanded a high standard of musketry, at which the cavalry was proverbially inadequate, and the GOC (an infantryman) lost no time in telling the officers of the cavalry brigade what he thought. He was aware too of the lack of machine guns (not put right until the war), and of a shortage of trained men in every arm. When Grierson's division was put on a war footing in 1909—as a training exercise—men and equipment had to be borrowed from all over the place. The trouble lay, partly in the inadequacy of arms production and of the number of recruits, and partly in the system of voluntary service itself. Since men were trickling in from the depots all during the year, no unit had all its members at the same stage of training and proficiency. Moreover, home units were continually being milked of drafts for the benefit of those stationed abroad. The ideal, from the military point of view, was compulsory service: by which, sufficient men would have been forthcoming for all purposes, and the annual intake of recruits received and trained together; but that of course was a political question, to which the Liberal Government of the day was unlikely to accede.

*　　*　　*

Even so the War Office was far from being idle. It is one of the ironies of history that the Liberals (always regarded as a pacific party) have provided some of the best architects of the Army, and put through many of the most important military reforms. Haldane, in office 1905–12, was one of the greatest of Secretaries of State for War. It was he who empowered Grierson (then Director of Military Operations) to start conversations with the Belgian and French General Staffs as early as 1906. He then proceeded to make definite plans—regardless of the absence of a political decision—by which, in the event of a war with Germany, the British would send an Expeditionary Force to Europe. Hitherto a campaign on the Continent had not been seriously considered. Back in the 1890s invasion had been regarded as the chief danger. It was then laid down that the Regular Army should have ready two corps for mobile warfare, in addition to various auxiliary forces mainly engaged in static defence. If necessary the regular troops were also to be available for service abroad, presumably within the Empire; and this is what happened at the outset of the Boer War.

Haldane encouraged the new strategy, taking tentative shape in the War Office, and made the necessary decisions.

'The continued occupation by a friendly nation like the French of Dunkirk, Calais and Boulogne, the vital Northern Channel ports of the Continent, was therefore an object upon which to concentrate. The accomplishment of this implied that we should have an Expeditionary Force sufficient in size and also rapidity of mobilising power to be able to go to the assistance of the French Army in the event of an attack on the Northern or North-Eastern parts of France. . . We had therefore to provide for an Expeditionary Force which we reckoned at six great divisions, fully equipped, and at least one cavalry division. We had also to make certain that this force could be mobilised and sent to the place where it might be required as rapidly as any German force could be.'[3]

The reorganisation of the Regular Army was debated in Parliament during 1906 and finally set in motion in January 1907. A second task, as momentous as the first, then awaited the Secretary of State—the creation of the Territorial Army as an effective auxiliary force in support of the Regulars. There were many difficulties. Although the existing Militia and the Volunteer units had already demonstrated their weaknesses, they were fiercely defended—especially the Militia—by a battery of determined Colonels, mostly on social grounds. Fortunately Haldane had powerful support from the General Staff, notably from Douglas Haig, then Director of Military Training. Haig had already made his mark as Director of Staff Duties in 'providing a central doctrine for the training for war',[4] and in furthering the issue of new training manuals. He now stood behind Haldane in his conception of the Territorial Army as an army complete in itself, with a full complement of artillery, engineers, and supporting services.

Despite strong opposition, the Territorial and Reserve Forces Act came into operation in April 1908. It provided for a Territorial Army of 14 divisions, 14 cavalry brigades, and corps troops, administered by County Associations, with the men enlisting for Home Defence, and for foreign service only in case of emergency. It was well supported from the first, and within two years had reached a total of 276,000 all ranks. Its efficiency was soon far in advance of the old Militia and Volunteers, and ensured the basic defence of this country, without which no one would have dared send the BEF off to France or anywhere else. The Act also provided for a Special Reserve for the Regular Army—quite distinct from the Territorials—and most of the Militia and the Volunteers found their way into one or other of these two new organisations.

*   *   *

Such very briefly was the background of reform to Wully's tour of duty at Aldershot 1907–10, a period tightening with political tension and the new alignment of power in Europe. Naturally all this legislation made a powerful impact on the Aldershot Command, which was expected to produce a large part of the BEF and to carry out the appropriate training and preparation. Wully's role, therefore, as Chief of Staff was of vital importance, a fact of which he was fully aware. To emphasise it he became active as teacher and propagandist. In lectures to units and in private conversations he never tired of discussing the implications of strategy, of explaining the function of Operations and the value of Intelligence, and of saying what the Army was up to and what it would have to do in the clash that was coming. In 1909 he made another private reconnaissance of the Belgian frontier, this time with Smith-Dorrien and Rawlinson, a future Army Commander, motoring all along the Meuse, through Spa, to Arlon and the borders of Luxembourg. On their return Wully and his chief were involved in a ludicrous mishap:

'It was about 6 am, and only a few ramshackle and out-of-date cabs were to be had. We got into an old hansom, and, driving up the steep slope into the old Waterloo Station, both shafts broke and the cab fell over backwards and was merely supported by the driver's seat. The driver, it seemed, rolled down the hill, but we were practically sitting on our shoulders with our legs sticking straight into the air, and so tightly wedged that we were unable to move. Luckily the horse was only too glad to stand still. At last an old man came along and was surprised to find us both laughing. We were extricated without much damage.'[5]

Since Aldershot was near London, and the showplace of the British Army, it attracted large numbers of visitors of every kind—journalists, foreign and colonial officers and missions, and of course Royalty. Edward VII came in 1907, 1908, and 1909, and was well liked and respected. His visits, however, caused Wully a good deal of worry. As His Majesty was in tender health and did not ride, a dummy scheme always had to be arranged, so that he could see the troops in training everywhere from his motor car. On most occasions he was accompanied by his son, the future King George V, with whom Wully struck up a warm and lasting friendship.

In contrast to his father, George was a simple, rather austere, person of conservative tastes and habits, who got on well with people of character similar to himself, regardless of their social position. Hence his popularity with the Socialist Ministers of the 1920s, few of them Radical and none of them pretentious, and hence too his liking for Wully. He was heard to say on one occasion that he would not attend manœuvres unless Wully took him round. Wully not only returned these kindly feelings, but in a very human way enjoyed being friends with the King. It was to stand him in good stead for the rest of his life.

There is a revealing anecdote about their unaffected relations with one another. On the day after the 1912 manœuvres, Wully was told that the King wished to see him, and learned that he was to receive the honour of Knight Commander of the Victorian Order.

'I was more than surprised, somewhat nervous, and quite ignorant as to what I was expected to do, but Wigram [the equerry] came to the rescue, drew the sword he was wearing, handed it to the King, and told me to kneel down. Having duly knighted me the King put out his hand, and not knowing what else to do I shook it, rising to my feet at the same time. I ought to have kissed it, of course, as a sign of homage, but the King was probably quite as pleased to see me shake it. The incident brought a broad smile over the faces of the onlookers, and I beat as hasty a retreat as I respectfully could.'[6]

The King was indeed delighted!

*   *   *

In the summer of 1910 Wully was appointed Commandant of the Staff College, in succession to Henry Wilson, the new Director of Military Operations at the War Office. He found that the College had made great strides since his own student days barely twelve years earlier. There had, of course, been a great deal of criticism of the Staff in the Boer War, some of it genuinely applicable to the methods and standards of staff training. A great deal more, however, derived from the fact that there had not been enough trained officers to go round, so that far too much staff work had fallen on regimental and Army Service Corps officers who had never been near the Staff College. Moreover, some of the senior commanders had been no nearer!

Since then the number of students had significantly increased, and the curriculum had been reanimated under two outstanding Commandants—Rawlinson (1903–6) and Henry Wilson (1907–10). Rawlinson had shown himself fully aware of tactical and technical developments, not only from the Boer War but also from the Russo-Japanese campaign of 1904–5 when combined operations were carried out by military and naval forces. He was also 'blessed with an extremely attractive personality, a handsome appearance, high social standing, and more than an average share of this world's goods . . . he brought a youthful debonair spirit with him, for he was only forty when he took over his duties.'[7] Wilson was no less dynamic, inspiring his admirers and provoking his detractors by his brilliance. He made his students appreciate the full function and purpose of the General Staff recently created, and the need to formulate a system and a doctrine. His admiration for the French Army was already in evidence, and as related he took the initiative in 1909 of visiting General Foch, and thus of renewing staff conversations between the two Armies.

Wully was utterly different, both in character and in method, to his predecessors. In some ways he was their superior, for by now he had both an unrivalled knowledge and mastery of staff duties, and he had also become a practical trainer of men.

'He had no time or affection for abstract theory, for evasion of the point. Nothing irritated him more than an attempt to obscure a perfectly clear issue by a cloud of words. . . A clear thinker himself, he sought to encourage logical appreciation of every military problem, and bade his students beware of being confused and misled by minor considerations, or an inclination to indulge in abstract contemplation, in preference to evolving a definite plan of action. He detested the craze for high-sounding phrases, "pivot of manœuvre", "interior lines", "offensive-defensive", and when Wully expressed distaste he expressed it forcibly. Any shirking of a difficulty was instantly detected. Students must get at the heart of a problem and prove the practicability of their solution by working it out in its fullest details. In fact he left nothing to chance and increased the thoroughness of instruction a hundredfold.'[8]

Clarity of purpose, thoroughness of method, and strict attention to detail without losing sight of the goal: these, in brief, were Wully's three principles. Of the last he wrote:

'Details, so-called, were thought to be petty and beneath the notice of the big-minded man, and yet they are the very things which nine hundred and ninety times out of a thousand make just the difference in war between success and failure.'[9]

Later Foch was to say of him: 'Robertson bâtit petit, mais il bâtit sûr.'

Wully would not have been ashamed of that. As to clarity, even the appellation 'Staff College' irritated him, since the aim was to train officers for command as well as for staff work. 'War School' was his suggestion, but he failed to get it accepted.

Wully's sense of realism showed itself in many ways: in the number and efficiency of the exercises that he ran, and even in his attitude to the theory of warfare.

'The training regulations dwelt with great persistence on the importance of the offensive, and the idea of fighting on the defensive was thought to be so obnoxious . . . that, for some time past, it had been deemed politic to leave defensive training severely alone. . . I made it an almost invariable practice at all staff tours and other exercises on the ground to create a situation that entailed taking measures for retreat. . . The great difficulty attaching to operations of this nature is to reconcile two conflicting aims—the husbanding of one's own resources and the infliction of loss upon the enemy— and it can only be overcome if the commander possesses sound judgment and a powerful iron will; if the staff are accurate in their calculations and untiring in their efforts; and if the troops possess great mobility, high morale, confidence in their leaders, and good fighting capacity in general. . . If we have this practice, the operation will not then come as a surprise to the troops in war; they will understand better what they are expected to do; and they will recognise it as being a form of war which may have to be adopted by an army.'[10]

Prophetic words! Wully rammed these lessons home by taking students round the lesser-known battlefields of the Franco-Prussian War—those near Amiens, Orleans, and Le Mans—which had been fought by partially trained and hastily raised French troops, after the opening campaign was over and lost; and he questioned a senior French officer (the local corps commander) who had taken part in them as a young man. The conversation led to a formal reception at which Wully's host made a long speech (duly translated) eulogising the British Army, and to which Wully was obviously expected to reply!

'Having been taken unawares, and being at all times incapable of making a public speech on the spur of the moment, I felt that the only thing to do was to put on a bold front and try to score by replying in French. I knew that my vocabulary was very limited, and that my French pronunciation was execrably bad, but there seemed nothing for it but to do or die. After talking for the space of some ten minutes, and having tried the effect of a few jokes—which apparently were not understood and certainly did not amuse—the proceedings became distinctly flat, and as a total collapse seemed imminent I made a last despairing effort not to be beaten. I apologised for my ignorance of the French language, regretted I could not say half what I wished to say, and added that, being unable to speak further, I would call on my officers to sing a ditty commonly heard at similar reunions in England. I then proposed the health of our host and asked the officers to sing "For he's a jolly good fellow". They responded with even more than the usual amount of noise and discord, and all that the French officers could grasp of the performance was a repetition of the same words. Next morning I bought the local newspaper in order to see what kind of an account was given of the entertainment. The corps commander's speech, a very good one, was reported *verbatim*. Mine was not. I did not expect that it would be. But the reporter credited me with a far better speech than the one I had actually delivered, and added that, at the end of it, I called upon my officers to sing the well-known English song of which the chorus was "For thou art a very good man"![11]

Although the students at Camberley all respected and feared Wully, they also loved him. He inspired respect because he was a master of his profession and a teacher of unexampled thoroughness, and affection because he also knew when to let up. One student,[12] who afterwards served with distinction in France and acted for a time as Wully's Military Secretary in 1919, left this personal note, which illustrates well the two sides of Wully's character.

'He was a great Commandant, very severe yet at the same time very nice, human and encouraging. We were all frightened to death of him, yet admired him greatly and were fond of him. He taught us a lot and made of some very junior officers, like me, people who could do staff work in war well.

'We were worked pretty hard the first year, a good many lectures and a lot of tactical exercises out of doors in which we covered immense distances on bicycles, and on occasional days one was told to accompany Wully in his car, when one had his individual attention and was thoroughly put through it. . . On one such occasion, the lot fell on me, acting the part of cavalry commander, and I seemed to do nothing right all day. In the evening writing orders in the pub we were staying at, and feeling rather crestfallen, the old man passed by and said to me, "The cavalry did not do too badly today, and I know I gave you a pretty bad time. How are they?" I answered, "Feeling a bit sore and licking their wounds, but determined to give the enemy hell tomorrow, sir." He said with a broad grin, "That's the spirit, boy, but it is somebody else's turn to come with me tomorrow."

'Later we went to North Wales for four days to do a bit of Indian Frontier work, and walking back from the mountains just before dark the Commandant turned round, called me up to him and said, "Point out on the ground where you would post your outposts tonight." After a quick look round I duly did so, and he said "Thank you, that will do well." We went back to the pub, had a bath and dinner, did our work and went to bed. I had just gone nicely to sleep, when I was woken up by a knock on the door and told by one of the Instructors that the Commandant wanted to see me at once, and that I need not dress. I found old Wully in a dressing-gown in his bedroom, and he said, "You are now in command of the outposts you posted this evening," and handed me a message from No 2 Picket which read as follows: "Am being heavily attacked in front and both flanks stop running short of ammo." I said, "What is the rest of the message, sir?" He answered, "I don't know, I expect their signal lamp is broken. What will you do?" I answered, "I should send a company up to help and relieve them." He replied, "I thought you would do that. You will find Col. Malcolm waking the rest of the students and telling them to dress. You do the same and lead them up to the relief of No 2 Picket." We all started off in a bad temper and luckily I had marked on the map where I had put the pickets, and by the grace of God, after the devil of a climb in the dark, we arrived at the top of the right mountain half-an-hour before dawn. We were then told to go home independently, breakfast would be at 8 am, and we would start work again at 9 am. Very good for us but very trying, and thank God it was not raining!'[13]

Although Wully enjoyed the social side of his job, and he and his wife were kind hosts, he was badly handicapped in this matter by his lack of resources. In those days the Commandant was expected to dip into his private means in order to entertain on the scale expected of a man in his position. Both Rawlinson (a rich man) and Wilson (a comparatively poor one) had done so. Wully had no objection to entertaining, in fact he was excellent value at a dinner party, but since he had no money of his own at all, he was compelled to cut social engagements to the bone. This may have been the reason why Wilson had advised against him as his successor, or it may have been the general antipathy which the two men felt for each other, and continued to feel for the rest of their lives. In any event it was exacerbated by two incidents.

'On arrival at Camberley Wully found on the hall table a bill from Henry Wilson for £250 for various items he was leaving behind. Robertson had not £250 in the world, so he wrote to Wilson's predecessor, Rawlinson, to enquire what had happened when *he* handed over. "Rawly" replied: "That fellow Henry! My wife built that greenhouse and gave it to Lady Wilson. My wife put in those rose trees and gave them to Lady Wilson. The furniture is the gift of past Commandants and goes with the house. You had better dig up the potato patch and see if the seed potatoes are still there".'[14]

Wully got his own back by cutting Wilson dead at the first Staff College Garden Party held during his commandantship, a deliberate insult which hurt Wilson deeply. In sum neither incident reflected much credit on either party. Be that as it may, one of the most practical services that Wully rendered to the College was to have the remuneration of the commandant raised, so that he could fulfil his social obligations without private loss. Ironically, the order only came through after he

1. Thomas Robertson

2. Ann Robertson

3. Thomas Robertson at his shop door in Welbourn

4. Will Robertson as a corporal
in 1879 . . .

5. . . . and as an officer in
India, 1890

had been promoted, though not paid as, Major-General, and on the very day that he ceased to be Commandant; but at least his successors benefited. Besides this, he made other notable improvements. In 1910 the Staff College was still dependent for administration upon the Royal Military College, Sandhurst, next door. Since, however, students already numbered 120 and directing staff 15, and plans were in hand to take in a large number of Dominions officers, Wully now felt he had a strong case for an administrative assistant of his own, and he succeeded in having an adjutant appointed. This relieved him personally of a lot of chores and allowed him more time and scope as a teacher. As a corollary he submitted proposals for enlarging the buildings and extending the recreation ground, most of it being done after he had left, and in a pinchpenny manner—but that was not Wully's fault.

When he left Camberley in the late summer of 1913, his term of office complete, he left a deep and lasting impression upon all who had served him as student or instructor.

*   *   *

Over fifty years old, Wully was now long overdue for a field command. Once more, however, he was to be baulked of his ambition, this time by appointment as Director of Military Training at the War Office. He was deeply disappointed, but comforted himself with the promise made him by Sir John French, CIGS, that he would be given command of the 1st Division at Aldershot, when the post fell vacant in the summer of 1914 under a year hence. So sure was he of the prospect that he sent his furniture to Aldershot and rented a furnished house at Byfleet. He then took up staff duty again at the War Office on October 9th.

At that time the chief business of the Directorate included the training of all troops stationed at home, home defence itself, and the education of officers and cadets. In the main, major revisions of policy regarding most of this work had recently been agreed, and so—knowing that his tenure of office would be short—Wully was content to implement rather than experiment. It was not in his nature, however, to be complacent, and he left on record sharp criticism of two important points of organisation. One was the system whereby a separate and independent Inspectorate kept watch on the state of training, and reported to the Army Council without reference to the CIGS, under whom the DMT worked. In Wully's view this was a wasteful and pointless dualism. It deprived the DMT of seeing the results of his own work, and even of keeping contact with the troops he was supposed to be training and stored up all kinds of mischievous possibilities. The other was simply the multiplicity of home commands, with no less than seven GOCs, all operating independently. No C-in-C Home Forces existed, and none was contemplated even in war, when the CIGS would in effect act in that capacity. This seemed to Wully to be utterly wrong, inviting confusion and danger, particularly in the event of emergency. It is of interest that both these problems found an early solution under the pressure of war, now looming near.

As it happened the confusion over defence was shown up within six months of Wully taking office, and in a most unexpected manner. The cause was the so-called Curragh Mutiny of March 1914, of which the background needs some preliminary explanation, since it was inextricably entangled in Irish politics. The full story has been told elsewhere,[15] but the principal facts are as follows.

* * *

During the latter half of the 19th century, a variety of legislation was passed with the purpose of improving conditions in Ireland, particularly in the matter of land ownership and tenant right. Gladstone, however, as leader of the Liberal party, was convinced that there was a moral duty to go further, and give the Irish a Parliament of their own. To this end he introduced the first Home Rule Bill in 1885. It caused furious passions, not only on the part of the Conservatives but within his own party as well, with the result that the Bill was thrown out, and the Liberals divided into two factions—the Gladstonians or Home Rulers and the Unionists. In 1893 he made a second and more successful attempt in that the Bill was passed by the House of Commons but failed in the Lords. Soon afterwards the Liberals lost office and stayed out until 1905, when they were returned to power with an overwhelming majority, and with Irish Home Rule as one of the main planks of their platform. Their first concern, however, was with social reforms at home, in the prosecution of which they came up against such bitter opposition that two further elections (both in 1910) had to be held, and the Parliament Act of 1911 passed to limit the powers of the House of Lords. By now the Liberals had lost their working majority, and depended upon the votes of their allies to stay in power; and it was mainly due to pressure from the eighty or so Irish MPs, led by Redmond, that the third Home Rule Bill was introduced early in 1912. This was to cause as great, if not greater, hostility than that aroused earlier, and added fresh fuel to a furnace that was already well alight.

Events now moved with the fatality and force of Greek tragedy, although neither side ever quite believed that the other meant to force the issue. The Cabinet calculated that enactment would be delayed until the middle of 1914, allowing for two rejections by the House of Lords, after which the latter House would no longer have the power to prevent the Bill from becoming law; and that was more or less what happened. During all this time, however, the Protestants of Ulster (more precisely the Six Counties of north-east Ireland) led by Sir Edward Carson, declared their determination to resist all attempts, legislative or otherwise, to tie them to the rest of Ireland, which was predominantly Roman Catholic. For them Home Rule meant Rome Rule, and they would have none of it. They were given powerful support by the Conservative party, led by Bonar Law, a Presbyterian of Ulster stock, and by many prominent persons who, for social, religious, or political reasons, held strong views about Ireland or just hated Liberalism and all it stood for. The Government had its hotheads too, notably Lloyd George and Winston Churchill, both of whom ironically enough had wanted to exclude Ulster before the Bill was drafted—it might have saved much heat if they had had their way. Once committed, however, both men made a series of pugnacious speeches, no less provocative than those of their opponents. Asquith, on the other hand, exerted a moderating influence. Although determined to see the matter through, he repeatedly tried to come to terms with the other side, but without success. King George V, too, played an admirable part in the background. He was in a most invidious position, being constantly appealed to to exercise the Royal Prerogative on behalf of one side or the other; and he did all he could to bring them both together in an endeavour to find some formula for solution.

By December 1913 the situation was so threatening that a conference was called at the War Office by Sir John Seely, successor to Haldane as Secretary of State for War, of all the GOCs. Among them was Sir Arthur Paget who commanded the troops in Ireland, a stupid, arrogant, quick-tempered man. No one was less fitted than he to handle a delicate situation, involving the loyalties of officers and the explosive atmosphere of a country torn by religious and political dissensions. He floundered from the first, and was totally unable to follow Seely's ambiguous exposition of a soldier's rights and duties, in the event of the Army being called out in Ulster. Nevertheless, he was directed to go back and 'make the position perfectly clear to all concerned', and was held personally responsible should any outbreaks of indiscipline occur.

The New Year opened ominously. The Ulster Volunteers numbered nearly 100,000 and they had a £1 million fund behind them. Carson was as belligerent as ever, inspecting 'his troops', and making speeches with a fine sense of the dramatic. Moreover, he was well informed as to the military preparations of the Government, thanks to the activities of no less a person than the Director of Military Operations, Henry Wilson, who was playing the part of stool pigeon and telling his Conservative friends of all that was going on at the War Office. An extraordinary situation, but then everything was being turned upside down, when the most upright citizens were taking the law into their own hands as a matter of course. The Opposition even made strenuous efforts to refuse passage to the Annual Army Act, a move that particularly angered the King. If successful, it would have meant that the Army would have had to be disbanded, and the Government deprived not only of the means of defending the Empire—a small matter, apparently— but of enforcing its will in Ulster—which was far more to the point. The last hope of conciliation seemed lost when, on March 9th, Asquith proposed an amended Bill which offered to exclude Ulster from the Irish Parliament for a period of six years, but this too was effectively and dramatically turned down by Carson in the House. This refusal prompted the Government to action at last, and a special Cabinet committee was called. As a result Paget was instructed by letter on March 14th to post troops for guard duty over stores, guns, and ammunition dumps about northern Ireland. A few days later the Navy was ordered in similar terms, both to cooperate with the Army in the movement of troops, and to send two cruisers to help guard Carrickfergus Castle, where the ammunition stocks were said to be in danger of attack. All this was to take effect on March 20th, a Friday.

Meanwhile, the curtain was going up. On March 18th Paget reported to the War Office for detailed briefing as to the kind of hostile action he might have to deal with—raids, riots, and the like, even some concerted action by the Ulster Volunteers, although this last was regarded only as an extreme possibility. Whatever sort of a fool he made of himself afterwards, one cannot but feel sympathy for Paget at this moment, and it was only human—though highly mistaken—that he should try to modify his brief before returning to Ireland on the night of the 19th. In this he succeeded and managed to extract one vitally important concession out of Seely, to the effect that in the event of an operation any officer *domiciled* in Ulster would be allowed to 'disappear' and be reinstated afterwards. However, if any others refused duty, they would be dismissed the Service. With that he had to be content, but it was sufficient—as things turned out—to spark off the 'mutiny' that followed. On this same day, the 19th, much else was going on. At the Curragh Camp, near Dublin, orders were received to issue ball ammunition to the entire garrison, while back at the War Office an argument was going on as to which Directorate would be responsible for making the necessary arrangements and issuing the orders. The three principals involved were the DMO (Wilson), who dealt with operations *outside* the United Kingdom, the DMT (Robertson), who dealt with operations *inside*, but only as home defence against attack from overseas, and the A-G (Ewart), whose duty was to provide troops in support of the civil power. In the end Wully lost out, and so it fell to him to take the appropriate action.

Like many others Wully never really believed that either side would be so foolish as to step over the edge, but he was sharply critical of the Government for placing the soldiers in such an invidious position. 'Soldiers cannot be treated as if they had neither souls nor consciences, and to expect them to undertake a duty which may lead to shooting down those with whose ideals and religion they are in sympathy is to expect a great deal.'[16] He believed that if everyone sat tight, the whole thing would fizzle out—not a strictly logical piece of thinking, but a shrewd one, and characteristic. Moreover, he at once began to ask a number of pertinent and practical questions.

'Are we supposed to be going to war with Ulster; that is, will the troops be on "active service"? If we are not going to war what are we going to do, as the case is obviously not one of suppressing civil disorder because there is no disorder at present? If we are going to war, is mobilisation to be ordered, and what ammunition, supplies, and transport are the troops to take? What instructions are to be given to the General in command regarding the nature and object of his mission?'[17]

Some of these questions could not be answered, indeed they never were. But they did help to induce those in supreme authority to face facts, and to reduce the whole thing to the absurdity it was or should have been.

Friday March 20th was the critical day. Paget had summoned a meeting of senior officers in Dublin, among them Major-General Sir Charles Fergusson, commander of the 5th Division, and Brigadier-General Hubert Gough, commander of the 3rd Cavalry Brigade, both from the Curragh, the latter a young forceful officer and future commander of the Fifth Army in France. To them Paget gave an account of the situation and of the preparations in hand. It was not a clear speech. In one breath he hinted that the country would be ablaze on the morrow. In another that no aggressive action must be made by the troops, who would nevertheless take up stations as a precautionary measure. The onus of aggression rested on the Ulstermen. He then communicated the offer to contract out, open only to those officers *domiciled*, i.e. who had their homes in Ulster. Any others refusing duty would be dismissed the Service. He concluded by ordering them to inform their subordinates. Although both men were deeply disturbed, Fergusson and Gough reacted differently, the former conceiving it to be his duty to obey (on the primary grounds that this was an order from the King), the latter deciding to resign. At a second meeting after lunch, which Gough did not attend, Paget gave details of the reinforcements to be sent from England, and reiterated that the whole plan was by way of precaution and demonstration. The Government buildings in Belfast were to be occupied, guards mounted or strengthened at vulnerable points, and the troops generally held in readiness, nothing else.

Fergusson then returned to the Curragh to find that Gough, who had preceded him, and most of the cavalry officers, were preparing to resign, only five or so being qualified to contract out. The majority of officers of other units, however, whom Fergusson personally interviewed on this day and the next, agreed reluctantly to obey him. When Paget heard about Gough, he immediately informed the War Office, whence a telegram was received about midnight, directing Gough and two of his Colonels to report to London immediately. This they did, taking the boat on the following Saturday night, the 21st. Meanwhile, on the morning of that day, Paget had gone down to the Curragh to talk to the cavalrymen personally. Hitherto, difficult though his brief was, his handling of the situation had been neither firm nor tactful, and he had made matters worse by personal innuendos, mainly directed at Gough. His new speech was a farrago of contradictions and irrelevancies, tinged with emotional bluster. Troops were to be sent in to Ulster, but would not fight. In the event of resistance, the men were to lie down and refuse to fire, or turn round and march back to barracks, while he and his generals would parley with the other side (whom he referred to as the 'Hibernians') under a white flag. On the other hand he was ready to 'hold the line of the Boyne' until reinforcements arrived from England. Why then, he asked, indulge in false sentiment by resigning? If anyone did, he could expect no mercy. By this time nobody was quite sure what Paget had said exactly—indeed doubt remains to this day—but the general impression was that there would be a show of force, only to dissolve directly the bluff was called. None were convinced. They had no intention of taking part in a pantomime battle, which at best would turn into a farce, at worst into real warfare. So the resignations stood, and nothing remained but for Gough and the

Colonels to report to the War Office. By this time the news had begun to leak out, and some newspapers were hinting that trouble was afoot.

A typical recollection of the confusion that reigned is provided by Sir Edward Beddington,[18] then a subaltern serving at the Curragh. He had dined with Gough, his brigade commander, on the night of Thursday March 19th, 'a very cheerful party, and the conversation was the usual, hunting, polo, point-to-points, and not a word of politics.' Early the next day Beddington crossed over to England for the weekend, staying at a large country house. 'As we were nearing the end of dinner, the butler brought me a telegram reading much as follows, "All officers of regiment have resigned rather than take part in operations against Ulster stop we were given our choice stop wire your decision." I asked if I might write a reply and wrote, "Will do the same as the others stop what is it all about." The question had never been talked about at all in the regiment, so I was completely in the dark. . . There was nothing in the papers on Saturday about it, and the Sunday papers never reached my host. . . The next morning (Monday) I had to motor to Crewe to catch the Irish mail, and the first I knew of the affair in any detail was what I read in the papers in the train to Holyhead. However, the porters at Crewe had noticed the name of the regiment on my suitcase and given me three hearty cheers, to my surprise. When I asked what it was all about, they said, "Your regiment refused to go and fight Ulster, here's luck to you all".'[19]

It remains to summarise the rest of the story. On Sunday March 22nd Gough had an inconclusive interview with Ewart, the Adjutant-General. The next day he saw French, CIGS, and was half-persuaded by him 'to wipe the slate clean and go back to Thursday evening', but only if given a *written* assurance that neither he nor his colleagues would ever be asked to take part in any operation against Ulster, in support of Home Rule. Thereupon French took him along the corridor to a frosty interview with Seely, the Secretary of State, who, however, eventually agreed to Gough's request. A message was then duly drafted and approved by the Cabinet, though it was extended after the Cabinet meeting, and further amended—at Gough's insistence—by French alone. Meanwhile, furious debates were

being conducted in Parliament, the Press, and in private conversations up and down the country, deploring or defending
Gough for his act of 'mutiny'. But all this was really beside the
point, for Gough had won the day. He and the other officers
were reinstated, the Army was not called upon to 'occupy'
Ulster, and the immediate crisis was averted. Seely, French, and
Ewart all resigned, and Asquith took over the portfolio of War
himself. In September the Home Rule Bill became law, but its
provisions were suspended until the end of the war, when the
Irish Question was 'solved', not by the North, but by the South,
in the two civil wars that led to the establishment of the Irish
Free State. The North retained its separate entity and Parliament, in collaboration with Westminster, as it still does today.
And so the 'final' solution of the Irish Question is constitutionally
no nearer now than it was in 1912–14, though the passions have
died down—and that is an essential preliminary to any constitutional settlement.

What would have happened had Paget behaved less ineptly,
and had Seely not conceded the offer to contract out, with the
obvious implication that the Government was not sure of its
ground, and could not rely on the loyalty of its Irish and Protes-
tant officers? Gough admitted afterwards that if he had been
ordered to go north, he would have done so. That was the tactical
mistake. At the same time military measures in Ulster, with or
without violence, would hardly have dispersed the underlying
dissensions about Home Rule. The fact was that both the
Government and the Opposition had manœuvred themselves
into impossible positions, and the soldiers found themselves the
playthings in a highly dangerous and irresponsible war game.
Wully's phlegm—though it riled Henry Wilson—part-instinc-
tive, part-intentional, was as practical an attempt as any to lower
the temperature and avoid a tragedy.

In France, 1914–15

EARLY in the summer of 1914 Wully warned young Edward Beddington (then a subaltern in the 16th Lancers, and a graduate of the Staff College) that he was to come to the War Office to 'help get the Cavalry Division ready for the annual manœuvres'[1] in September. That year they were to take the form of *the retirement of a force before an enemy of superior strength involving the passage of the River Severn*. The scheme, mainly devised by Wully, never of course came to anything, and Beddington was advised to stay with his regiment, since a similar operation was performed about that time in real earnest in northern France. But the preparatory work was not wasted. It gave Wully yet another opportunity to study the technique of retreat, although on this occasion he could hardly have foreseen all the difficulties, or that the movement would last all the way from Mons to the Marne.

By now he was in two minds about his own future. His hopes of commanding the 1st Division were fast disappearing. If war broke out, the DMT would automatically become chief staff officer to the defence forces at home, and it seemed unlikely that another officer would be given the job at this late stage. As it happened he was not left behind in England after all. At the last moment there was a reshuffle of the higher appointments. Archibald Murray, originally earmarked as QMG to the British Expeditionary Force, was chosen by Field-Marshal Sir John French, Commander-in-Chief, to be his chief staff officer (CGS), in place of Grierson who took command of II Corps. I Corps went to Haig, and the Cavalry Division to Allenby. Wilson became Sub-Chief (Major-General, GS) to Murray. On grounds of ability Wilson should probably have had Murray's job. He had latterly done more than anyone to make contact with the French and, at staff level, prepare the BEF for its role in France. But Asquith would not hear of it. He had neither forgotten nor forgiven Wilson's intrigues during the Ulster troubles earlier in the year. And so it came about that Wully was appointed QMG to the BEF, stepping into Murray's shoes once again. He duly reported to the Hotel Metropole in Northumberland Avenue where GHQ was mobilising, and crossed to France on August 14th.

Before this, Europe had burst into flames. The timetable of events affecting the BEF had begun on August 2nd, when Germany first demanded passage for her troops through Belgium. The next day she declared war on France, and on the 4th the first patrols entered Belgian territory. By midnight a state of war existed between Germany and Great Britain. By the 12th all the major European powers concerned, except Italy, were at war. The volcano had blown its top at last.

The British Army began mobilising on August 3rd. Plans for this and for the subsequent transfer of the BEF to France, where it was to take station on the left of the French line, had long been prepared, and in great detail. Everything proceeded smoothly and with the utmost efficiency. Main parties began to cross the Channel on August 12th, and the whole force had been landed by the 17th. Not a man was lost by enemy interference. Indeed the Germans had practically no knowledge of what was happening—neither of the strength of the BEF, nor of its location, nor of the timing and direction of its moves—as they found to their discomfort later. However, not all the original plans were carried out as intended owing to the intervention of the new Secretary of State for War, the legendary Lord Kitchener.

It will be recalled that when Seely resigned after the Curragh affair in the previous March, Asquith added the portfolio of War to his own duties as Prime Minister. This was an astute move, designed to allay political passions, and it succeeded very well. But clearly the arrangement was only a temporary one. On August 2nd Asquith deputed Lord Haldane, then Lord Chancellor and former War Secretary, to handle Army affairs on his behalf, and to put through mobilisation. Haldane complied, but made it clear that he had no wish for a second spell at the War Office. He and certain other members of the Cabinet, not to mention a popular clamour in the Press, all advised that Kitchener should take over. Asquith agreed.

Not everyone was in favour of the appointment, however, not even Kitchener himself. For the last forty years he had spent almost all his service abroad, in India and Africa (north and south), where one success after another had contributed to a seemingly impregnable reputation: enhanced, it must be said, by a magnificent physical appearance and proud bearing. He was the Ideal Soldier. On the other hand his long sojourn in the East had nurtured a sense of despotism and secrecy, an innate egotism, and a sheer oriental delight in personal splendour. His one remaining ambition was to become Viceroy of India, where he had already recast the military system as C-in-C, and in the process had brought about the resignation of the then Viceroy, Lord Curzon. In addition his absence from England had cut him off from all the major Army reforms, effected between the Boer and the First World Wars. He did not hide his disapproval of them. He thought the Regular Army far too small, and the Territorial Army beneath contempt, an entirely erroneous opinion based on preconceived notions about part-time soldiers. This was to have unfortunate repercussions later.

It is not surprising, therefore, that his principal critics were to be found among the senior Army officers at home, who were now to become his subordinates and colleagues. They were well aware of his opinions, qualities, and weaknesses, particularly his arrogance and pathological inability to delegate or co-operate. His way of working was to arrive, more or less intuitively, at decisions by himself, and then require his orders to be carried out. Consultation, in its full and proper sense, was almost unknown to him; and when he gave advice—as fellow members of the Cabinet were soon to find out—it usually took the form of a pronouncement. All this had served pretty well in the past, as his glittering career seemed to prove. But the past had been of a kind that one man, admittedly outstanding, was able to dominate—defeating ill-armed and ill-organised Sudanese at Omdurman, for example, or even wearing down the Boers, for although Kitchener had made many mistakes during the South African campaign, the ultimate outcome had concealed his errors in a cloud of success. But Kitchener was now 64, and the new war beginning had very little relation to the past, in terms of scale and technique. It was never capable of being dominated by one man, and in trying to dominate it Kitchener revealed himself as no more than human in his failings. It was thus a personal as well as a national tragedy that his record of service between August 1914 and his death in June 1916 definitely diminished his reputation, which had stood so high till then. As was feared he attempted far too much, and filled the senior posts at the War Office—with a very few exceptions—with compliant officers who were unable to stand up to him; indeed, most of the ablest had already rushed off to France. Action of this kind contributed directly to his decline from power, and to the appointment at the end of 1915 of Wully Robertson as CIGS, in which capacity he was to supplant Kitchener as chief military adviser to the Cabinet.

All this, however, lay in the future. Meanwhile, the country was delighted to learn that Asquith had persuaded Kitchener to join the Government. On August 3rd he had actually boarded the cross-Channel steamer at Dover, when summoned to London by telephone. Two days later he was formally appointed Secretary of State for War, the first active soldier to sit in the Cabinet for nearly a century.[2] He soon proved that, with all his defects, he was still capable of arriving at some astonishingly far-sighted decisions. One was that, so far from being over by Christmas, as the majority seemed to think, the war would last at least three years and involve millions of men. And he proceeded to launch a recruiting drive that enabled him to start sending drafts and divisions of freshly-trained troops into the line within a matter of months. Another followed his remarkably accurate appreciation of forthcoming German moves through Belgium. He argued that the Germans would never have taken so serious a step—after all it was that that had brought Britain in—unless they had meant *from the first* to stage their main attack in that quarter. He was not impressed by the French offensive in Alsace-Lorraine, launched at the outbreak of the war for patriotic rather than for strategic reasons, nor by the argument that the Germans would be too busy defending themselves against the Russians in the east to do anything substantial in the west. On the contrary he believed they wanted to win the war quickly in the west, and by an all-out attack on the northern flank.

That being so, the tiny BEF would stand right in the path of the main onslaught, and would need to profit from every advantage of time and space. In view of our late declaration of war, was it right to concentrate the force so far forward at

Maubeuge, as originally planned, and risk envelopment before it was ready? Was it not better to concentrate at Amiens 70 miles or so further back? After protracted argument at a Council of War, Kitchener finally gave way on this point. In fact the BEF did manage to get into position just in time—by August 20th—thanks partly to efficient transport arrangements, but also to the fact that Belgian resistance held up the Germans four or five days longer than expected. But he had his way over the question of committing the whole strength of the BEF, namely six infantry divisions and one cavalry division. Foreseeing the possibility of losing the entire force at the first impact, he decided to hold back two of the infantry divisions, Nos 4 and 6, as reinforcement and reserve when the situation warranted. He was bitterly opposed, and only yielded to the extent of allowing the 4th Division to arrive in time for the battle of Le Cateau on August 26th; but the 6th did not enter the line until the second week of September. Kitchener's decision was a disputable one, and informed opinion has never yet agreed about it. But in his general view of the strategy and opening moves of the campaign in the west, he was absolutely right, the only senior officer on the Allied side to be so.

Briefly, the Germans did mount their main offensive in the north, with forces far superior in men and equipment to the Belgians, the British, and the French Fifth Army opposing them. The Allied commanders, especially the French, completely misread the situation, and believed almost till the last moment that the initiative lay with *them*. Then came the awakening. On August 20th the main part of the Belgian Army retired into Antwerp. By the 21st the French offensive in the south had been halted and thrown back, and their Fifth Army was under attack on the River Sambre. On the 22nd the whole of the French centre and left was in violent conflict with the enemy and retiring. On this day British cavalry first made contact with the Germans, and II Corps (3rd and 5th Divisions, and 19th Infantry Brigade) moved up to the line of the Mons–Condé Canal, with I Corps (1st and 2nd Divisions) to the rear on the right. The roads were filling with refugees, and all the troops were tired after marching long distances on cobbles in the hot sun. Between the British right and the French left, a gape of nine miles had appeared, filled only intermittently with cavalry. There was a mental vacuum too, due to the inability of Sir John French and General Lanrezac, commander of the French Fifth Army, to agree or even to understand one another. The scene was set for the battle of Mons on August 23rd.

* * *

Let us now follow the movements of Wully at GHQ. On August 14th he crossed to France and spent the night at Amiens. On the 15th he went on to Paris, where he put up at the Hotel Crillon.

'The manager, M. Décquis, placed the best rooms at our disposal, and gave us what I have always thought to be the best dinner I have ever had. He produced an equally good English breakfast at five o'clock next morning, and when I asked him on leaving for the bill he replied he would send it to me at Berlin. . . I went to Berlin after the war, but I have not yet received the bill.'[3]

On the 16th Wully was one of the party that visited General Joffre at Vitry-le-François, and on the 17th he arrived at Le Cateau, where GHQ settled into a large school in the centre of the town.

'I and the four officers of my staff were billeted in a small house close by, the owner being a kind-hearted old lady who occupied the adjoining house. Woodroffe [ADC] quickly got our small mess into working order, and saw that nothing was lacking in the way of either food or drink. Our soldier-cook—still a dark horse—played up well, and was assisted by the woman cook of our landlady, though by what means they were able to understand each other's language was a mystery. This difficulty once led to a rather noisy altercation, which called for the intervention of Woodroffe. Hearing heated arguments taking place in the kitchen, in the most extraordinary mixture of French and English, he proceeded there to enquire what was the matter, and found the two cooks engaged in a tug of war at opposite sides of a frying-pan of potatoes which were to be cooked for breakfast. It transpired that the kitchen fire had refused to burn properly, and that the French cook was trying to explain to ours that she had a good fire next door and would take the potatoes there to cook, while our man was under the impression that she wished to appropriate them for herself, and he was determined not to let them go at any price. Woodroffe restored peace, and we got our potatoes by the required time. About a week later, when the German troops were nearing the town, I was able to repay the hospitality of our landlady by sending her off in a motor in the direction of Paris, as she had no other means of getting away.'[4]

At Le Cateau Wully devoted most of his time to visiting areas through which the troops were moving.

'Some fifty per cent of the infantry was composed of reservists just called up, and as most of them were not in hard condition, the blazing August sun and long stretches of white dusty roads made marching and the carrying of some 60 lbs of kit and equipment a heavy burden. All the more reason, therefore, why the Quarter-master-General's staff should be active, and personally see to it that there was no shortage of food or water, that the billets and bivouacs were as good as could be found, and that the transport conveying the requirements of the troops should reach its destination in good time. It was my purpose to ensure that this was done.'[5]

Wully was fully aware that, for his department, no less than for the fighting troops, the most difficult days lay ahead. What was going to happen? Although the official view still discounted a strong German offensive in the north, and proposed that the British and French should attempt to envelop the German right, there were already rumours to the contrary: in short, that the enemy

'. . . had larger forces north of the Meuse than the French seemed to think, and if, instead of our enveloping his right, he should succeed in enveloping our left, our line of communication would be seriously endangered, and we might in consequence be compelled to abandon our sea-bases at Havre and Boulogne, and establish others further to the south. Moreover, I knew before leaving England that Lord Kitchener was of the opinion that we were concentrating too far forward.'[6]

Wully had no doubt at all that his duty was to *prepare for the worst*, and so to organise supply as to keep the troops fully fed and provisioned, whatever happened. In the event of static warfare or an advance, this would be a comparatively simple matter. In the event of a retreat, quite the opposite. He therefore summoned Robb, Inspector-General of Communications, to GHQ, and on August 22nd—one day *before* the battle of Mons —made such preparations as he could. The vital decision affected the ports. Clearly, if the BEF retired, it would or

6. The incidents at Dir during the Chitral Campaign, 1895, as depicted in the *Daily Graphic*

7. Welbourn School, where Will Robertson earned sixpence a week as a pupil-teacher

8. A group at Aldershot in 1909. The front row includes King Edward VII, centre; Grierson, second from left; Mildred Robertson, third from left; Smith-Dorrien, fourth from left; Lady Smith-Dorrien, in white dress; French, third from right; and Wully, extreme right

should not do so by the way it had advanced—from the Channel coast. Kitchener had instructed French to 'support and co-operate with the French army', in other words to conform to Joffre's plans, and keep contact with the French Fifth Army on the right. This meant that the line of retreat would be inland, and that the advanced Channel ports might have to be abandoned. As history has recorded, Wully's appreciation proved remarkably accurate, and his decisions no less wise. Amiens was given up almost at once as a forward base, and was occupied by the Germans on August 31st. On the 24th all further movements through Havre and Boulogne were stopped. Three days later Boulogne had been cleared of stores, and on the 29th a new sea-base designated at St Nazaire on the west coast of Brittany, serving a new inland base at Le Mans. Meanwhile, a quantity of men and material awaited transshipment at Havre. All—20,000 officers and men, 7000 horses, and 60,000 tons of stores—were transferred west in the first four days of September.

Timely as these moves were, they incurred much dislocation and disorder.

'In the hurry and confusion attending evacuation of the original bases, the ships had been loaded on no system except that of getting out of the place as rapidly as possible, the Germans then being at Amiens and their advance parties pushed forward in the direction of Rouen. Different kinds of stores were inextricably mixed; machine guns were on one ship and their tripods on another, while the articles wanted first were, as often as not, at the bottom of the ship, below sacks of oats and bales of hay, and therefore were the last that could be got out. Moreover the establishment of a new base, even at a good port, is a matter which demands considerable time and previous preparation, and in many respects St. Nazaire happened to be particularly inconvenient and deficient of the facilities required.

'Another factor which militated against the prompt supply of food and stores was that we did not control the railways we used, and could not expect to do so. Trains were allotted to us daily by the French authorities, they were necessarily restricted in number, and the time and place of their arrival were very uncertain, as in the circumstances they were bound to be. The trouble was aggravated when they could no longer pass through Amiens and had to proceed to the front via Paris, for besides the exodus from that city which was then taking place, Joffre was transferring masses of troops from his right to his left, and for these and other reasons there was a widespread congestion and dislocation of railway traffic. I found that the only sure way of getting trains up by the time they were wanted was to send the indefatigable Percival [DAQMG] down to Paris by motor, and for him to board the train and compel the station-master to send it forward. Many a time he did this, and was instrumental in producing food for the troops, which but for his efforts they would not have received.'[7]

Of course everything was vastly aggravated by the retreat itself, which lasted from August 24th until September 5th, from Mons to a position behind the River Marne, SSE of Paris, a marching distance of more than 200 miles. It is not necessary to retell this epic, except in outline, since full accounts already exist. In brief, apart from two pitched battles, one of encounter at Mons on August 23rd and a delaying action at Le Cateau on August 26th, both fought by II Corps, the retreat consisted in the main of numerous small-scale engagements by units of the tiny BEF, relentlessly harrassed by an immensely superior enemy, which sought to entrap and destroy the whole force. That the British succeeded in fending the Germans off and reaching the Marne, depleted but intact as a fighting force, was due to the amazing courage and endurance of officers and men, to their high state of training (especially in the handling of the rifle), and to the coolness and competence of the majority of unit and formation commanders.

By way of illustration of some of the unit fighting—in this case the cavalry—above all of the magnificent morale which permeated the whole BEF, I quote the following extracts from the Beddington Memoir.

August 26th. Captain Beddington was now 2nd-in-command of C Squadron of 16th Lancers

'I was sent off with 2 troops and 2 guns of E Battery RHA under John Gough (not the Staff College teacher), to find a position whence we could enfilade the Germans as they debouched uphill from Le Cateau. We found a lovely place and John did rare execution with his guns: I could see it well, being on his left in case the Germans came and attacked from that direction. By about 1 pm John had used up all his ammunition and all he could collect locally, which was not much as his guns were 13 pounders [the cavalry field-piece], and I was wondering what to do next when a signaller came up about 1.30 pm with a message to say the regiment was moving East by South, and I was to rejoin bringing Gough and his guns with me. The Regiment had an hour's start of me, but I had the luck to come up with them at Beaurevoir about midnight. We marched all night and reached St. Quentin at midday 27th August: we got rations and forage there but owing to a false alarm we were hurried off to Itancourt, and finally billeted there for the night. It was on these long days that in the hot weather one got fearfully thirsty and dry: I found that biting the apples on the roadside trees, sucking the juice and not eating the apples, was an excellent refresher.

August 28th

'We moved southwards towards Jussy, after some scrapping with unenterprising German cavalry that did us no harm, and reached there about 5 pm, after crossing the Crozat Canal. About 6 pm Charles Campbell told me he wanted me to take 2 troops on outpost, and that he would relieve me soon after dawn with his other 2 troops. . . I made up my mind to look for a place whence I could picquet the German billets and thus not be surprised. I found the ideal spot about 3000 yards N. of Jussy at a railway bridge, quite close to Montescourt where I knew the most advanced Germans were billeted. I had the bridge put into a rough state of defence, i.e. loopholes in the parapet facing north and sandbag cover to the two flanks, with a wire entanglement across the road under the railway bridge (the wire and posts came from the French farm fences), and with trip wires across the road some ten yards away both North and South. Meanwhile I searched the few houses of Montescourt and was lucky enough to find a baker whom I ordered to bake 50 loaves forthwith: he refused, so I put a Corporal in charge of him and told him he would be shot if the loaves were not ready by midnight, which of course they were.

'The night was quiet until about 11.30 pm when someone was challenged, approaching from Jussy. He did not bother to answer and was lucky to escape being shot, but he fell over the trip wire and turned out to be the Squadron Quartermaster Sergeant, wheeling a barrow load full of sardine tins sent me by Charles Campbell. At midnight we issued rations. . . The work on the bridge was finished, and I posted 10 men under Jack Wodehouse to hold it and let everybody sleep, but to wake me at the first alarm. . . I was wakened at 3.30 am (August 29th) and told that enemy cavalry were moving on the bridge from the North. It was still dark and I had some difficulty in restraining the men from opening fire. When they got really close to the wire, about twelve yards, I ordered fire to be opened. The effect was complete surprise. One officer and 9

men were killed and others wounded, and the survivors turned
back; of course we had no casualties. . . As it got light, a German
mounted patrol under an officer appeared on our left flank between
us and a wood. I told a Corporal and 2 men to shoot at them, and a
lucky shot hit and knocked out the officer's horse at a range of about
500 yards. I told the Corporal to bring him in, the others having
disappeared into the wood. . . The prisoner was unhurt, a delightful
Prussian Guards Cavalry Division Captain, who spoke English
well. We chatted and his only complaint was that his capture was an
awful foul, for none of his men could hit a haystack at 500 yards,
let alone a cantering horse. Shortly afterwards Charles Campbell
arrived with two more troops, and I rode back to Jussy, accompanied
by the prisoner on a spare horse, to take command of D Squadron,
to which I had been appointed the previous evening.'

At GHQ the atmosphere was often tense and sometimes
confused. Sir John French was at odds with General Lanrezac,
the French commander on his right, and the former quickly
got the impression that he was continually being let down by
the rapid French retirements. The fact was that both men were
suffering under the appalling strain of command, and their
judgment was often impaired. In the end Joffre intervened to
replace Lanrezac, while Kitchener had to come over to France
himself, to make sure that Sir John did not pull the BEF out
of the line at the very moment when Joffre was preparing his
counter-attack on the Marne. Others were feeling the strain,
too, and reacting in their own fashion. Murray, the CGS,
competent but highly strung, collapsed at least once through
sheer fatigue, while Henry Wilson—always ebullient—was
inclined to make macabre jokes about the fate of the BEF.

Wully, on the other hand, was a rock of calm and resource.
He said little, worked himself and his subordinates to the limit
of endurance, and only occasionally let out some caustic comment on the way things were going. He never lacked a grim
sense of humour and he never lost his nerve. Typical is his
reference to an incident which occurred when GHQ had
moved for the fourth time in a few days—from Le Cateau to
St Quentin, to Noyon, to Compiègne, to Dammartin, and
subsequently twice more to Lagny and to Melun, the end of
the retreat.

'As can be imagined our personal feeding arrangements were

rather sketchy and uncertain during the hurry of the retreat, but at Dammartin we hoped for better things and were looking forward to the enjoyment of a roast leg of mutton for dinner. Suddenly, however, the order was given to move to Lagny, and as it was then seven o'clock we had to go off without any dinner at all, the leg of mutton, just ready for eating, being packed up in a newspaper and taken away on the floor of a motor lorry. It was none the worse next day, except for being cold.'[8]

As for his work, he blew to bits any idea that he suffered from overcaution or was rigid in his methods. In his own words:

'In the retreat a large amount of clothing and equipment were either lost, captured, or thrown away . . . and it was my duty to see that they were immediately replaced. The ordnance regulations were of the most stringent red-tape description, and before stores were allowed to be issued, commanding officers had to render, sometimes in triplicate, elaborate "army forms" setting out their demands and giving full reasons for them. It was absurd to suppose that this procedure could be adhered to when the troops were constantly at close grips with a pursuing enemy; when the wretched forms, with all other army stationery, had perhaps been left behind or thrown away; and when the commanding officers, killed, wounded, taken prisoner, or for some other reason could not readily be found. There was no authority at all, to the best of my memory, for the free issue of clothing to officers. They were expected to get it, I imagine, as in peace, from Savile Row or other places inhabited by the military tailors of London.

'The senior ordnance officer at GHQ was at first terribly perplexed to know what to do. . . He must often have thought me most irrational and unsympathetic, for I would listen to nothing about his regulations, so long as officers and men were going about bareheaded for want of a cap, or had their backs exposed to drenching rain for lack of a coat. I insisted that the missing articles must be replaced at once . . . and said that the entire responsibility would be mine if he got into trouble.

'The distribution of supplies was another difficulty as it became impossible to know where particular units might be. I could only guess . . . send their food there . . . and a further supply to other probable places, in the hope that if the first consignment did not reach them, the second would. The expedient was also adopted of dumping supplies—flitches of bacon, sides of beef, cheese, boxes of biscuits—alongside the roads so that the troops might help themselves as they passed.'[9]

Wully's brilliant improvisations worked well. Although many of the stores were inevitably lost—and incidentally led the Germans to believe the BEF was in headlong rout, which it was not—the chief aim was achieved. Unhappily, there was another by-product of war, which clogged the movement of the troops on the roads and nearly put paid to Wully's frantic efforts to supply them—the refugees.

'The flight of these fugitives was a strange mixture of tragedy and comedy. All the men were old or very young; the children, some laughing, some crying, went by in droves; and tired mothers, carrying their infants on their backs, crawled along the hot and dusty roads with fear and despair on their terror-stricken faces. Two, three, and even four generations of a family sometimes could be seen making their way together to the rear, some on foot, others riding in farm-carts, donkey-carts, ox-wagons, on bicycles, in perambulators, according to age and circumstances, whilst the household effects and farm stock with which they were accompanied were of the most varied description. Cows, sheep, goats, pigs, fowls, geese, ducks, cats and dogs, carried or driven, were amongst the number, and vehicles of every kind, from a wagon to a wheelbarrow, were brought into use and laden with every imaginable article from beds to bird-cages. As if to intensify the distress and misery of the scene, the distant sky was black with smoke rising in dense clouds from the burning villages . . . but a few hours before . . . the homes of those who were now fleeing from them, knowing and caring not where, so long as they were safe from the Hun.'[10]

*　　　*　　　*

But the immediate agony was nearing its end. The enemy offensive was over-reaching itself. On August 30th, von Kluck, commander of the First Army on the German right, swung SE away from Paris, in an attempt to entrap the French Fifth Army and roll up the troops holding the centre of the Allied line. By this manœuvre he gave a respite to the Allied left— the French Sixth Army under Maunoury forming up NE of Paris, the Paris garrison under Galliéni, and the BEF, next in the line, withdrawing over the Marne. All these troops—of whose condition and strength the Germans were largely ignorant—escaped the net, and constituted the main part of the counter-stroke launched by Joffre on September 6th. It was touch-and-go even then, partly on account of personalities. As noted, Lanrezac had to be replaced (by the dynamic Franchet d'Esperey), while Sir John French—by now convinced that the BEF was too battered to continue the fight—had first to be overruled by Kitchener, and then cajoled by Joffre to conform to the plan. Even Joffre had to some extent to be primed by Galliéni as to the timing of the move.

It is no part of this narrative to describe in detail or discuss the moves and might-have-beens of the battle of the Marne, or of the battle of the Aisne which followed it, for Wully was not involved in the operational planning or execution of either. It is sufficient to record that, in reacting to the Allied attack, the German First and Second Armies (on the enemy right flank) allowed a gap to open up between them, into which the BEF marched. Although not conducted without sharp fighting, it was a move more in the nature of a by-product of battles elsewhere, than a major offensive on its own. None the less, it was of the utmost importance. The threat it offered impelled the whole German retreat, and had it been launched with greater violence and élan by fresh troops, the consequences might have been catastrophic for the Germans. Even so by September 13th the BEF had succeeded in crossing the River Aisne, an advance of some 70 miles. On the 14th, however, the arrival of German reserves, released by the fall of Maubeuge, brought the movement to a halt. Thereafter trench warfare developed, and in this part of the line stalemate set in.

Meanwhile both sides engaged in groping efforts to outflank each other to the north. So far as the British were concerned, the main body of the BEF was pulled out of the line early in October and sent up to Flanders, to the general area west of Lille, where it was immediately involved in costly attempts to push east—to anticipate or even get round the Germans, or alternatively to prevent the enemy breaking through to the Channel ports. However, there too deadlock soon set in, the line running roughly from Givenchy northwards to Armentières, Wytschaete, and Ypres, where a new British force arrived from northern Belgium on October 14th. This force, IV Corps, had earlier been shipped direct from England in a belated attempt to hold up the Germans round Ghent and Bruges, and indirectly to assist the Belgian Army in the defence of Antwerp, where a scratch force of British marines had also been sent at the eleventh hour. After Antwerp capitulated on October 10th, the Belgians established a permanent defence line on the River Yser, north and south of Dixmude near the coast, while IV Corps moved down to Ypres as described. It was joined a week later by I Corps (the last formation to leave the Aisne), by the Indian Corps at the end of October, and by the 8th Division from England early in November. This gave the BEF a total of ten infantry and three cavalry divisions, most of them brought up to strength by considerable drafts sent over during the last four months of the year. Finally three more divisions were added before the end of December.

The majority of these troops took part in the First Battle of Ypres, which lasted from October 19th to November 14th. This was in effect a series of desperate engagements up and down the British line, the French assisting round Ypres itself, with the German Fourth and Sixth Armies, which strove repeatedly to break through. They very nearly succeeded in doing so. It was the last phase of open or semi-open fighting, and such trench warfare as developed had to be improvised. The trenches themselves were shallow, hastily dug under fire with inadequate means, not continuous, and protected very little by wire. The Germans were much superior in numbers (about 2:1 overall), and had a far greater complement of machine guns, heavy artillery, and most other material. They also had the advantage of higher ground to the east. The British, however, made full tactical use of woods, ditches, and other cover, in a generally inferior position. They excelled as always with the rifle and a limited amount of field artillery, although the ammunition was deficient in both quantity and quality. They were also well led and staffed, and the few reserves were employed with the utmost economy and effect. All displayed the most astonishing bravery and staying power, so that when the fighting died down at last, the front (though dented here and there) was still intact, and the threat of a major disaster in the north had been averted. But the cost had been appalling. Of the force that had landed in August barely one officer and thirty men per battalion survived, in sum only just sufficient to maintain the framework of the army in the field, and help train the drafts and the new citizen army being raised at home.

*   *   *

On November 15th the French took over the Ypres salient, and the BEF consolidated along a continuous front from near Wytschaete in the north to Givenchy in the south. Thereafter the fighting subsided, and both sides settled down to construct trenches and rearward defences, and organise services. Only minor actions were fought until the spring of 1915. The respite was badly needed. Heavy rain fell in the first half of December, and conditions deteriorated. Nevertheless, much was done to rest and re-equip the men, and—where necessary by improvisation—to make good the deficiencies in supplies.

The fact was, as Wully well knew, that production at home was nowhere near what was needed in France. Since the Aisne fighting in mid-September, he had been waging a dour battle of his own with all the administrative and supply problems generated by the Army's move northward. First came the move itself, which was partly his responsibility. The cavalry went by road, the infantry by rail—but to destinations hard to determine at the outset, since all depended on how far west the enemy had penetrated. In the end arrangements answered reasonably well, and the men were involved neither in a running battle with German patrols nor in a surfeit of marching. GHQ moved up to Abbeville on October 8th, and to St Omer shortly afterwards. Havre was restored as the principal port and base. There was also the problem of the British troops retiring from Belgium. 'It took us some days properly to get hold of these contingents, find out where they were, who they were, and what they had with them'[11]—a pregnant statement, as anyone knows who has been involved in a comparable situation.

The fighting that preceded Ypres, above all the First Battle of Ypres itself, put an enormous strain on supply and communications. Stocks of ammunition ran down like water, especially of the 18-pounder gun and 4.5-inch howitzer, the staple field artillery. On November 16th Wully told von Donop, the Master-General of Ordnance, that the stock of 18-pounder ammunition had fallen alarmingly, and that an allowance of ten rounds per gun per day was barely possible.

'As to 4.5" ammunition I can say nothing. The figures speak for themselves and it seems hopeless.'

On November 24th he added:

'The total stock . . . is only about half the regulation allowance, and that allowance, as we already know, is much below what is required for a war of the present nature. . . It is sad to think that we have provided guns which fire ten or more rounds per minute, while our output is less than ten rounds in twenty-four hours. Artillery is dominating this war. . .'[12]

At the worst moment he had to reduce the ration to *three* rounds per gun per day, but this was just a symptom of the chronic shortage that bedevilled the BEF for months to come. It was a similar story in regard to gun spares, and to trench mortars and grenades. On December 24th Wully wrote:

'Our troops are very greatly handicapped in this matter. Every corps without exception has several times reported that their men are simply bombed out of their trenches and other localities. No sooner do they capture them than the Germans bomb them out. . . When do you think that some of the 200 additional mortars referred to in my earlier letter are likely to be ready?'[13]

To help fill the gap, mortars were manufactured at the Royal Engineer and Ordnance workshops at Havre, and grenades or 'jam pots' compounded on the spot out of gun cotton, nails, and other unlikely and unreliable materials. Even rifles were short, though not specifically in France. They were urgently needed for the new units training in England, and for formations elsewhere. To this end every weapon possible was gathered up from the wounded and the dead, and passed back to base armourers or to workshops at home.

Weapons and ammunition were not the only things in short supply. Wully sent a constant stream of urgent demands back to Cowans, QMG at the War Office, for practically everything that a soldier needed for his existence in the bitter Flanders weather: trench stores of every description, material for revetments, wire, wire cutters, field cables, braziers, uniforms and underclothing, blankets, boots, socks, coats, comforts, hose tops for Highlanders. . . Soon the response began to flow, unofficial as well as official, and troops were to be seen dressed up like Christmas trees, wearing a wild variety of headgear, mufflers, skin waistcoats, and oversize greatcoats. Wully wrote to Cowans on November 21st:

'The weather still continues very cold. The snow has not moved and the frost is severe. There are many cases of frostbite. . . As regards boots in general they must be very large sized, and so must jackets and trousers. The men simply stuff on all the clothes they have, and they are becoming pretty numerous in view of the large amount of gifts sent up, and a great deal of room is required both in the boots and in the clothes. The men never grumble at having too large boots, as they can always put on two or three pairs of socks.'[14]

In due course storage became a problem, and some restraint had to be exercised. Sleighs were refused, and an offer of 50,000 Japanese hand warmers by the *Daily Express*! One of the most welcome and necessary improvements was the bath houses, set up in factories or other large buildings in the rear. Here men came out of the line for a wash and change of underclothing, and had the lice baked and ironed out of their uniforms.

Some of the chaos was unavoidable, the outcome of the Marne retreat and recent battles, and was soon cleared up. But there was a deeper, more serious aspect. Pre-war planners had made a bad mistake about the provision of machine guns (the BEF only had two per battalion), trench mortars and grenades, heavy artillery (almost non-existent), and even field artillery. They had completely miscalculated ammunition requirements, which were soon to rocket with the development of trench warfare—all of which would take some two years to make good. But the Government, and the nation behind it, were also to blame, for public opinion before the war would never have sanctioned the scale of preparation, in terms of either men or material, needed for an emergency such as this.

Moreover, false optimism was still abroad, both in England—Kitchener and Churchill excepted—and in France. At GHQ Sir John French talked blithely, even at the most desperate stage of the Ypres battle, about driving the Germans across the Rhine, if only Kitchener would send him the necessary men and material. Neither he nor Wilson believed in Kitchener's forecast of a long war, or that it was right to train entirely fresh citizen armies. French, of course, was actuated by sentiments other than professional disagreement. A touchy man, he had deeply resented Kitchener's visit to France at the critical juncture of the Marne, also the dispatch of a separate force to

Belgium to help save Antwerp, and he was convinced (not without reason) that Kitchener sought to act as if he were C-in-C and CIGS combined, as well as Secretary of State for War: after all, Kitchener was the senior Field-Marshal in employment, entitled to wear uniform, and still the hero of the public. It must be said, too, that French and Wilson were not alone in their conviction that the Germans would be defeated soon, or at least that the BEF would shortly make a big advance. Most of the senior staff and commanders thought likewise, including Wully, and many of their opposite numbers at home as well. Cowans, for example, in his letters to Wully, frequently added a postscript in a half-joking half-impatient tone, on the lines of 'Do get a move on' and 'Don't let the men throw away their new clothing when you go forward.'[15]

By December 1914, it had become clear that Murray, CGS to the BEF, whose health and temperament had not stood up well to the events of the last few months, would have to be replaced, and rumours began circulating as to his successor. The obvious choice was, again, Wilson. He was able, full of ideas, spoke French well, and got on with the French High Command. Sir John supported his candidature strongly. But Wilson's reputation for intrigue, in particular his activities over the Curragh and his outspoken criticisms of Kitchener, bedevilled his prospects as before. Asquith had not altered his opinion of him, and obviously Kitchener was no friend. And there were others against him. Haig, for instance, made an adverse comment in his diary, but noted at the same time that Wully—whose name was now being suggested as an alternative—could not be spared. At Christmas it seemed that, for lack of agreement, Murray would have to stay put.

But the BEF was steadily expanding in strength and status. It now consisted of eleven infantry and five cavalry divisions, most of them at full complement. As from December 26th it was reorganised and redesignated as follows:

First Army (General Sir Douglas Haig)
　I Corps (Monro), IV Corps (Rawlinson), Indian Corps (Willcocks)
Second Army (General Sir Horace Smith-Dorrien)
　II Corps (Fergusson), III Corps (Pulteney), 27th Division (Snow)

Cavalry Corps (Allenby)
Indian Cavalry Corps (Rimington)

Too much was at stake for the matter of the succession to be postponed much longer. On January 17th 1915 General Joffre visited GHQ at St Omer for a conference, at which both Wilson and Wully were present. In the afternoon the two men were out together in a car, discussing the morning's business. They then talked about Murray and his job. Wilson (who already knew he would not get it) told Wully that he would refuse the appointment, if offered it, and intimated he thought it likely it would now be offered to Wully. According to Wilson, Wully showed great reluctance, and begged him to use his influence with Sir John not to make the offer. He too, Wully said, would have to refuse, since he feared Sir John would fail and bring him down with him. So runs Wilson's account, concluding, 'The chance of a lifetime, and two men in one car, both refusing it!'[16] Nine days later, to Wilson's considerable surprise, Wully did accept, and Wilson was appointed Chief Liaison Officer to the French GQG (High Command).

How accurate Wilson's record is in detail, we can only guess, but the substance seems correct. In his Autobiography, published in 1921, when Sir John French was still alive, Wully wrote more circumspectly:

'In January 1915 the Commander-in-Chief asked me to become Chief of the General Staff in place of Murray, who was about to return to England. The offer was a tempting one, as it meant an increase of pay as well as of position, but I did not wish to accept it. I had become interested in my work, I knew that the Commander-in-Chief had previously asked for another officer to succeed Murray, which was sufficient proof that I was not his first choice, and although he had appeared quite satisfied with me as Quartermaster-General, there was no certainty that either of us would be equally happy if I became his Chief of the General Staff. I therefore asked to be allowed to stay where I was, and after further discussion a final decision was, by my request, deferred for a day or two. In the end I realised that it was my duty to put personal considerations aside, and on the 25th of January I took up the new post, being succeeded as Quartermaster-General by Major-General Maxwell.'[17]

There is nothing difficult or dishonest in reconciling these two accounts, for they do not fundamentally disagree; but it is necessary, too, to enter into the atmosphere and the relationship between the two men. Wilson and Wully had disliked each other for a long time, for they were utterly different in temperament and make-up. On this occasion, however, they found common ground to the extent that both thought Sir John French inadequate as C-in-C, regarding him as reckless, touchy, and impulsive, and insufficiently educated or gifted to control large formations, especially in association with an ally. At the same time Wilson (an Irishman like his chief), with all his flair, verve, and social assurance, was on easy, intimate terms with Sir John, messed with him, and was confident of handling the old man, whatever he did. Wully, on the other hand, was not so sure of his ground. He knew himself to be blunt and reserved, economical in speech and gesture, and less pliant temperamentally. Socially he was far less adept, although he never allowed himself to be browbeaten, however arrogant French might be. The fact that he had been a NCO when the latter was a rising regimental officer worried him not at all. On the contrary, he was proud of having come up from the ranks, and was sure on that account that he knew the Army better than anyone else—it added to his stature and was an important element in his formidable character. But it was for that reason too that he hesitated, since he distrusted French's professional competence and personal qualities as a commander, and doubted whether he—or anyone else—could counteract these disabilities as chief staff officer. He foresaw the situation arising, perhaps again and again, in which loyalty to his chief would conflict with his judgment as CGS, and he shrank from the prospect. In the end he mastered his reluctance, as he said, and there is no reason whatever to doubt the sincerity of that statement. It was a decision compounded of conscience, natural ambition, and response to a challenge. He accepted the appointment.

* * *

Wully became CGS to the BEF on January 25th 1915. What were the prospects of the war?

Lord Hankey related that although there was no organisation for the supreme direction of Britain's part in the war, comparable in scope and efficiency to the one set up later, yet a War

Council had been formed by Asquith at the end of November 1914, and that this body did advise the Cabinet on the problems and policy of direction, including strategy.[18] Moreover, two Memoranda touching strategy had been circulated by early January 1915, one by Hankey himself, the other by Lloyd George. Although composed without mutual reference, they had many important points in common. They agreed, for example, that following the First Battle of Ypres a deadlock had been reached in the fighting in France, that it was a waste of life and effort to continue to attack, and that some new tactic must be tried. Hankey suggested that either a new weapon must be evolved to overcome the defensive power of trenches, barbed wire, and machine guns—he hinted, *inter alia*, at the tank—or a new front must be opened up elsewhere. His plan was to attack Turkey and to bring in all the Balkan states against her: a manœuvre that would keep Bulgaria on the right side, and bring aid both to Serbia (still holding her own against Austria) and to Russia in the Caucasus. Lloyd George wanted an offensive against Austria, either in the Adriatic region or through the Balkans from Salonika.

In opposition to these ideas was a plan submitted by Sir John French, in which he refused to admit the inevitability of deadlock in the west. He contended that the German line *could* be broken, provided he had enough artillery ammunition, especially high explosive, and proposed an attack along the coast of Flanders, supported by the Belgians and the British Navy. In general he supported Joffre in the belief that the Germans should be attacked as soon as possible, preferably before the spring, while their main effort was being concentrated against the Russians; after that it might be too late. It should be added that Joffre and most of the French commanders were also influenced by other considerations, above all by the natural and burning desire to rid France of the enemy, whatever the cost.

The War Council discussed all these and contingent proposals during the first half of January, and arrived at two main decisions:

first, to mount a naval attack on the Dardanelles in February, a proposal advanced by Churchill.

secondly, to prepare for the Flanders operation, but to postpone the final decision until the beginning of February.

In the end the Flanders operation was negatived by Joffre, who wanted the BEF to support him in his own offensive plans; but the Dardanelles plan went forward, and the outer forts were bombarded on February 19th. Such was the start of the disastrous Gallipoli campaign, which dragged fitfully on for the rest of 1915. As a strategic conception it was imaginative and full of possibilities, although the capture of Constantinople would not necessarily have put Turkey out of the war, as Mustafa Kemal was to prove in 1919–21. As an operation, however, it was never properly planned, and the execution broke down again and again through lack of preparation and control. Although originally intended as a naval action— making no demands upon military resources—it was realised soon after the first bombardment that the Army would have to take part too. And so, after a second naval attempt on March 18th—which only just failed—a military expedition was hastily mounted under the command of Sir Ian Hamilton. Five divisions were landed on April 28th and gained a foothold, but no more. A second major effort with a dozen divisions was undertaken in August, but after coming tantalisingly near to success this broke down too. Stalemate ensued, and after an agonising autumn of indecision the whole force was evacuated —miraculously without further loss—in December 1915 and January 1916. Total casualties, however, amounted to over 200,000 killed, wounded, and missing, and a vast quantity of material was lost besides.

The strategic and political consequences were, perhaps, even more damaging. Had Gallipoli succeeded, the whole Balkan situation might well have been transformed, as had once been hoped. As it was, Turkey gained a new lease of life, and Bulgaria joined the Central Powers, and helped annihilate the Serbs. Too late a Franco-British force was sent to Salonika, where it not only failed to save the Serbs, but barely managed to keep out the Bulgars. Furthermore, the Salonika front continued to absorb Allied troops and resources, without any material benefit, almost till the end of the war. It was to be regarded by Wully, when CIGS at the War Office, as a running sore and a military mistake of the first magnitude. The entry of Italy into the war on the Allied side in May 1915 did little to offset this tale of disaster.

So much for a brief reference to the main military events outside France, in so far as they affected the British war effort in 1915. Several historians state that once the decision had been made to undertake land operations in the eastern Mediterranean, then everything should have been concentrated there, and the west should have been allowed to remain quiescent. But that was not practical policy, as was shown by what happened in France. Small as it was, the BEF found itself involved in no less than three offensives—Neuve Chapelle (March 10th–13th), Aubers Ridge and Festubert (May 9th–25th), and Loos (September 25th–October 16th). Although all were costly and abortive, and none made any significant impression upon the Germans, they were entirely induced by pressure for offensive action in concert with the French. And this takes no account of the Second Battle of Ypres, a defensive action of fearful intensity, April 22nd–May 25th.

Briefly, Kitchener (who was primarily responsible for military strategy), and the War Council at his back, were facing a dilemma that bedevilled the whole strategy of the war. Should the main effort be made in the east or the west? In 1915 both were tried, and both failed utterly. The truth was that Britain was ready, neither for a one-front nor for a two-front campaign, yet she was committed to war. Moreover, once committed, it was impossible to contract out of action altogether, and less and less possible to disengage on any one front—even partially—and from France least of all, as events were to show.

What then were the Western arguments, which prevailed in the end?

Geography

Germany and her allies—the Central Powers—were located in a bloc in the middle of the Continent, with continuous land communications between them. Germany held the predominant position. That meant she could quickly, economically, and effectively reinforce any front, for offence or defence, by *interior* lines.

The Allies were located on the circumference of Europe, and so had to depend on longer, *exterior*, lines of communication, many of them by sea. This involved the use of shipping and a far greater expenditure of time and resources: in short, a much heavier and more complex logistical burden, mainly borne by Britain.

The War so far

Germany had held the initiative since the start. By the end of 1915 she had captured large areas in the east, west, and south-east. But she had broken through in no vital spot, for although Serbia had been eliminated, her defeat did not affect the main issue.

Germany was near the peak of her effort, France and Russia were at or past theirs, while Britain and her empire had not yet reached hers. On balance, then, the situation favoured the Allies, in that their potential resources were the greater. On the other hand, Germany was in a powerful defensive position. Therefore it was to her advantage to try to exhaust the Allies by entrapping them in subsidiary fronts. Gallipoli, Salonika, Italy, the Middle East, made no impression upon her, for she could resist sideshows indefinitely. In this way, even if she could no longer win, she could certainly not be defeated.

The Future

France and Flanders remained the *vital* front for both sides, because a decision here could end the war. At one point the line was within 50 miles of Paris, and a German break-through would be immediately fatal. On the other hand a German collapse would have a similar, though not quite such a quick, result. This is what actually happened in 1918.

For Britain, as for France, the western front was the easiest to support in terms of men and supplies. Logistical problems were smaller. Moreover, it was advantageous to train formations in country similar and near to the battle areas, where the troops could also act as reserves in case of emergency.

The Allies were numerically superior in the west, and would soon be so in terms of material as well.

Much valuable French territory remained in German hands. This, and the fact that France had sustained the main effort of the war so far, had all told on her powers of resistance. It was therefore essential to back her in her own country to the uttermost, and throw the Germans out as soon as possible. Her morale might not survive a policy of indefinite defence.

The war could only be won by offence—by fighting hard, and by concentrating every effort on the decisive front. There was no way round that. Whatever the techniques evolved to master trench defences, heavy casualties had to be anticipated and endured, and the whole strategic plan sustained by a determined effort of will, carried through to the end.

Once the Germans had been beaten in France, then all the other fronts would fall in automatically. But if the Germans won in France, then no other front would count, and the war would be lost.

Such, in brief, was the Western case. Naturally it appealed most forcibly to the men in France. Sir John French and most of his subordinates, including Wully, were convinced Westerners, they could hardly be otherwise. The BEF was steadily gaining in strength and would rise to 36 divisions by the end of 1915. How were the troops to be employed, if they did not fight? Their whole *raison d'être* was to assist the French, who were mounting offensive after offensive. If the BEF was reduced, or stood tamely on the defensive, it might cause a breach with the French Army, let alone the French Government. And—whatever Sir John's faults and exaggerations—was he not justified in saying that it was far too *early* to decide that the German line could *not* be broken? What might not yet be done by new methods and plenty of ammunition? The French at least were determined to try. It was incumbent on him to do likewise.

Kitchener generally concurred, although he was fully aware that the BEF could make no large-scale effort before 1916. He never had any faith in the Dardanelles expedition until it was too late. If possible, he would have preferred to abstain from all offensive action until the nation was ready, and until a strategy had been formulated with the means to prosecute it. But that was a familiar problem in history, rarely capable of ideal solution, to be experienced again by the British Army in France and Norway in 1940, and in Greece in 1941. As it was, the failures in east and west during 1915 contributed directly to Kitchener's decline from power and popularity, no less than the shortage of munitions, for which he was also held personally responsible.

*   *   *

Munitions were an involved story. It was realised, almost at the outset of the war, that artillery requirements had been grossly miscalculated, and a Cabinet committee was formed in

October 1914 to try to improve the position. It achieved very little, partly because Kitchener insisted on keeping things under his own hand. By January 1915, moreover, the outlook was obviously deteriorating. The trades unions were objecting to the dilution of labour, thus impeding the expansion of production, and Kitchener had been quite unable to change their attitude. In February Lloyd George circulated a trenchant Memorandum on the subject, and in March Sir John French made out that the attack at Neuve Chapelle had failed for lack of shells. In fact the attack failed for other reasons, but he was using a popular argument as a cover for the failure of the operation, and of his own optimistic predictions in particular. There was, however, a very real shortage overall, especially of heavy guns and ammunition; and this problem was unresolved. In April a Munitions Committee was set up under the chairmanship of Lloyd George, upon which Kitchener was represented, but it did not carry enough weight to be effective— although Lloyd George himself made good progress with the trades unions. The crisis finally came on May 14th when, on information supplied privately by French, Lord Northcliffe attacked Kitchener in the Press, accusing him of starving the Army of shells. In so doing he hoped to drive Kitchener out of office altogether, for that was the real object of his campaign. He failed, but his action contributed to the demise of the Liberal Government five days later, and to its replacement by a Coalition.[19] When the new Government emerged, it contained a Ministry of Munitions with Lloyd George at the head, while Kitchener was entirely relieved of this responsibility. Although the new Ministry profited materially from the latter's work—a fact not generally recognised—there is no doubt that Lloyd George infused order and a blast of urgency, and succeeded where Kitchener had failed. The crisis was truly desperate but improvement agonisingly slow. The BEF survived the shortage of artillery ammunition only by the narrowest of margins, and a whole year was to pass before there were enough guns and shells to make possible warfare of the scale and shock desired by the Westerners.

* * *

Such was the background to the part played by Wully in 1915. At the very outset he was keenly aware of the strategic dilemma in which the BEF was placed. In broad terms, for a small force in such a vulnerable position, defence—and a period of build-up—was the only obvious course. Yet the BEF was soon to be involved in fierce fighting once again, due essentially to its subsidiary role in the conduct of the war in France. Wully wrote afterwards:

'A defensive policy was not practicable, and yet it is true that our armies were not in a condition to fight with any good prospect of obtaining decisive results.'[20]

Broad strategy, however, was not then his concern, although he never ceased to think about it and soon felt compelled to make his views known more widely. But in January 1915, it was the immediate situation that mattered, and Wully began characteristically by reorganising his own office, simplifying procedure, and choosing his own men: among them, Colonel Frederick Maurice, who became head of the Operations branch in April with the rank of Brigadier-General. Since the two men combined into a formidable and famous partnership, both in France and later at the War Office, and were both imbued with the same aim—the winning of the war in France and nowhere else—it is necessary at this point to bring Maurice into closer view.

Frederick Barton Maurice (familiarly, Freddy Maurice) was the eldest son of General Sir Frederick Maurice, a distinguished Professor of Military History at the Staff College, and grandson of the Reverend Frederick Denison Maurice, Christian Socialist, and founder of the Working Men's College. Like his father and grandfather, Maurice was a man of unswerving probity, who guided his life literally and without exception according to the dictates of conscience. So much so that in 1918—as will be told—he deliberately sacrificed his professional career for the sake of a principle in which he passionately believed. His Army service had been exemplary. Eleven years younger than Wully, with all the advantages of his class, a quick brain, even temperament, and ability for hard work, he moved quickly up the ladder of promotion. Starting in the infantry in 1892, he went as a special service officer to the South African War and was promoted brevet major at the age of 29. He entered the Staff

College in 1902, and afterwards held a succession of staff jobs including that of a GSO2 in the Directorate of Staff Duties at the War Office under Haig. In 1913 he served as an instructor at the Staff College during the last nine months of Wully's Commandantship, and it was then that their close friendship and professional association began. When war broke out he went to France as a GSO2 on the staff of the 3rd Division, which—with the other components of II Corps—was involved in all the heaviest fighting of the retreat. The strain was such that the GSO1, Colonel Boileau, committed suicide, to be succeeded before the end of August by Maurice, who throughout had stood the test with nerves of iron. Seven months later he was appointed to GHQ, and in 1916 he rose to the rank of Major-General at the age of 45. His only misfortune was that he never held any important command in either peace or war. In this—like Wully—his talent for staff work and sheer efficiency told against him, and he moved inexorably on from one staff appointment to another. The two men, so different in physical appearance, social background, and personal demeanour, were yet a perfect foil for one another. This was their bond. They were partners, possessed of a mutual instinctive understanding, invigorated by the same consuming devotion to the Army. They thus formed a single unit, stood together and were treated together (by soldiers and civilians alike) in all the fearful pressures of the next three years.

Here is a first-hand description of Maurice (in 1916), written by Major-General Sir Edward Spears, then acting as a liaison officer attached to the French Sixth Army.

'As imperturbable as a fish, always unruffled, the sort of man who would eat porridge by gaslight on a foggy morning in winter, looking as if he had enjoyed a cold bath, all aglow with soap and water, just as cheerful as if he were eating a peach in a sunny garden in August.

'A very tall, very fair man, a little bent, with a boxer's flattened-out nose, an eye-glass as flat and not much rounder than his face, and a rather abrupt manner. A little *distrait* owing to great inner concentration, he simply demolished work, never forgot anything, knew everything, was quite impervious to the moods of his chief, the accurate interpreter of his grunts and groans, and his most efficient if not outwardly brilliant second. No man ever wasted fewer words or expressed himself when he spoke with greater clarity and conciseness.

'An admirable character, the soul of military honour, with a deep sense of civic duty inherited from a family which placed service to the country and to the people of the country above all else, he too suffered acutely from the tactics of the politicians and their too subtle methods.'[21]

As yet, however, neither Maurice nor Wully had had much to do with politics. That would come later. Meanwhile Wully noted:

'Maurice . . . was . . . possessed of quite exceptional talents. He was particularly well read in military history, had a thorough grasp of the principles of strategy and tactics, and, what was more to the point, held sound views regarding their practical application. He could express himself temperately and clearly both verbally and on paper, and he devoted every spare minute of the day and night to thinking out how best to beat the formidable enemy in front of us. There was . . . a great deal of thinking to be done at the time, for not much daylight was yet visible.'[22]

Their problem was the role of the BEF, and how best to advise Sir John French in his relations with General Joffre, the actual—if not formally acknowledged—Generalissimo in France. Moreover, Joffre was inflexibly determined upon the offensive, and Sir John—handicapped by his own impulsive character and indeed by his own convictions—was in no mood to stand up to him.

*   *   *

Joffre's aim was to reduce the huge German salient between Rheims and Amiens, by attacking towards the railway arteries that fed the whole occupied territory. Early in 1915 he planned three offensives: in Artois, Champagne, and the Verdun-Nancy areas. He asked the BEF to participate in the first by an attack towards Aubers Ridge, SW of Lille, in co-operation with the French Tenth Army, next in line to the south. Sir John agreed both to this and to an earlier request to relieve some French formations round Ypres, which were required by the Tenth Army for the offensive. In the event, however, he was unable to carry out the relief—he had been counting on the arrival of two further divisions, one of which was diverted to the Dardanelles —with the result that the Tenth Army had to contract out of the operation altogether. In fact the French Artois offensive was put off until May. Knowing this, Sir John might have been expected to postpone his plans as well, but for various reasons—principally, to show what the British could do—he made up his mind to 'go it alone'. It was an unwise decision, for the British attack—now isolated and always limited in scale—could only have been effective if launched simultaneously with the larger French undertaking. As it was, such success as it achieved served to warn the enemy of what to expect next time, and of this full advantage was taken.

The operation lasted three days, March 10th–13th, and was carried out by troops of the First Army under Haig. It was in short Haig's battle, and the plans that he made foreshadowed in many respects the system developed in later, far larger, battles. He proposed two objectives: first, the capture of the village of Neuve Chapelle, and then an advance to Aubers Ridge itself. He concentrated all his artillery (372 guns) on a narrow sector of the front, and prepared to assault with a superior force of infantry (48 battalions) against thinly-held positions. Two cavalry corps were held in reserve. The first day was a success. The bombardment was well prepared and executed, and achieved complete surprise. Most obstacles were obliterated, and the infantry pushed through the gap to capture Neuve Chapelle as planned.

But that was as far as they got. Instead of exploiting the success at once, attempts were made to clear the flanks before continuing the advance, with the result that the enemy had time to bring up reserves and establish a new position, which held out against all further attacks on March 11th and 12th. The operation then came to a halt. Casualties were heavy (some 12,000), and only a small dent had been made in the German line. None the less, there were a few consolations: the efficiency of the bombardment and the success of the break-in, the spirit and determination of the infantry, and the proof that the BEF, hitherto engaged almost exclusively in defence, could also act effectively in offence. Neuve Chapelle did much to raise morale, and impress allies and enemies. But clearly there was much to learn, especially in the development of a battle, and in converting a break-in into a break-through. The strategic results were negligible.

Wully put his finger on some of the weaknesses at once—on the need for closer co-operation between staffs, and for greater initiative among subordinate commanders. To Callwell, DMO at the War Office, he wrote afterwards, 'We had a good show at Neuve Chapelle, but it ought to have been much better'.[23] He did not claim, however, that the battle had to be stopped solely through lack of artillery ammunition, as did Sir John. This was not true. Requirements had been estimated and stocks accumulated beforehand, and these did not prove insufficient for a short offensive. To say, as Sir John also did or was supposed to have done, that with enough shells he could always be certain of blasting his way through the enemy line, proved nothing and meant very little. Battles did not, even later in the war, depend entirely upon bombardment, but upon a whole host of considerations of which the use and weight of artillery was one.

Although Neuve Chapelle did not break down for the reasons advanced by Sir John, it did very seriously deplete the stocks of ammunition and cause renewed anxiety on this score. Wully knew that the utmost care was necessary, not only for general replacement, but to allow the BEF to renew the offensive in the same area in May, in conjunction with the French effort in Artois, as originally planned. He was therefore understandably resentful of the growing demand for men and munitions for the Dardanelles, reacting as it did upon the resources of the BEF in France. Although wrong in dismissing the expedition out of hand as of no strategic value, he was completely justified in suspecting that it was ill prepared and ill executed. He wrote to Callwell:

'I have never thought that the Fleet would get through the Dardanelles and do not think so now. To my mind such an attempt is a ridiculous farce, and we all know the accuracy of the sailors' shooting. . . As to the Dardanelles, I stand to win five shillings from the Chief in the course of three days unless we have achieved our object. I am prepared to lay odds to any extent and to anybody, but have not been able to find a single taker here.'[24]

He had known that the offensive in May (Aubers Ridge on May 9th and Festubert from May 15th to 25th) was to be anticipated by a second desperate onslaught at Ypres, his anxiety would have been even more acute, and his resentment even more bitter. But that was not the worst of it. Early in May, in the thick of the fighting, the BEF was compelled to send to the Dardanelles out of its own slender stocks a substantial quantity of 18-pounder and 4.5 ammunition. Such things were better not known in advance.

The Second Battle of Ypres, which lasted from April 22nd to May 25th, surprised the Germans almost as much as the Allies. A major battle grew out of a local attack, in which for the first time the Germans tried out the use of gas. They had made no serious provision to exploit the success it brought them—indeed their strategy was to stand on the defensive in the west for the whole of 1915—and so they bore all the guilt of introducing a frightful new weapon, without really profiting from its use. The Allies suffered from a series of mistakes and from some bad luck. No notice was taken of a prisoner who gave specific warning of the attack, while shortly beforehand good French troops had been relieved by two second line divisions (one of French Territorials, the other of Africans) in the north of the salient, where the German attack came in. Everywhere else round Ypres the British were in position again, with two corps of the Second Army under Smith-Dorrien, the Canadians on the left.

The gas was released from cylinders against the French on the afternoon of April 22nd, and the line gave way at once, leaving the Canadian division entirely exposed. A flank was immediately thrown out and reserves brought up, so that somehow the gap was filled, but only just in time. It was a wonderful piece of initiative and improvisation, backed by sheer dogged determination, and it saved the day. Had the Germans followed up with their usual vigour, they could not have failed to take Ypres and so cut off all the British troops in the salient to the east. In fact they were tactically, as well as strategically, unprepared, had no proper respirators themselves, and stuck to a rigid system of limited objectives, by which the infantry advanced only so far as the artillery had prepared the way. They held out, however, against all counter-attacks, and these proved very costly operations indeed. Thus the British found themselves, shortly after the start of the battle, in what was obviously an untenable position—a constricted salient, overfull of troops, exposed on three sides to superior German artillery. Accordingly, when it became clear that the lost ground could not be regained, Smith-Dorrien, the Army commander, asked permission to retire to a less vulnerable position, in conformity with the new line.

To this, Sir John reacted in the most extraordinary fashion, and ordered Smith-Dorrien to hand over command of all the troops round Ypres to Plumer, one of his subordinate corps commanders, with the brusque warning that not a yard of ground was to be given up. In mitigation it may be said that Sir John's action derived partly from a wish to satisfy Foch, Joffre's deputy, who was continually exhorting him to attack. But it also sprang out of something less excusable—a rankling resentment of what had happened at Le Cateau on August 26th 1914, when Smith-Dorrien (then commanding II Corps) had waged a successful delaying action against orders. Relations had deteriorated ever since, but the fault lay squarely with Sir John. This became painfully evident when, shortly afterwards at Ypres, he was compelled to recognise the force of Smith-Dorrien's request, and actually sanctioned a withdrawal from the salient. Even then it was only partial, and by that time many more lives had been lost.

Eventually on May 6th Smith-Dorrien simultaneously offered his resignation and received abrupt dismissal from GHQ; and he left for England forthwith. For Wully it was an altogether distasteful episode, and just what he had feared when he first became CGS. He knew Smith-Dorrien well, had served under him at Aldershot, liked him personally and respected him professionally. He had been in close touch with the battle all along, sending staff officers (Maurice among them) up the line to receive reports and transmit orders on the spot. He had seen very well what was happening but was quite unable to move Sir John, who refused to see Smith-Dorrien, and actually had the letter of dismissal signed and sent by the Adjutant-General, Macready.

There now follows a story, long current in the Army, though usually considered apocryphal, albeit characteristic of Wully. Lately, however, it has been confirmed by a spectator of the incident.[25] According to the account, Wully—less disgusted by the dismissal than by the way it was to be done—decided to break the bad news to Smith-Dorrien himself. In his view it was the least that was due to a wronged commander and a personal friend, and it was a step, moreover, that called for the utmost understanding and tact. In all innocence, therefore, he came to the conclusion that he was the man best fitted to do it. The account then runs:

'We were standing talking somewhere in front of the Ypres salient, when Wully drove up in his car, pulled Smith-Dorrien aside and remarked, loud enough for us all to hear, "'Orace, you're for 'ome". And home he went.'

The sad thing was that Second Ypres did not peter out quickly or come to a sudden standstill once the initial impetus was over, but was prolonged by attack and counter-attack of the utmost ferocity until May 25th, when both sides stopped from exhaustion and lack of artillery ammunition. The British were literally down to their last few rounds of everything but shrapnel, while their casualties amounted to nearly 60,000 officers and men. The Germans suffered about half this loss, and also ran short of shells. But whereas their shortage was purely local and temporary, the British were in far worse case. Moreover, many lives could have been saved had Smith-Dorrien been listened to in the first place. As it was the salient remained, in attenuated form, but with most of its disadvantages. True, much blood had been shed to preserve this, one of the last stretches of Belgian territory not occupied by the Germans, but sentiment never justified slaughter on this scale, nor were there any tactical or strategic compensations.

The fact that a major battle flared up unexpectedly at Ypres did not upset the original plan to launch a new attack towards Aubers Ridge in the south, in conjunction with the large-scale French offensive, now retimed for early May. The operation was allocated once again to Haig and the First Army (consisting of ten divisions) and was designed *inter alia* to draw off local German reserves from the French front. Tactically it was a repetition of Neuve Chapelle, with appropriate variations of site and method, by which it was hoped that the lessons of the earlier battle would be absorbed and applied. On this occasion it was proposed to break in north and south of the village of Neuve Chapelle, after a short surprise bombardment as before, though with a larger number of guns. The air arm was given wider tasks of reconnaissance, artillery spotting, and

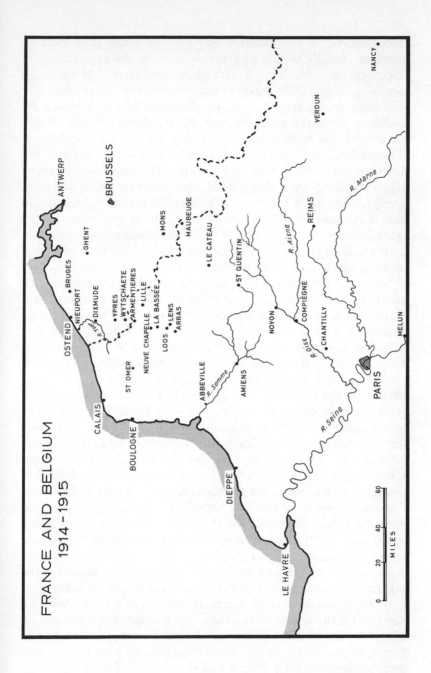

FRANCE AND BELGIUM
1914 – 1915

bombing, while the infantry was allotted some close support artillery (mainly trench mortars) to assist in the exploitation of successful attacks. The British, however, were not alone in profiting from their earlier experience. On their side the Germans made very careful preparations to resist attack by building powerful defences and by reinforcing their troops. As a result the opening attack on May 9th was a costly failure. The preliminary bombardment entirely failed to destroy the German wire and fortifications, so that the assaulting infantry was decimated by well-directed machine-gun fire from relatively undamaged positions. The British not only lacked the necessary heavy artillery, but the results of fire were inadequately observed, and much of the ammunition proved defective owing to faulty fuses. Only a few minor lodgments were effected, and the battle had to be broken off at the end of the first day.

Since the French were making encouraging progress further south, it was essential that the offensive be continued; and so a week later a new attack was mounted, this time in the area of Festubert, a short way to the south of Neuve Chapelle. On this occasion methods were revised. Instead of a brief opening bombardment, there was a prolonged programme of shelling (on the French model) for three days before the first infantry assault on the night of May 15th/16th, and the results of fire were carefully observed. Objectives were limited to only 1000 yards ahead, and the momentum of the attack was sustained for some ten days. Technically it was attended by better results, although no significant success was obtained. Here and there German positions were taken, well prepared and defended though they were, and the enemy was compelled to build a new line and throw in reserves as hoped. But in the end the attack came to a stop, generally for the same reasons as before, and particularly for the lack of weight in artillery support. Casualties were correspondingly heavy.

Between May 9th and 25th the First Army lost some 28,000 officers and men. Added to the 12,000 lost at Neuve Chapelle, and the 60,000 at Second Ypres, it resulted in a round total of 100,000 for the spring offensives of 1915 alone. May marked in effect the final efforts of the old Regular Army, fighting as a homogeneous body. It had been in action for nine murderous months, during which time it had demonstrated over and over again its skill in manœuvre and use of weapons, above all its astonishing morale. Without that it would have never held together, in face of a crippling inferiority in material, especially after trench warfare had set in. From now on, however, the new citizen army began to take shape, with the arrival of complete Territorial and New Army (Kitchener) formations, and with the rebuilding of the old divisions with entire drafts of newly-trained men. The veterans were progressively rationed out, at the various levels, throughout the whole force; and so helped gradually to create a new army, which in the course of time and hard fighting acquired most of the efficiency of the old.[26]

*   *   *

As the fighting died down on the British front at the end of May, Wully began once more to assess prospects and results. What had been achieved so far? In terms of ground gained, or even of serious damage to the enemy, very little—and all at high cost. But that was part of the price that had to be paid for acting as handmaid to the French, who themselves had made only small advances, and sustained infinitely greater losses, in their recent offensives. It was of course a very great disappointment, and made the casualties all the harder to bear. Had the French had even a moderate success, then everything would have been demonstrably worthwhile, and it would have been unthinkable for the BEF not to have played its part. Success or no, the experiment had to be tried. None the less, it was not an utter failure. Sir John had not been entirely wrong in claiming that the German line could be breached. Wully wrote to Call-well on May 31st:

'We know that we can break the front because we have already done it on two occasions. . . There are three phases to be got through. The first is to carry the trenches and for that plenty of ammunition and a good supply of infantry are necessary. The next phase is to get through the defended localities. . . The third phase means sufficient infantry and a reasonable amount of field artillery to exploit the successes gained in the first two phases. You cannot expect the same divisions to go on fighting day after day for weeks. They have to be withdrawn and given a rest, and other divisions put in their place. What is really wanted is sufficient ammunition and sufficient men to continue pushing without a pause, and this we have not yet had.'[27]

In short, the technical lessons were being slowly and painfully learned, but Wully realised that a lot of time would have to elapse before the BEF acquired the means and the skill to apply them to the full. He refused, however, to allow the suffering and the horror of this type of warfare to blind him as to the absolute need to work out a successful form of attack, and thereby to gain a decision in the west. But now there was a new and unpalatable development, which was to prolong the whole process into the years ahead.

As a direct result of the spring fighting, the Germans began hurriedly to double the strength of their defences by building a second line several miles behind the first, well sited and heavily wired, and generally out of effective range of artillery. From July onwards, every day that passed, the new system grew stronger and more formidable, and so inevitably raised the total of resources required to overcome it. It also threw Western strategy into the melting-pot. Should not the Western Allies attack again before the enemy line became absolutely unassailable, and while the main German strength was committed in the east? That certainly was how Joffre looked at it. Wully, however, took the opposite view, not because he had lost faith in winning the war in the west, but simply to permit the BEF to husband its strength. The very fact that the Russians were being driven pell-mell out of Poland sharpened his fear lest the Germans decide at any moment to break off battle against them, and return to the offensive in the west. In that case, he said, the BEF was in no state to withstand an all-out attack. It was desperately short of armament and ammunition, and had suffered very heavy losses. And although new divisions were arriving, the men were inexperienced and needed extra training before entering the line. Furthermore, nothing had been done to reconnoitre lines of retirement or construct a new defence position in the rear. He was not being over-cautious. It was common sense, while you were weak, to prepare for the worst. He had been one of the few who had foreseen the retreat in August 1914 and acted ahead. Both his instinct and his intelligence warned him that something similar might happen again, before the BEF had found its feet. In a word—consolidate now and get ready to attack later—nothing else.

Sir John, however, would not take a firm line, and it was from this moment, at the end of May, after he had had time to reflect on the results of the spring offensives and consider further the whole management of the war, that Wully began to make his views known in higher places. Sir John was reckless, he told Hankey on June 1st, when the latter was on a visit to GHQ;[28] and in a letter dated July 4th he communicated his fears on defences to Kitchener himself.[29] As yet, however, he did not have Kitchener's ear, nor did he really want it. For one thing he abhorred the Dardanelles affair and was fast losing confidence in Kitchener's strategic grasp. For another, although he had little respect for Sir John and was deeply worried about the situation in France, he was still reluctant to by-pass his chief. This is clear from his correspondence with the King. The two men, it will be recalled, had been on good terms since Aldershot and Camberley days. George V—essentially a simple, unpretentious person who took to men of a similar character— liked Wully and respected him as a soldier. Since the beginning of the war he had kept in touch by letter, through the medium of his equerry, Major Clive Wigram, and of his private secretary, Lord Stamfordham. He wanted to know what was really happening in France, and was particularly upset by the bad relations between Kitchener and Sir John. Wully's replies were factual and guarded at first, but far more open as from the summer of 1915, as the following extracts show:

Wigram to Robertson, July 11th 1915

'H.M. has told me to write to you to ask if you think the recent meeting at GHQ was a success, and if it is likely to bear good fruit. H.M. is so anxious to establish cordial relations and good will between the War Office and GHQ. H.M. hopes you had an opportunity of a talk with Lord K at GHQ, and that you were able to explain the difficulties on the spot.

'We returned yesterday from a visit to the Grand Fleet—such a happy family party. The C-in-C beloved and trusted by all. Oh! if we could only get the same feelings of comradeship and mutual service between the parts of the Army abroad and at home. . . *Your* presence at home inspired much confidence, and these visits must be repeated as often as possible.'

The meeting in question took place at Calais on July 6th, and is referred to shortly, but Wully had no opportunity of talking to Kitchener. However, he kept Wigram *au fait* with events in France, and on one occasion at least committed a deliberate indiscretion.

Robertson to Wigram, August 6th 1915

'I am very anxious about the present situation. . . It is the effect of the Dardanelles which disturbs me. Unless the enterprise is shortly stopped, the chances of obtaining a reasonably successful issue to the war will be doubtful. We should do just enough to enable us to get away, and then come away *at once*. The effect of this withdrawal in Egypt, India, etc is beside the point, for we shall lose them if we lose here, and we shall not and cannot win here unless we are given the necessary means. We have not the means to conduct war in both places. . . Sir John has just returned, but has not enlightened me as to what our policy is really supposed to be. I have asked him to send home *his* views on the situation, so that the Government may realise how they stand. But he declines to do so. He says, and I daresay quite correctly, that his views are already well known, and that it is a waste of time to repeat them. I had prepared, for his assistance, a short note on the situation, but he declined to read it even. He said that he knew it, and of course he does. But a deliberate and reasoned statement should nevertheless be of use. I do not for a moment suggest it should be shown to His Majesty and it must *not* be to anyone else as it has not been read, as I have said, by the C-in-C. If the views of the General Staff here are likely to be of any help they should be asked for officially. I cannot refrain from sending the paper to you however, because I think that unless ammunition is sent here to enable us to cooperate with the French in a week or two's time, and so relieve pressure in Russia we may fail to win.'

Wigram to Robertson, August 8th 1915

'Many thanks for your private letter and notes. I am very glad you have sent me these as I have shown them to H.M., and Lord K, and Lord K is coming down here to discuss the situation with H.M. tomorrow.'

Wigram to Robertson, August 10th 1915

'I think Lord K was impressed with your memo, and he studied it because he knew H.M. would question him! . . The King feels that the more you can see of Lord K the better, and H.M. hopes that the relations between the GS at GHQ and at the WO are friendly and correct. Their views should be identical as far as possible, and the GS at the WO should not advise Lord K without your knowing what advice is being offered. The GS at GHQ should send a survey of the situation once a fortnight or once a month, and you should come home as often as possible. Lord K does not understand the GS, but was quite ready to read your memo.'

Robertson to Wigram, August 11th 1915

'As regards the Notes I sent you on the situation and what you say about keeping touch with the War Office, I am afraid that is impossible so far as Notes of the above kind are concerned. It would never do for the General Staff to send their views to the War Office unless they first had the approval of the Commander-in-Chief, and as I told you he declined to send the Notes, because, he said, his views were already known. I can only repeat therefore that if the views of GHQ here are needed they must be sent as those of the Commander-in-Chief. Any other course would lead to difficulties. There can only be one C-in-C in an Army.'

Wigram to Robertson, August 13th 1915

'There ought to be a standing order that Lord Kitchener should have the views of GHQ through the Commander-in-Chief once a fortnight or once a month.'

Robertson to Stamfordham, undated

'I believe that Sir John is now, in a sense *trying* not to annoy Lord K, but we need far more than that. The worst of it is that, I suppose, the Government pay no heed to his opinions. He is a discredited nonentity, I take it. I hope it is not so. If they do *not* trust him, they should replace him. If they *do* trust him, they ought to take his advice, or at any rate ask for it if they do not get it.

'He, moreover, has never really sincerely, and honestly concerted with the French, while they regard him as by no means a man of ability or a faithful friend, and therefore they do not confide in him. Joffre and he have never yet been a mile within the heart of each other. Further, he has never fully laid his opinions before the Government. He has too much taken the stand of doing as *he* wishes, and telling the Government nothing. I have been very concerned about this for a long time past.'[30]

Although Wully was aware that a new offensive would have to be mounted in concert with the French sooner or later, he did not alter his view that it should be delayed as long as possible. That delay was essential was borne out by at least one conference among the many that took place during the summer between Allied leaders and staffs. It was the one held at Boulogne on June 19th and 20th, under the chairmanship of Lloyd George, at which the requirements of trench warfare were realistically assessed. To produce the requisite ordnance, in the proportion of one heavy to two light field guns, and all the ammunition as well, would take not much less than a year. In addition it was now being calculated that, in order to break through the new German defences, any future offensive by the BEF would have to be of the order of 36 divisions, attacking along a front of 25 miles, backed by appropriate fire power. In view of this and of the munitions forecast, and of the manpower situation (still lagging owing to the retention of the voluntary system), there could be no prospect of effective British participation in France before the spring or summer of 1916.

Nothing, however, deterred Joffre, who was planning another attempt to cut into the great German salient in France with renewed attacks in Artois and the Champagne. Since early June he had been demanding that the British take over a stretch of line south of Arras—which was agreed—and co-operate in the offensive by attacking in the Loos-Lens area on the boundary of the British First and French Tenth Armies. Both Wully and Haig (in command of First Army as hitherto, and by now acknowledged as the ablest British formation commander) demurred: partly for reasons already mentioned, partly for tactical ones—the ground was unsuitable and the defences known to be extremely strong. For a time the two men managed to persuade Sir John not to give way in detail, but in the end—having yielded in principle to Joffre's demands—he had to surrender in detail as well. Meanwhile respite came from another quarter.

On July 6th Asquith and Kitchener came over to Calais in an attempt to co-ordinate strategic plans with the French leaders. Sir John attended, but not Wully who was kept out of the inner council, though he was apprised of the decisions taken. It seemed that Kitchener dominated the proceedings by sheer force of personality and gained some important concessions. One was that Joffre should postpone his offensive, at least until another major effort had been made at Gallipoli. If this succeeded, then the whole character of the war might be altered. If it failed, then it was privately agreed that Joffre should have his way in the west, with the implication that the BEF would comply with his plans. In fact Joffre never relaxed his intentions for a moment, but continued to make preparations for an autumn offensive as if nothing new had ever been decided. In any case he did not have to wait long.

On August 6th Hamilton launched a new assault at Gallipoli which, although it came very close to success, ended up no nearer Constantinople than before. Within ten days Kitchener returned to France. Gallipoli had failed finally (as it turned out), and the Russians were suffering a whole catalogue of defeats on a scale which made it doubtful whether they could go on fighting much longer. It was against this background of disasters that Kitchener finally gave way, and exhorted the BEF to fall in with Joffre once again: in short, to launch an attack for which it was not ready, and in which its commanders— even Sir John—did not believe. Such were the origins of the battle of Loos, September 25th–October 16th 1915.

In outline, six divisions were to attack on a front of some six miles, from La Bassée Canal in the north, to a point opposite the village of Loos and the suburbs of Lens in the south. On either flank a division was detailed to capture the German strong points, well sited among the wooded and built-up areas of the mines. There they would protect the other four divisions, which would advance over the undulating plain in the centre, not by fixed objectives but exploiting success as it came, with a view to bursting through the German lines of defence and enveloping Lens, in concert with the French attack from the south. Much depended on the use of gas, designed to offset the lack of artillery fire power and demoralise the enemy. Haig wrote to Wully beforehand:

'Without gas the front of our attacks must be reduced to what our guns can satisfactorily prepare, with the results normally attendant on small fronts; namely, concentration of hostile guns on point of attack, large losses and small progress. In my opinion, under no circumstances, should our forthcoming attack be launched without the aid of gas.'[31]

On the latter point, however, Haig had to be overruled, since the attack formed part of the combined offensive with the French Tenth Army, and he was instructed to have ready a limited alternative plan. The attack had to go in, but everyone appreciated the vital importance of gas, and Haig was given a good deal of latitude in the matter of timing.

As it happened the weather was favourable, but only just. After a preliminary bombardment of four days, and arduous preparations to install the cylinders, gas and smoke were discharged on a faint wind early on September 25th. In the south the cloud carried forward successfully so that Loos was overrun, and a strong defensive flank secured by the 47th Division more or less as planned. This had a direct bearing on the advance of the next division, the 15th, which nearly broke through round Hill 70. In the centre the cloud was wayward, and the attack only achieved partial success with limited advances in two areas. In the north the wind was adverse, the cloud blew back and disorganised the attack, so that no defensive flank was secured. In short the passage of the gas roughly determined the pattern of the attack, which failed in the north, but gained a clear tactical success in the south. Such was the position by midday on September 25th, and all now depended on the follow-up, for which fresh troops were needed. They were not there, and the lack of them lost the battle.

By design Haig had no immediate reserves of his own, since it was clearly understood that he would have the use of three divisions from the general reserve. Unfortunately Sir John kept them under his own hand too far back, and when he did allow them to be rushed up, the German defences had stiffened and it was too late. But worse was to follow. Two of the reserve divisions were green, and had never been in battle before. Staff work was faulty, and the men arrived tired, hungry, and thirsty, with no clear idea as to where they were or what they had to do. They were then thrown in—with tragic results— and the situation had to be restored by the last division in reserve, the Guards.

By September 27th the battle was virtually over, only a small bulge had been made in the German line, and the real opportunity had been missed. Nevertheless, the operation was continued, in conformity with the French offensive (itself another expensive failure), until the middle of October, though without tangible gains and at great cost. Altogether the British lost 50,000 officers and men in the main attacks alone, more than twice the casualties of the enemy, for whom in the end it was a clear defensive success. And yet, at one point, Loos had been a near-victory, and proved once again that the BEF, if properly led and equipped, was fully capable of success. It was, however, a conclusion that had long ceased to require proof, and certainly did not compensate for the high price that had to be paid. This battle shook the whole structure of the British command, led to the dismissal of Sir John French, and hastened Kitchener's abdication from power at the War Office.

In France it was the last straw. Sir John had proved yet again that he was unequal to the job. He was headstrong, inept, and simply not endowed with the right qualities to command a large British army, either in association with a preponderant ally—indeed, Joffre barely bothered to consult him any longer, but merely made demands—or in any of the circumstances of a desperate war. After Loos, moreover, he ran out of ideas, and frankly lost hope.

Besides this he had repeatedly shown himself to be a small-minded man. Jealous of his authority, he was always trying to assert himself. We have seen of his resentment of Kitchener, but he was suspicious of his subordinates as well, and at times vindictive towards them; for example, his treatment of Smith-Dorrien. Towards Wully he blew hot and cold. In early days he tried to put him in his place, snub him socially, and refuse abruptly to discuss professional problems. None of this made much impression upon Wully, whose persistence was proverbial. Haig related how on one occasion Wully had to be shooed out of the room because, fearful of whatever foolishness his chief might commit next, he always made a point of being present whenever Sir John saw any of his senior commanders.[32] Later Sir John relaxed a little, for he could not deny Wully's ability and worth, and he knew full well that he could not do without him.

Sir John also took credit too readily for what was not his—for the operational plans of Neuve Chapelle and Loos, for instance, both of which were worked out by Haig. And he told lies when he made mistakes. The worst example of this arose at Loos, when he reported in his official despatch that he had made the reserves available several hours earlier than in fact he had. This was of course the crux of the whole battle. Haig felt so bitterly about it that he told most of the story to Kitchener in a letter dated September 29th, and repeated it more fully to Lord Haldane when the latter visited him in France on October 9th.[33] He also took the matter up formally with GHQ, but got no satisfaction whatever. In essence he maintained that, despite repeated requests, Sir John had not acted until too late and had prevented Wully (who was fully aware of what was needed) from acting either; that he had allowed untried formations to be used; and that he had stationed himself some 25 miles away from, and out of communication with, GHQ at St Omer, and so was unable to exercise control over the battle.[34]

Kitchener needed no convincing about Sir John. The two men had been at loggerheads for a long time, so much so that since July Kitchener had privately been consulting Haig behind Sir John's back, and soon afterwards he made contact with Wully too. Moreover, behind *him* stood Asquith and—as we have seen—the King, who were both party to this curious arrangement. Wully and Haig already had a common, though undeclared, understanding, but it was an awkward and equivocal situation for them both, particularly for Wully who had to serve Sir John more intimately than Haig. After Loos, however, they both felt impelled to speak their minds.

Loos ended on October 16th. On the 17th Wully and Haig had a critical meeting. Wully had just returned from a week at the War Office where, at Kitchener's request, he had been acting as consultant to the General Staff, and had attended several meetings of the Cabinet. It was the first time he had been asked formally for advice, although various people (besides the King) had been consulting him informally for several months. As far back as June 30th he had on request supplied a member of the Government with a note outlining a new War Council, or small inner Cabinet, of key Ministers and professional advisers, as a more efficient instrument for conducting the war.[35] And he had been making his influence felt within the War Office itself by correspondence with Callwell since the beginning of the year, and latterly with Murray, the new CIGS.

It was high time that fresh advice was brought in. The war was going very badly everywhere. By the end of October Kitchener's position as virtual dictator of military policy was visibly collapsing. Gallipoli had failed for the second time, the landing of a force at Salonika seemed a desperate expedient, and in France Loos had proved a great disappointment. Kitchener seemed unable to make up his mind on any definite course of action, allowing himself to be driven along by the mere march of events. A strong party in the Cabinet wanted to get rid of him, and he was almost ready to go of his own accord. But Asquith felt otherwise. He wanted to keep Kitchener for the magic of his name, and for support in staving off conscription, a step which many Liberals regarded as politically disastrous and a betrayal of principle. But he did insist that Kitchener rehabilitate the General Staff at the War Office, to allow it to function once more as the instrument of operational planning and control, for which it had been originally designed.

Kitchener gave in. He had already sacked the CIGS, Wolfe-Murray, a conscientious officer who had done his best, but who was described, nevertheless, as an 'overpaid nonentity'. Kitchener hardly ever consulted him at all, and had only appointed him in the first place because, at the beginning of the war, most of the senior officers had rushed off to France. 'I suppose', Kitchener was reported then to have said, 'there is nobody else but Wolfe-Murray.' The new CIGS was Archibald Murray, Wully's predecessor as CGS to the BEF, and lately acting as Deputy CIGS. Murray had not been a success in France, where neither his health nor his temperament had stood up to the strain of the opening months of the war; and he was a man beset by bad luck, as events would shortly show. But there was no doubt as to the value of his work at the War Office. Hankey praised him highly, and described him as a real 'St John the Baptist' to Wully, who succeeded him at the end of the year. Indeed, during the three months he held office as CIGS (September 25th–December 23rd), he went far to putting the General Staff on its feet again. Thanks to him, strategic and logistical problems relating to the various fronts were scientifically studied almost for the first time, and a series of excellent papers produced, one of which (dated December 16th) was later referred to by Wully as the 'Bible of the war'. It was of course a clear exposition of the Western case! Kitchener, however, still found it difficult to consult his subordinates; it had never been in his nature or experience to do so, and even Murray was unable to stand up to him in a crisis. For that reason the latter was dubbed 'an old woman' by Haig, but unfairly so. True, he did not have a granite character such as Wully had, but even Wully did not try conclusions with Kitchener, until the latter had been further shorn of authority, and their mutual relationship set down *in writing*. The following extract from a letter, written by Murray to Sir Ian Hamilton after the war, is revealing of the whole situation.

'Though you have a very good idea of the War Office in 1914 and 1915, you cannot know as well as I do the awful state it was in during the latter years under that past master of disorganisation, Lord Kitchener.

'In March 1915 I took up the work of Deputy CIGS and saw the work of the War Office from the inside. My own particular task, until I became CIGS was almost solely connected with the organisation and training of the New Armies, necessitating constant travelling. The Military Members of the Army Council never met as a Council. Sclater, the Adjutant-General, was entirely under the thumb of Lord Kitchener. . . Wolfe-Murray, an able soldier and a courteous gentleman, knew little of GS work, and Kitchener daily bewitched him with his fantastic schemes and kaleidoscopic ill-judged orders. Jack Cowans (QMG) went his way serenely doing excellent work and only objecting to be sent for before 10 am.

'Lord Kitchener, I judge from a daily experience covering ten months, was quite unfit for the position of Secretary of State. At the beginning of each week he was fairly capable of standing the strain, but by Fridays, when he vanished until Monday to Broome Park, he was worn out.

'I cannot describe to you, working with him day after day, how impossible I found him. He never had his CIGS, AG, and QMG in his room together and told them what he wanted. No, he sent for them in turn and gave his instructions, telling each of them as little as possible, whilst he kept the threads in his own hands. There was only one branch of the work that I got on well with him and that was the "K" [New] Armies. Here it was "hands off my own troops, they must have every chance". For the Territorials, their history, organisation, and customs he cared nothing. He would at any time break them up and send them anywhere poorly armed and trained, and inadequately equipped. No "K" Division left the country incomplete.

'The Cabinet did not believe in him and curiously enough he was afraid of their meetings, and tried to reduce to writing beforehand all he meant to say and confess on any particular subject. He seldom told the Cabinet the truth and the whole truth. Especially he kept them in the dark as to the monthly intake necessary to keep 70 Divisions in the field. It was not until he left for the Dardanelles [in November] that I gave the true numbers, showing that without conscription the numbers available, or likely to volunteer, were far below requirements.

'Gradually the Cabinet gauged his value and insisted on his presenting to them papers on every subject prepared by the General Staff and not edited by him. Here I came in. For three months I wrote papers on every theatre of war and re-established the General Staff. But the full value of the General Staff did not come until Lord Kitchener left for the East, when for the first time the Army Council began to function and the General Staff worked hourly in touch with the War Staff of the Admiralty. The Military Members met every day and work went fast and satisfactorily. The Cabinet, I was told, was getting all they wanted. On Kitchener's return he sacked me, but fortunately Robertson had gained a strong position with the Cabinet. . . Of course I did not like being superseded, when as a matter of fact I have never in my forty years service done better work than I did during the three months I was CIGS.'[36]

*　　　*　　　*

At their meeting on October 17th Wully told Haig that, when in London, Lord Stamfordham had rung him up from Sandringham and sounded him on behalf of the King about the replacement of Sir John. Wully had refused to commit himself, either to Stamfordham, or it seems to the King whom he saw shortly afterwards. He wanted first of all to consult Haig, hence their present meeting. Haig's reaction is recorded in his Diary in the following words:

'I told him at once that up to date I had been more loyal to French and did my best to stop all criticisms of him or his methods. Now at last, in view of what had happened in the recent battle over the reserves, and in view of the seriousness of the general military situation, I had come to the conclusion that it was not fair to the Empire to retain French in command on this the main battle front. Moreover, none of my officers commanding Corps had a high opinion of Sir J.'s military ability or military views; in fact, *they had no confidence in him.* Robertson quite agreed, and left me saying "he knew now how to act, and would report to Stamfordham". He also told me that the members of the Cabinet who had up to the present been opposed to removing French had come round to the other opinion.'[37]

The two men thus laid their cards on the table at last. And they went further than discussing the command of the BEF. In this and subsequent conversations and correspondence, they agreed to press for a change in the whole conduct of the war. Firm Westerners, they were convinced that France was the only front that mattered, and that everything else should be subordinated to it. Gallipoli should be given up, and Salonika eliminated as soon as possible—certainly no more troops should be sent there, as the French were demanding. Above all, a comprehensive strategic plan should be worked out by the General Staff in London and strictly adhered to. In fact the CIGS had already produced at least two appreciations advocating a Western policy,[38] but Murray was said to have been overruled by Kitchener who had ordered him to recommend the despatch of eight divisions to Gallipoli from France; further, that the Cabinet had accepted the recommendation. Whether the story was true or not, the implications boded ill for the future of the General Staff, particularly now that Kitchener was supposed to have 'rehabilitated' it. Fortunately the despatch of the eight divisions remained an academic matter, since it had afterwards been decided to send out a senior officer to make a preliminary report. Haig understood from Wully that Kitchener had chosen him for the job, but that 'owing to a possibility of requiring me to replace Sir John French, General Monro [commander of Third Army] was fixed upon'.[39] Nothing more was said on the subject for the moment, but on October 24th Haig made up his mind that Wully was the best man to become CIGS, as he would be certain to stand up to Kitchener.

'The Government seems quite incapable of deciding on a sound military policy and sticking to it. A sound military adviser, a man of character, must be found to advise them.'[40]

Haig expressed his conviction to the King, then on a visit to France, and also repeated his criticisms of Sir John French. Later he told Lord Esher that Wully should be appointed CIGS, with power to advise the Cabinet direct, and that the best thing to do to Kitchener was to appoint him Viceroy of India.[41]

Meanwhile, events were working themselves out. Monro took Hamilton's place in the Dardanelles and—primed it was said by Wully—recommended that the whole operation be abandoned. Kitchener would not hear of it, and on November 4th hastened out to the Mediterranean himself. The Cabinet devoutly hoped that he would not return, but that instead he might accept some such post as C-in-C of the whole Middle East area. No such miracle occurred. Once arrived at the Dardanelles, however, Kitchener had reluctantly to admit that Monro had been right. Even so he could only bring himself to consent to a partial evacuation, and then confused the issue further by urging that the evacuated divisions be sent to capture Alexandretta, to open up yet another Turkish front. Fortunately the Cabinet was stung into rejecting this proposal, though not before Wully had told Haig that he thought Kitchener had sent them all mad. In the same letter he added:

'Do you know that French is in bed again till Wednesday. I think the first thing is to get you in command.'[42]

By now Wully was fully in Asquith's confidence, was giving the Cabinet oral and written advice, and was lending a lot of weight to Murray at the War Office. His most important contribution was a cogent Memorandum, dated November 5th, written at Kitchener's request, and sent in his absence abroad direct to the Cabinet. It set out all the Western arguments, and proposed that the functions of S of S and CIGS should be clearly distinguished and defined, backed by a proper Staff, so that 'there should be one military authority responsible for advising His Majesty's Government regarding military policy in all theatres.'[43]

Murray did not see this paper in advance, and Wully felt uncomfortable about it, as his covering letter to Asquith made clear.

6th November 1915

'Dear Mr Asquith

Before I left England on Tuesday last Lord Kitchener asked me, as a result of some long conversations we had together, to write him a paper giving my views on the conduct of the war, stating fully and freely what measures should, in my opinion, be taken in order to win. He particularly told me to hold nothing back.

I have just finished the paper, and as he has left the WO temporarily I send it to you, because there is no time to lose.

The paper really trespasses on the domain of your Chief Military Adviser—Sir A. Murray—and therefore I feel considerable hesitation in sending it to you, as it is desirable that you should receive advice from the responsible officer only. On the other hand it may be useful to you, at any rate as regards the nature and effect of operations on this front, and if you can agree to treat it as personal no harm should be done by sending it. As a matter of fact, I believe Sir A. Murray would agree with it.

Another reason for sending it is that I feel so strongly we *can* win through if only we decide what is the right thing to do, and then resolutely stick to our decision and refuse to be diverted from it by the many specious temptations which always beset those responsible in time of war.

I remain

Yours truly

W. R. Robertson'

In fact Wully's relations with Murray remained undisturbed throughout, but his position at this time was as equivocal as Haig's. Neither of them was acting according to the strictest rules of etiquette—but, then, no more were the leaders with whom they were treating, or the King himself. But there was no doubt that, on grounds of professional knowledge and experience, shrewd thinking, and sheer force of character, Wully was quickly establishing himself as the future 'chief military adviser' to the Government. There remained, however, the problem of Kitchener.

Kitchener came back to England at the end of November, and immediately offered to resign. Asquith persuaded him not only to withdraw his offer, but to stay on as S of S with much reduced powers. He had already lost control of munitions, now he was asked to hand over strategy—the key executive function—to the CIGS, who—Asquith had now decided—was to be Wully, in place of Murray. It was a humiliating position, and Kitchener showed greatness in accepting it. He sent for Wully at once, told him what had been decided, and explained the whole position to him in general terms in a lengthy conversation at his quarters in York House.

Fortunately the two men respected and liked each other. Wully was pleasantly surprised by the frank manner in which Kitchener admitted his own faults, and what might have been a frosty interview turned out full of promise. However, he refused to be lulled by generalisations.

'I was much impressed by his outspoken manner, and felt that I was in the presence of a man whose character was totally different from what I had been led to suppose; but I still thought it would be best for both of us, and for the country, if before finally deciding we came to a definite understanding, in writing, on the particular points regarding which I was in doubt.'[45]

Kitchener assented, and Wully went back to France where he composed a long Memorandum, in which their relative powers and positions were clearly and ruthlessly expressed. In the covering letter, dated December 5th, he wrote:

'As regards our conversation yesterday, I am really very grateful you should think me a possible selection as CIGS. I have sent you a separate letter on the subject today. I particularly wish to apologise for its apparent abruptness. It reads the reverse of pleasing, but I must send it as it is, as I have to start at once for Chantilly. It was written in a great hurry, and I am afraid it is rather characteristic of my blunt way of saying things. Please excuse it.'[46]

The essence of the Memorandum may be summarised as follows:

(1) There should be a supreme directing authority or War Council (previously outlined by Wully in his paper of June 30th—see page 130—and not to be confused with the advisory committee the Cabinet, November 1914 - May 1915—see pages 104-5). This Council should formulate policy, choose the men to execute that policy, and supervise the conduct of the war.

(2) The War Council should receive all advice on matters concerning military operations through one authoritative channel only —the CIGS.

(3) All operation orders should be issued and signed by the CIGS under the authority of the War Council, *not* the Army Council. Likewise all operational communications from GOCs should be addressed to the CIGS.

(4) The S of S should confine himself to the raising, maintenance, and equipment of the troops.

(5) Such a system would ensure greater security, as well as efficiency.

(6) The CIGS should have certain assistants to relieve him of all but his essential work, and to represent him when necessary. He must have time to think quietly.

(7) A C-in-C Home Forces should be appointed to command all army units in Great Britain. He should be on the same footing as a C-in-C abroad, and in the same relationship to the CIGS.

Kitchener's inclination on reading this Memorandum was, once more, to resign. On constitutional, as well as personal, grounds he could not stomach continuing as S of S without any executive function other than that of feeding and clothing the Army—even equipment was now largely the responsibility of the Ministry of Munitions. He did, however, recommend Asquith to accept Wully's terms, and suggested that he himself might stay on as a member of the War Council [or its then equivalent, the War Committee—see page 146], though not as S of S, and give all the help possible from there. He thought that Lord Derby would best succeed him at the War Office.[47] This really did seem final, but now it was Wully who took the initiative once again.

'His [Kitchener's] letter reached me at St. Omer about seven o'clock in the evening, and as I knew he was passing through Calais at eleven o'clock the same night on his way to Paris, I got into my motor after dinner and went to Calais to meet him. He greeted me very cordially, albeit a little sadly, I thought, and with an air of disappointment. I came at once to the point and said that whatever happened I could not hear of his leaving the War Office, since there was no one who could fill the position which he held in the country, and I begged him to discuss with me the paragraphs in the memorandum to which he objected. As his train was due to start almost immediately for Paris he asked me to go with him. I jumped in, and we sat up talking till two o'clock next morning, the conversation being resumed after we had breakfasted in Paris.'[48]

Wully insisted that the existing system was cumbrous and a sham. The Army Council consisted of eight (later increased to eleven) members, in addition to the S of S, and all had the right to be consulted before operation orders were issued. In practice they were not so consulted, and could not expect to be, except where it affected their own departments. Operations were the business of the General Staff and of no one else, and this should be recognised, as it was already in all first-class armies. It followed that the CIGS should bear the responsibility of the work of his own department, sign the orders, and communicate with the commanders in the field.

'When I had explained the proposal in this way to Lord Kitchener, and cleared up the other points with which he was not at first in agreement, the offending paragraphs in the memorandum . . . were amended in a manner satisfactory to both of us.'[49]

What happened was that the wording was modified to the extent that the CIGS should sign orders 'under the authority of the Secretary of State for War', which did not alter the fundamental point that the CIGS remained responsible to the War Council, not the Army Council. The paragraph defining the limitation of the S of S's powers was cut out—though in reality it operated just the same. The revised Memorandum is printed in full in Appendix A.

And so the matter was finally resolved. Asquith gave his blessing and Kitchener never interfered with strategy again. He called the compact 'Our Bargain' and stuck to it faithfully. Wully became CIGS on December 23rd, and the new arrangements were regularised by an Order in Council dated January 27th 1916. The two men remained close friends and colleagues until Kitchener met his death on the way to Russia in the following June.

Meanwhile, another important bargain had been struck. During Kitchener's absence in the Mediterranean in November, Asquith had taken charge of the War Office and had made up his mind not only to resolve the question of CIGS, but to replace Sir John French as well. Haig knew nothing of this decision until Wully informed him privately of it on November 25th, and nothing further until December 3rd, when Kitchener

7ᵗʰ Decʳ

YORK HOUSE.
Sᵗ JAMES'S.

My dear Robertson
        Many thanks for your frank
letter, I took it this morning to the P.M.
and recommended him to accept your
terms — He quite agreed with me that it
was of course impossible for me to retain
the responsibility of S of S. without any execution
work as regards the war & with my functions
curtailed to the feeding & clothing of the
Army. The munitions ministry do all
the rest of the work you consider should
be done by the S of S. — The P.M. will
I think agree though he said he wanted
time to consider the matter & from
what he said I may be still a member

TRANSCRIPT

My dear Robertson; Many thanks for your frank letter. I took it this morning
to the P.M. and recommended him to accept your terms—He quite agreed with
me that it was of course impossible for me to retain the responsibility of S of S
without any executive work as regards the war and with my functions curtailed to
the feeding and clothing of the Army. The Munitions Ministry do all the rest of
the work you consider should be done by the S of S.—The P.M. will I think agree
though he said he wanted time to consider the matter and from what he said I may

of the War council though not as S of S
in that case you may rely on me
to always do my best to support you in
carrying out the difficult task you
will have before you -
This change will come at a suitable time
As you know I told my colleagues I could
not remain responsible as S of S if the troops
were kept at Salonica and that is apparently
what is to happen - I suggested to the P.M.
that Derby would do well as S of S. I feel
sure you would get on well with him
and be loyally supported, he now does the
recruiting so knows about that part of
his work - Yours very truly

Kitchener

I have no doubt the P.M. will send for you
soon

be still a member of the War Council though not as S of S. In that case you may rely on me to always do my best to support you in carrying out the difficult task you will have before you.

This change will come at a suitable time. As you know I told my colleagues I could not remain responsible as S of S if the troops were kept at Salonica and that is apparently what is to happen. I suggested to the P.M. that Derby would do well as S of S. I feel sure you would get on well with him and be loyally supported, he now does the recruiting so knows about that part of the work.

Yours very truly, Kitchener. I have no doubt the P.M. will send for you soon.

told him he had been recommended to succeed Sir John. In his letter to Kitchener of December 5th, Wully wrote:

'Sir John tells me that he sent in his resignation to Mr Asquith yesterday.'

And he added surprisingly

'He tells me that he has recommended me to succeed him [Sir John]. But this would not do either from the point of view of seniority or experience in the command of troops.'[50]

Asquith made the official offer of the command in France to Haig on December 8th. It was accepted, and on the 19th Haig formally took over.

By Christmas 1915 the two architects of the Western school of strategy had won a complete victory. It now remained to see what they would make of it.

Chief of the Imperial General Staff:
December 1915 to December 1916

DIRECTLY Wully walked into the War Office, he made himself felt—but his first day was a miserable one.

'The reforms commenced with the room assigned for my own use in the War Office, the first and only day spent in it being quite the most exasperating day of my life. The telephone, which I have always detested, rang incessantly, and a constant stream of people of both sexes and all grades—girl typists, wives of officers, Members of Parliament, boy-scout messengers, general officers—entered the room, one after another, unannounced, either to see me on some trivial matter or someone else whose room they thought it was. To attempt to work under such maddening conditions was worse than useless. Lucas [ADC] realised the position as well as I did, and by nine o'clock next morning he had taken possession of another room for me, from which all telephone apparatus was expelled, and access to which could only be gained through an ante-room where he or my private secretary kept constant guard so that I might be left in peace.'[1]

Wully's first task was to establish the authority of the General Staff beyond all doubt as the supreme planning organism of the Army. To this end Murray had already done a great deal, but he had only been CIGS for three months, and he had always been handicapped by his subordinate relationship to Lord Kitchener. Now that Wully had overcome the latter difficulty, he was in a position to go much further than Murray had ever been empowered—or had had the force of character—to do, and he acted accordingly. He began by settling his own status in relation to that of his colleagues. Although it had been agreed that he should replace Kitchener as chief military adviser to the Government, it did not follow apparently that he should have precedence in the Army Council, the body set up in 1904 to manage Army affairs. This was an anomaly from every point of view, not least because the CIGS had originally been intended, *by virtue of his appointment*, to act as First Military Member of the Council. Latterly, however, this position had been accorded to the officer senior in rank—whatever his appointment—and so it came about that Wully found himself on arrival in third place. It was of course entirely illogical and intolerable. Since, said Wully, it was the business of the CIGS to advise the Government where to send the troops, and to send them there, it followed that the QMG—for example—should feed them. 'It was not the job of the QMG to lay down where the food should be sent, and then for the CIGS to send the troops there to eat it.'[2] But Kitchener, unpredictable as ever, wanted to preserve the *status quo*; and in the end Wully had to be promoted from Lieut-General to the temporary rank of General,[3] in order to gain the necessary authority and precedence.

Next Wully turned to changes under his own hand. He was anxious to reshape certain sections of the War Office on the lines of GHQ in France, an organisation he had himself helped to create under the test of active service, and to install some of his own men. For example, he introduced a General Staff registry for operational messages, hitherto lumped along with the rest in the civilian registry, without any effective system of priorities. He also split the Operations Directorate into two—Operations and Intelligence—bringing over Maurice as DMO, though for a time he retained Callwell as DMI. Callwell (former DMO and I) had for long been his most reliable contact in London, and he was to prove invaluable in the following months as a guide to War Office ways. Soon Wully gave him other jobs—sent him to Russian GHQ twice in 1916, for instance—but finally appointed Macdonogh in his stead. Both Maurice and Macdonogh had held corresponding posts in France, likewise Whigham who became Deputy CIGS, and they formed the backbone of the new team. Others came over too. In all they composed a body of tried and trusted staff officers, who knew Wully and his ways as well as he knew them. Under him they not only restored and expanded the functions of the General Staff, but gained for it that recognition which Wully was never tired of asserting it must have as the instrument of direction of a great Army. Such had long been the case, of course, in France and Germany. Not so in Britain. Although a General Staff system had been in being since the Esher reforms of 1904, the machinery had only slowly come into operation, while in 1914 Kitchener had thrown it out of gear, as already explained. It was only now that it was allowed to function properly again, and for the first time *under the conditions of war*: itself the very purpose and justification of an Army and a General Staff. For this, history must give great credit to Wully Robertson.

Without an efficient organisation and a staff upon whom he could absolutely rely, Wully would have found the job impossible from the start. As it was, the pressures were so complex and so powerful that he was only just able to withstand the strain. In the end they were to break him as they broke Lord Kitchener, though for different reasons and in different circumstances, as will be related.

Essentially there were two sources of friction, both inherent in the situation surrounding the CIGS, and both in this instance operating to his detriment. The first related to personalities. Wully was by no means an easy man himself. Yet even he, formidable and self-reliant as he was, needed all the sympathy and support of those at the top in order to master the fearful problems that beset him day after day. Such support progressively diminished, so that already by the end of 1916 he was in a position of isolation. So long, however, as Kitchener was alive, all went fairly well. Kitchener stuck by the Bargain to the letter, accepted the reduced powers of his ministerial post without demur, and backed Wully in the War Committee and the Cabinet. There was a bond of professional solidarity between the two men, and they respected and liked each other personally. Moreover, Wully 'absolutely played the game by his official superior but real colleague; he behaved to him as if he acknowledged his subordination.'[4] In a less degree also, the presence of Asquith as Prime Minister, who was always fair (though not dynamic) in his handling of men and affairs, was a stay and a comfort. Against this, the antagonism of Lloyd George (as Secretary of State for War, July–December 1916, and Prime Minister after that) grew so devastating that it wore Wully down, and ultimately drove him out. It will be said, no doubt, that strong personalities are bound to conflict and cause friction; that this was just a private misfortune and a comparatively minor episode in a war that was won in the end. In fact it was very nearly lost, and precisely because the political and military leaders were at civil war among themselves. It was a lesson well learned when the Second World War was fought. As Lord Ismay wrote:

'. . . there were none of the hateful intrigues or bitter animosities which disfigured the councils of the First World War. Of course there were moments when tempers were frayed, . . of course there were times when the soldiers resented the continuous, but not always unsalutary, prodding of their political Chief. But . . . I can testify that the War Cabinet was a band of brothers, and that the relations between Churchill and his official advisers, both civil and military, were characterised by mutual understanding, esteem and affection.'[5]

The second source of friction resided in the actual machinery for directing the war effort as a whole. In regard to the Allies as a team, no permanent arrangements of any kind for their common co-operation existed before the Inter-Allied Supreme War Council, set up at the end of 1917. In regard to Britain alone, such machinery as existed was faulty and incomplete. This was surprising in that the Committee for Imperial Defence, fathered by Balfour in 1902 and nurtured by Hankey, was an imaginative and far-seeing body, and made many of the necessary preparations for a war with Germany. But it miscalculated the size and nature of the national effort needed for a world war, particularly as to the planning of resources in men and material, and it never worked out an 'efficient higher administrative apparatus to replace the peacetime Cabinet procedure'.[6]

Soon after the war began, the Committee of Imperial Defence sank into abeyance, while the Cabinet carried on as best it could. It ran into difficulties at once, and had to resort to various expedients to make the administration more efficient. These have already been mentioned. They consisted chiefly of a succession of advisory committees, whose decisions were usually confirmed by the Cabinet, to the extent that they came to possess a kind of executive power of their own. They were:

War Council: November 1914–May 1915
Dardanelles Committee: May–October 1915
War Committee: November 1915–December 1916

None of them was satisfactory. Although intended to be small and streamlined, they all grew big and cumbersome, while their proceedings were inadequately recorded and circulated. The title 'Dardanelles Committee' was itself a comment on the limited view of the war, taken by the Government at the time.

It was not until Lloyd George set up his War Cabinet in December 1916 that anything approaching efficiency emerged. This body consisted originally of five men, most of them Ministers without departmental responsibilities, free to give their minds to the business of running the war. Although they had to call in others for specialist advice, thereby swelling their numbers whenever they met, it was nevertheless a much more effective system. Moreover, the War Cabinet was 'completely equipped with a supporting secretariat and sub-committee organisation as used by the Committee of Imperial Defence . . . and was in essence a democratic form of constitutional dictatorship by Lloyd George.'[7] Of this, and of its expansion into the Imperial War Cabinet, more later.

Wully was of course intimately affected by these changes, chiefly as they reacted on the new status which he had won for the CIGS by the Bargain with Lord Kitchener. As Lord Beaverbrook put it:

'. . . in reality two Secretaries of State were appointed. One, Lord Kitchener, with the nominal leadership, was to discharge all those duties which would appertain to the Secretary of State in time of peace, the other, General Robertson, was to conduct the war. . . This privilege [of direct access to the Cabinet] made his [Robertson's] position practically co-equal with his colleague and far superior to the position of the First Sea Lord towards the First Lord of the Admiralty.'[8]

The Bargain was to bring much trouble: not only with Lloyd George, who violently objected to playing second fiddle in his own department, but in constitutional terms as well. In short Kitchener had given away more than he ought, at any rate by peacetime rules. Since the Secretary of State was responsible to Parliament for the Army, then he had to answer for everything that the War Office did. True, munitions had already been removed to a separate Ministry, but that did not affect the issue. Operations and the raising and maintenance of the troops remained. By allowing the CIGS to deal direct with the Government on operational matters, the S of S allowed himself to be by-passed in regard to the most important business of the War Office, which was constitutionally *all* his parish. This is what Lloyd George objected to when he succeeded Kitchener in July 1916, and with a good deal of justification. It created a situation between him and Wully which was exacerbated by their profound disagreement on strategy, and by their temperamental differences as well.

On the other hand there was undoubtedly a strong case for changing the constitutional procedure, which had been conceived in peacetime, and in a previous age. This was war, and war of a kind never experienced before in terms of technique, urgency, and scale. The problems were such that the Cabinet had continually to consult its Service chiefs direct. A new situation had arisen that demanded a new solution. The one presented by Wully was only tolerable if the CIGS and S of S worked in harmony, and agreed above all on strategy. Curiously enough, Lloyd George never discovered the real solution, even when he became Prime Minister and had the power to provide one. In December 1916 he appointed Lord Derby to take his place at the War Office under precisely the same conditions as before, and then set about devising other ways round the impasse. He eventually hit on one at the end of 1917—a device and not a solution—and he used it to push Wully out.

The real solution was only discovered after the war, first with the creation in 1923 of the Chiefs of Staff Committee, where the Chiefs of Staff of all three Services (the RAF had been created in 1918), backed by a Joint Planning Committee, met as a team to work out strategic problems in common, and advise on defence as a whole. From then on machinery existed for producing and presenting 'a corporate, coherent and comprehensive strategy to the Government'.[9] The design was completed in the Second World War when Churchill, as Prime Minister and Minister of Defence, acted as chairman of a body known as the Defence Committee (Operations), on which the three Service Ministers always sat, with the Chiefs of Staff in attendance, and to which the COS Committee was responsible. Ultimate authority rested with the War Cabinet as before. That solved both the constitutional responsibilities and the official relationships of Ministers and Service Chiefs, and at the same time removed many of the causes of personal friction as well.

*   *   *

But all this is anticipating. In 1914–16 there was no Inter-Service organisation for the formulation of strategy, and therefore no comprehensive plans.

'What actually existed . . . were separate departmental projects placed before a confused Cabinet: some of them designed only for the first few weeks of a minor campaign in France and quickly overwhelmed in the rush of events; some hastily improvised almost singlehandedly for political reasons by Churchill and Lloyd George. . . All these lacked both the careful staff consideration which modern war required, and the backing of vast reserves of manpower, equipment and supplies. The result was a jogging series of stop-gap attempts to meet crises as they arose.'[10]

In other words Ministers either had to choose between the experts as best they might, or act as amateur strategists themselves—a game which many of them were only too pleased to play, at any rate as regards *military* operations. As Wully said sardonically, since the Navy was or pretended to be a technical Service, naval officers were adept at taking cover behind a smoke screen of scientific jargon, which rarely failed to bamboozle a civilian boarding-party. Indeed about the only exception was when Lloyd George imposed his will on the Admiralty in April 1917 over the convoy system, and insisted on changes in the structure of the Naval Staff. In fact the Admiralty had no General Staff structure comparable in concept or quality to that of the War Office. None the less, it seemed to Wully that anyone could lay down the law about *military* strategy, start new fronts, or move formations about the world regardless of logistics. Every suggestion, however silly, had to be investigated by the General Staff, involving a lot of unnecessary work and nervous energy. Wully bore the brunt of this himself, and it told on him heavily.

'At 11 am on practically every day of the week, except Sunday, I was required to attend the meeting of the Cabinet, War Committee, War Cabinet or whatever . . . in order to report the events of the past 24 hours; to predict, when requested, what they might be during the next 24; and to elucidate or justify such General Staff recommendations as awaited Government sanction.

'The First Sea Lord was not called upon to make such lengthy statements and explanations as myself. He had less to talk about, and naval phraseology was less easy for Ministers to understand. Theoretically our respective statements were supposed to be made at the beginning of the meeting, so that we might get back early to our offices. But they were often postponed because some unexpected question had cropped up . . . an objectionable newspaper article . . . an awkward question in the House of Commons . . . fear of industrial troubles . . . criticisms of military matters gleaned by Ministers during a visit to the front, or received in a letter from a constituent, or heard at a dinner-table on the previous evening. When at last the agenda paper was reached, the business in hand might take a long time to settle or, when settled, the Prime Minister might ask me to remain in case I should be wanted in connexion with some other subject. . . Thus it came about that I seldom left the meetings before 1.30 pm, and serious encroachments were made upon the time available for other work.'[11]

The pity of it was that, even with slightly better machinery, much of this pressure upon Wully might have been relieved and personal relations preserved. As it was its very cumbrousness— its amateurishness—widened the general gulf between civil and military, 'frocks and brasshats' as Henry Wilson called them, and helped breed an atmosphere of mistrust and intrigue that was never eradicated. Nor were the policies and personal loyalties always clear-cut. While the soldiers usually stuck together as professionals and Westerners, Henry Wilson excepted, the Ministers were a mixed lot of party adherents who differed deeply on many issues. Asquith, wise and respected though he was by almost everybody, was simply not strong enough to hold them all together; while Lloyd George, with all his war-winning virtues of dynamism and drive, encouraged enmities and intrigues on the principle of 'divide and rule', and incurred more distrust on the part of the Army than anyone.

None the less—according to Hankey, an admirably fair and acute observer, who held the key position of Secretary to the War Committee—Wully made a very good impression.

'The War Committee was admirably served by Robertson who was a tower of strength to them. His policy, if not very inspired, was always definite and his advice, therefore, always consistent. He was an admirable administrator and, once a decision was taken, the Committee could rely on him to carry it out. He proved far more adaptable than had been expected to political considerations, and in cases where these were paramount, he was willing to recognise the fact and to conform his policy without giving way on what he considered essential. His relations with Asquith and the Committee were, therefore, as good as could be wished.'[12]

As a Committee man, however, Wully suffered—like Haig— from one damaging defect: damaging, that is, to himself and to the interests he represented. Although he had a clear, shrewd mind, knew what he wanted and why, and wrote excellent papers, he was relatively inarticulate. Hankey wrote:

'In speech he was slow and deliberate. He never uttered an opinion which he had not thought out. He would address international conferences in correct French (carefully written out as a rule) and with an English accent. He would nearly always meet the brainwaves of the nimble-minded French politicians with a negative, so that eventually they gave him the nickname of *"General Non-Non"*.'[13]

It was this characteristic that aggravated English politicians too, especially Lloyd George, an instinctive man of action, who thought and felt fast, and thus put Wully at a disadvantage. Wully was baffled by the quick unpredictable shifts of debate, resented them, and even suspected those whom he considered responsible for them. On such occasions he would take refuge in silence and scowls, or in a series of grunts, fearsome disapproving sounds, which were the armour of a deliberate thinking and deliberate speaking, but never a dim-witted man. However, when handled aright, all this defensive mechanism would dissolve. Hankey had had early experience of this before the war, when Wully was Director of Military Training.

'It was at a meeting of the Home Ports Defence Committee, of which I was *ex officio* chairman, and he the senior military member. He was sitting on my left, the senior naval member being on my right. It was Robertson's first attendance at the Committee. Almost immediately he sat down he turned round in his chair, half left, and took no part in the proceedings, showing thereby how much he disapproved of so humble a person as myself being in the chair! I determined not to quarrel, and conducted the business without taking any notice. Before the next meeting I paid him a visit, and, without referring to his attitude at the previous meeting, asked his advice as a senior officer and more experienced man on how to approach the questions on the Agenda. From that day onwards we remained good friends, and during the war, even in circumstances of great delicacy, we remained on the best of terms and kept in closest touch.'[14]

Hankey added:

'But perhaps his greatest quality, transcending his great powers of work, his mastery of principle, his organising capacity, and his judgment of men, was "character". His was a dominating personality. . . It was this which made him a tower of strength to the War Committee. It was this which enabled him to retain his post in difficult times for more than two years, when he had to give place to a more nimble and versatile mind.'[15]

Socially Wully soon became immensely popular. People loved him for his simplicity, his uninhibited speech, his absolute faith in Britain's ability and will to win the war, his massive physical appearance. Here indeed was John Bull in person, English to the core, shrewd, suspicious of frills and foreigners, intolerant of shams, robust, reliable, and human; above all, a man of the people, who—for all his dazzling success—remained one of them. Thus, they gave him their trust and affection, wrote him dozens of letters, and showered invitations upon him.

Wully thoroughly enjoyed all this—he would not have been human or himself if he had not—but he did not allow it to affect his judgment or his bearing in any way. At the same time such popularity did help sustain the strain of office, and he turned it to good account. He became an honorary member of half a dozen London clubs, and was happy often to take Mildred off for the weekend to one or other of the country houses where they were invited, notably to the Pirries at Witley Park. Most important of all was the use of a town house. When Wully first came to London, he and Mildred took a flat in Queen Anne's Mansions, but early in 1916 Sir George Fowke offered them the free tenancy of No. 4 South Street, off Park Lane, and this became their home until November when they moved into Kitchener's old quarters at York House, St James's Palace. They stayed there for two and a quarter years, until February 1919, a whole year after Wully had left the War

Office, when the place was needed for the young Prince of Wales. George V, always a staunch friend, could hardly have done Wully a more useful kindness. It was these, and similar acts of friendship, that made it practicably possible for him to live up to his official position, and to make good his entire lack of means outside his Army pay.

But if any people of money or title thought that, because of hospitality, they could put Wully under obligation, they were soon disabused. Repington, the military correspondent, related:

'I chaffed him about the Society ladies who pursued him. He told me that he had been the recipient of innumerable invitations to lunch from one lady, who in her importunity pursued him to the War Office, but he succeeded in resisting her blandishments. His "pursuer" had tried to work on his wife, but had failed: but he understood the game, and was determined to stand clear of politicians, their wives, and the other great ladies who sought to lionise him for their own purposes.'[16]

Another time, he attended the celebration of Italian Day at the Ritz.

'People having parties included the Italian Ambassador, Prince Victor Napoleon, Lady Bagot, Lady Massereene and various others. Afterwards a Vaudeville, and Lady Constance Stewart Richardson posed and contorted and danced, in few clothes and with bare feet. She looked like a white dervish. Lady Strafford declared that she was playing John the Baptist, and that the contortions represented her attempts to find locusts and wild honey. Had a short talk with Prince Victor and Princess Clementine. Many fled when Lady C. danced, including Sir William Robertson, who, when asked whether he did not think that she had a very fine leg, replied that "it was just like any other damned leg".'[17]

Wully never forgot his own people. He kept in constant touch with his brother, Tom, and sister, Emily, to whom he was the same Will they had always known. Of his son Brian, who had passed out of RMA, Woolwich, early in the war, he was justifiably proud. In 1915 the boy—still under 19 and thus ineligible for the front—had served for a time as ADC to his father. Subsequently, after a period of duty with his Corps, he served as ADC to Haig during the Somme battle. Thereafter he did a spell on the staff of XI Corps, and he ended the war as an infantry brigade-major, winning the MC and DSO.[18]

* * *

Wully lost no time in setting about the War Committee. On December 28th, five days after his appointment as CIGS, the Committee formally approved his plea to regard France and Flanders as the main theatre of operations, and to make preparations for an offensive there in co-operation with the Allies. This confirmed the plans made earlier in December at Chantilly for three main offensives—in France, Italy, and Russia—all to go off as nearly as possible together in the following spring. For Wully it was not only a great triumph but a great relief, and he lost no time in telling Haig the good news in France. After months of vacillation and disastrous campaigning, he was free at last to salve what he could from the various fronts and redeploy British strength. But it was a very heavy task. France apart, British forces were committed on no less than five fronts about the world, some of them in bad case. All required major feats of reorganisation.

In the Dardanelles the campaign had already been lost. Anzac and Suvla had been successfully evacuated, but Cape Helles was still being held, partly to satisfy the Navy, partly in the hope of tying down a substantial body of Turkish troops in the peninsula. Wully rejected both these pretexts outright. In his view, 'to continue hanging on to the place merely because we were afraid to leave it, was not only a waste of men, but . . . a constant source of anxiety.'[19] He therefore gave the order to go, and by January 9th 1916 nearly 40,000 men and most of their artillery had been extricated without serious incident or loss, thanks largely to good nerves and the brilliant handling of commanders on the spot. And so one sombre chapter was finally closed.

Egypt had two battlefronts, with troops engaging Senussi tribesmen raiding in the western desert, and others facing the Turks who occupied Sinai and threatened the Suez Canal from the east. The defence of the Canal and of Egypt generally was of course vital to British strategy, and early in the war the garrison had been increased to over four divisions. With this force the C-in-C, Sir John Maxwell, had acted offensively against the Senussi and repelled a spirited Turkish attack on the Canal in February 1915. Some of the enemy actually gained the west bank, but they were all killed or taken prisoner in the end. Thereafter the east front became quiescent, and Maxwell relied on a purely static defence along the Canal itself. A number of troops were drawn off to the Dardanelles, and Egypt served generally as a base for operations in the Eastern Mediterranean and the Balkans.

At the end of the year events took a new turn. The Dardanelles were evacuated, the majority of the troops returning to Egypt, and Murray (Wully's predecessor as CIGS) was given the command of the east front. He was also charged with supervising the operations at Salonika and with reorganising the Dardanelles detachments. This meant that there were to be two commanders in Egypt—Murray in the east, and Maxwell in the west—a dual arrangement decided by Kitchener, to Wully's dismay and disapproval, though matters were soon put right. In January 1916 Murray was relieved of all operational control at Salonika (in favour of Sarrail), though the administrative responsibility remained; and in March he assumed sole command in the Middle East. Maxwell went home to deal with the Easter Rising in Ireland.

Wully refused to treat Egypt as a major theatre of war, or even admit that it stood in any serious danger at all. He made it clear to Murray that his primary task was to reorganise and re-equip the troops, in order to transfer as many trained formations as possible to France, and only secondarily to deal with the enemies on the spot. Murray fulfilled these requirements to the letter, but the size and complexity of his task, and thus the measure of his success, was never fully recognised. When he arrived, troops were still pouring into the country from the Dardanelles, some units had disintegrated, many of the men dejected or indisciplined. Within six months he had not only got them into good order and good heart, but had also 'exported' ten of his best divisions (nine to France, one to Mesopotamia), three independent infantry brigades, 11,000 Indian troops, and nine batteries of heavy artillery. An eleventh division was sent to France early in 1917.

By then he had left himself with three under-strength infantry divisions, plus the elements of two more, all relatively inexperienced, and two good cavalry divisions which, unlike the static warfare in France, were to play an important part in the mobile operations against the Turks. He was badly off for heavy guns and aeroplanes. Yet with rapidly decreasing forces he completed the subjection of the Senussi (taking Siwa in February 1917) and drove the Turks out of Sinai. The logistic difficulties were immense. Sinai was a desert—sand in the north, gravel and clay in the centre, mountains in the south. The best plan was to push along the coast and establish a line about 100 miles east at El Arish—El Kossaima. This guarded most of the tracks likely to be used by the enemy, and reduced the front from 80–90 miles (on the Canal) to about 45. The move depended upon communications and water, and Murray set to work to provide both, calling upon the reserves of Egyptian industry and labour and importing the rest, mostly rails, pipes, and machinery. By February 1917 he had reached the frontier, having laid nearly 400 miles of railway, 300 miles of metalled and wire-mesh roads, and 300 miles of pipes. Since wells were unsuitable, all the water had to be drawn from the Sweet Water Canal back in the Delta, pumped under the Ship Canal and piped east: a vast undertaking involving the construction of filtration plants, pumping sets, and reservoirs, in addition to the laying of the pipe line. Moreover, many of the pipes arrived rusty, with wrong threads, and had to be adapted *in situ*. All this was done. Without it and the other essential services, neither men nor animals could have survived.

Meanwhile the enemy was not inactive. Russian successes in the Caucasus in the spring had made it unlikely that the Turks would renew their offensive against Egypt. Yet they managed two minor actions: a successful one at Katia in April, where they cut up some British cavalry, and an unsuccessful one at Romani in August, where they lost half their force of 15,000 men in casualties and prisoners. After that Murray took the offensive, capturing El Arish in December and Rafa on the frontier in January 1917. He was also concerned with another front. In June, Hussein, the Sherif of Mecca, had sprung the Arab Revolt in the Hejaz, taking Mecca itself and three ports on the Red Sea. His son, Feisal, was in active command. But the impetus soon started to peter out when Medina resisted. Here the Turks were well entrenched and had sufficient strength to recapture all that was lost, if the moment came. At first Murray thought little of the Arabs' chances. He was an orthodox soldier with an orthodox view of warfare, and he refused all demands to send British troops in force to Arabia. But when T. E. Lawrence, self-constituted liaison officer to Feisal, asked him for other sorts of help, he allowed himself to be persuaded. Personally he took unkindly to Lawrence's arrogance and Arab dress, but he confirmed him in his appointment, and consistently supported him with arms and equipment, supplies, instructors, and gold. Those were the commodities most needed at that juncture. Later Allenby, who got on with Lawrence far better, was in a more favourable position both to help him on a larger scale and be helped by him in terms of guerilla fighting.

And so, after a year in command in Egypt, Murray had done all that Wully had asked him to do, and more. Unfortunately, his very success in the east opened up possibilities in Palestine, for which he was neither prepared nor briefed, and it led to his undoing after the two battles of Gaza in March and April 1917.[20]

Further east, in Mesopotamia, a campaign that had begun well was now sliding towards disaster. After a bold advance during 1915 towards Baghdad, a force from India under General Townshend outran its strength and communications, was compelled to retreat, and then shut itself up in Kut-el-Amara. All attempts at relief failed, and at the end of April 1916 the force had no option but to surrender. The whole expedition had been managed and mismanaged by GHQ India, and in February in desperation the War Office took over. By then it was far too late, and Wully could do nothing to prevent the final issue. He did, however, see to it that the front was reorganised and in August handed over to a first-class commander, Maude, who had been the last man to leave Cape Helles. Maude was to make ample amends by recapturing Kut in February 1917, and by going on to take Baghdad a month later.

The fourth front, in the Balkans, had opened in October 1915 as a Franco-British effort to save the Serbs, which failed. It then deteriorated into a purely defensive operation round Salonika, with an international force composed of French, British (five divisions), Serbs (the remnant of the Serbian Army, after its retreat through Albania and rehabilitation on the island of Corfu), Italians, and Russians. The commander, Sarrail, a

Frenchman, was a controversial figure who owed his appointment to political pressure at home. He himself dabbled in Greek politics, a subject of infinite variety and uncertainty, which nearly involved the Allies in disaster. In due course a pro-Allied Government was set up at Salonika by Venizelos who, however, only gradually established his authority. The Greek Army was undecided in its loyalties. When the Bulgars attacked in August 1916, one Greek corps stationed on the right of the British in Thessaly surrendered, and eventually all Greek troops had to be taken out of the line. Later they were re-formed, and proved themselves stoutly in the final battles of 1918. Meanwhile, the front alternated between spasmodic attacks and complete inertia, locking up large numbers of Allied troops at infinitesimal cost to the enemy.

It was just as Wully had expected. It had become obvious to him early on that, although the Salonika force outnumbered the enemy, it was unable to break through the front, embedded as it was in difficult mountainous country, poorly served by communications, and favourable to defence. Moreover, it was a purely peripheral campaign. What, he pleaded again and again, was the point of keeping troops there at all? Malaria caused far more casualties than bullets or shells. Far better transfer the men to France, or even to some other front, where they could influence the war. Indeed, he was quite prepared to abandon the Balkans altogether, arguing with force that it would pay the Allies to do so. But he never got his way. He was invariably baulked by the French, who were determined to keep their hold on that part of Europe. Even Joffre—doughty Westerner as he was—supported Salonika, though for political not military reasons. Wully wrote:

'For about three years it [Salonika] absorbed a large Entente force which contributed nothing material to the winning of the war, beyond detaining two or three German divisions of inferior quality, and a number of Bulgarian divisions who would probably have objected to serve outside the Balkan Peninsula. This is a hard statement to make, remembering the privations and sickness our troops experienced, and the fine work they performed in the offensive of September 1918, but the fact remains that the Bulgars were defeated on the West Front and not in Macedonia. . . The entire campaign, in fact, was complicated and tiresome, and more conferences were held . . . in regard to it than to any other military question.'[21]

The fifth front was in East Africa where, under the skilful leadership of von Lettow-Vorbeck, the Germans had been conducting a remarkably tenacious campaign since the outbreak of war. By the spring of 1916 their territory was still largely intact, and it was decided to call in the help of the South African Government and General Smuts. Operations then began to take a turn for the better. They remained, however, painful and protracted, partly owing to the difficult climate and country, partly owing to the ingenuity of the enemy who managed to stay in the field right up until November 1918. Indeed, comparatively large forces had to be deployed to deal inconclusively with a small and elusive foe. But by European standards the numbers were small and casualties low, and in relation to the general strategy of the war, East Africa was a sideshow. Wully never allowed it to be anything else.

*   *   *

So much for the strategic commitments that had, somehow or other, to be subordinated to the great offensive soon to be launched in the west. But although strategic planning might to some extent be simplified in this way, nothing could be done without an adequate supply of men and arms.

Thanks to Kitchener's earlier efforts and, above all, to Lloyd George's at the Ministry of Munitions, production was now coming along fast, though not so fast as to sustain any large-scale attack before the middle of the summer; and this became increasingly clear as the months passed. Even when the Somme did go off, there was barely enough. The expenditure of ammunition was colossal, many guns and shells proved faulty, duds littered the battlefields, while barrels burst or wore out prematurely: the result of sheer inexperience in manufacture and forcing the pace in the factories. Nevertheless, by early 1916, the immediate crisis of ordnance production seemed to be over.

As to men, this was a more complex story and largely a political one. It will be recalled that, at the start of the war, Kitchener had by personal appeal succeeded in attracting a large number of volunteers, and that he had continued to rely on the voluntary system all during 1915. There is little doubt that he was right, if only because so many joined up in the first twelve months that it would hardly have been possible to train and equip any more. Unfortunately there was little attempt at selection, and anyway volunteers always mean waste, since too many brave spirits and skilled men are sacrificed in the first rush. Apart from this, the Government—and the nation—were almost totally committed to the idea of voluntary enlistment, some (like Asquith) believing in it on principle, others clinging to the mistaken notion that the war would be won before the supply of volunteers dried up.

By the middle of 1915, however, the situation was obviously deteriorating. The losses in France and Gallipoli, the gradual realisation that the *whole* effort of the nation was needed to fight a world war, all pointed in one direction—compulsion. But the Government would not have it, and continued to believe that the nation would not have it either, even though the National Registration Act of August 1915 revealed that there were still plenty of men available for service. In October came the Derby scheme, by which men were *invited* to volunteer in groups according to age, youngest first, single before married, all staying in their employments till called. The scheme had some success, but by the end of the year the crisis was coming back again, and it was obvious that the Government would have to make another move. As a first step, it asked the General Staff for a clear forecast of future requirements.

At this point Wully took over as CIGS. It was one of the first questions he had to deal with, and he took good care *not* to commit himself to any hard-and-fast reply. He did, however, point out to Kitchener that simply to fill up some 70 under-strength British divisions (half of them in France), and keep them filled up, there would have to be a monthly intake of about 130,000 men.[22] The Cabinet then set up a committee to thrash out the whole subject of military and financial needs. The committee worked fast, and by early February 1916 it had been agreed that the Army should aim at 62 full-strength divisions in the field by the end of June, with three months reserves, plus 5 divisions for home defence, without reserves. So far so good, but that was only half the answer since, as Wully pointed out, the flow of recruits was insufficient to make good

even this estimate.[23] The Military Service Act of January 1916,
yet another half-measure, had already proved inadequate.
While making service compulsory for all single men between
the ages of 18 and 41, it exempted the married, and left out
Ireland completely. Meanwhile, all the Derby groups were being
called up, so that in many cases conscience was penalised and
the injustice was widely felt. Finally—after further delay and
much reluctance—Asquith gave in, and a new Military Service
Act came into force on May 25th, which applied to everyone
within the existing age limits, *including* married men and
widowers with dependents. Asquith and his supporters had
been completely mistaken in gauging the temper of the nation.
Compulsion was inevitable, and the great majority had long
accepted the fact. Now they welcomed it with relief.

Compulsion did not, however, come in time for the Somme,
of which the brunt was borne by volunteers. Nor did it ever
satisfy the needs of the Army as a whole. Indeed, the problem of
manpower plagued the General Staff until the very end of the
war, and for two reasons. One derived from certain anomalies
within the Army itself. The fact, for instance, that time-expired
Regulars could still leave the Colours, and were doing so at the
rate of 5000 a month as late as the summer of 1916. Or, again,
the absence of legal powers to transfer men from one branch of
the Service to another. Such things were nonsensical in war,
and Wully dealt with them as expeditiously as he could. But he
was unable to stop uncontrolled competition for personnel by
the various arms, and he failed to induce Lloyd George, when
Secretary of State for War, to enforce a proper system of
allocation through the medium of the Army Council.

The second reason resided in the situation outside the Army,
where the struggle was even more chaotic. Tribunals continued
to exempt a large number of men of service age. Ireland was
never touched, and although a Manpower Distribution Board
was set up in August 1916 to work out some system for the
economic use of labour, it proved ineffective. Nor did the
Ministry of National Service, created a year later, do any
better so far as the Army was concerned. By then the ghastly
losses in France were having an effect, not only on the numerical
strength of the Army, but on the attitude of the Government
to strategy and tactics. It was given forcible expression by

Lloyd George, who had long believed that the generals were wasteful of men, and that trench warfare in France would never lead to victory. And so, unable to impose his views on Wully or Haig, he sought to put a brake on them by controlling their sources of manpower. In short, manpower became a weapon in the dispute between Westerners and Easterners, never satisfactorily resolved. The final crisis came early in 1918, as will be told.

There was yet another reason. All agreed that the country needed to be in a strong position when the war ended, and not find itself—as France would—materially and spiritually exhausted. Kitchener held this view, using it as an argument against compulsion, telling Wully:

'Don't hurry things so. What we should aim at is to have the largest army in Europe when the terms of peace are being discussed, and that will not be in 1916, but in 1917.'[24]

Wully accepted the aim, but not the conclusion. Fortunately.

*   *   *

Meanwhile the planning went ahead. Since the offensive was primarily the responsibility of the commanders in the field, Joffre and Haig wasted no time in getting down to work. But there were a number of differences to be resolved first.

One was the *form* of the offensive.

Joffre wanted a series of 'wearing-out' or 'wearing-down' battles (*batailles d'usure*), before the main attack, to draw in and consume the enemy reserves: in short, battles of attrition, on the lines of the French offensives in 1915. He also made it clear that he looked to the British to do the job, since the French had already suffered enormous losses and were running short of men. Haig disagreed.

He conceded the value of raiding and harassment on a small scale, both to gain a moral superiority over the enemy and, if possible, to capture strong points. But long-drawn-out engagements before the main attack might merely result in the attackers being worn out first, while giving the defenders enough time to make good their losses before the set piece. He did, however, favour diversionary attacks a short time—say one or two weeks—beforehand, to deceive the enemy as to the weight and place of the main effort, and to induce him to commit his reserves prematurely. As to the main attack itself, he abhorred the pattern of annihilation favoured by the French. He preferred an all-out punch to burst through the enemy line, followed by exploitation with cavalry. For that reason alone he wanted as much time as possible for preparation—to accumulate material and train his men—in order to give the punch the greatest possible power, and so to finish the job quickly. The irony of it was that, when the punch was finally delivered on July 1st, it failed to burst through the German lines, and the Somme did deteriorate into a desperate drawn-out agony of annihilation, far worse than anything experienced before. Nevertheless, Haig's main intention seemed sound, and after a good deal of discussion he managed to persuade Joffre of it at a conference at Chantilly on February 14th.

On the second point—the place of the attack—he was unsuccessful, and therein lay much of the tragedy of the Somme. Early on Joffre had suggested a series of alternative offensives, the Somme to be one, in a renewed effort to puncture the great German salient in France: a variation—providing that more than one alternative came into play—of the strategy of 1915.[25] So conceived the Somme had possibilities. Alone it had none, since it was located at the apex of the salient, where even a break-through would only flatten out the forward curve of the enemy line. Moreover, this was an area where no serious fighting had taken place for a long time, and where the Germans had managed to construct an immensely strong system of defence, with two lines built and a third a-building, sited along ridges with an excellent field of fire, and bristling with strong points and deep dug-outs hewn out of the chalk. Serious as these objections were, even they might have been overcome had the Somme been supported elsewhere. But Joffre's intentions were not solely strategic. He wanted to ensure that the British would be involved on a grand scale for the first time, and when and where he wanted. Since, at that time, the boundary between the two armies lay along the Somme river, his plan made certain of this.

Haig had other ideas altogether. He preferred an attack further north in Flanders which, if linked to a landing operation up the Channel, offered clearer strategic possibilities—the retirement of the enemy along the vulnerable coastline and the rolling-up of his northern flank. Part of this plan was to be attempted in 1917, but Joffre would have none of it in 1916, and Haig had to give way. He did so because he had been formally instructed by Kitchener to co-operate with the French as closely as possible. The French, in fact, were still the predominant partners, and Haig did not feel justified in challenging them on this point at this early stage in his new command. Later in 1916, after the German offensive at Verdun had put paid to practically all idea of alternative French offensive action, it was found impossible to withdraw from the Somme commitment. Not only had the preparations gone too far, but it had become imperative—militarily and emotionally—to help relieve the appalling pressure at Verdun. Hence the operation remained in isolation, with all its disadvantages magnified and intact.

Thirdly, timing. Any ideas about an early spring offensive soon evaporated before the realities of the situation, as it developed day by day. It was quickly realised that supplies of munitions would not be adequate before the summer at least. Likewise every extra day that could be gained for the training and assembly of troops was obviously essential. Another factor was the advent of an exciting new weapon—the armoured fighting vehicle or 'tank'. Thanks to the efforts of a handful of pioneers and the far-sighted patronage of men such as Hankey and Churchill, the latter using Admiralty funds, development had so far advanced that it was possible to stage a secret demonstration at Hatfield Park in February 1916. Everything went off very well, and the ability of the new machine to deal with trenches and obstacles won official approval—and an immediate order for 100 tanks. Most important—though Wully was reserved—Haig was enthusiastic, and asked for as many machines as possible for use in the offensive. In the end he got 48, but of these only 36 took part in the attack of September 15th, with inconclusive results. That Haig was severely criticised for using them when and how he did, prematurely in fact, does not concern us here. The point of relevance is that he welcomed the invention and wanted the machines, and that their availability influenced his own ideas as to the timing of the Somme. Without doubt he would have preferred to wait longer, but in this matter—as in so much else —he was not a free agent.

Abroad preparations for the Somme were affected by two groups of events: namely, the other Allied and the enemy offensives. The Allies, it will be recalled, had already agreed to co-ordinate their efforts by launching three offensives in the early part of 1916, in Italy, Russia, and France. The timing, however, went astray. In Italy plans were disrupted by an Austrian attack in the Trentino in May. In Russia the Brusilov offensive started well against the Austrians in June, and brought some relief to the Italians, but although it duly forced the Germans to transfer some fifteen divisions to the east, it did not seriously distract them in France. For, in France, it was not the Allies who took the initiative, but the Germans. On February 21st 1916 they launched a massive attack against the hinge of the French line at Verdun, and sustained it for five murderous months. It was a deliberate attempt to destroy men and morale by saturating the defences with artillery fire of such weight and concentration that the French were compelled to throw in all their reserves simply to stave off collapse. In short, this was *par excellence* a battle of attrition. Casualties on both sides were enormous, and although the Germans never succeeded in breaking through, they came very near to doing so. In the process they so depleted French strength, that Joffre had not only to rely on the Somme alone, but prevail on Haig to advance the starting date to July 1st, some two months earlier than the British commander had hoped.

*   *   *

For Wully, as for Haig, the Somme represented the first great test of Western strategy. It dominated the thoughts and actions of them both. And so—during the months that preceded, accompanied, and followed the battle—it revealed much of the shape and substance of their characters, in the way, for example, they reacted to people and events, and particularly to each other.

On the surface both men had a great deal in common. They were regular soldiers, at the top of their profession and at the height of their careers. Their work was essentially inter-dependent, and they relied upon each other almost without question. They held similar views about the war, and they agreed about the superiority of the British race and the role of the British Army. They disliked politics and mistrusted most of the politicians, retreating on occasions into either a defensive contempt or a stonewall silence: an attitude aggravated by the difficulty they both experienced (Haig, especially) in expressing themselves in speech, although on paper they suffered from no such handicap. Wully wrote admirably clear and reasoned Memoranda, while Haig was at his best in his private Diary and correspondence. Both were often exasperated by the French, as they had reason to be, but they both liked and respected Joffre. In this Haig was the more understanding of the two, and he showed greatness at times in the support he gave to some of his more difficult French colleagues.

In the final judgment both were big men, though insular and conservative. The reasons for their conservatism sprang from utterly different sources and backgrounds.

Haig was a born aristocrat, impervious in his social assurance and in his sense of mission to lead the British Army to victory. He had a simple faith and a simple morality, inculcated by his upbringing and sustained by the sermons of his Presbyterian chaplain, George Duncan. His presence was striking. He looked the leader that he was, and there is absolutely no doubt that he commanded the loyalty and respect of the Army in France, casualties and criticisms at home notwithstanding. Secure in himself and his post, he never sought to justify his actions in public, but was content to leave judgment to history.

Wully too was sustained by his religion, absorbed and inherited—as we have seen—from his mother, to whom he had been devoted. A straightforward Anglican, he rarely missed church and he was well acquainted with his Bible. Otherwise his assurance was of a different kind to Haig's, deriving not from the privileges of birth, but from their absence—from the very fact that he had made his way alone. Although the social order had impeded him, he did not reject it, at least in its essentials. He believed in it because he believed in social stability, and because he had mastered society. That struggle had been a tremendous, but not impossible, test of character, and he had shown what good gifts and sheer guts could do. All this had left its mark upon him—upon his bluntness and gruffness and homeliness—and turned him into the formidable person that he was. He feared nothing and no one, and deferred only to a very few: to the King, to Asquith and Kitchener in the Government (and these with reservations), and to only one man in the Army—Haig.

Why Haig? It is not easy to answer. It lay in a combination of circumstances: in the accident that Haig was his senior in the Service, who had commanded armies in the field while he himself had never had a command at all; in his belief that Haig was the one man who could win in the west and so win the war; in the fact that Haig was a 'grand seigneur' with a presence and a standing that impressed even Wully. Their full relationship comes out in the almost continuous correspondence—several letters a week—that passed between them for more than two years. Even before Kitchener's death, Wully was consulting Haig on a host of subjects other than those connected with the business in France, and looked to him more than to anyone else for backing and advice in his own job.

From his side Haig offered all the help that his character and abilities allowed. But he lacked imagination in that he never fully grasped what Wully was up against, and he never overcame a stifling reserve. Although he carried an immense burden of responsibility himself, Haig was nearly always surrounded by friends and protected from interference at home. He was undisputed master in his own house. Even in his most difficult dealings with the French, he had the advantage of treating with men of his own profession. And so, at times, he appeared extraordinarily insensitive to Wully's problems.

Wully, on the other hand, was in a far more lonely position than Haig. His responsibilities were multifarious, and often intangible, as well as crushing. He had to grapple, at national level, with appalling problems of manpower, material, and strategy, and answer for the progress—or lack of it—of all the fronts, in France and everywhere else. Inasmuch as this was all part of the job of the CIGS, Wully did not complain. What he found hard to bear was the unending struggle to secure official support, or to get the Government even to face up to some of the problems which he was desperately trying to solve. Some of the trouble was due, as described, to inefficient machinery, and to the fact that members of the War Committee played at strategy on their own, displaying both an ignorance of logistics and a reluctance to go all out in fighting the war. But the petty sniping and squabbling upset him almost as much. 'They regard me', he told Haig, 'as an optimistic ass when not as a stupid soldier. They think—and many say—that all soldiers are stupid.'[26] It resulted often, not in the outright rejection of his advice—which would have been logical—but in various methods of getting round it: hesitation, procrastination, and intrigue. Months and years of such pressure all bore upon Wully and, after Kitchener's death, upon him almost alone. That was why he turned increasingly to Haig, as the only man in his profession who could help him, and as the commander whom his own efforts were aimed at helping most.

He wrote to Haig on December 31st 1915:

'I am doing all right on the War Committee but it is difficult to keep one's temper. At the last meeting Balfour weighed in with a proposal that as the Western Front was so strong we should transfer all possible troops to cooperate with Russia on the Eastern Front! Words failed me and I lost my temper.'

On January 5th 1916:

'It is deplorable the way these politicians fight and intrigue against each other. They are my great difficulty here. They have no idea how war must be conducted in order to be given a reasonable chance of success, and they will not allow professionals a free hand. As you know the War Committee last week approved of certain conclusions [to make France and Flanders the principal theatre of war] which I have sent you. Balfour as a member of the Committee, also approved of them, but rather against his inclination. Not being able to talk the War Committee round to his point of view he has now written a long Memorandum to the Cabinet arguing quite contrary to the War Committee's conclusions. He has several supporters, as every other member of the Cabinet always has no matter what the question may be. Lord K asked me to write a rejoinder but this I have declined to do. I have taken up the position that the General Staff views have already been set forward at sufficient length, and that I have no more to say as regards the strategy to be adopted; that the recommendations of the General Staff have been approved by the War Committee, and until the War Committee tell me that they intend to withdraw their approval there is no action for me to take.'

But the matter did not rest there, and for the next three months Wully had to fight to hold the War Committee to its decision, in the knowledge that all the preparations going forward might yet be cancelled.

On January 13th:

'There is a fairly strong party in the Cabinet opposed to offensive operations on your front in the Spring or indeed at any time. One wants to go to the Balkans, another to Baghdad, and another to allow the Germans "to attack us". I have used all the arguments you or any other soldier would use, but not with complete success. In the War Committee decision [of December 28th] I sent you a few days ago you will see that we are to make every effort "to prepare" for offensive operations in the Spring. In the original draft I put we are to make every effort to "undertake" offensive operations in the Spring. By a decision made today . . . it has now been watered down to the effect that we are "to prepare" for offensive operations in the Spring "but without committing ourselves definitely to them". In general there is a great deal of wobbling, and it is bound up with the question of the size of our Army, a matter which is not yet settled. . . The fact is they are not showing the necessary grit and determination to see the thing through, now that the shoe is beginning to pinch a little. As a matter of fact it pinches exceedingly little in this country yet. It is scarcely noticeable.'

The fact was that it was impossible to prepare for an offensive, of the type and scale envisaged in France, *without* commitment. For the Somme vast dumps had to be accumulated, camps and railway lines laid out, and the troops trained to attack sections of the enemy line on specially prepared lay-outs behind the lines. It all took months of effort, and Haig never had enough time as it was. But neither he nor Wully were able to convince the Government of this.

At the end of March, the Somme still undecided and time running out, Wully tried once more to force the issue. In a paper dated March 31st, he asked the War Committee to 'decide at once and definitely'.[27] Four days later, Haig (at Wully's request) asked for official authority to concert an offensive with Joffre, and submitted his plans for the Somme. On April 7th Asquith, pressed by his generals and by the French, finally assented. Yet there was much misgiving. Haig's plans came in for heavy criticism, and the impression remained that the Government still held back.[28] So much so that on April 14th, on a visit to London, Haig asked Wully and Kitchener once again: 'Does H.M.'s Government approve of my combining with the French in a general offensive during the summer?' He only got half an answer even then. 'They both agreed that all the Cabinet had come to the conclusion that the war could only be ended by fighting, and several were most anxious for a definite victory over German Arms.'[29] In fact the War Committee did not know *what* it wanted, but by this time a formal decision had ceased to matter very much. Events at Verdun and opinion in France were making a British offensive so necessary, that henceforward both Wully and Haig felt free to concentrate upon it.

Yet there was never enough time, while some of the preparations—at one stage considered adequate—turned out quite the opposite. For example, although Lloyd George had transformed the production of arms and ammunition during the previous twelve months, and had in good faith predicted the end of shortages from May onwards, he was proved wrong—both as to the quantity and in many cases the quality of guns, fuses, and shells.[30] On the other hand, although conscription came too late for the Somme, which was fought largely by volunteers, Wully did manage to send 19 additional divisions to France between January and July. This expanded the BEF to some 60 divisions, and enabled Haig to launch the main attack with 18 divisions of the Third and Fourth Armies. Wully would have got together even more men had he had his way, for instance, in reducing or converting the cavalry, but he was unable to overcome Haig's opposition. Although both were cavalrymen, Haig had far more faith in the role of this arm, useless though it had become in the conditions of siege warfare, and he was counting on it specifically for the pursuit stage of the Somme, when it was hoped to regain manœuvre in open country.

The other source of trained men that eluded Wully was, of course, Salonika. Not only was he unable to bring the five British divisions home and shut down the front, but he found himself involved in a wearing contest with Joffre and the French Government over reinforcements and the prospects of a Balkan offensive. Salonika, more than anything else, sharpened

Wully's innate and native suspicions of the French, who never ceased to be the subject of numerous naive exchanges between him and Haig. At heart Haig differed little from Wully in this matter, though he showed far greater tact in his handling of individual Frenchmen. Even so, neither of them ever quite knew where they were with any of their Allies.

Wully wrote to Haig on January 5th:

'I am very pleased to hear you like Joffre. I always got on well with him. He is not brilliant but he is sound and honest. As a whole the French commanders and staff are a peculiar lot. Now and again in some respects they are quite good, but on some occasions they are most elementary and unpractical. The great thing to remember in dealing with them is that they are Frenchmen and not English-men, and do not and never will look at things in the way we look at them. I suppose that they think that we are queer people. It is a big business having to deal with allied commanders and one has to keep oneself in check and exercise great tolerance.'

Such sentiments served also to strengthen Wully's instinctive belief in British superiority and to write, 'I am more convinced than ever that it is we who will have to finish this war, and therefore in every way we possibly can we must take the lead, or at any rate refuse to be led against our judgment.'[31]

No doubt, too, it was insularity as well as professional caution that prevented Wully and Haig from accepting General de Cas-telnau's warning of a German attack at Verdun, though Haig acted at once when the attack broke on February 21st, relieved the French Tenth Army on his right, and offered to counter-attack should the situation become desperate. Thereafter the pressure on Verdun, at first irregularly, then with relentless force, determined the final timing of the Somme and the size of French participation in it.

May was the critical month. On the 2nd there seemed no urgency, and Joffre told Haig that no attack need be mounted before July 1st. On the 4th Clemenceau, Chef du Comité Militaire du Sénat and a strong critic of Joffre, impressed on Haig the need to wait until all was ready; and such too was the sense of a report on French Parliamentary opinion received about a fortnight later. Meanwhile, on the 6th, Haig talked the situation over with Wully and agreed to hold off as long as possible. Soon, however, the mood began to change, as losses mounted towards a catastrophic total and the defences of Verdun crumbled, one after the other. On the 24th Joffre sent Haig a message in despondent terms. The Somme must not be delayed beyond the beginning of July, and the French effort there would have to be reduced. Wully and Haig privately agreed to comply if it came to the worst, otherwise to postpone the attack until August 15th when the British would be far better prepared. On the 26th Joffre, Wully, and Haig all met, and Joffre repeated his sombre appeal. When Haig mentioned August 15th, Joffre blew up and shouted that 'the French Army would cease to exist if we did nothing till then'. Seeing, therefore, that the worst had indeed come, Haig agreed to advance the date of the offensive to July 1st or thereabouts, and the conversation ended amicably—though not before Wully had put in some pointed words about Salonika.[32]

Since the French were so hard pressed, he asked, why then persist with this useless front in the Balkans? Now more than ever was the moment to bring the troops back to France, where they were so urgently needed. Once more Joffre begged the question by referring it to his Government. Three times in the next three weeks Salonika came up for discussion by Ministers, but even then they were unable to arrive at any definite decision. There were few doubts about the Somme, however. Verdun seemed to be on the point of falling, and the atmosphere in France had become tense with renewed suspicion about British good faith. When *would* the British Army intervene?[33] Besides, the time had surely arrived for the concerted Allied offensive, agreed at Chantilly the previous December. Though shaken by an Austrian assault, the Italians counterattacked in the Trentino in the middle of June, while a few days earlier the Russians had launched a real thunderbolt under Brusilov. In the end, after last-minute delays, the Somme did go off on July 1st, and pressure on Verdun immediately relaxed.

Such was the chancy manner in which Western strategy entered its first great test. Few great operations of war are planned, let alone conducted, without fault; but the Somme suffered exceptional handicaps *before* it was launched. Preparations were compromised at both ends of the time-scale: at the beginning by the fact that the British Government clutched hold of the brake in a panic effort to stop the battle being fought at all; at the end by the fact that the French Government and commanders cut the brake cable in two, for precisely the reverse reason. In the meantime Wully and Haig mobilised means and resources as best they could, in the face both of these, and of all the other, hazards relating to material and manpower, and were compelled to fight before they were ready. Now that the history of 1916 has fallen into perspective, we can see how the original plan was eroded by events; how the Somme was prised off into isolation and expected by itself to achieve the hardest of all victories: namely, the defeat of an enemy in a defensive position of exceptional strength, without any real prospect of strategic gain; and how finally it was left to tactical ingenuity and to the courage and blood of hundreds of thousands of men upon the battlefield to see it through.

*   *   *

The Somme lasted for four and a half months, from July 1st till November 18th. Although fierce fighting rarely ceased on any part of the front, the pattern was not so much that of a single continuous offensive, as of a series of attacks mounted at different points and at different times, in a persistent effort to maintain momentum and exploit success wherever the enemy gave ground. In short, though planned otherwise, it became a long-drawn-out contest of attrition of appalling agony and crippling losses, suffered (so far as can be ascertained) in almost equal proportions by both sides.[34]

Haig's original plan was to make an all-out assault along eighteen miles of line, between Gommecourt in the north and Maricourt in the south, with eighteen divisions belonging to Allenby's Third and Rawlinson's Fourth Armies. The majority of the men were New Army volunteers and Territorials, grouped under Rawlinson. The operation was concerted with an attack by five French divisions on the British right astride the River Somme, and preceded by an intensive bombardment which lasted from June 24th till July 1st. What happened then is generally regarded as the greatest single tragedy of the war. The British lost nearly 60,000 men on the first day alone, of whom one-third were killed, and only succeeded in making small penetrations in the southern sector; elsewhere they made vir-

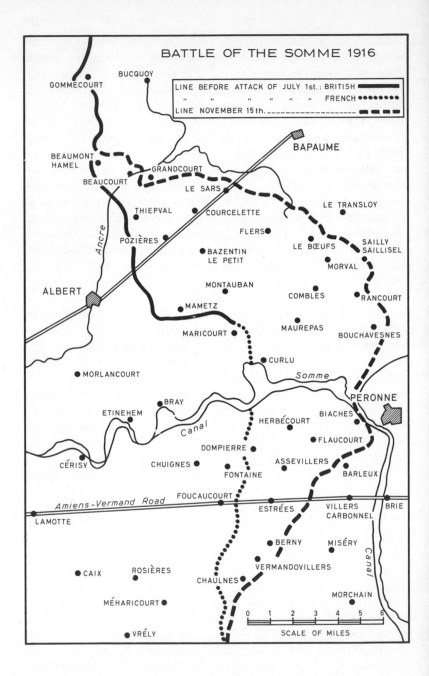

BATTLE OF THE SOMME 1916

LINE BEFORE ATTACK OF JULY 1st.: BRITISH ▬▬▬
   "   "   "   "   "   FRENCH ●●●●●●
LINE NOVEMBER 15th. ▬ ▬ ▬ ▬

GOMMECOURT
BUCQUOY
BAPAUME
BEAUMONT HAMEL
GRANDCOURT
BEAUCOURT
LE SARS
LE TRANSLOY
THIEPVAL
COURCELETTE
FLERS
POZIÈRES
LE BŒUFS
SAILLY SAILLISEL
BAZENTIN LE PETIT
MORVAL
Ancre
MONTAUBAN
COMBLES
RANCOURT
ALBERT
MAMETZ
MAUREPAS
BOUCHAVESNES
MARICOURT
CURLU
MORLANCOURT
Somme
PERONNE
BRAY
BIACHES
ETINEHEM
HERBÉCOURT
Canal
FLAUCOURT
DOMPIERRE
CÉRISY
CHUIGNES
ASSEVILLERS
BARLEUX
FONTAINE
FOUCAUCOURT
Amiens–Vermand Road
ESTRÉES
VILLERS CARBONNEL
BRIE
LAMOTTE
BERNY
MISÉRY
CAIX
ROSIÈRES
VERMANDOVILLERS
Canal
CHAULNES
MORCHAIN
MÉHARICOURT

0 1 2 3 4 5 6
SCALE OF MILES

VRÉLY

tually no progress at all. On the other hand the French did well, in the main because they had more concentrated artillery and better trained infantry.

The British failed initially for a variety of reasons. The artillery fire, though heavy in comparison with the past, was not heavy enough; nor was it otherwise effective. There were too few batteries for such a long and deeply defended front, too many gun and ammunition failures, no smoke shells, and hardly any gas. As a result, although vast damage was done to the enemy, especially to his communications, the first-line defences survived, while the second-line were hardly touched. Furthermore, close co-ordination between artillery and infantry had not been perfected—the creeping barrage was to evolve out of this bitter experience—so that German machine-gun crews were able to emerge from their dug-outs relatively intact, and take terrible toll of the advancing British infantry. In other ways too the infantryman was heavily handicapped. So overburdened with kit (60 lbs or more), he was only able to move at a slow walk across far too long a stretch of open ground, sometimes uphill, into the mouth of well-sited positions, before which the wire was all too often uncut. Unlike the French, who had been in and out of action for a long time, knew how to advance in irregular groups and short bursts, taking cover wherever they could, and making full use of supporting fire, the young British soldiers were altogether too raw. They lacked battle experience, while their training (most of it done in England) had been unrealistic. The Germans were amazed to see lines of British troops, with officers in front, keeping rigid parade-ground intervals—until the machine guns began to chatter, and the men fell in swathes. Sheer courage, displayed all along the line in the highest degree, and superiority of numbers, were no substitutes for tactical skill, nor could they ever be in siege warfare.

This is not the place for a detailed description of the Somme. The story has been told *in extenso* in many other books. All that is relevant here is a résumé of the salient facts, and an appreciation of the influence of the battle upon the progress and direction of the war.

Briefly, then, once the initial shock was over, and all hope of a quick break-through given up, the offensive changed character. Fresh drafts and units came into the line and, gaining daily in tactical skill and battle experience, kept up the tempo against the enemy. All through July and August fresh attacks were mounted in one sector after another and small advances made, with the object of so wearing down German resistance that a second massive assault might yet succeed. In September prospects improved. The French extended their front south of the River Somme, and on the 15th Haig launched a twelve-division attack in the centre, putting in tanks for the first time. The secret had been well kept, for the three dozen machines that managed to reach the front surprised the British troops almost as much as the German. Haig entertained the highest hopes of them, and continued to back them after the battle was over. Wully was sceptical, writing to Haig on August 29th:

'I hope the Tanks prove successful. It is rather a desperate innovation.'

The immediate results were certainly disappointing. The attack gained some ground, and although at one moment a decisive success seemed in sight, in the end the operation petered out under rain and against German reserves. Most of the tanks were knocked out or failed mechanically, and in tactical terms they were wrongly handled. But their moral effect was very great, and the experience won contributed directly to their technical improvement and tactical successes later in the war. Strong criticism can, however, be levelled against their being used in such small numbers, and thus in squandering the element of surprise. Fortunately the Germans failed entirely to appreciate their potentialities.

At the end of September the weather broke, and the battlefield became a sea of mud. Operations continued, however, though on a reduced scale, all through October. Finally, after a few dry days early in November, seven divisions attacked astride the River Ancre in the north and made important though limited headway. After that, bad weather set in again and closed the campaign down. At long last the Somme was over.

Was it all worthwhile? There can be no single simple answer, since it is impossible even now to reconcile two conflicting sets of conclusions. It is possible only to balance one against the other, and leave the record and resolving of it to posterity and private reflection. Judged by the appalling casualties and small amount of ground gained in an unimportant sector, the answer is 'no'. A whole generation of rising manhood was wiped out or maimed, and since many of the men were volunteers it included much of the flower of the nation. Judged in the long-term—by the relief it afforded to Verdun,[35] and gauged against the admission of the German Chief of Staff, Ludendorff him-self, when he said that by the end of 1916 'the German Army had been fought to a standstill and was utterly worn out'—the answer is 'yes'. In the final reckoning, therefore, it may be argued that—had it not been for the Somme—the German Army might never have lost the war at all.

But one thing is clear. Wully and Haig were prisoners, as well as proponents, of their own contentions. The Somme was the product of the Western school of strategy and of their military leadership. They felt compelled to stand by it together, while it was being fought, no less than before it was fought. The con-duct of the battle was entirely Haig's. Whatever blame is ascribed to him for the débâcle of July 1st, posterity will also measure him by his decision to fight on. The very absence of success and the huge cost in human life emphasised the size of that decision. Some hold that, once the true situation had become known—say, before the second main attack on July 14th—then the offensive should have been stopped, and that it was sheer callousness to continue. Indeed, horrific memories of the Somme (and of other battles, such as Third Ypres) left such an impression upon the minds of politicians (such as Churchill) and certain young officers (such as Wavell, Alanbrooke, and others), that it exercised a marked influence upon their whole attitude to strategy when their turn came to command in the Second World War. On the other hand, some hold that in deciding to continue Haig exhibited immense moral courage, and proved himself a great leader. Moreover, it is beyond all doubt that he inspired trust in those who served him, whatever their rank and however badly the battle was going. And it was his spiritual stamina, his determination to achieve a result in the end, that sustained the whole campaign.

For his part Wully was no less involved. While the conduct of the battle was Haig's, Wully had equally to bear responsibility for backing him to the uttermost, shielding him from criticism and interference at home, yet fully aware of the fearful cost. That too was a burden of dreadful weight, for it was in Wully's power, as it was in Haig's, to stop the offensive at any time.

The two men stand before history in these terms.

* * *

In London the Somme was the sombre backcloth which darkened every official meeting and every major event after the beginning of July. No one knew exactly what was happening in France, only that the advance was agonisingly slow and the cost in casualties colossal. In the War Committee all turned to—and some upon—Wully, holding him responsible for, and expecting him to pronounce upon, all that was taking place. He had known that this would happen, of course, but whereas hitherto he had been able to rely upon Kitchener, and to a less extent upon Asquith, now he was almost entirely alone.

Kitchener was dead, drowned when the cruiser *Hampshire* struck a mine off the Orkneys on the way to Russia on June 6th. His death came as a fearful shock to ordinary men and women in every part of the British Empire, for in their eyes his legend was undimmed. His colleagues knew of course that, as a leader and administrator, Kitchener had long passed his zenith, indeed had revealed many damaging weaknesses of character. None knew this better than Wully, who had in effect displaced him. But Wully had come to respect Kitchener and had leaned heavily on him all the time they worked together. The Bargain, faithfully kept, had proved a boon to them both. Now it looked like being dissolved, for after keeping the portfolio of War in his own hands for a few weeks, Asquith handed it over to Lloyd George, who had always said he would refuse to go to the War Office, if it meant accepting Wully's terms.

But he did go. A fortnight before the new appointment took effect,[36] the two men had a word together, followed by an important exchange of views, beginning with a letter from Wully dated June 24th, in which he explained and justified the Bargain. He repeated almost word for word the terms he had proposed to Kitchener six months before.[37]

Lloyd George replied on the 26th with an able and forceful statement, spattered—as might be expected—with a few barbs. While protesting that he had no wish to alter things as they stood, he yet made clear the reasons for his opposition. Everything devolved upon the status and powers of the Secretary of State.

'The holder of the seals of office retains his ultimate responsibility for the War Office. The Prime Minister, Parliament and the Country must hold him accountable. The position of the Secretary of State in relation to the Government on the one hand and the War Office on the other, is, and must be, very much the same as that of the First Lord of the Admiralty in relation to the Government and the Board.

'Applying this consideration to your paper I would first point out that you do not specifically provide that the Secretary of State shall be kept informed of everything. Perhaps the expression is not intended to bear the meaning it appears to convey, but in paragraph 4 you speak of the Chief of the Imperial General Staff ensuring that the Secretary of State shall receive "at all times full information of *all that he should know*"—that is, in regard to communications dealing with operations. The Secretary of State must, in my opinion, receive copies of *everything*.

'Again, you say, very properly, that all advice concerning Military operations should reach the War Committee through one authoritative channel only, namely, the Chief of the Imperial General Staff. But you omit to say at what stage the Secretary of State is to be informed of the character and terms of that advice. It is clear to my mind that the Chief of the Imperial General Staff should always explain to and discuss with the Secretary of State the lines on which he is framing such advice before it is tendered to the Committee. The First Sea Lord discusses all questions bearing on naval strategy with the First Lord before his recommendations are submitted to the War Committee. It would be humiliating and intolerable if I were to hear your policy expounded for the first time at the War Committee. Friction could only be avoided by complete self-effacement on my part as a member of that Committee. I only wish to have the same voice in the discussion with you of war policy on land as Mr Balfour now has in the settlement with his advisers of operations at sea. Political considerations (I mean international politics) and questions of equipment—both in my sphere—are just as essential to the decisions of war problems as knowledge of military strategy.

'Again, to take another class of question, namely, appointments of Commanders-in-Chief, Commanders of Armies and of officers in analogous positions. You say that these should be made by the War Committee on advice given by the Chief of the Imperial General

Staff to the Secretary of State. I admit that both the War Committee and the Chief of the Imperial General Staff have necessarily a large share in this business, but I am not sure that I understand you to recognise fully the Secretary of State's responsibility. It seems to me that, while the Secretary of State must be fully advised by the Chief of the Imperial General Staff and must obviously be largely influenced by such advice, yet, it should be for the former to bear the burden of convincing the War Committee and the Prime Minister where necessary, and of gaining their support of the submission which, in due course, it is for the Secretary of State to make to the King.'[38]

In short, Lloyd George put his finger on the old sore, although he offered no cure. Even so a cure could never have been effected solely by a new and better formula, much though one was needed. Goodwill was essential. That had always been part of the Bargain with Kitchener, but it was now to vanish in a cloud of temperament and mutual suspicion, to reappear only after Lord Derby had succeeded Lloyd George at the War Office at the end of the year. The constitutional formula, however, remained unchanged.

In his reply Wully showed great willingness to meet Lloyd George's objections, or mitigate the contradictory nature of their official relationship.[39] He gave an immediate assurance that the Secretary of State would be kept informed of everything that 'it would be worth his while to know'; and that he personally would always discuss beforehand the advice he proposed to give to the War Committee. Naturally he gave nothing fundamental away, but he left no doubt as to *his* goodwill. As he said:

'After all, a system qua system amounts to very little. The whole crux lies in the way in which it is carried out, and whoever may become Secretary of State I can promise him the loyal co-operation of myself and the whole of the General Staff.'

Unhappily, elsewhere in his letter, Lloyd George betrayed in advance his prejudice against the Army, and in several ungenerous phrases.

'Up to the present our fifty divisions have barely (and not always) held their own against the German thirty divisions. . .

'I am in entire agreement with you as to the inefficiency of the system by which the War had been conducted up to the date of the resuscitation of the General Staff. Perhaps it is too early to expect results from the new arrangement, and although the six months which have since elapsed have not produced any conspicuous military victories, yet the real test of the new methods is at hand, and I have every hope that a substantial victory will justify them.'

Wully rejoined:

'As you know it is less than a month that we have had in France as many as the 50 divisions you mention, and for want of heavy guns and ammunition and for other reasons we have necessarily been on the defensive. Troops acting on the defensive are bound to lose ground now and then, and in course of time to lose the war. That is why all soldiers and sailors hate it as by it alone they can never hope to win. . . We began the war with a Force of only 6 Regular divisions, and 14 imperfectly trained and equipped Territorial divisions, with no heavy artillery worth mentioning. We are now beginning to make good our grave deficiencies, and to have a reasonable chance, which we have never had before, of showing that we can fight as well as the Germans can. What the actual result will be I certainly shall not attempt to prophesy. No one can be sure of success in war, especially when dependent upon New Armies. But whatever the result may be . . . no Army could have done more than ours to make itself efficient, and I have the fullest confidence in the Commanders and Staff in France, as I have in the brave British men who have so patriotically come forward to fight for their Country under the most adverse conditions. They thoroughly deserve all the help, trust, and sympathy people at home can give, and needless to say these are the most necessary when the most needed.'

For the time being Lloyd George held his fire. The Somme was the first real test of his relations with Wully, as it was of Western strategy as a whole. He would wait for news. The War Committee waited likewise. Wully, too, was waiting. Early in July he went over to France to see Haig and pick up what he could, but it was too early to glean very much. On the 7th he began to press Haig, since he in turn was being pressed, the first of a series of letters in which he urged Haig, for both their sakes, to tell him all he could as often as he could. Haig was remarkably reluctant. True, the situation was obscure, and there was nothing very concrete or encouraging to say, certainly nothing about a big and successful advance. Even so Haig made the least of what there was. By nature cautious, he had small conception of what lay behind Wully's insistence, and no idea at all of public relations. All during July, when the British Army was waging its biggest battle yet, and sons and fathers were falling in their thousands, people at home had to make do with a series of laconic communiqués, and of course with thousands of telegrams that told a family that its man was missing or dead. But the Government itself was hardly any better served. In desperation Wully appealed once more to Haig on July 29th, although— knowing the burden that Haig was bearing—he managed to write in a restrained and reasoned way.

'The Powers that be are beginning to get a little uneasy in regard to the situation. The casualties are mounting up and they are wondering whether we are likely to get a proper return for them. I do my best to keep the general situation to the front, and to explain what may be the effect of our efforts, and I ask them what alternative could be adopted in place of our present efforts—more especially having regard to our allies. I also try to make them think in German of the present situation, But they will persist in asking me whether *I* think a loss of say 300,000 men will lead to really great results, because if not we ought to be content with something less than what we are now doing, and they constantly enquire why we are fighting and the French are not. They argue it is mainly a question of numbers and big guns. The latter we have not yet in sufficient numbers, and the former is affected by whether we are losing more than the Germans. I am sorry to worry you in this way but it is necessary you should know what is passing. I really know very little as to your present appreciation of the situation, and think it necessary you should send me another secret statement of your views. It is probable that you will be sent for in the course of a week or so, if matters continue much as in the last fortnight, in order to tell the War Committee what you think. In general, what is bothering them is the probability that we may soon have to face a bill of 2 to 300,000 casualties with no very great gains additional to the present. It is thought that the primary object—relief of pressure on Verdun—has to some extent been achieved.'

Haig's comment on this *cri de coeur* was contained in three sentences, which he scratched across the foot of Wully's letter.

'Not exactly the letter of a CIGS. He ought to take responsibility also. I have no intention of going before the War Committee while this battle is going on.'

On mature reflection, however, he did sit down and write just the sort of report that Wully had been asking for, summarised in his Diary as follows:[40]

'(*a*) Pressure on Verdun relieved. Not less than six enemy Divns, besides heavy guns have been withdrawn.

(*b*) Successes achieved by Russia last month would certainly have been prevented had enemy been free to transfer troops from here to the Eastern Theatre.

(*c*) Proof given to the world that Allies are capable of making and maintaining a vigorous offensive and of driving enemy's best troops from the strongest positions has shaken faith of Germans, of their friends, of doubting neutrals in the invincibility of Germany. Also impressed on the world, England's strength and determination, and the fighting power of the British race.

(*d*) We have inflicted very heavy losses on the enemy. In *one* month, 30 of his Divns. have been used up, as against 35 at Verdun in 5 months. In another 6 weeks, the enemy should be hard put to it to find men.

(*e*) The maintenance of a steady offensive pressure will result eventually in his complete overthrow.

Principle on which we should act. *Maintain our offensive*. Our losses in July's fighting totalled about 120,000 more than they would have been had we not attacked. They cannot be regarded as sufficient to justify any anxiety as to our ability to continue the offensive. It is my intention:

(*a*) To maintain a steady pressure on Somme battle.

(*b*) To push my attack strongly whenever and wherever the state of my preparations and the general situation make success sufficiently probable to justify me in doing so, but not otherwise.

(*c*) To secure against counter-attack each advantage gained and prepare thoroughly for each fresh advance.

Proceeding thus, I expect to be able to maintain the offensive well into the Autumn.

It would not be justifiable to calculate on the enemy's resistance being completely broken without another campaign next year.'

This report was read over by Wully to the War Committee on August 5th and thereafter circulated to members of the Cabinet. It was well received and elicited a warm message of support, which Wully passed on to Haig. Meanwhile, Wully had himself been arguing the case in similar terms, and to such effect that even Lloyd George appeared content, though only for the moment.

'LG is all right provided I can say *I* am satisfied, and to enable me to do this it is necessary you should keep me acquainted with your views. I dont want your plans and you can rely on me acting discreetly. But if I have to depend almost entirely upon Press Communiqués, my opinion is regarded as not much more valuable than that of anyone else, and indeed it is almost impossible to give an opinion. So if you could manage to send me your views—as briefly as you like—say once a week, I think matters would be more satisfactory.'[41]

Haig then relented a little, and when he received the War Committee's message of encouragement on August 9th, he responded warmly and freely acknowledged the debt he owed to Wully.

'I am most grateful to you for all your efforts in our behalf, and I fully realise what a most difficult task you have in keeping the military view uppermost in the Cabinet. I shall of course send you my views periodically of the situation here, and also at any time you may feel the need of a document from the front.'[42]

Both men, of course, were being subjected to tremendous strain, but this contretemps need never have arisen, had there been a regular flow of confidential reports from GHQ. If Haig needed any further proof of Wully's difficulties, or of his absolute loyalty to himself and the BEF, he had it repeatedly from an old friend—Lord Esher—whom he had known since the days of Army reform in the early 1900s. Esher, wearing a uniform all of his own, had installed himself in Paris as a kind of private ambassador, much to the annoyance of H.M.'s accredited representative, Lord Bertie of Thame, but he was in a position of great influence, and always seemed to be in the know. On August 7th he wrote to Haig:

'Clive tells me privately that Robertson was a bit "rattled" by the politicians. They actually asked him to "certify that the offensive would attain its objects". This is a demand which I should imagine had never in the whole history of war been made upon a soldier. But the old man responded gallantly, and "certified" accordingly.

I myself do not believe that Robertson has or ever has had any arrière pensée, and that he is heart and soul anxious to back you for all he is worth, and smash Germany.

He is shrewd and of Scottish blood, and knows full well that we have no one except you who can carry through to the end with prudence and high resolve this fight to the death.

If the combination of you and Robertson were to fail, no other is possible, and we may as well hand over to Joffre, or make peace. In any case, this old man alone stands between you and vacillating political counsels.

The Duke of Wellington would have been upset, over and over again, between 1810–14 if he had not had *one* man, i.e. Wellesley, in the Cabinet who supported him.

No C-in-C can withstand stabs in the back, which he is bound to get from people at home, unless he has someone to interpose a shield. This, I believe, (until it is conclusively proved to the contrary) Robertson will do.

Then, on the other hand, I am certain that any soldier situated as he is, in the mephitic atmosphere of the W.O., requires inspiration and breaths of fresh air from the C-in-C in the field. This he amply gets from you, and he should be saturated with it as freely as possible!'[43]

*   *   *

Had the Somme been the only controversial event in the latter half of 1916, or turned out a minor rather than a major disappointment, then the Coalition Government might not have foundered, as it did, at the end of the first week of December. However, so many troubles were reaching a state of crisis during the autumn, yielding such a volume of criticism, that an explosion became inevitable.

Abroad a new front had opened up, with the entry of Rumania into the war at the end of August. To all appearances her action was of great benefit and promise to the Allies, with her resources of oil, strategic position, and not inconsiderable army. Yet she quickly disintegrated when it came to the test. She was chronically short of war material, and depended for supplies on the immensely long and chaotic route via Archangel and the Russian railway system, which had already all but collapsed. Indeed, Russia herself was in no condition to maintain even her own troops, let alone those of an ally. Above all the Rumanian plan of campaign was ill-timed and ill-conducted. Too late to profit from the impetus of the Brusilov offensive in the Carpathians, it consisted principally of an attempt to occupy Transylvania, in itself a political rather than a strategic move of any real consequence. Retribution was quick, for the

Germans reacted with remarkable speed and efficiency. Despite their commitments in France, Italy, and the east, they assembled two Armies of German and Austrian troops and counter-attacked at the end of September, pushing forward with such speed and success that they captured Bucharest on December 6th, and forced the remnants of the Rumanian army north-eastwards into Moldavia, where it sheltered with the Russians and took no further effective part in the war. Meanwhile, another enemy force, mainly Bulgarian, had come up from the south and occupied the province of Dobrudja. And so within four months a promising new front had collapsed, the enemy had made substantial material and strategic gains, and Rumania—as Lloyd George bitterly observed—had gone the way of Serbia and Belgium.

Although unable to save Rumania from defeat, the Western Allies had not been totally inactive. A military convention had been signed, supplies assigned and despatched, and plans made to launch a supporting offensive from Salonika. It will be remembered that the latter had been under active consideration shortly before the Somme began. As always Wully had strenuously deprecated any serious move, in general because he was a Westerner with his eyes firmly fixed upon the great new battle shortly to start in France, in particular because Milne, the British commander at Salonika, had advised that a reinforcement of some ten to fifteen divisions would be necessary for any real prospect of success. A commitment of this size was logistically and strategically out of the question, and Wully brusquely refused it. With the advent of Rumania, however, a new Balkan situation was created, and even Wully had to admit that something must be done.

None the less, the Allies were no better able to attack effectively at Salonika than in the past. Moreover, relations with Greece were as critical and confused as ever, various measures —mostly hostile—being mounted against her all during 1916, in order to ensure her neutrality, if nothing worse. In June the Greek Army had been formally demobilised, though a number of units remained on the frontier at war strength; they made no attempt, however, to prevent the Bulgarians from occupying territory in the north-east. At the end of September, Venizelos set up a pro-Ally Government (first in Crete, then in Salonika),

9. Wully and his son, Brian

10. Mildred Robertson

11. Wully, facing car, on manœuvres at Hinton Waldrist in 1909

12. With Haig in France in 1916. Wully is sixth from left

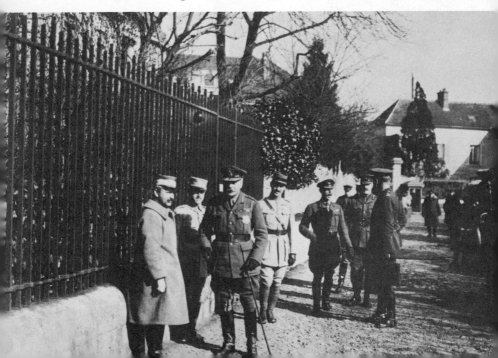

and began recruiting an army of his own. On September 18th, however, a Greek Army Corps had surrendered to the enemy at Kavalla, and the Allies retaliated with an ultimatum to the Royal Government in Athens, involving the seizure of the fleet and a landing at Piraeus. Even then many more months were to pass before the situation was resolved—with the general recognition of Venizelos and the forced departure of the King (in June 1917)—and Greece won over as an effective and combatant partner.

In view of these events, it is not surprising that the attack launched by Sarrail in September failed to affect the course of the war in the Balkans, although it achieved a local success at the western end of the front, where the French and Serbian troops got as far as Monastir on November 19th. Elsewhere the British contingent was confined to minor actions and demonstrations, and to dealing with the dangerous situation created by Greek defections. None of this diverted the Bulgarians from joining in the attack against Rumania, nor did it distract the enemy offensive against her at other points. At an Allied conference held at Boulogne on October 20th, it was agreed that— despite Lloyd George's vehement protestations—little further could be done to help Rumania by any country except Russia, her neighbour; and although men and material were promised and sent (including one British division), Salonika remained a mirage. Some, like Wully, never thought of it as anything else. Others, perhaps the bulk of public and political opinion, were bitterly disappointed.

*   *   *

In the last four months of 1916 public dissatisfaction with the war found formidable expression in the words, actions, and very personality of Lloyd George himself. Here was a dynamic politician of such radical mind and intense patriotic fervour that his frantic frustrations were bound to end in eruption and blow either himself or the Government to pieces. The fact that most of the problems besetting the Coalition were the heritage of unpreparedness in 1914, and beyond quick solution, was beside the point. Lloyd George was a volcano, and in following his bursts and flashes all through the autumn of this darkening year, we are watching an elemental force almost out of control.

Thus in his assessment of the Somme, Lloyd George moved spasmodically from suspicion before the offensive opened on July 1st, to doubt and impatience in August, to certainty by the end of September that the whole enterprise was so much useless butchery. He did not immediately state what he thought, but one extraordinary incident clearly showed the way his fluid Celtic mind was flowing. In the course of a visit to Foch in September he asked him why the British, who had gained no more ground than the French, had suffered much heavier casualties: a technical question which drew a technical answer. But the sting lay in the sequel. What was Foch's opinion of the ability of the British generals? Foch's reply was studiedly non-committal, but it was clear to him that the question had been purely rhetorical. Soon afterwards he told the whole story to Haig, Haig to Wully, and the fat was in the fire.[44] Wully was deeply incensed and was ready to have it out with Lloyd George then and there.[45] Haig, however, played the whole incident down and persuaded him to say nothing, but the damage had been done.[46] As to Lloyd George, so far from letting the matter drop, this was but the prelude to the drama enacted in February 1917, when he as British Prime Minister connived at placing the BEF under French command, in such a manner as virtually to reduce Haig to the status of Adjutant-General.

Events in the Balkans have already been related and Lloyd George's strategic dreams described. He had always wanted to make a big front out of Salonika, arguing that a few days expenditure in men and ammunition on the scale of the Somme would suffice to win a victory over the Bulgars. He refused to listen to Wully's contention that the best way to help the east was to keep up the pressure in the west, or that it was impossible to take a dozen divisions out of the line in France, find the shipping to transport them to Greece, and pitch them forthwith into the attack in a difficult, mountainous, unfriendly country, all so as to turn the march of events in Rumania. He pressed Wully hard, and the conflict came to a head in an angry exchange of letters on October 11th, in which Wully complained that Lloyd George disregarded and even argued against his advice to the War Committee; while Lloyd George protested that he, as Secretary of State, was free to take whatever line he thought right.[47] The real quarrel was not of course about the Balkans, but the familiar one about their official relationship and private incompatibility.

In the course of his letter, Lloyd George also accused Wully of divulging confidential information to the Press, and assumed an air of great injury. It was true that Wully privately told his troubles to Repington, military correspondent of *The Times*, and that Repington passed a good deal on to his employer, Lord Northcliffe.[48] Further, that Lord Northcliffe was a wayward, power-seeking proprietor, who sought to influence the Government, on occasions in an indefensible manner. But Repington did not give away anything vital, or write anything that any competent observer could not have reconstructed for himself from conversations in clubs and current rumours. Indeed, much more was communicated by generals to correspondents in the Second World War, and often with good results.

Nothing further came of this particular incident, but by early November Lloyd George was talking openly of resigning. Stopped by the Somme and the Balkans, he now cast about for another means of getting his way. He turned to Russia. Although the Russians were the only Ally that had won any substantial victories on the Continent so far, conditions were fast deteriorating behind the front, and losses in men and material had been colossal. The country sorely needed help, but the chaos of her communications and the incompetence of her régime caused deep concern in the west. What were the facts? It was for this very purpose—to find out exactly what was happening—that Kitchener had set out in early June and died at the outset of his journey. Since then the Brusilov offensive had swept westwards like a heath fire and burned itself out, though without causing irreparable damage to the enemy. On November 3rd Lloyd George persuaded the War Committee that a conference needed to be held in Russia, and that an Inter-Allied Mission should attend it, with Wully as a member. Wully categorically refused to go. He saw in this only a plot to get him out of the way, and to enable the Secretary of State to seize the reins in his absence. Moreover, a new and vital meeting was to be held at Chantilly in mid-November to decide plans for 1917. It was essential that he stay. He therefore canvassed all his friends, sent word to the King, and finally made a desperate appeal to Asquith himself.

'The more I think of it the more I feel it would be absolute folly for me to go. Alexeieff refused to come here because he could not get away; Cadorna and Joffre I am sure will not go, and yet the work they have to do is not comparable with that which falls upon me. I have larger forces in Salonika than anyone else; and operations in Egypt, Mesopotamia and East Africa calling for daily attention, besides France. Further our army is still very much in the making; we are in the midst of introducing conscription; and there are a multitude of questions regarding training and provision of officers, organisation, and preparation for next year to which I alone can attend. Further I have nothing to see Alexeieff about. I have no questions of strategy to discuss with him, and I have no assistance to offer him, more than he already knows about.

'The temporary cessation of fighting in France does not affect the question. My chief business is the control of all operations, organisation, and the coordination of preparations for next spring. To go away now would be fatal to these matters, I think, and so does Haig and my Staff. . . To put me for a month or so out of touch with the five commanders in the field and several others and also with the War Office would involve such loss of control as could never be regained. In short I cannot do the work I ought to do as CIGS if I go away, and no one can do it for me. I hope most earnestly you will not now ask me to go.'[49]

The appeal was successful, and the crisis passed. On the next day the delegation left for France. In Hankey's words:

'We started for Paris on November 14th. Asquith and Lloyd George were the only Ministers to attend the conference, but Robertson and Maurice accompanied us as they were to attend the conference of generals and staffs, which was to be held simultaneously with the political conference but at Joffre's headquarters at Chantilly. In spite of the peculiar delicacy of the situation we were an extraordinarily cheery party. Here was a Prime Minister, beset with incredible difficulties, both external and internal, with a disunited Cabinet, and subjected to bitter and acrimonious Press attacks; a Minister of War, an active critic of the policy of the Government of which he was a member, and at loggerheads with his own Chief of Staff; and finally the said Chief of Staff, who was out for war with his chief "without kid gloves on". Yet, as Lloyd George was fond of recalling, it was an extraordinarily harmonious and almost hilarious party which travelled that day to Paris. True, a shadow came over the party as we passed the great war cemetery at Etaples, already terribly full, and Asquith's thoughts, we all felt, had turned to his brilliant son Raymond who had lately fallen on the Somme. Shortly after, however, Robertson restored general merriment by calling out "There's a fine pair of pants for you, Prime Minister", pointing to some back-yard, where there hung on the clothes line a pair of unmentionables of gigantic proportions and indescribable hue!'[50]

To all intents and purposes the conference at Chantilly was a repetition of the one held there eleven months earlier, in December 1915. Wully and Haig both attended, together with the military representatives of the other Allies, under the chairmanship of Joffre. They reached only one conclusion of importance, namely that France should remain the principal theatre of war, and a new offensive be mounted there not later than mid-February 1917; thereafter the general offensive be renewed on all fronts within as short a time as possible.

These proposals were duly approved by the Ministers in Paris, and all seemed satisfied except Lloyd George, for whom they amounted merely to a continuation of the slog and slaughter he so utterly abhorred. Moreover, they crystallised in him the decision henceforward to fight for the revision not only of strategic policy, but of the very method of conducting the war. He was convinced that the Cabinet, and in particular the War Committee, as then constituted, were incapable of doing the job. The machinery was wrong and some of the men were wrong too, and he said openly that unless they were changed we should lose the war. The Government was already under heavy fire through the activity of commissions set up to enquire into the Dardanelles and Mesopotamian campaigns, and through the mounting pressure of problems relating to manpower, production, shipping, food, and much else; and there was widespread feeling, inside and outside Parliament, that Lloyd George was right.

This is not the place in which to record the meetings and manœuvres that led up to the resignation of Asquith and the fall of the Coalition Government on December 7th, or to try to unravel the complex negotiations between Lloyd George and the other leading personalities during the three weeks that preceded that event. All of this has been told in detail elsewhere.[51]

Although not directly concerned, Wully had a shrewd idea

of what was going on, if only because the enforced absences and commitments of the Secretary of State at this time brought him some relief. He cannot have believed, however, that a man of Lloyd George's calibre would be likely to disappear from the scene. As to the cause of the crisis, he was in harmony with the idea that the War Committee should be reformed or replaced. As far back as the summer of 1915 he had himself advocated a far smaller body for the effective prosecution of the war, and now he was brought into the discussion again—shortly before the Government fell—at an informal breakfast meeting at Lord Derby's house, at which Lloyd George was also present.[52] When, however, he first met the new War Cabinet, he described the five members to Haig as 'quite as bad [i.e. talkative] as the old lot',[53] but he freely admitted that the new machinery was a vast improvement.

Personally, Wully regretted the departure of Asquith, whom he had always respected for his integrity and his wisdom, and from whom he had received a great deal of support. There was no one in the new Cabinet upon whom he could rely to the same extent. Specifically Asquith left at a most inopportune moment for, to Wully's great satisfaction, the War Committee had just approved a proposal to introduce universal national service. In Wully's view the measure was essential in order to render effective the existing legislation on military service, and so make it possible to draft—from industry and other occupations—larger numbers into the Army, which was again running short of men. At the end of October it was estimated that the BEF alone was 80,000 under strength,[54] irrespective of the wastage on other fronts, the fighting requirements for 1917, the expansion of other arms and services, and the steeply rising commitments of industry and transport—all set against the background of Britain taking over more of the burden of the war.

So viewed, manpower was of immediate urgency, particularly as it affected the Army which, in Wully's view, could alone force the decision on land. A month later he agreed with Lloyd George that a Memorandum, signed by the Military Members of the Army Council, be handed to the Secretary of State for submission to the War Committee; and this was duly done on November 28th. This highly important document stated *inter alia*:

'. . . unless steps are taken *at once* by His Majesty's Government to introduce some better system of utilizing the manhood of the nation, untrammelled by the conditions that in practice now nullify to a great extent the object of the Military Service Acts, it will be impossible after April next to keep the armies up to strength.

'At present the monthly intake of recruits is some 20,000 below requirements, and it is estimated that the total number of recruits for 1916 will be 95,000 short of the number which the Cabinet Committee agreed in February last could be placed at the disposal of the Army by the end of the year.

'For the year 1917 the following men are required:

Infantry. Newly-trained men, exclusive of returned sick and wounded. Category A.	584,000
Other Arms. Ditto	216,000
In addition for Categories B.1 and C.1 about	140,000
Grand Total	940,000

'The Ministry of Munitions require a reinforcement of about 250,000–300,000 hands (all ages, including about 100,000 women) to enable them to complete the new programme (including steel, but excluding Admiralty and Board of Trade shipbuilding, and also RNAS requirements).

'There are still in civil life over $2\frac{1}{2}$ million men of military age, exclusive of Ireland, and given therefore a proper organisation of the man-power of the country, there appears to be no reason why the above 940,000 men should not be forthcoming. We suggest that the military age should be raised to 55 years and that all men up to that age should be utilized for such national service as H.M. Government deem to be essential to the effective prosecution of the war.'

What happened next is best recorded by Wully himself:

'To my surprise the Memorandum met with practically no opposition when, on November 30th, it came before the War Committee for consideration. Mr Asquith . . . clearly showed that he was not prepared to oppose it; the other Ministers present, whatever they may have thought, said scarcely a word against it; and within a few minutes the policy of national service was approved in principle, a committee was appointed to work out the details, and the War Committee placed on record that they attached great importance to the enactment of the necessary legislation before Christmas, 1916. No better day's work was done in London at any time during the war.'[55]

And to Haig he wrote jubilantly:

'I have managed to frighten the Government pretty badly the last few days, and today, within an hour, they decided to place every man up to 60 [sic] years of age, at the disposal of the Government for national service. The women are also to be "compulsed". No more weekend leave for soldiers *at home*; civilian traffic (joy-riders) to be stopped; express trains etc to be taken off; unnecessary merchandise to be stopped. All this will give you your rolling stock —*when* you can get it across the Channel. These are drastic measures. They are to be worked out within a week, and Parliamentary sanction obtained before Christmas.'[56]

A telling answer, it seemed, to critics—such as Esher—who complained that Wully was neglecting his duty in leaving Army recruitment in the hands of a subordinate officer, the Adjutant-General, who was quite unable to cope with the passive resistance of other Government departments.[57]

Alas, Wully rejoiced too soon. Within a week the Government had resigned, and although Lloyd George had approved of the Memorandum and voted for it in the War Committee, as Prime Minister he hesitated. True, he announced in Parliament on December 19th, that 'the War Cabinet have unanimously adopted the conclusions come to by the preceding War Committee',[58] but his subsequent actions failed to match his words. In short, the new policy was watered down, and universal national service was not adopted until the spring of 1918. As suggested earlier, manpower was an important element in the strategic struggle between Westerners and Easterners, and—for whatever reason he supported the Memorandum at first—Lloyd George now had second thoughts. For Wully it was a bitter disappointment.

It was, however, but one incident—one facet of the destructive relationship that had sprung up between the new Prime Minister and his chief military adviser: a tragic omen for the future of a great country at war, and a personal tragedy too. It might seem that the two men would have been natural allies, sharing as they did the common ground of humble origins, powerful characters, and self-made careers crowned with success. But it was not the case, for they were hopelessly divided by the chasm that separated 'frocks' and 'brass-hats', by the passionate radicalism of Lloyd George who had grown up to regard the Army as an autocratic anomaly, and by the stern conservatism of Wully, who looked upon civilians as interfering amateurs.

To conclude. Wully's position at this critical juncture of the war was aptly summed up by Esher, writing to Haig on September 25th:

'He [Wully] is consumed by dislike and suspicion of Lloyd George. At this I am not surprised for he realises that any day this impetuous little man might take the bit between his teeth, and insist upon some strategical move entirely at variance with the military policy that is now achieving such remarkable results.

'Robertson's position is strong in the country, because since Kitchener's death he stands for the antithesis of the "politicians", who are suspected of self-seeking. But he is weak in the War Council [Committee] where he cannot count upon the support of anyone. . .'[59]

Nor did it seem, in December, that he would be likely to do better with the newly-formed War Cabinet.

Chief of the Imperial General Staff:
December 1916 to May 1917

WHEN Lloyd George became Prime Minister in December 1916 he abolished the War Committee, as he said he would, and set up a small War Cabinet of five men—himself, Bonar Law, Arthur Henderson, Lord Curzon, and Lord Milner—to direct the war. As Chancellor of the Exchequer and Leader of the House of Commons, Bonar Law was the only one to carry departmental responsibilities; otherwise all were free to devote their entire energies to the task, meeting daily to receive advice, deliberate, and take decisions, relying upon the superb service of the new and enlarged Secretariat under the irreplaceable Sir Maurice Hankey. Thereafter, the improvement in the machinery, as well as in the momentum, of government was most marked. Agendas and reports arrived promptly, proceedings were properly minuted and circulated, and subordinate committees were strictly controlled. The arrears of the autumn were materially reduced, and a vast volume of new business done. Much of this was due to the efficiency of Hankey and the dynamism of Lloyd George, but much also to the accumulated experience of the past two years, grafted on to the wisdom inherited from the old Committee of Imperial Defence. Moreover, the new organisation was sufficiently well-founded and sufficiently elastic, both to respond to the moods and moves of the new Prime Minister, and to allow for its own expansion into the Imperial War Cabinet (first meeting in March 1917), and again to accommodate the numerous Inter-Allied Conferences, which largely at Lloyd George's behest now proliferated.

So far as strategy was concerned the new War Cabinet found itself committed to the decisions taken at Chantilly the previous November: a renewal, in short, of the offensive in the west early in 1917, in concert with similar moves in Russia, Italy, and possibly the Balkans as well. The kaleidoscope, however, was already shifting, and in Lloyd George's view at last offered opportunities for escape from the Western policy he so abhorred.

First, there were the manœuvres for peace on both sides of the front. The fall of Bucharest on December 6th had prompted the Central Powers to attempt negotiations from a position of strength, apparent if not real. Likewise, on the Allied side, high hopes of the Somme had earlier encouraged Wully, Esher, and Haig, as well as members of the Government, to discuss the shape and aims of the Peace Conference, should the enemy suddenly sue for terms. Wully presented his ideas in a General Staff Memorandum of August 30th, both as to the political settlement and the military armistice. Neither need detain us here, for nothing came of them. Of greater interest was his concern lest the French call the tune, and his attempt to galvanise the War Committee into readiness. To Esher he wrote:

'I confess that I have anxiety when I think of the day on which we may be seated round the Council Table discussing the terms of peace. I am not thinking so much of the enemy as of the Allies. I do sincerely hope that we shall be strongly represented when that day comes, but I do not see how we can be unless certain important changes take place.

'As regards our increasing strength in France, it is not possible for the French to have it both ways. The stronger we become the more predominant we become. I hope, and I certainly intend to make us as strong as possible. As I have said above, my chief anxiety is that the effort of our Armies are making may be sacrificed, or at any rate not sufficiently rewarded when the day of reckoning comes.'[1]

In substance Esher agreed with him, but told Haig:

'Old Wully as the representative of military considerations will never do. His ignorance of French alone is a fatal drawback. No one but you can take the place that K [Kitchener] would have filled.'[2]

How wrong he was! Although certainly less tactful, Wully proved far tougher than Haig in contests with the French, and his anglicised speech was no disadvantage on such occasions. But all this was academic talk. As the Somme ground to a halt, so faded any hopes of dictating terms to the Germans, and quite different sentiments took their place. The Marquess of Lansdowne, Minister without Portfolio, actually advocated a negotiated peace and published a letter to that effect. Needless to say it caused much indignation, not least in Wully, who referred in a Memorandum to

'. . cranks, cowards, and philosophers, some of whom are afraid of their own skins being hurt, whilst others are capable of proving to those sufficiently weak-minded to listen to them that we stand to gain more by losing the war than by winning.'[3]

But there was never any real 'danger' of peace, owing to the intransigence of both parties. After the United States had independently sounded out their intentions, it transpired that, whereas the Central Powers offered no reparations and the restitution of only part of their conquests, the Allies entertained nothing but the complete restoration of occupied territory and large indemnities besides. In fact there was never any hope of coming to terms. Indeed, failure to negotiate served merely to harden the Allies and hasten the German decision to launch unrestricted U-Boat warfare, as from February 1st 1917. And this in turn was instrumental in bringing the USA into the war on April 6th.

Lloyd George did not take the German peace offer very seriously, although he was at pains to present the Allied case, quickly but judiciously, both to Parliament and to President Wilson. He was too passionate a patriot to entertain any unworthy compromise and, heavy and hateful as the cost was, he was determined to win the war. He therefore sought other means of slipping the bonds of Chantilly. Baulked for the moment in France and the Balkans, and with the Russian Mission provided for, only one European front offered immediate scope—Italy. To his mind it offered great possibilities and so, on his initiative, a meeting in Rome was fixed for the first week of January. This was not to be yet another isolated conference, but the first of Lloyd George's attempts to hammer out a system between the Allies for the unified direction of the war, strategic, economic, and political—an overdue and altogether admirable intention. The fact that he also designed it as a device to get round the Westerners and unseat Wully and Haig was, of course, far less admirable. However, before the Allied representatives left for Rome, the kaleidoscope had already altered elsewhere, this time in France.

When the Coalition Government was falling in London, a similar crisis was coming to a head in Paris. It all centred upon the person of Joffre, who had commanded the French Army— and in effect decided the Continental strategy of the Western Allies—since the outbreak of the war. But Joffre had been in the saddle too long. In the opinion of many of his countrymen he had become far too powerful, and his HQ at Chantilly had usurped many of the functions of the Government in Paris. Although he got on well with Wully and Haig, and with most other Allied representatives, he had become impatient of advice and dictatorial towards his own Ministers. Since the Marne, moreover, he could boast no large-scale victories by French arms. Instead he had conducted a series of costly offensives without any compensating recovery of occupied territory. The Germans were still in possession of some of the richest provinces of France, and they were still far too close to Paris. He was blamed, too, for unreadiness at Verdun and for an equivocal attitude towards the Balkans. Although primarily a Westerner he had supported Sarrail, though not sufficiently to enable him to gain a decision. He was, therefore, suspect as to strategy, and even as to the sincerity of his intentions. And anyway a general who wins no victories has to reckon with popular reaction sooner or later.

That reckoning was now at hand. Briand's administration fell on December 8th, but Briand himself remained to reconstitute it, setting up a Comité de Guerre to run the war on much the same lines as the new British War Cabinet. He tried to retain Joffre by appointing him Technical Adviser to the Government, in addition to his existing position as Commander-in-Chief of the French Army as a whole. As C-in-C of the French Armies of the north and north-east, however, Joffre was replaced by Nivelle, a subordinate commander with a brilliant record at Verdun. But the new formula was not destined to work. General Lyautey, the new Minister of War, who had made a great reputation in North Africa, objected to the post of Technical Adviser on the ground that it would conflict with his own duties, nor did he get on with Joffre personally. At the same time Nivelle was permitted direct access to the

Government, thus by-passing his own superior. In the face of these moves, clearly intended to render him powerless, Joffre resigned. His resignation was accepted and, with the honorary title of Marshal of France, he passed out of history. It only remains to record that Haig, mindful of Joffre's great service to the Allies in his capacity of *virtual* Generalissimo in the west, tried to persuade Briand against the change, but failed.

The substitution of Nivelle for Joffre did not lead to any surrender of Western strategy, quite the reverse, but it did entail a radical recasting of plans. But although Haig and Wully knew of what was afoot, and at a conference in London at the end of December the French pressed the BEF to take over more front to enable Nivelle to prepare his attack, Lloyd George averted serious discussion until the wider problems of strategy had been thrashed out at Rome.

The British representatives left London on January 1st. They included Wully and Henry Wilson (nominated for the Russian Mission), but not Haig (now a Field-Marshal), since France was not directly to be discussed. On the 2nd they were joined by the French delegation in Paris, and the two parties travelled on together in the same train. They had a busy evening talking, and Hankey related a comic, though somewhat discouraging, anecdote about Lyautey, the new French Minister of War.

'The journey was an incessant series of conferences in conditions of great discomfort owing to the heat and noise. When we were all retiring to bed in a state of complete exhaustion we received a message that Lyautey wished to discuss another important matter. We dressed again and trailed down the swaying and jolting train to his saloon, where we found the general studying a large map of Egypt and Palestine. We listened while he rapped out in sharp, staccato sentences an interminable series of platitudes on the campaign in the Sinai Peninsula. No one made any comment and we retired as soon as we could to our sleeping berths. As we retraced our footsteps Robertson growled out to Lloyd George—"That fellow won't last long!" And he didn't! A few weeks later he got into trouble for refusing information to a parliamentary commission and was packed back to Morocco.'[4]

Wully added this footnote:

'Lyautey . . . is a dried up person of the Anglo-Indian type who has been in the colonies all his life and talks of nothing else. He talks a good deal. He has no grasp whatever of the war as yet and I should doubt if he remains long where he now is.'[5]

Immediately on arrival at Rome, Hankey was sent round post haste to sound out Cadorna, the Italian Commander-in-Chief, about the Prime Minister's pet new project: the loan of 250–300 heavy British guns from France, and a similar number from the French if they would let them go, to back up an Italian offensive through the Julian Alps. But Hankey was too late. Wully—to whom the project was anathema for the usual reasons—had got in first and 'got at' Cadorna, and had already left him when Hankey arrived. Thus Cadorna was wary, and at the subsequent meetings made difficulties about returning the guns in time for the Western offensive. He was also apprehensive of provoking the Germans, who had not hitherto appeared in any force against him. The French, too, were lukewarm, and in the end the Prime Minister's attempt to galvanise this front came to nothing. He had, however, sown the seed, which duly germinated and grew into a fully-prepared plan for transferring British and French troops to Italy in case of need: a wise precaution that paid good dividends after Caporetto.

In other respects the Conference proved hardly more fruitful, largely because Wully refused to be drawn into sideshows, and thereby reiterated the strength of his own position.

'While at Rome we talked of practically nothing else but Salonika and Greece, and at one time I began to fear that after all we should be sending two further divisions. The French and Russians both fought hard for them and Briand held forth very eloquently for three quarters of an hour. The Prime Minister told me about this and when I expressed the hope that he would decline to send more divisions he did not give me a very definite answer. I therefore thought it necessary to warn him quite plainly that I could never consent to signing the necessary order for sending more. He was rather annoyed at this and described it as holding a pistol at his head. I did it for his benefit as I did not wish him to commit us in an International Conference to a promise which I myself had definitely decided that I could having nothing to do with.'[6]

Greece was then in the thick of the crisis over her attitude to the war, and Sarrail had come over to Rome breathing fire against her. Wully described him as a

'. . . fine looking, handsome man of the swash-buckler type. He completely captivated the Prime Minister who has formed the opinion that he is an exceptionally good man. In my opinion he is a man who may one day pull off a good coup, but he is quite as likely, perhaps even more so, to do the reverse and to land us into difficulties. I am quite sure he means to have trouble with Greece if he can possibly create it, and I do not think he would regret having a few troops cut up if that would suffice to bring about a row. . . We do not want a war with Greece if we can possibly avoid it. . . It would be as bad as going into Afghanistan. . . It would be like attacking a swarm of wasps.'[7]

Happily Lloyd George persuaded Sarrail to regard this unfortunate country as a potential ally, instead of a potential enemy, and act accordingly. Wully also referred to a matter of far greater significance than at first appeared, a foretaste, in short, of the Nivelle affair.

'Briand brought up a proposal for placing Milne [GOC British troops in Greece] definitely under Sarrail's order, and the Prime Minister seemed to think this was necessary. I was sent for to give my opinion and I gave it pretty plainly. I told them that we could not possibly put British troops really under a foreign general. That the thing was not practicable because our General could not be forced to comply with the orders of a foreign general. There is no law behind such a proceeding, and moreover our Government could not possibly divest itself of its responsibility for our troops and they could only look to our General to see that the right thing was done. After a good deal of talk it was decided that Milne should be to Sarrail as Gouraud was to Ian Hamilton [at Gallipoli], and orders to that effect are being sent to him. As a matter of fact it makes practically no change in the present arrangement.'[8]

The conference finally agreed to rearm and re-equip Russia, and to continue to concert action by more frequent and regular consultation, a first step towards the permanent organisation founded at Rapallo in the following November. Despite the disasters that were to befall her, Italy was a fortunate country for the Prime Minister, for she provided the means by which he achieved his principal purpose: the unified direction of the war.

13. Kitchener, left, with Wully, centre, in London on Anzac Day, 1916

14. With King George V and Queen Mary at Aldershot in 1916

15. Wully and Maurice, centre, leaving the Hotel Crillon after the
Allied Conference in 1917

16. In Cologne with Joffre in 1919

For the moment, however, Lloyd George found himself frustrated yet again. Failure to mount a grand offensive in Italy, or to alter the situation in the Balkans, threw him back upon the only alternative—France—and upon what proved to be his only whole-hearted venture into Western strategy. He did not, of course, place himself unreservedly in the hands of Wully and Haig; that would have been too unnatural. Things had already reached such a pitch in his relations with these two men that he would have sacked them both, had he dared. He did not dare, because they had the backing of the Army and enjoyed the trust of most of the nation, and because he knew very well that he was unable to find adequate substitutes. He turned, therefore, not to his own generals, but to the new star, Nivelle, and sought to use him as a means of controlling military policy. The extraordinary story that follows is a classic example of the way in which Lloyd George resorted to devious, on occasions frankly dishonest, methods in order to achieve sound and honourable ends.

*   *   *

General Robert Nivelle had risen quickly. Starting the war as a Colonel, an artillery specialist, he had made a big reputation at Verdun, first as a corps commander and then as the Army commander in charge of the front. When German pressure relaxed in the summer of 1916, he contrived a series of limited but highly successful attacks with comparatively small forces (never more than three or four divisions), backed by deep and intense artillery bombardment and creeping barrages. In this way he recaptured a good deal of ground and several forts and strong-points, some with emotive names such as Fort Vaux and Fort Douaumont, and all at comparatively low cost. In fact the last of these attacks was launched at the very moment when he was waiting to take over from Joffre. By December 1916, therefore, Nivelle's stock stood high, both publicly and professionally. Publicly because he had won some real French victories, he not Joffre. Professionally because he had won them by scientific methods which he had clearly demonstrated. What remained to be proved was whether a plan for using small forces against a tired enemy could be applied on a large scale and in different circumstances. Nivelle made the mistake of *assuming* that it could. It led him to believe in the *mathematical* certainty of his own formula, and simultaneously inflated his own ambitions in a highly dangerous manner.

These dangers were not apparent to his colleagues at first. They were well masked by his strong, open face, his attractive manner and power of persuasion, above all by his ability to speak fluent English learned from his English mother. He made an excellent impression upon Haig, who thought him 'a most straightforward soldierly man',[9] when they met for the first time at Cassel on December 20th, soon after Nivelle had taken up his new command. In fact Nivelle was wasting no time in putting over to Haig *his* version of the offensive, which differed materially from the one agreed with Joffre a month earlier.

The Joffre plan had envisaged a repetition of the Somme on two fronts, each of 20–25 miles in length, the British to attack between Vimy and Bapaume in the north, the French between the rivers Somme and Oise in the south, with a defensive gap of some eight miles in between. Secondary diversionary attacks were planned by the French on the Aisne and in Upper Alsace. At the same time the British agreed to extend their line southwards towards the Somme, and to maintain offensive pressure against the enemy in the valley of the Ancre during the winter months. An important corollary to these operations was yet another, of familiar lineage, dear to Wully and Haig, as indeed it was bound to be to most British leaders, political, military, and naval: a campaign to clear the Channel coast. The plan had been coming forward in one form or another since the end of 1914, and it had much to recommend it. The strategic advantages of turning the enemy flank in Flanders were obvious, but there was a powerful naval interest as well. To protect the constant flow of men and arms to France was a heavy commitment. The Navy was already at full stretch policing the high seas, and would soon be tested to near breaking-point by the U-Boat offensive of 1917, which brought Britain to within measurable distance of starvation. Thus the capture of the ports of Zeebrugge and Ostend, and the possibility of clearing the Germans right out of Belgium, would assist the Navy as much as the Army, and directly bear on the safety and fighting potential of the nation.

This time there seemed a real chance that something would be

done, and—following an instruction of the War Committee[10]—
the whole matter was thrashed out in earnest at a meeting held
at the War Office on November 22nd 1916, attended by Wully,
Haig, and the Admiralty representatives. The findings were
confirmed by Asquith the next day, and the plan then went[11]
before Joffre who gave it his general blessing. After further discussion it crystallised into a proposal for a military offensive
eastwards from the Ypres salient, combined with a later landing
from the sea, all to go off a few weeks after the main offensive in
the south. This was of course the latest version of the plan for
the Third Battle of Ypres (commonly known as Passchendaele),
which in the event did not get going until the end of the following July.

The main reason why the Flanders offensive was to be postponed yet again derived from Nivelle and his new plan. Briefly
he proposed to follow up the Somme, not by repeating the
pattern of attrition—first exhausting the enemy and then breaking through when the point of exhaustion had been reached—
but by destroying the main strength of the German Army in
France by a massive knock-out blow of such proportions that it
would ensure decisive success within a matter of hours. In the
unlikely event of failure, the whole operation would be called
off at once at minimum cost. And there were other important
changes. Joffre had proposed two main zones of offensive, one
British, one French, the former to be the larger on the understanding that the British would continue to take a heavier share
of the burden of the war in France. Nivelle proposed three: two
as before to engage the enemy and absorb his reserves, but the
third—further south on the Aisne, formerly regarded as a subsidiary action by Joffre—would follow as the main blow, smash
through the enemy front, and open the way for pursuit by a
'mass of manœuvre' of 27 divisions, held in reserve, all French.

To allow this reserve to be formed, Nivelle asked Haig to take
over yet more line, this time a distance of some 20 miles (as the
crow flew) right down to the Amiens-Roye road (extra to the
extension already agreed with Joffre and taken over), all to be
done by January 15th. The British would still be needed for the
preliminary engagement and for the exploitation battle, but to
compensate for the extension of their line (and thus for the extra
troops required to man it), he suggested that the winter opera-

tions on the Ancre be given up and the Flanders plan put off. He argued that the latter would not be necessary, if his offensive succeeded, for the Germans would be compelled to get out of Belgium anyway. At the worst it could always be mounted later in the year. One thing was abundantly clear. This was to be principally a French operation, with a French victory at the end of it—a patriotic consideration and, one suspects, a personal one as well, with Nivelle as the great architect and master mason of it all.

Haig's first reaction was not unfavourable. He liked Nivelle as a man, and wrote off his extraordinary optimism as natural French exuberance. Moreover, although Nivelle's plan had an uncomfortable resemblance, at least in outline, to his own which had failed so disastrously on the Somme on July 1st 1916 —the idea of the knock-out blow—he recognised that the circumstances were different, allowing for better preparation and execution, and conducted on a bigger scale. It was also comforting to be told that the French were willing and ready for another gigantic effort. He may also have submerged his doubts in the thought that the Germans might after all be at the end of their tether in France, and that this would prove the *coup de grâce*. In fact, as Ludendorff later admitted, the Germans *were* greatly depleted in men and morale as a result of the Somme, and the pressure soon to be exerted against them on the Ancre excited their worst fears lest the big battle should start up again almost at once. Ironically, the substitution of Nivelle's plan for Joffre's gave them just the breathing-space they needed. In February and March they used it to great effect by evacuating a dangerous salient, laying waste the territory they had recently occupied, and retiring to a shorter fortified position of formidable strength—the Hindenburg Line—where in due course they decimated the great French attack and destroyed all Nivelle's hopes. It also had an indirect bearing on Third Ypres, for had the latter been launched in the late spring of 1917, as originally intended, instead of the late summer, it might never have bogged down in the appalling sea of mud to which the August and autumn rains reduced the clay fields of Flanders.

Haig did not dislike Nivelle's plan in its general form, indeed, he accepted it, but he was deeply concerned about the extension of his front. He therefore answered Nivelle on December 25th, indicating agreement in principle, but limiting the extension to 8, not 20, miles. Nivelle was irked by Haig's reluctance, and pressed his point through the agency of Ribot and Thomas, the French Ministers who visited London on December 26th and 27th, though without result. On December 31st Haig met Nivelle again and restated the position. He would take over 8 miles by early February, not 20 miles by January 15th as Nivelle had first demanded. As to the future, everything depended on reinforcements, but he implied willingness to take over the remaining distance should he get the men. In return he asked Nivelle to relieve him in a similar manner when it came to the Flanders operation. Nivelle was friendly, seemed satisfied, and gave the assurance asked for. In fact he was far from content, and tried to waylay Lloyd George on his return from Rome in order to renew his demands. All he got, however, was agreement to thrash the matter out anew at a meeting in London on January 15th.

All this time Wully was on the watch. He was being pressed by the Prime Minister to send British troops to several fronts—Italy, the Balkans, even Egypt—but although he got his own way at Rome, his very success there served only to strengthen Lloyd George in the decision to go all out with Nivelle. As a Westerner Wully was, of course, always disposed to reinforce the BEF, but he disliked Nivelle's peremptory demands at the outset, distrusted his plans, and feared his cavalier ideas of security. To Haig on December 28th he wrote:

'As regards Nivelle it would appear that either on his own initiative or by the instructions of the French Government he is going to keep them fully informed of all his arrangements with you, and will get them to put pressure on us when he and you do not agree. He very stupidly sent to the French Government his whole plan which he had previously given you. This was sent to our Foreign Office and was hektographed off in the usual manner, and I suppose there are now dozens of copies of the paper about London to say nothing about Paris. . . I myself did not intend to send it even to the War Cabinet.'

And to Wigram on January 12th:

'You may have heard of the difficulty which has arisen between Nivelle and Haig with regard to the extension of our front. As usual the French wish us to take over a great deal more line and at the same time prepare for a big offensive. This happened on every occasion when I was in France, but Joffre and Lord French usually came to a satisfactory conclusion. On this occasion however Nivelle has appealed to the Prime Minister. He wired to us en route from Rome asking the Prime Minister to see him. He declined to do so unless Haig were present. Nivelle has again returned to the charge, and is coming over here on Monday to see the Prime Minister—Haig will be there also. I think it particularly bad form on Nivelle's part to do this, and also it introduces the politicians into military matters.'

Wully was also disquieted by the possible effect of Nivelle's plans upon the Flanders operation, and questioned Haig specifically on this point in a letter dated January 1st.[12] Haig replied on January 6th, enclosing a copy of a letter written by him to Nivelle that same day, in which he included the following sentences:

'It is essential that the Belgian coast shall be cleared this summer. I hope and believe that we shall be able to effect much more than that, and within limitations of time I will cooperate to the utmost of my power in the larger plans which you have proposed.

'But it must be distinctly understood between us that if I am not satisfied that this larger plan, as events develop, promises the degree of success necessary to clear the Belgian coast, then I not only cannot continue the battle but I will look to you to fulfil the undertaking you have given me verbally to relieve on the defensive front the troops I require for my northern offensive.'[13]

Since no one could control the course of Nivelle's offensive, not even Nivelle, his reply to Haig on January 11th—for all its clarifications and assurances—made the position no clearer. But at least the two commanders were generally agreed about the form of the offensive. Only the reliefs remained undecided, and of course the date when operations would start. Such was the situation on the eve of the conference in London on January 15th and 16th.

*　　　*　　　*

Lloyd George was only too ready and willing to be captivated by Nivelle. He had reconciled himself to the idea of another offensive in France; he liked Nivelle's plan because it was conceived as a quick decisive battle, involving a minimum of casualties, and because the French were to be in charge; he liked Nivelle himself because he was a French, NOT a British general, who had won victories, because he spoke English fluently and presented his case clearly and persuasively, and because—it was said—he liked the shape of his head![14]

On the 15th Lloyd George saw Wully and Haig in advance of the main meeting, made unfavourable comparisons between the British and French Armies, and pressed them to accede to Nivelle's demands. Nivelle appeared in the afternoon, when the ground was gone over again, Haig continuing to stand out for five extra divisions: namely, 27 to hold the extended line and 35 to conduct his share of the offensive, 62 in all. No decision was reached, but Nivelle was pressed to stay till the morrow, when the Prime Minister returned to the charge. Wully sombrely summed up all the objections, not only to the extension, but to the basis of the plan itself. He did not believe that the Verdun formula could be applied automatically to a battle of this scale. The fronts were too wide, and the German defences too deep, to ensure decisive success within Nivelle's promised 48 hours. By then, even if things had gone well, much more time and effort would be needed to complete the operation. It was bound to resolve itself into a series of limited advances and complex adjustments. No one could arbitrarily break off a battle of this kind at an early stage, unless it had either succeeded miraculously or failed miserably. Nivelle was being much too optimistic. Moreover, any attack involved losses, and this plan simply meant that the French would have larger losses than the British, not that losses would be avoided altogether. Finally, what was to be the fate of the Flanders operation, so vital to British security?[15]

Wully argued in vain. In the end he was overruled by the War Cabinet. Haig was told that the extra divisions would be forthcoming, and that the new line must be taken over by the first week in March. The general offensive would begin not later than April 1st. A Memorandum, embodying these decisions, was drawn up and signed by Wully, Haig, and Nivelle, who had thus got his way at the cost of two weeks' delay by the reliefs.[16] He returned to France, privately confident that he could repeat the manœuvre whenever he wanted, and appeal to Lloyd George over the heads of his advisers. For his part

Lloyd George was no less delighted, and instructed Wully to inform Haig that the Government expected him to fulfil the agreement 'in the letter and in the spirit'.

Unfortunately, the difficulties that arose during the next few weeks slowed down the military preparations, and made it seem—anyway to Lloyd George and Nivelle—that Haig was dragging his feet. Transport was the chief trouble. The continuous expansion of the BEF and all its services, and the immediate build-up for the forthcoming offensive, were proving too much for the communications system, especially the railways, which were still under French control, a responsibility not passed to the British until March. In addition Boulogne harbour had had to be closed for a time owing to the sinking of a ship at the port entrance, while the hard weather and subsequent thaw played havoc with the canals and roads. Thus, within a week of the London meeting, Haig felt compelled to warn Nivelle that the hold-up might affect the date of operations. At the same time Nivelle had been apprised in advance of the details of Haig's plan for the British attack between Bapaume and Vimy, with which—for technical reasons—he found fault. All this strengthened him in his private resolve to enforce his authority over Haig in order to ensure the precise execution of his own master plan. However, although a dictatorial note had already crept into his *written* communications to Haig, nothing unpleasant occurred at a meeting between the two men on January 29th, when the situation was calmly and reasonably discussed.

Nevertheless, conditions did not improve, and on February 14th Haig sent Wully a plaintive telegram, asking for a high-level Ministerial conference to straighten out the transport tangle and settle the operational matters it affected. He added that he was hoping to see Nivelle again in two days' time. Wully was disturbed.

'So long as Ministers take part in the discussion of plans of operations we shall always have trouble of the worst kind I am sure. Soldiers understand each other, and I have some hope that Nivelle will see you and that the two of you will come to a satisfactory agreement. The problem seems perfectly simple. The railways have broken down and until we can get them right we ought not to go off.'[17]

Nivelle did see Haig on February 16th and seemingly with good results. They agreed that no attack should start until the railway problem had been solved: a decision that rendered unnecessary the kind of conference Haig had first asked for, since it was now purely a matter for the experts. None the less, the arrangements were not altered, and a meeting between the leading soldiers and politicians was fixed for February 26th at Calais. Things were to turn out very differently to that which either Wully or Haig had expected.

*   *   *

The fact was that Lloyd George, the British Prime Minister, and Nivelle, the French Commander-in-Chief, had been hatching a secret plot to place Nivelle in supreme command of both Armies in France. Their intermediary was Commandant Bertier de Sauvigny, who represented GQG (French High Command) at the War Office: that is, 'he was accredited to Sir William Robertson and not to any Minister, and his duties were purely military, or so the British soldiers thought.'[18] In fact he was in contact with Lloyd George, and had a lengthy conversation with him on February 15th, Hankey also being present. On this occasion the Prime Minister expressed his profound confidence in Nivelle and stated that he wished him to make use of all the forces on the French front, British as well as French. According to de Sauvigny, he then said:

'There is no doubt that the prestige which Field Marshal Haig enjoys with the public and the British Army will make it impossible to subordinate him purely and simply to the French Command, but if the War Cabinet realises that this measure is indispensable, they will not hesitate to give Field Marshal Haig secret instructions to this effect, and, if need be, to replace him if he will not give the support of all his forces when this may be required, with complete understanding and compliance. It is essential that the two War Cabinets should be in agreement on this principle. A conference should be held as soon as possible, for although the date by which the British Armies will be ready has been retarded by a fortnight owing to the congestion of the French railways, it is nevertheless so near that we must take a decision as soon as possible.'[19]

Well aware of the implications, de Sauvigny said nothing to the War Office, but reported direct to his superiors. It is not certain whether Lyautey saw his report, or understood it if he did, but Nivelle of course did, and on the strength of it drew up precise proposals for the 'take-over' of the BEF, and brought them along to Calais. There was yet another adept piece of subterfuge.

'General Robertson did not attend the last meeting of the War Cabinet held before the conference, on Saturday, February 24th. He had been told that he need not come, which was unusual when military matters were to be discussed. Suspecting nothing and having plenty to do, he remained at work in the War Office, little guessing that on Mr Lloyd George's proposal the decision had been taken in principle to place the British armies under General Nivelle.'[20]

Everything was therefore ready for this astonishing, paradoxical, move; for although the deal was crooked, the game was good. The idea of unified command was undoubtedly sound, and Lloyd George was far-sighted and patriotic in promoting it, but he could hardly have set about his task in a worse manner. He was proposing, without the knowledge and agreement of his own soldiers, to place the French contingent commander over his British counterpart (to whom, incidentally, he was junior in rank), and—as later transpired—in such a manner as to deprive the latter of many of the normal responsibilities of his own command. This was quite different to that which happened a year later, when a separate Supreme Commander, Foch, a man of tried worth and experience, was placed over both the British and the French field commanders, Haig and Pétain respectively: an appointment, it may be added, made at Haig's request.

The conference opened at 3.30 pm on Monday February 26th in the bleak Gare Maritime hotel. Present were: Lloyd George, Hankey, Wully, Haig; Briand, Lyautey, Nivelle; assistants and advisers. The first session was devoted entirely to the transport problem, which soon became a tussle between the technicians, punctuated by comments from Haig and Nivelle as to the effect of transport upon operations. Lloyd George then recommended, and it was agreed, that the technicians retire into committee and leave the principals free for further talks after tea. At 5.30 pm they reassembled, and Nivelle made a set speech about his plans for the offensive. It was all familiar stuff, no one demurred, and nothing new was said. Lloyd George, it seems, then became restless, referred pointedly to the value of a unified command, and turning to Nivelle added: 'Let us speak with the utmost frankness.' Nivelle, embarrassed, could only reply with a piece in praise of Haig and a vague reference to the need for a convention defining their relationship as commanders. Lloyd George pounced on this, asked him to be more precise, and to return later with proposals in writing. By this time, according to Spears (to whom Wully described the conference in later years), the two British generals had become uneasy, but they still did not realise what lay in store.

The conference then broke up to allow Nivelle to 'formulate his proposals', though they were, of course, already drafted and reposing in his brief-case. The Prime Minister took Hankey for a long walk. When they got back, shortly before 8 pm, they were joined by Briand, Lyautey, and Nivelle, who thereupon handed over the required document. It amounted to this:

(1) As from March 1st Nivelle would exercise command over the BEF in respect of all operational and contingent matters (planning, execution of plans, grouping of forces and boundaries, and the disposal of relevant resources).

(2) At GQG Nivelle would have the services of a British Chief of Staff, with appropriate staff, and of the Quartermaster-General. The former would act as the link with the War Office, and be the channel through whom Nivelle would transmit his orders.

(3) Only disciplinary and personnel matters would be retained by Haig, who would thus be reduced to the status of an Adjutant-General.

It was a staggering document. Totally unrealistic, to say the least. Did Nivelle really imagine that the British would allow their great Army to surrender its independent existence, kick its beloved commander downstairs, and reduce itself to the level of the Foreign Legion? The amazing thing was that Lloyd George did seem inclined to accept the proposals as they stood, although they must have gone far further than even he had ever contemplated. Hankey was horrified. How on earth would the generals take it? Here is Spears' account:

'General Robertson dined with General Maurice [DMO]. As he finished he was handed a translation of the Nivelle proposals. As a stimulus to good digestion they were a failure. Wully's face went the colour of mahogany, his eyes became perfectly round, his eye-brows slanted outwards like a forest of bayonets held at the charge —in fact he showed every sign of having a fit. "Get 'Aig", he bellowed to The Monument [Major Lucas, his ADC].[21]

'General Robertson, ten years after that night, could not master his anger when he recalled it. His eyes would grow dark and his eye-brows bristle as with the eye of memory he gazed once more on General Nivelle's proposals.'[22]

Haig arrived and, like Wully, was stunned by what he read. Thereafter they began to react differently. Haig was deeply hurt, but felt that any criticism of his might savour of 'saving his own skin' as Commander-in-Chief, so he retreated within his armour of well-bred reserve and detachment. By contrast Wully became very angry, inhibited by no such idea that it might be ungentlemanly behaviour, and it was as much due to his irate resistance, as to the astute compromises put forward by others, that the day was eventually saved for the British Army in France. The two men went straight along to see the Prime Minister, and a stormy scene ensued. Lloyd George made things worse by announcing that the War Cabinet had *already* agreed to the principle of unified command (at the meeting on February 24th, which Wully had been told he need not attend), and that Nivelle *insisted* on Henry Wilson becoming the British Chief of Staff at GQG under the new scheme. For the soldiers that was the last straw, and when Wully countered with a series of pertinent questions about the constitutional legality of the whole idea, Lloyd George blew up too. 'You must have worked out a scheme and be in agreement with the French by 8 o'clock tomorrow morning', he is reported to have said, and showed them the door.

Wully's immediate reaction was to resign in disgust, but soon realised that he was needed now more than ever to defend the interests of the Army. He turned to Maurice, who henceforward played a vital part—together with Hankey on the other side of the fence—in finding a way round the *impasse*. However, Maurice's first effort as compromise failed, for a most unexpected reason.

'Maurice set to work on a counter-proposal which he submitted to his chief, and together they took it to Haig. They found him very unwilling to discuss it. He was reluctant to participate in the negotiations, or even to make suggestions. He said several times that this was a political matter which concerned the CIGS and not himself, that it was in fact a discussion concerning the appointment of a Commander-in-Chief, and that therefore he could not take part in it.'[23]

Maurice went on working. Hankey was busy too. He was in an awkward predicament. His belief in a unified command had already alienated Wully and Haig, but his opposition to the Nivelle proposals put him at a disadvantage with the Prime Minister. So he too wrestled with a draft, knowing that unless he could persuade Lloyd George to give ground a little, the attitude of the soldiers—whether they resigned or not—might force the hand of the War Cabinet. Before going to bed he had a formula ready. Wully did not sleep well and summoned Maurice in the early hours for further talk. At 6.0 am he sent The Monument to Nivelle to ask for an interview, but Nivelle, already dressed, obviously aware that trouble was brewing, came along himself. Wully went straight to the point. Why on earth had he not been consulted before the scheme was submitted to the Prime Minister? Such a thing had never happened in Joffre's time. He was amazed it could happen now. Nivelle then gave a masterly performance. He expressed painful surprise. Did not General Robertson know? The idea had not come from *him*, but had been agreed by the two Governments before the conference, who had instructed him to work out the details. This he had done. He had not imagined for a moment that General Robertson had been kept in the dark.

Wully and Maurice believed Nivelle absolutely, as did Haig later. Indeed, Nivelle's duplicity was not fully revealed until after the war. Moreover, he then proceeded to elaborate to Maurice alone a highly tendentious account of all that had preceded the proposals, placing the onus of blame upon the politicians and Bertier de Sauvigny, and weeping crocodile tears for Haig, whom he again extolled. During this moving speech, Hankey had paid a call on Wully, who was not in a good mood.

'I had my formula typed by Sylvester, first thing, and saw Robertson at 8.0 am. He was in a terrible state and ramped up and down the room, talking about the horrible idea of putting the "wonderful army" under a Frenchman, swearing he would never serve under one, nor his son either, and that no one could order him to. He had not slept, for the first time in the war, he said. I could do nothing with him, so left him.'[24]

Hankey then had breakfast with Lloyd George, who had also slept badly.

'I tried to frighten him by the probable results of Robertson's and Haig's impending resignations, and he was affected, though he swore he was not going to be beaten over this. Then I warned him he could not fight on the basis of the outrageous French document and he agreed and asked me to draft something on which he could fight. This was the psychological moment to pull my formula out of my pocket. He read it, accepted it. . .'[25]

Meanwhile, Haig had done some drafting, though not very helpfully. He gave Wully a note suggesting that either matters be left as they were, or that the British Armies be placed under the French Commander-in-Chief. In the latter case the British Commander-in-Chief and GHQ would disappear, a drastic change 'fraught with the gravest danger'. Haig then retired once more into his den. Wully put the paper in his pocket and, taking Maurice with him, went along to beard the Prime Minister on his own. They had another stormy encounter. Haig's fatalistic alternatives infuriated Lloyd George, but

'Wully was not easily overridden . . . and he never fought so hard as when defending Haig. He was fighting a rearguard action now, but a highly aggressive one. He did not hesitate to speak his mind at having been kept in ignorance of the Government's decision. . . He argued that General Nivelle was totally inexperienced in handling large bodies of troops. . . How could this Frenchman be made responsible for the safety of what were to all intents and purposes the total forces of Britain and of the Empire? . . What would the Dominions say? . . Was it constitutional to place British soldiers under anyone not holding the King's Commission?'[26]

Lloyd George did not give way. He displayed Hankey's draft, with its important amendment that Nivelle should exercise command over the British Armies *for the duration of the forthcoming offensive only*. Unfortunately Wully was in no mood to consider it. His blood was up. He refused to budge, and his obduracy produced another explosion in the Prime Minister, who threatened there and then to stop the conference, and lay the whole matter before the War Cabinet.

'Hands in belt, his enormous eyebrows bristling, flat-footed and raging, Robertson propelled himself out of the room. His movements were those of a charging elephant depicted in a slow-motion picture. Again he contemplated resignation, but after a talk with Maurice he thought better of it.'[27]

Maurice, who was already playing an invaluable part as moderator and counsellor to his chief, now made his most important contribution to the whole conference. He suddenly recalled a precedent which, if embodied in Hankey's draft, seemed to offer a workable solution. It was the agreement by which Gouraud, as commander of the French troops at Gallipoli, had both conformed to the orders of Hamilton, the C-in-C, and retained the right to appeal to his own Government. The principle had again been invoked at Rome to adjust the relations between Milne and Sarrail at Salonika. Why should it not apply now? Maurice lost no time in telephoning the War Office for the exact text of the original agreement.

This was the turning-point. Wully now began to thaw out towards Hankey and studied his draft with care, while Hankey undertook to persuade the Prime Minister to agree to the Maurice amendment. Confabulations between all parties continued, but a practical compromise was now in sight. Once assured that Haig would still have to obey Nivelle's orders, Lloyd George not only accepted the revisions, but rejected Nivelle's original demand for a British Chief of Staff and Quartermaster-General at GQG, substituting a representative Mission with a senior officer at its head. Although the appointment was not agreed until after the conference, it was ultimately given to Henry Wilson, lately in Russia; and in him Nivelle got the man he wanted. Haig, now mollified by both Lyautey and Nivelle, continued his resistance for a time, but in the end he allowed himself to be persuaded, mainly by Wully, and signed under protest. All the other principals signed too. The agreement consisted in essence of four main points:

(i) The general direction of the campaign would be in the hands of the French Commander-in-Chief.

(ii) Haig would conform to the overall plan.

(iii) If at any time Haig considered that the safety of his Army was endangered or its success prejudiced by this plan, he was free to act as he thought fit and appeal to the CIGS and the War Cabinet.

(iv) While conforming to the overall plan, he was free to direct operations on his own front.

The conference closed with the briefest of references to the transport problem, for which ironically it had been called in the first place. In fact, transport matters were already on the mend before Calais, and the technicians did the rest on their own. Salonika was also mentioned—and dismissed!

*   *   *

Calais did not finally settle the dispute between Haig and Nivelle, for two reasons. One was the German retirement to the Hindenburg Line, and its effect upon Allied plans. The other was Nivelle's continued attempt to treat Haig as a subordinate in the literal sense of the term.

News of the German move actually reached Calais on the second day. The *Siegfried Stellung* was a prepared position of formidable strength, constructed up to 20 miles behind the existing front, over 70 miles long, running from near Arras in the north to near Soissons in the south. Its purpose was defensive: eliminating salients, shortening the line, and economising in men. The retirement had originally been planned for March, and in the main it took place then, but British pressure on the Ancre during January had caused such anxiety that the starting date was advanced. It was these initial moves, opposite the British sector of the front, that gave the clue to what was happening, and caused Haig to question the validity of Nivelle's operational plans.

Meanwhile, Nivelle was exhibiting extreme irritation. On February 27th, the very day the Calais Conference came to an end, he sent Haig a brusquely-worded letter, fixing Cambrai as the objective of the British attack, April 8th as the date of that attack, and demanding details of the plans of both Haig and his Army Commanders. He also listed the names of several officers whom he wanted appointed to the British Mission at GQG, among them Henry Wilson (as already requested) and

John Davidson, Haig's own DMO. Nivelle's letter was tactless and peremptory, written in the style of a superior officer giving orders, not of a colleague addressing the commander of a great national Army, who had made the *beau geste* of complying with his policy. The letter was deeply resented at GHQ and Haig waited a day or two before replying. On March 3rd he sent Wully a copy of this letter, together with a covering note and an operational appreciation of his own. He suggested that the German withdrawal might be the prelude to a counter-offensive in the north, where Allied defences were comparatively weak. Should not, therefore, the Nivelle plan be re-examined? In any event he felt he must take the necessary precautions in that area, but since his hands were now tied, he would have to invoke the saving clause of the Calais agreement, so that he might act as he thought fit for the safety of his Army. On the next day he sent Wully two more letters in the same vein, and also replied to Nivelle, enclosing a copy of the appreciation forwarded to London. He issued the warning that he might not now be ready to attack by April 8th, and asked Nivelle what changes he had in mind for the overall plan of offensive.

All this was very ill received by Nivelle, and his displeasure was increased by an adverse report from des Vallières, French representative at GHQ, as to Haig's general attitude and intentions. In his reply of March 6th, he discounted the extent and implications of the German retirement, flatly disbelieved in any counter-offensive, whether in Flanders or anywhere else, and stood firmly by his own plan and dates, allowing for modification only in the Arras area. He then reported the whole affair to the French Government. As a result Briand addressed a long telegram of complaint to Lloyd George on March 7th, accusing Haig of trying to avoid the Calais agreement, and insisting on Henry Wilson's appointment.

This telegram was the ace of arrogance and defeated its own purpose, but it would never have been sent had Briand not felt sure that Lloyd George was trying to neutralise Haig, if not actually get rid of him. However, the atmosphere in London had already changed, thanks largely to Wully who had been extremely active ever since his return from France. First he enlisted the support of the Army Council. Then he told members of the War Cabinet, collectively and individually, exactly what had happened at Calais, and what they had let themselves in for, as a result of their decision of February 24th, made in his absence and without his advice. He repeated all the arguments and made all the most telling points. Neither he nor Haig *approved* of the Calais agreement. Their signatures simply meant that they agreed to the method of carrying it out. If they had not signed, they might have seriously embarrassed the Government, but did the Government realise what it had done? Once battle was joined, it was no use relying upon any saving clause, for events would take their own course.

'Supposing a situation arose whereby the Channel Ports and Paris were threatened, was there any doubt which General Nivelle would consider the more important? . . What control had the British Government over Nivelle? None, absolutely none. The rugged old man stumped up and down Ministers's rooms, or glowering at them from under his enormous eyebrows banged the table and repeated over and over again that Nivelle was answerable to the French Government alone, and that therefore the French and not the British Government was the supreme authority over our army. Was that what was wanted? he growled, baring his teeth in the alarming way he had: well, if so, tell the country.'[28]

All this had a marked effect upon men like Milner and Curzon, and even upon Bonar Law, who was determined to back Lloyd George to the hilt. Outside the War Cabinet, Derby talked of resigning, and at the Foreign Office Balfour made clear to Cambon, the French Ambassador, what was at stake. If the experiment of putting both Armies under a French commander failed for lack of tact and understanding, then it might prove impossible to repeat it. As to Lloyd George himself, he passed perceptibly from active hostility to Haig to something approaching toleration, in the face of French intransigence and of rising doubts on his own side. But it is clear that had not Wully taken the stand he did, then the Prime Minister might have dismissed Haig in the early days of March and ridden out the consequences. In that case the French would have asserted their authority by default.

Wully did not, however, defend Haig with his eyes shut. Without giving an inch where it mattered, he also advised moderation. He pressed Haig, for example, not to oppose the appointment of Henry Wilson, and to see Nivelle personally once again. He did not really believe that the two men were so far apart—inasmuch as both realised that the original plan would have to be modified in some respect, as a result of the German withdrawal—and he was anxious to take these purely military matters away from the politicians and return them to the soldiers. He did not at first get his way. Further communication between Haig and Nivelle on March 9th showed that an *impasse* had been reached, and on Lloyd George's insistence a new 'Calais' was called in London on the 12th, to work out the application of the old Calais agreement.

This time the atmosphere was very different. Wully was alert and on the attack, most of the War Cabinet were with him, while the Prime Minister himself was no longer so well disposed towards Nivelle or French pretensions. Nevertheless, Lloyd George conducted the preliminaries with his accustomed skill and vitality, and eased the way forward by seeing both Haig and Nivelle privately in advance, and by prevailing on Haig finally to accept Henry Wilson. At the main meeting, however, matters went less well, and on Wully's suggestion the soldiers repaired to the War Office to hammer out their differences once and for all. Here Wully was undoubted master of the field. Discussion centred upon the functions of the British Mission and the method of communication between Nivelle and Haig. Nivelle wanted to send his orders via London, while Lyautey preferred the Mission to be attached to him in Paris. Wully would have none of this, and insisted on direct contact between the two field commanders, with the Mission doing the proper work of intermediary and liaison. It was all the most uncompromising common sense.

'The French generals held different opinions on important points, the British were perfectly clear as to what they wanted, with the result that General Robertson, on whom the main burden of the negotiations fell, carried the day through sheer honesty of purpose, directness and character. He could at times be quite eloquent and persuasive, especially when it was a question of brushing aside non-essentials and revealing the central facts. Upon such occasions he would speak for a considerable time in a deep slow voice without taking breath; he would then stop, his lungs would fill audibly and rather asthmatically, and baring his teeth he would smile a smile that always made me think of the ogre's expression when he declared with relish that he "smelt the smell of an Englishman"; then he would start off again. This does not sound like a method that would make proselytes, and it would certainly not have galvanised multitudes, but it was extraordinarily effective because of the man's tremendous personality and huge reserves of strength. Upon this occasion it won the day, and there was little left for the politicians to say when the memorandum drawn up by the soldiers was submitted to them.'[29]

The new agreement was duly signed on March 13th. Haig added a rider to the effect that he fully intended to play his part, provided that he and his Army were treated as "allies and not subordinates", and that the duties of the Mission might have to be modified by experience. So ended this phase of the first attempt to formalise a system of unified command. It may well be said that the whole enterprise was unnecessary, since under Joffre unity had already been achieved on an informal basis. It was true that Joffre had commanded the loyalty of his Allied colleagues out of personal respect, but he also exercised authority by reason of the predominance of French power on land. Now Joffre was gone and the balance of power had materially altered. It was impossible to replace him on the same basis as before. There were, therefore, good grounds for attempting some new and formal structure, and the attempt might well have succeeded had not Lloyd George and Nivelle resorted to tricks, and had Nivelle shown restraint and goodwill after the Calais agreement. But—as has already been demonstrated elsewhere in this book—no agreement, however carefully worded, can hope to work without mutual tact and esteem; and this, too, was the burden of a letter which Wully wrote to Nivelle, with the best intentions, on March 13th.

'For some time past we have been working at and drawing up conventions, but the most essential thing of all is that we should work together with cordiality and that we should have complete confidence in each other. This is worth more than all conventions on paper.'[30]

The reply he got was a sour one. Nivelle was a lesser man than Joffre. He was so blinded by ambition that he allowed himself, not only to be irritated by the British generals, but he completely misinterpreted their natural caution, and was convinced it amounted to bad faith. His resentment went to extraordinary lengths against Haig. As commander of the BEF, Haig had both the right and the duty to draw his own conclusions about the first stages of the German withdrawal. His suggestion that the enemy might use some of the divisions drawn into reserve by this manœuvre to stage a counter-offensive in the north, was mistaken; but he was absolutely correct in stating that the Germans were retiring all down the front south of Arras, and that this necessitated radical modifications to the Nivelle plan. Not only was Nivelle loath to admit the force of this argument, but he resented Haig putting it forward at all.

*   *   *

Just as Calais had been the summit of Nivelle's rise, so London was the start of his decline. Thereafter, a series of events *in France* contributed inexorably to his downfall, with the ironical result that within a few weeks he found himself looking to Haig for his surest support. It is not the business of this book to enter into every detail of the days before the battles of Arras and the Aisne in April and May 1917. Yet the salient facts must be related, since they bore upon the higher direction of the war, and thus upon Wully's thoughts and actions at the time.

On March 15th, two days after the London Conference, Lyautey resigned, to be followed by Briand on the 17th and the fall of the French Government; a bad blow for Nivelle, since Briand had been responsible for appointing him C-in-C, and for backing him and his plan to the limit. The new Government was led by two men of very different outlook: Ribot, the Prime Minister, a financier; and Painlevé, the Minister for War. Painlevé, in particular, had deep doubts about the offensive, and sought principally to reduce French commitments and avoid further losses. Yet hesitant Ministers were not in themselves sufficient to deter Nivelle. Far more serious was the turn of events on the front, and the doubts of the French Army Group Commanders—Franchet d'Esperey (GAN: Groupe des Armées du Nord), Micheler (GAR: Groupe des Armées de Réserve), and Pétain (GAC: Groupe des Armées du Centre), who were to conduct the battle.

All during March, the German retirement gathered momentum. Interrogations of prisoners, the discovery of empty trenches, the conflagration of villages behind the enemy line, reports of every kind poured in from the British, and from their neighbour, the GAN, stationed opposite the larger of the two German salients, now quickly deflating. But still Nivelle was unmoved. Franchet d'Esperey was like a hound straining at the leash. He saw that unless he acted at once, the attack which he was mounting under the Nivelle plan would hit the air, and the Germans would gain the safety of their new line relatively undisturbed. He was not given his head until March 15th. By then it was too late; moreover, German devastations and booby-traps, and their rearguards, rendered the advance a comparatively slow and painful business; and it was clear that this part of the offensive would have to be recast.

None the less, it was an exhilarating experience recovering large areas of French territory, devastated though it was, and the Allied Press made a resounding victory out of it. Even Nivelle appeared to be caught by the contagion, but that was not the case with his principal subordinates, or even with certain members of his own faithful staff at GQG, who regarded the German move with foreboding. Would not enemy reserves now be available to strengthen his position at both ends of the Hindenburg Line, where the main British and French attacks were to go in? Particularly at the southern end, on the Aisne, where formidable new defence works had lately been observed? Did it not mean one thing, that the Germans were shrewdly aware of Allied plans?

But Nivelle seemed unperturbed. From an excess of caution, he now plunged into a paroxysm of impatience lest the Germans escape him, and retire even *beyond* the Hindenburg Line, before he could launch his great attack. Urging the British to keep pace with the GAN, he developed his theme at a conference on March 19th, and switched large contingents of men and material southward from the GAN to the GAR, in order to put even greater punch behind the grand assault, and exploit even more effectively the pursuit that would follow. This improvisation represented the first major break in his own meticulous preparations, and at a second conference on March 26th it was patent that the Army Group Commanders were badly worried. D'Esperey knew that his part had gone by the board, and that he could no longer provide the diversion upon which Micheler depended. As for Micheler himself, who commanded the greatest concentration of force of all, he was now doubtful of his chances and evasive in his manner. Pétain, whose Group, next in line, was to attack on the front east of Rheims, was frankly sceptical of the whole operation and never hesitated to say so. Nivelle, however, brushed all opposition aside and fixed anew the timetable for the attack: the British would open at Arras on April 8th, followed successively by the French Army Groups at intervals of several days. The only deterrent, which even he could not summarily dismiss, was the atrocious weather.

Meanwhile, another stream was beginning to flow against him. On March 24th Painlevé visited Haig, and gained a good impression of the efficiency, as well as of the morale, of the British troops and their commander. Here were no raw amateurs as he had been led to expect, and he paid close attention to the view of the battle which Haig put before him: not a quick break-through, but a series of limited advances, in short another struggle similar to the later stages of the Somme. This was the very thing that Painlevé feared most, and on his return to Paris he suffered a further shock in receiving a report (the Freycinet Report), which purported to originate with the staff of the GAR. It said briefly that in the changed circumstances the Nivelle plan would not work, and that it would only result in disappointment and severe casualties. Painlevé then took the irregular, but understandable, step of consulting the Army Group Commanders behind Nivelle's back. They only succeeded in deepening his depression, d'Esperey and Pétain repeating their criticisms, while Micheler for once spoke out frankly: his attack would make some headway, but it would not break through.

As a result of these interviews the French War Committee called Nivelle to Paris and put the case before him on April 3rd, but once again Nivelle carried the day by sheer force of confidence and personal conviction. Two days later the whole farce was played over again. On the 5th Painlevé received a new note, this time from Colonel Messimy, a former Minister of War, who (it was said) based his conclusions on a conversation with Micheler. It was the same story as before—the Nivelle plan was over-optimistic and out of date, and it could only bring disaster. The Government could not afford to ignore this second warning any more than the first; and so a full and final conference was called for April 6th at Compiègne, the new French HQ, to be attended by members of the War Committee, Nivelle, *and* his Army Group Commanders.

It was not a pleasant or even a convincing meeting, although a conclusion was indeed reached, namely that the offensive would go off as planned. Nivelle played his accustomed role, and both d'Esperey and Pétain were as plain spoken as before, but Micheler was confused and nervous and spoke ambiguously. It was, of course, an invidious thing to criticise one's commander to his face and before others; nevertheless, Micheler left an impression of moral cowardice. The arguments that carried most weight embraced the Allied situation at large. Revolution had broken out in Russia in mid-March, the Czar had abdicated, and it was doubtful whether the Russians would even stay in the war, let alone mount another offensive. The Italians were fearful and inactive. In short, the grand strategy of Chantilly had collapsed. Moreover, the U-Boats were gaining the upper hand, and only the declaration of war by the USA afforded a brighter prospect, but it would plainly be a long time before the Americans could take an effective part in the land fighting. Since, therefore, the war seemed once more to be swinging in favour of the Central Powers, it was essential to retain the initiative by striking now, and by striking so hard as to transform the whole of the Western front. Finally, the conference was reminded, the British were already committed, for the preliminary bombardment at Arras had begun.

*   *   *

As it happened, the weather was so bad that it was agreed to postpone the attack by one day, from April 8th to Easter Monday April 9th. Haig was as usual calm and confident, though aware of Nivelle's difficulties and of the precariousness of the French part in the offensive. He did not, of course, share Nivelle's desperate optimism, nor did he ever lose sight of the Flanders operation. He wrote to Wully on April 8th:

'I hear Nivelle has had trouble. Some of the French Govt wished to forbid the French Offensive altogether. But Nivelle has gained the day. I think this indicates the instability of purpose of our French Allies! and if anything goes wrong Nivelle will disappear!

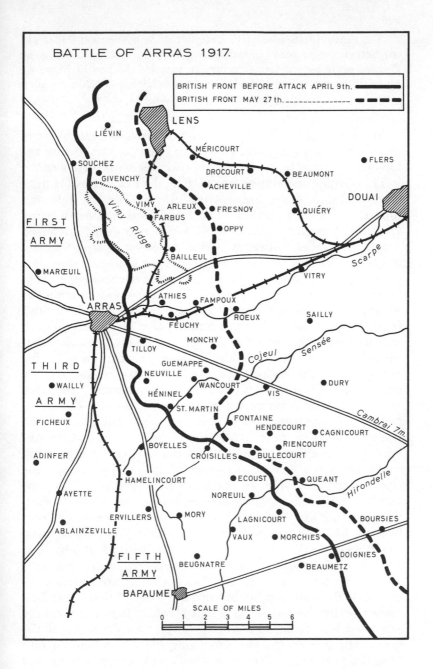

BATTLE OF ARRAS 1917.

BRITISH FRONT BEFORE ATTACK APRIL 9th. ——————
BRITISH FRONT MAY 27th. -----------------

LIÉVIN

LENS

MÉRICOURT

FLERS

SOUCHEZ

GIVENCHY

DROCOURT

BEAUMONT

ACHEVILLE

DOUAI

VIMY

ARLEUX

FRESNOY

QUIÉRY

FIRST

ARMY

FARBUS

OPPY

Vimy Ridge

BAILLEUL

MARŒUIL

VITRY

Scarpe

ATHIES

FAMPOUX

SAILLY

ARRAS

ROEUX

FÉUCHY

MONCHY

TILLOY

Cojeul

Sensée

THIRD

GUEMAPPE

NEUVILLE

WAILLY

WANCOURT

DURY

ARMY

HÉNINEL

VIS

FICHEUX

ST. MARTIN

FONTAINE

Cambrai 7m.

HENDECOURT

CAGNICOURT

ADINFER

BOYELLES

RIENCOURT

CROISILLES

BULLECOURT

HAMELINCOURT

ECOUST

QUEANT

AYETTE

NOREUIL

Hirondelle

ERVILLERS

MORY

LAGNICOURT

BOURSIES

ABLAINZEVILLE

VAUX

MORCHIES

FIFTH

DOIGNIES

ARMY

BEUGNATRE

BEAUMETZ

BAPAUME

SCALE OF MILES

0 1 2 3 4 5 6

'The grave question which I have to decide in the next few weeks is whether the present operations are likely to result in freeing the Belgian ports by the late summer. If, say, by the end of May, we are still before the line Lille–Valenciennes–Hirson–the Meuse, then preparations should be begun for the switch elsewhere.'

At Arras Haig's plan was to capture the northern hinge of the Hindenburg Line, and break into open country before the Germans were able to consolidate their rearward defences.

The opening assault was launched by the First Army (Horne) on the left and by the Third Army (Allenby) on the right and proved a brilliant success. The Canadians captured Vimy Ridge, just north of Arras itself, while two corps advanced nearly four miles eastwards astride the River Scarpe. Further south the attack went less well. In sum the Germans were tactically surprised and, in places, almost overwhelmed, so that by the end of the first day only a few men stood between the British and a break-through. For several reasons the British failed to profit from the opportunities they had themselves so magnificently created—due to the appalling weather that turned the torn battlefield into a morass, congestion of traffic, exhaustion of the troops, lack of effective liaison, and rigidity on the part of certain staff officers and commanders, who were at a loss to improvise once the set piece was over. Failure to press home the attack on April 10th and 11th allowed the enemy reserves to come up and consolidate the line. Moreover, with few concessions of importance, the Germans succeeded in containing all further attacks mounted against them during the rest of April and May. In the south the Fifth Army (Gough) fought a series of desperate actions, mainly round Bullecourt, where the initial assault had broken into the Hindenburg Line; but here, too, the battle petered out in the end. When the fighting closed down in the last week of May, the British had advanced 1–5 miles on a front of over 40 miles, captured 20,000 prisoners and more than 250 guns, for a loss of over 150,000 men. German casualties were probably not far short of this. Haig had known before the end of April that his effort here was virtually expended, and he began at once to prepare for the switch to the north. His sole reason for prolonging the Arras fighting into May was to assist and encourage the French, in a vain hope that

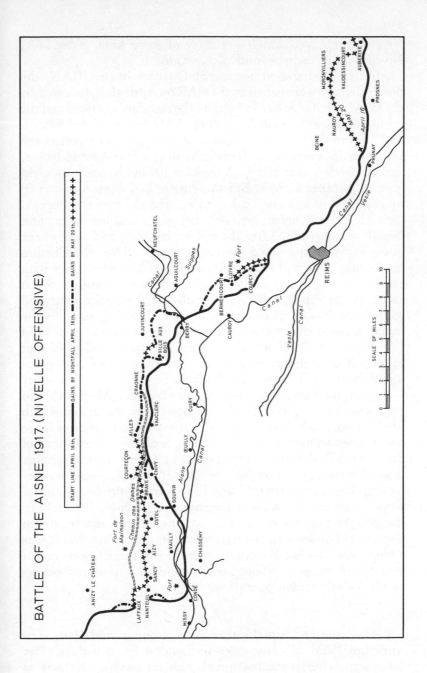

BATTLE OF THE AISNE 1917. (NIVELLE OFFENSIVE)

START LINE APRIL 16th. ——— GAINS BY NIGHTFALL APRIL 16th. ——— GAINS BY MAY 20th. +++++++

SCALE OF MILES

0 1 2 3 4 5 6 7 8 9 10

ANIZY LE CHÂTEAU

Fort de Malmaison

LAFFAUX

NANTEUIL

SANCY

AIZY

VAILLY

CHASSÉMY

Fort

CONDÉ

MISSY

Chemin des Dames

OSTEL

BRAYE

CHIVY

SOUPIR

ŒUILLY

CUIRY

COURTEÇON

AILLES

CRAONNE

VAUCLERC

VILLE AUX BOIS

JUVINCOURT

BERRY

Aisne

Canal

Suippes

Canal

AGUILCOURT

NEUFCHATEL

CAUROY

BERMERICOURT

LOIVRE Fort

COURCY

Canal

Vesle

Canal

Vesle Canal

REIMS

PRUNAY

BEINE

NAUROY

MORONVILLIERS

VAUDESSINCOURT

AUBERIVE

PROSNES

Vesle

Canal

May 20

April 16

Nivelle might yet snatch a victory of some kind. Tragically, Nivelle was already beyond effective aid.

After an abortive attack on St Quentin by.the GAN, the main offensive was opened by the GAR on April 16th, followed by the GAC one day later. Judged by the standards of the time, the result could not be called a failure. After four days the French had captured 20,000 prisoners and 150 guns, compelled the Germans to evacuate a large salient (Laffaux-Condé-Braye) and fall back on the Hindenburg Line behind it, and also yield ground in other sectors. But the enemy had been forewarned by captured orders and bad security, and the promised break-through did not occur, neither after 48 hours, nor later; and Nivelle was forced to alter the whole character and aims of the offensive by conducting a limited operation to free the Chemin des Dames ridge and relieve Rheims, and this indeed met with some success. But the cost was enormous—nearly 100,000 casualties by April 25th alone—and the disappointment and consequent loss of morale even greater. It led directly to the replacement of Nivelle on May 15th and the appointment of Pétain, first as Chief of Staff in Paris and then as C-in-C, and to a host of transfers and dismissals among staff and com-manders. It led also to outbreaks of mutiny in the French Army —the first on April 29th, the majority between May 25th and June 9th. In fact, the Nivelle offensive was the spark which fired a long train of accumulated unrest—due to lack of leave and proper welfare behind the lines, indifferent treatment of the wounded, defeatist propaganda, and general war fatigue. It was Pétain who saved the day, by suppressing disorder, cor-recting the worst abuses, humanising some of the conditions of service, and visiting a large number of units himself to talk to the officers and men. In this way he helped materially to restore confidence and the will to continue fighting, but it was a long, slow process. For many months the French were in an acutely precarious position, and this had an important bearing on Haig's subsequent operations.

*   *   *

Let us now pick up the threads in London and Paris. On April 9th Painlevé came over to London for two days. The Compiègne conference had given him no comfort, he was as apprehensive as ever about the forthcoming offensive, and deeply depressed by the Allied situation at large. He unloaded all his worries upon the Prime Minister, and found he had come to the right person at the right time. Not only did Lloyd George infuse him with his own indomitable energy and courage, dark though the horizon was, but he also impressed upon him the only possible advice about Nivelle at that late hour: namely, let him fight his own battle in his own way. That day the first reports came through from Arras, and Painlevé shared in the general upsurge of delight at the British Army's success; it boded well for the Aisne.

The next afternoon he paid a visit to Wully at the War Office. Their conversation touched on many of the subjects broached the previous day, notably the prospects in Italy and the Balkans. Wully reiterated his well-worn views. Greek politics remained as difficult and tangled as ever, and it was best to keep out of them. Although Sarrail was mounting another offensive, nothing conclusive could be expected from that front, if only because the U-Boats—now at the height of their depredations—rendered it absolutely impossible to transport the additional material and reinforcements which would be necessary to gain a decision. As to Italy—here Wully held his ground as firmly as ever, though much had happened since the Rome Conference at the beginning of the year. At the end of January, Cadorna had submitted his plan for an attack towards Trieste, backed by Allied troops and guns, but had been told that no such project could be entertained at least until after Arras and the Aisne. Next, Nivelle had gone to Italy in February, followed by Wully himself towards the end of March. Neither thought highly of the Italians, and it was due to Wully's representations that some of the more elderly commanders were replaced. He also issued a warning that the further the Italians pushed eastwards, the more they would lay themselves open to being cut off by an attack from the north— the very situation, in fact, created later by Caporetto. Cadorna, however, stuck to his plan and, supported by detachments of Allied heavy guns, eventually took the offensive in mid-May (Tenth Battle of the Isonzo, May 15th to June 8th), but it was all too late to be of any help to the fighting in France. Meanwhile, Foch had also gone to Italy early in April to work out a plan for reinforcing the Italians should the Germans attack. Wully was not against the idea in principle, but he told Painlevé that no troops could be sent now. The British and French Missions attached to Italian GHQ would keep him and the French War Office fully posted. Since Cadorna had claimed that he could hold up any attack through the Alps for three weeks, no emergency would be irretrievable for lack of time, though in the event it was to turn out a 'damned close-run thing'. He expressed his real feelings to Haig in a letter sent that night:

'I impressed upon him that what we must do was to insist on the Italians taking the offensive and of defending their own frontier if attacked, and that there could be no question of sending divisions, either French or British, at present. It would be folly to send them.'[31]

Although Wully had disposed of Italy for the time being, anyway so far as Painlevé was concerned, he had not done so for Lloyd George. On the very next day, April 11th, the Prime Minister met Ribot at Folkestone, and heard from him in closest confidence of the peace proposals lately put forward by the Austrian Emperor Karl. Although in the end these proposals came to nothing, for reasons which need not be investigated here, they served to strengthen Lloyd George in his firm belief that a large-scale Allied attack upon a faltering Austria from Italy held great possibilities. Moreover, he was privately determined that this should be the next step, should Nivelle fail, not Flanders.

As to Nivelle, Wully could now afford to be generous. All he had said and done at Calais, and all his warnings to the War Cabinet, had been justified up to the hilt. Handing the BEF over to Nivelle really meant handing it over to the French Government, and here they were trying to cancel a great offensive at the last moment, regardless of the fact that the British were already committed. The Arras attack, important though it was, formed only one part of the grand design. It would never have been launched in isolation. As it was, the whole plan was in serious jeopardy.

'. . . poor Nivelle is going into action with a rope round his neck. It is a horrible predicament for a Commander, and the worst of it is that one of his Army Commanders in the attack is not in favour of it. However the French may do better than I fear they will, in these circumstances. They are certainly beginning the fight under great disadvantages because of the cold water that has been thrown on Nivelle's plans. No more foolish or cruel thing can be done than to crab a man's plans once they have been approved. In fact no plan should ever be crabbed. It should either be accepted or rejected, and if accepted criticism should be silent.'[32]

He stated categorically that, if the French failed, it was essential to regain complete control over the BEF as soon as possible. This was an overriding necessity and he made it the subject of a Memorandum to the War Cabinet on April 17th, emphasising yet again the 'advisability of acquiring a greater share both in the diplomatic and military management of the war.'[33] Haig, of course, needed no persuading, but both agreed that they must wait for the right moment before taking action.

Everything therefore depended on the course of the fighting in France. What was happening? Wully found the obscurity and the waiting very hard to bear. But whereas the lack of news from the French was understandable, it was not so in the case of the British. Once more Wully found himself at the mercy of Haig's reluctance to pass on anything but the most laconic reports, and in desperation he sent Maurice over to France to find out what he could. His anxiety was evident in his next letter dated April 20th. It revealed again, too, his astonishing diffidence towards Haig, the only man in the British Army to whom he, the bluntest and most forthright of men, felt unable at times to speak his full mind.

'It is because Ministers are so apt to jump from one thing to another that I have occasionally in the past asked you to keep me informed a little as to what you have in your mind, so that I can meet their arguments in the way they would be met if you were here. I am not for one moment complaining of the want of information, as I have not felt the want of it recently and I shall get all I want, I have no doubt, when Maurice returns. I am merely saying what I have said before, namely, that it is necessary for you to tell me anything you care to tell me so that I can keep these people quiet.'

By now it was four days after the start of the French offensive, and he had no need to wait upon Maurice in order to sum up the situation over there. He saw it all only too clearly, and set down a reasoned and perceptive statement of the theory of warfare, as it had evolved on the Western front.

'I only wish to goodness the French had learned the lessons of the war as well as you have, and had realised that you cannot smash right through the deep and strong defences in the course of a day. Nivelle's prophecy of doing the trick in 24 to 48 hours and then pushing up a lot of other divisions was always to my mind most ridiculous, and I could never understand why he should have made such a statement. It is coming home to roost now and will be his undoing if he is not careful. It was a very silly theory for him to have advanced, and he seems to have entirely wasted the lessons of the last two years and a half. You know, I imagine better than most people, that every war has its own peculiarities and in certain important respects is totally different from its predecessors. To my mind no war has ever differed so much from previous wars as does the present one, and it is futile, to put it mildly, hanging on to old theories when facts show them to be wrong. At one time audacity and determination to push on regardless of loss were the predominating factors, but that was before the days of machine guns and modern armament. Of course there must still be audacity and determination to push on otherwise nothing would be done, but there is no doubt that in these days these qualities must be governed, and in practice they undoubtedly are governed, by the effects of modern fire and modern entrenchments. Your recent splendid operations are a proof of this so far as I at this distance am able to judge, for it seems to me that your success was mainly due to the most detailed and careful preparation, to thorough knowledge of the ground by battalions and batteries and the higher units, and to well observed artillery fire. It seems to me that these factors will continue to the end of the war to be vitally essential, and if they are not so regarded success will be rather in the nature of a fluke, and will probably entail heavier losses than will justify the few hundred yards of trench or additional village gained.

'I cannot help thinking that Nivelle has attached too much importance to what is called "breaking the enemy's front". The best plan seems to me to go back to one of the old principles, that of defeating the enemy's army. In other words, instead of aiming at breaking through the enemy's front, aim at breaking down the enemy's army, and that means inflicting heavier losses upon him than one suffers oneself. If this old principle is kept in view and the object of breaking the enemy's army is achieved the front will look after itself, and the casualty bill will be less. I apologise for breaking

out in this manner into a sort of Staff College lecture, but after all
lookers-on do see something of the game, and I believe that if
Nivelle's mind had been working a little differently he would not
have contemplated for a single moment getting right through the
enemy's defences in a couple of days, or at any rate saying that he
would be able to decide at the end of two days whether his operations had been successful or not. I have just turned up a Paper I
wrote in January with respect to his plan, a copy of which I sent
you, and I find that I was rather a true prophet as to what might
happen to his operations. I am sorry I was.'[34]

On April 24th Haig saw Nivelle at Amiens and received his
assurance that the offensive would be continued. On the 26th
he drove to Paris. That night he wrote to Wully:

'I have seen M. Ribot and also M. Painlevé. The former authorised me to tell you "that there is no intention on the part of the
French Govt to stop the offensive."

'I saw M. Ribot alone and he told me that he thought the moment
was not at all suitable for making a change in the higher command.
So I presume that Gen. Nivelle will remain in.

'Painlevé on the other hand struck me as anxious to put Pétain
into Nivelle's place.

'Which of the two (Ribot or Painlevé) will win the day it is
impossible to say at this moment.

'I found Painlevé much excited and had almost made himself
believe that the French had been defeated on the Aisne! Ribot was
quite calm. Both seemed greatly relieved by the confident feelings
which I expressed, and the *facts* as to the enemy's condition which
I put before them.'[35]

Haig also made clear to the French Ministers, as he had done
to Nivelle at Amiens and earlier, the prime need to clear the
Belgian coast before the autumn, and that he counted upon the
French Army to support him in this, the Flanders operation, in
the same way as the British Army was lending support now.
His concern was given added weight by the U-Boat campaign,
of which the news got worse every day. Wully wrote on April
26th:

'The situation at sea is very serious indeed. It has never been so
bad as at present, and Jellicoe almost daily pronounces it to be hopeless. There may soon be a serious shortage of food in this country,
and this has to be taken into consideration in regard to all theatres
of war.'[36]

Events were now moving towards a climax. On April 27th Lloyd George told Wully they must have a conference with the French very soon to clear the air. Wully passed this news on to Haig the next day, and received his reply by return on the 29th.

'Our plans in France will want careful handling. But my difficulties are for the moment increased by my not knowing who is the French Commander-in-Chief! Tonight I hear Pétain is to be "Adjutant General" or CIGS, with Nivelle still in Command in France.

'But whoever the nominal or actual C-in-C may be, we will be confronted with one and the same policy viz. that dictated by the French Govt. This policy, I feel sure, is to be based on avoiding losses while waiting for American reinforcements! Pétain calls this system "the aggressive defensive" and doubtless in his mind he imagines that the British Army will do all the "aggressive" part, while the French "squat" on the defensive.

'I hope to send you a paper tomorrow night giving my views on the situation. Meantime I think that the time has nearly come for me to take up the "alternative plan" in earnest. With this in view we should ask the French to relieve some of our Divisions on our right, while we relieve their Divisions on the Belgian Coast. But pressure on the German front must not be relaxed in the meantime in any way. This seems to me of first importance for the success of *our* plan.

'If I cannot come to an agreement with the French C-in-C (whoever he may be) on this question, it may be necessary to settle the matter when the conference is held.'[37]

On April 30th Haig told Gough (one of his Army Commanders) he was 'preparing for the Ypres operations, and that he would command the northern half of these operations.'[38] On May 1st he sent off to the War Cabinet an appreciation on the 'present situation and future plans', in which he stated that the enemy must be worn down further until so weakened that he was unable to withstand a decisive blow. For that, however, the situation was not yet ripe. In practice the Flanders operation was the next big move.

'Success seems reasonably possible. It will give valuable results on land and sea. If full measure of success is not gained, we shall be attacking the enemy on a front where he cannot refuse to fight, and our purpose of wearing him down will be given effect to. We shall be directly covering our own most important communications, and even a partial success will considerably improve our defensive positions in the Ypres salient. This is necessary in order to reduce the heavy wastage which must occur there next winter as in the past, if our troops hold the same positions.'[39]

That same day Wully telegraphed to Haig to meet him and Lloyd George in Paris on May 3rd. The conference would start on the 4th.

*   *   *

To end this section we must turn towards a familiar figure, who had recently come out of a year's semi-obscurity to stride back to the very centre of the stage—Henry Wilson. There was never any doubt about Wilson's abilities—his agile brain, his good work at the Staff College and the War Office before the war, above all his command of French and excellent relations with senior French officers. He was an outstanding personality, but his defects were as considerable as his gifts; and he had made powerful enemies by his political prejudices and the restlessness of his mind, committing him on several occasions to unwise statements and actions. He was commonly looked upon as an intriguer. Moreover, though prescient, he had been unlucky in some of his forecasts, and so had never acquired the authority of a successful prophet. All this had impeded his career, notably in January 1915 when Wully had been preferred as Chief of Staff to General French. Nevertheless, Wilson's next appointment as French's Liaison Officer with Joffre had turned out very well, a post that suited him exactly, and he held it until the end of the year. At the general switch of high positions, however, which then followed, he entered a period of relative decline. Haig distrusted him, and as commander of IV Corps he was not a success, though it would be unfair to blame him for an unfortunate incident in May 1916, when one of his divisions lost ground and prisoners to a sudden German attack on a sector of Vimy Ridge. With the advent of Lloyd George his prospects improved, and shortly before Asquith resigned he was nominated chief military representative on the Mission to Russia under Milner. He attended the Rome Conference early in January 1917, shortly before the Mission departed, and returned from Russia on March 2nd, barely ten days before the Revolution broke out. He thus walked slap into the Nivelle affair.

It will be remembered that at the Calais Conference, which had just taken place, Nivelle had demanded Wilson as British Chief of Staff at GQG. Although Wilson had had no hand in this—he could not possibly have done so, being away in Russia—very naturally it did nothing to improve his standing with Wully or Haig. But Lloyd George was in favour of the idea, and when it was finally agreed to substitute a British Mission for a Staff, he insisted that Wilson should be in charge of it, with the title of Chief Liaison Officer, and he got his way. It was a repetition, in fact, of the post Wilson had held in 1915, but now—with the rise in size and status of the BEF—it had assumed far greater importance. Moreover, Wilson had a critically important role in interpreting Nivelle to Haig and Haig to Nivelle—alleviating Nivelle's arrogance and assuaging Haig's *amour propre*—and generally in establishing that mutual confidence between commanders, which was essential to the success of the offensive.

Soon after Wilson returned to England he heard the whole story of Calais from The Monument, and it filled him with foreboding. He disliked intensely the way he had been brought into the scheme of things and considered he had been placed in an impossible position. On March 12th he met Haig at the London Conference (called to straighten out the difficulties following on Calais), heard his version of the matter, and recorded his reply in his Diary in these terms:

'I first made my own position quite clear—viz., that I knew nothing of all these manœuvres. I thought them stupid, and I would not be mixed up in any way. I said that what was wanted was a *perfectly clear* definition of his position *vis-à-vis* Nivelle, and that once this was done there would be no place for me, and that, rather than accept an equivocal position, I would prefer going on half-pay, and I would go on half-pay. Haig said that he would not hear of such a thing and begged me to accept the post of Chief Liaison Officer.'[40]

In the end, according to his Diary, he was prevailed upon by a combination of Wully, Haig, Nivelle, Derby, and the King to accept, but he reserved to himself the right to resign at any moment.

Thus it was that Wilson was involved in the labour and actual *accouchement* of the Arras and Aisne offensives. He crossed to France on March 17th, the day that the Briand Government fell, attended Nivelle's conferences with his Army Commanders on March 19th and 26th—where he particularly noted Pétain's pessimism—and was soon aware that the new administration was having deep doubts of the whole offensive. Nivelle told him personally of all that had transpired at the final meeting at Compiègne on April 6th, two days after it had happened. When the Aisne attack was launched ten days later, he watched part of the fighting and soon realised that the promised victory would not be forthcoming. He felt sure then that Nivelle was doomed.

On April 22nd he lunched with Esher and expounded his ideas about the shape of future operations: There were three alternatives:

'1. Somme—i.e. wearing down the Boches.
2. Verdun—i.e. whirlwind attack.
3. Pétain—i.e. do nothing.

'We have tried 2 (Verdun), which has been a complete failure. There remain Somme and Pétain. To my mind the Pétain plan is one to be avoided, and a Somme, with intelligence, is our only chance.'[41]

All this tallied in essence with the way Wully and Haig were thinking. They all hoped that Nivelle would not be replaced at this juncture, and they all agreed that it was essential to keep up the pressure against the Germans. Such was the gist of the message which Wilson brought to Lloyd George at the end of April, when together with Wully he pressed the Prime Minister to speak in these terms at the conference in Paris on May 4th.

9

Chief of the Imperial General Staff: May to July 1917

THE events of the next three months—May, June, July: the prelude to Third Ypres—are not easy to disentangle. They were charged with pressures on both sides of the Channel, and their precise significance is still disputed. There were, however, a number of threads leading through the labyrinth. One was Haig's iron determination to fight in Flanders; another, Lloyd George's abhorrence of a 'second Somme' and preference for a campaign in Italy; a third, Pétain's caution. Around these, in an intricate skein, wound most of the actions and reactions of their colleagues.

On May 3rd Haig and Pétain had a preliminary meeting in Paris, at which Haig gave notice of his intentions in general terms, Pétain concurring. Later, the British commander saw Wully and Lloyd George, who had just arrived. The Prime Minister was for the moment well disposed towards Haig, but he was anxious lest the French give up all ideas of offensive action. On the 4th the morning was devoted to a conference between the generals—Haig, Wully, Pétain, and Nivelle—who appeared without difficulty to reach agreement along the following lines. The offensive would go on, the British to bear the brunt, but the French would give active support and take over part of the British line. As to method, no attempt at a breakthrough in the Nivelle fashion was contemplated. Instead, the enemy must be worn down by continual attacks with limited objectives, using artillery to the full. Details of all future plans were to be kept absolutely secret, even from the Governments. After lunch Haig

'walked with L.G. across the Seine to the trees of the Champs Elysées, expecting Robertson to join us under the shade for the day was very hot. Wully, however, found the combination of new breeches, riding boots, a big lunch and the hot sun too much for him to face a walk! So he got into a car after walking a few yards and went direct to the hotel. We accordingly went and joined him there, and the Prime Minister discussed the situation with us in the sitting-room.'[1]

Later that day and on May 5th the full conference confirmed the military decisions and reviewed the situation outside France, notably in the Balkans. Lloyd George made a strong speech in support of the generals and endorsed their demand for secrecy. As to Salonika, he now threw his weight into the scales *against* a big offensive there, for reasons heartily approved and already advanced by Wully. Whatever the pros and cons of the Balkan front, shipping had always been the controlling factor. With the U-Boats threatening the very survival of Britain herself, it had become urgently necessary to reduce the entire British land commitment in that area and save ships in the Mediterranean. Recently the Prime Minister had compelled the Navy to adopt the convoy system, and he was in process of forcing through far-reaching changes in the structure and personnel of the Admiralty. The whole subject, therefore, dominated his mind, and at Paris he was determined to have his way. He announced his firm intention to withdraw at least one British division and two cavalry brigades from Salonika, and rode down all the protests of the Allies. He also managed to restrain the French, (still bent on violence against the Greeks), while conceding them certain diplomatic advantages. His action led directly to the virtual settlement of the whole internal problem of Greece at the London Conference at the end of May, and to the events that emanated from that: namely, the expulsion of the King, the restoration of Venizelos as Prime Minister of a united country, and the full participation of the Greek forces in the war.

Wully was, of course, delighted. He told Esher that the Paris Conference was 'the best we have ever held'.[2] Calais had been abrogated at last, and now it seemed that the bogey of Salonika was being laid too. They were all agreed on the new policy in France, and that meant that the Flanders operation would go ahead. Moreover, it appeared that henceforward the British would dominate the direction of the war, as their military and naval preponderance and economic resources entitled them to do.

But appearances were deceptive. The Arras and Aisne offensives were within sight of closing down. Nivelle had only a few more days as C-in-C, while Pétain—whatever his sentiments at the conference—was deeply depressed about the future. The grim and hidden fact was that the French Army was on the edge of collapse. Although the worst was yet to come, some units had already mutinied, and Pétain had every right to be apprehensive. For the time being, however, the news was suppressed and the fighting prolonged.

Meanwhile, Haig was getting ahead with his preparations. On May 5th he sent a letter to Nivelle, explaining his intentions in greater detail, and asked him to be ready to relieve part of the line. He proposed to keep up the pressure at Arras, and launch a new attack on the Messines-Wytschaete Ridge early in June, as a necessary preliminary to the main offensive in the north later. Nivelle never replied to this letter, but before his dismissal on May 15th he indicated to Henry Wilson at Compiègne his willingness to help. On May 7th Haig saw his Army Commanders at Doullens, and gave them an account of the Paris Conference as it affected the BEF. Flanders was 'on', and would be divided into two phases as stated: first, Messines under Plumer; then Ypres under Gough, with Rawlinson to command the coastal attack. This was not, of course, the first time that the operation had been discussed at Army level. Plans had been drawn and redrawn at least since the beginning of 1916, but the campaigns of Verdun and the Somme had put paid to it that year. After the Chantilly Conference in November, however, it had been restored to the programme and—as already explained—secured to follow the British and French offensives in the south in the early part of 1917. Thus detailed planning had merely been resumed, and Haig's present discussion was—with a few modifications (notably Gough's appointment, a recent decision)—by way of confirming long and careful preparations.

But Flanders was an unlucky scheme, with an unlucky history, and clouds were soon gathering, seemingly to prevent its execution yet again. On May 12th Haig received a warning from Wully to the effect that the Russian débâcle and the unsettled conditions in France might affect the decisions reached in Paris. On the 14th Henry Wilson confirmed the melancholy fact that no one knew who really was in command of the French Army, though on the 15th the news of Nivelle's dismissal came through, and of his succession by Pétain. Foch was to take Pétain's place as Chief of Staff in Paris.

By this time the War Cabinet had become deeply perturbed. The minutes of the Paris Conference, as issued by the French Government, omitted any mention of agreement by the French to continue offensive action; and Wully was instructed to inform Haig accordingly. That same day, May 16th, he telegraphed to the effect that the War Cabinet would only support the British offensive 'on the express condition that the French also play their full part as agreed.' Furthermore, Haig was to make this clear in his talks with the French general in effective command, whoever he might be, Nivelle, Pétain, or Foch. Any idea of fighting alone—hence of incurring heavy casualties without adequate gains—would not be countenanced.[3]

Wully followed this up with a letter dated May 17th:

'I am afraid I have bombarded you rather with telegrams recently concerning your proposed discussion with the French Commander-in-Chief, whoever he may be, but the Cabinet are very anxious, and quite rightly so, about the matter. As you know, Pétain and Nivelle both made out at our Conference that they intended to fight; they also seemed to agree so far as they were concerned to the relief of the French divisions on the coast; and they also agreed to study the question of taking over part of your line. There is no doubt about it that at the back of the French mind there is a strong desire to avoid casualties, and after all that is only another way of saying that they do not want to fight. The Cabinet are quite consistent in the desire to support our views as to the necessity for continuing a real offensive action, but at the same time they are equally desirous of the French doing their share, because if they do not, it is quite clear you will have all the German divisions which can be scraped together on the top of you, and we shall find ourselves at the end of the year with depleted divisions and the French will not. This will not be good from many points of view.

'It is a very difficult matter for you to deal with because of course you cannot guarantee that the French will do what they promise, but you can form a pretty good idea; *and at any rate you should make your doubts known to the Cabinet if you have any.* . .'[4]

So everything depended upon Haig's interview with his French counterpart, Pétain, and a meeting was fixed at Amiens for May 18th. Before this Henry Wilson was commissioned to find out from Pétain himself whether he was empowered to speak and act with full authority, in other words—was he, Pétain, the man really responsible for future French plans and operations? Pétain's reply was unequivocal—yes.

At Amiens everything passed off surprisingly well. Haig was favourably impressed by Pétain's open manner and quiet, business-like answers; and he was reassured by his clear promise of support. Pétain began his part of the conversation by reaffirming his own position, and spoke with candour of the unrest in the French Army. None the less, he repeated his intention of fulfilling the Paris agreement and of supporting the British Army wholeheartedly. He had, he said, four attacks in preparation, and named two: one at Malmaison on June 10th (not launched till October), and another at Verdun timed for the end of July (actually August 20th). Haig then disclosed his own plans and handed over a summary and sketch. His intention was to break the enemy defences north and east of Ypres, capture Roulers and Thourout (with its important railway junction), and advance north-east to Ostend and Zeebrugge. The attack at Nieuport and the landing on the Belgian coast would follow, directly the main offensive had made ground. Pétain criticised these plans on the grounds that they were too ambitious. The objectives were too distant—Thourout alone was more than a dozen miles from the Ypres salient—and this contravened the agreement on 'limited' offensives. However, it was essential that the British should attack, and how they did it was their business. Haig replied that the operation was really a series of attacks, each with a limited objective, but it would also allow for the exploitation of success, once the enemy showed signs of breaking; moreover, the strategic possibilities were tremendous—the capture of the U-Boat bases and the clearance of the coast, leading to the recovery of a large part of Belgium, with its vital communications system serving the northern part of the enemy front. As to reliefs—Pétain was willing to hand over the coastal sector at Nieuport and for a Franco-Belgian force (altered later to the First French Army under General Anthoine) to co-operate on the left of the main offensive at Ypres. Elsewhere he could only agree to limited reliefs of the British line. As a result of this meeting, Haig reported to London his entire satisfaction that the French would co-operate in the full spirit of the Paris decisions.

But—as so often happened in negotiations of this kind—personal encounters proved deceptive. It had been so with Nivelle. It would be so with Pétain. Although Haig was reassured by the Amiens meeting, Henry Wilson was not. Wilson, furthermore, was far more knowledgeable of French affairs than Haig, and far more closely attuned to the mentality of the French leaders. He was aware, too, of the deep depression caused by the Aisne, the general war weariness of the nation, and the desire to avoid further casualties. He distrusted Pétain's promises of attack, and sure enough when the latter confirmed his verbal agreement with Haig in writing, the total of attacks had diminished in number, while their dates mostly failed to correspond with the British operations they were supposed to assist. The truth was that Pétain did not believe in the success of any *big* offensive in 1917, nor was he alone in this. He envisaged only small-scale fighting and spoiling attacks, while relying upon a final effort with American help in 1918. Furthermore, he was thinking in these terms before Amiens, and for a variety of reasons, of which the state of the French Army was only one. Finally, he and Wilson were antipathetic, and their antipathy led directly to Wilson's resignation as Chief Liaison Officer at GQG on June 26th. Thus an important link between the British and French High Commands, and their Governments, was temporarily severed, for although the Mission continued, no one could insert himself into the confidence of the French as Wilson could with Foch, or had done with Nivelle.

Any doubts, however, about Pétain's *immediate* intentions were quickly resolved by events. A week after Amiens, the mutiny in the French Army began to take a more serious turn. Pétain realised at once that half-measures would no longer do, and that it was useless to expect the men to go on fighting until radical reforms had been made as to conditions of service and, above all, to the provision of leave as of right. The Army would need a long period of rest and rehabilitation. Although the news was kept a close secret, and so successfully that it never reached the enemy in any tangible form until too late, Pétain had no hesitation in telling Haig. On June 2nd he sent him his Chief of Staff, General Debeney, with instructions to hold nothing back, and to say specifically that the Malmaison attack would have to be postponed. In fact, apart from 'artillery offensives' on the Aisne and in the Champagne, no French attack could be expected before the end of July. There was, however, no suggestion that the French would fail to play their part at Ypres.

Haig was now faced with a critical decision. Should he pass on the news to the War Cabinet or not? If he did, as *prima facie* it was his duty to do, then almost certainly he would be ordered to call off his own attack at Messines, now only five days away, since the Government had laid down that French support was a *sine qua non* in any British offensive action. On the other hand, Pétain's message was a military secret of the utmost gravity, and Haig well knew the consequences of divulging anything confidential to any but those who absolutely needed to know it. Nivelle's loquacity was only too fresh in his mind. In the end, confident that Messines would succeed and that its success would directly affect the reception of his larger plans for Ypres, he kept the information to himself.

By acting as he did, Haig undoubtedly left himself open to criticism. It may be argued, however, that not only was his action justifiable on the grounds given, but in fact justified by the result. The capture of Messines Ridge, a heavily-fortified position just south of the Ypres salient, was carried out with complete success by the Second Army (Plumer). This was *par excellence* an example of siege warfare with a strictly 'limited objective'. Preparations had been going on for over a year. Shortly after 3.0 am on June 7th nineteen huge mines were exploded under the German forward defences, followed by an artillery barrage of great depth and intensity. The principal position was soon taken, but the fighting continued for a week before the operation was over. Casualties exceeded 24,000, most of them incurred after the opening assault. At one point it was planned to exploit this success by gaining ground at the junction with the Ypres salient, and so improve the starting positions for the main offensive later; but the idea was abandoned. Whether the halt was tactically correct or not was, in fact, irrelevant. Haig could not proceed with the second phase at

Ypres without first securing the sanction of the War Cabinet; and that is what the next month was spent in doing.

Meanwhile, Lloyd George was by no means unaware of the way things were going in France. He had been doubtful of French intentions since the end of April, and his doubts were increased when, on June 8th, Henry Wilson reported personally to the War Cabinet his apprehensions of French morale, and the fact that Pétain had been unable to support Messines. Wilson also saw Wully. His message was emphatic and clear. It was absolutely necessary to win a victory somewhere, military or diplomatic, in order to keep the French in the war. He did *not* believe in waiting until 1918. While all this strengthened members of the War Cabinet in their resolve to stand by the policy agreed in Paris, it inclined the Prime Minister more than ever to seeking the required victory in Italy, or even in Egypt, where Allenby was shortly going to take over the command from Murray.[5] Lloyd George had never lost sight of the Italian plan, and it was enhanced at this time by the current (though limited) successes of the Italian Army at the Tenth Battle of the Isonzo, and by his knowledge of the secret Austrian peace proposals. Wully, of course, was totally opposed to any kind of Eastern solution, while members of the War Cabinet were divided. It was at this point of acute crisis and complexity that the Prime Minister decided to appoint a new body, the War Policy Committee, to undertake a comprehensive review and arrive at a considered strategic decision. Hankey wrote:

'The War Policy Committee consisted of Lloyd George, Curzon, Milner, and Smuts (who had just become a member of the War Cabinet), but Bonar Law was kept in the closest touch with their work and was virtually a member. I was the secretary, and I had to carry out this task without any assistance. The Committee had to conduct its investigations without interfering with the daily meetings of the War Cabinet, where day-to-day decisions had to be taken over a vast field. The new Committee, therefore, used to meet at an early hour and twice the members dined together and continued their deliberations late into the night. The Committee managed to hold sixteen meetings between June 8th and June 20th when the results of the enquiry were laid before a full meeting of the War Cabinet, and the final conclusions were reached.'[6]

Wully was one of the principal witnesses called by the Committee,[7] and was present at many of the discussions. He also took a leading part in the second and most important stage of all, as from June 19th, when for a whole week he and Haig defended the merits of the Flanders plan together. Indeed, his contributions to the summer discussions of 1917 all through were of historical importance, and revealed the deepening dilemma in which he found himself after the Paris Conference of early May.

* * *

At Paris Wully had been at the summit of his influence and authority. He had been proved superbly right about Nivelle. He had foreseen the fallacies of the Aisne, and he had stood almost alone between the BEF and an ignoble, impracticable scheme of command, connived at by his own Prime Minister. The conference of May 4th–5th had been his vindication— even Lloyd George had been his ally then—and he stood out as the man who had never wavered, stronger than ever in the trust and affection of the Army which he served. And so he stood, too, in the general mind of the nation which, ignorant of the stresses he had to withstand, looked upon him as a father-figure of immovable resolution and good sense.

But if Paris represented the end of a long struggle uphill, it also signalled the start of a gradual descent. Thereafter Wully found himself, not only conducting a familiar and wearing tussle with the Prime Minister, but subject also to disturbing reservations about the campaign in Flanders, to which as a Westerner he was strategically committed. In short, he was torn by a conflict of convictions, and in the struggle to resolve it he was ground down between the millstones of Haig and Lloyd George. In the end he supported Haig, as he was bound to do, but it cost him his influence and ultimately his job.

The Prime Minister's views on strategy were well established and well known. He saw no real prospect of beating the Germans in France, and hated the idea of further massive attacks and murderous casualties. He preferred to 'knock away the props', principally the Austrians, by concentrating Allied effort in Italy in order to take Trieste. Success there, if vigorously exploited, might help revive the stagnant fronts in the Balkans and Eastern Europe, cut Bulgaria and Turkey off from Germany and put them out of the war. After that all the Allies could round on the principal enemy together. Simultaneously he hoped to see the Turks driven out of Palestine, or at least give up Jerusalem, the capture of which—it was said—'would please the Welsh'![8] He was strongly opposed by both Wully and Haig on the grounds that the capture of Trieste would *not* mean the end of the Austrians, whom the Germans would never allow to collapse and whom they could easily reinforce by interior lines of communication. Moreover, the Italian front was highly vulnerable from the north, ill served by road and rail from France, and too restricted to allow the build-up of an overpowering concentration of force. Cadorna's competence was also in doubt. Finally, the weakening of the front in France, which the Italian project would entail, might well let the Germans through. The other fronts were largely a matter of logistics, but—apart from Russia (now a hopeless case)—they could never be decisive.

Haig's ideas were no less positive than those of Lloyd George, and totally opposed to them. He was sure that the Germans could be, indeed had to be, beaten in France. Despite the relief in the east afforded it by the Russian Revolution, he thought that the German Army had suffered severely in men, material, and morale, and would be unable to stand up to another big battering of the kind contemplated. He considered that a successful offensive in Flanders would not only stifle the U-Boats and reduce the nuisance of air raids on London, but might lead to a quick ending of the war on land. He felt certain that the BEF was the only army capable of doing the job, and that if necessary it could do it alone. This was, of course, a point of keen controversy. Haig had been specifically warned not to attack without French support, and although Messines had had to be a lone operation, there was no knowing whether Pétain would make good the rest of his promises. In the event they were ultimately, though tardily, fulfilled by Anthoine's First Army at Third Ypres, and by the local diversionary attacks at Verdun and Malmaison during the offensive. It is true that Haig had small faith in the value of such support (though it turned out useful enough in the end), and paid it little more than lip service in fulfilling the conditions laid down by the War Cabinet. In reality he was impelled by quite a contrary consideration: namely, the need to engage the main strength of the Germany Army in the west in order to protect the French in their weakness. He was encouraged to believe this for several reasons. One was Pétain's confidential revelations of the state of the French Army (which Haig never passed on to the War Cabinet) and the corollary that the British should attack and continue to attack, although Pétain did not ask for, nor did he believe in, a full-scale offensive such as Third Ypres. Another was Haig's own estimate of the decline in fighting power of the French Army, and in national morale, formed long before he heard the worst from Pétain, but afterwards confirmed by keen observers such as Henry Wilson and Esher. In the event all these considerations served his purpose, nor did their apparent contradictions render them invalid as *bona fide* arguments for Third Ypres. The French Army did give support and it did need protection; there was factual proof of both. The other difficulty related to Haig's belief in the deterioration of the German Army. If that was true, how could it be said to menace the French? The answer, in his opinion, was— time. Given time to recover, the Germans might renew the offensive in west or east, against the French temporarily unsettled after the Aisne, or against the Russians who were in a yet more serious predicament. By attacking that summer Haig believed he could not only relieve his two Allies and bring them through the winter, but go far towards defeating the Germans outright. Finally, he feared that if he stood on the defensive in France, the BEF might be milked of men and guns for the benefit of the Italians—to his mind a lunatic proposal.

So much for the two opposing views of strategy, east and west, as represented by Lloyd George and Haig at this stage of the war.

Although a Westerner, Wully held an intermediate position, Maurice beside him.

Broadly he stood right behind Third Ypres, as a long-agreed plan with real strategic possibilities. It had been awaiting execution at least since the Chantilly Conference of November 1916, not to mention its earlier history, and nothing that had happened since then had in any way diminished its urgency. Rather, the contrary. Wully accepted the arguments advanced by the Admiralty, agreed entirely with Haig about Italy, and as to Russia he told Repington:

'He doubts whether the Russians will do anything for a hundred years, for the nation behind the Army is no good for anything "except music and dancing and tommy-rot love stories".'[9]

But Wully did not go with Haig all the way. He did *not* believe that the BEF should fight unsupported, hence his urgent messages to Haig before the latter met Pétain on May 18th. Neither did he hold such sanguine views about the state of the German Army in France. Haig had been briefed by Charteris, Director of Intelligence at GHQ, always over-optimistic, while Wully relied upon Macdonogh at the War Office, a far more realistic adviser, with better sources of information. Wully was also doubtful of Haig's tactics, or rather of Gough's, whose Fifth Army was to open the battle. Haig had picked Gough (a cavalryman) for his youth and his dash, in preference to Plumer or Rawlinson, whom he considered too cautious. The choice was a hint of Haig's ultimate aim, a break-through and a pursuit, and bore a horrid resemblance to the pattern of the Somme and the Aisne, although the tactical method was declared to be that of the limited offensive. In other words each successive ridge or objective would be taken by a fully-mounted and defined attack, an adaptation of the Pétain principle to which Wully fully subscribed, though he did not acknowledge Pétain as the originator, saying rather it had evolved out of the experience of past fighting. The difficulty lay, of course, in limiting each step *in a continuous offensive*. Messines had been correct for it had been complete in itself. Third Ypres would depend on the success of each component step. What would happen to the battle if one of the components failed? If it was broken off, according to the book, then the campaign would halt without completing its strategic purpose, and a lot of lives and effort would have been expended for nothing. If it was kept going, then Wully feared it might indeed degenerate into a second Somme, a human holocaust that he was as concerned as the Prime Minister to avoid.

Then there was the terrain. Wully had a shrewd idea of the difficulties, both from his own knowledge of Flanders earlier in the war, and from the opinions of others. Part had been inundated already. The remainder, with its high water table, heavy clays, and intricate system of land drainage, was highly vulnerable to bad weather and to the destructive effect of artillery. Since bombardments and barrages had now reached an unheard-of intensity, Flanders was not a good place to conduct a siege battle. There was no lack of criticism on this score. Foch particularly had 'wanted to know who it was who wanted Haig to go on a "duck's march through the inundations to Ostend and Zeebrugge".'[10] Repington had also unwittingly warned Wully about 'Low Country fighting'.

'I said that you can fight in mountains and deserts, but no one can fight in mud and when the water is let out against you and, at the best, you are restricted to the narrow fronts on the higher ground, which are very unfavourable with modern weapons. I reminded him of our past failures in the low-lying lands, and urged him to keep away from them. He listened so attentively that I think some operation in this sense may be in the wind.'[11]

Even so it is rare that a single factor determines a plan, which is usually decided by a process of balancing pros and cons. Where else was there on the British front that had not either been worn out by earlier fighting (such as the Somme), or that offered such strategic advantages? Moreover, mud and water might not be such a bogey if the fighting was done in the summer when the ground was hard, as proved to be the case during the few dry spells of the actual offensive. In general, however, the weather for Third Ypres turned out appalling and the timing most unfortunate. Moreover, many good dry days were lost between Messines and the opening day of the offensive on July 31st, and again during the intermission in September, a loss which can bear both criticism and extenuation. But one of the ironies of the war derived from delays over which neither Wully nor Haig had any control, for instance the substitution of Nivelle's plan for Joffre's early in 1917, or at a local level the lack of readiness by the French First Army (Anthoine) due to the absence of a large number of men on leave, following Pétain's new dispensation. On the other hand the protracted discussions of Haig's plans, imposed by the War Cabinet in June and July, although unsettling for the C-in-C, did not—it is thought—affect the final date.

But Wully's chief reservation related to manpower, for apart from the human waste and horror of a siege battle, there was the primary problem of finding enough men to fight, let alone replacing them when killed or wounded. It will be recalled that at the end of 1916 the Army's requirement of men for 1917 had been estimated at 940,000—a figure accepted by the Asquith Government, together with the recommendation that the military age be raised to 55, and that all men up to that age 'be utilised for such national service as H.M. Government deem to be essential to the effective prosecution of the war.' For the soldiers this meant that, with reasonable allowance for other employments, the Army would have first call on all manpower. It did not work out that way. Under Lloyd George the terms were less strictly interpreted and other priorities admitted, particularly ship-building and agriculture.

Wully, however, never ceased to press his case by one means or another. In February 1917 he persuaded the Army Council to take the matter up again. By way of solution, the War Cabinet merely suggested reducing the number of battalions per division from twelve to nine as had already happened in Germany and France. This was no solution at all. Whereas the Germans had resorted to it to increase the total of their divisions, the French had done so because they were running out of men. Britain still had the men, if they could be extracted from other occupations, and they were desperately needed to bring the existing formations up to strength. Raising the total of divisions solved nothing, besides which there was a real shortage of trained staffs. Further representations followed and met with some response, but the monthly Army intake was running at about half the original estimate when, on May 31st, a new statement was submitted by the Adjutant-General.[12] In reviewing the shortcomings of the previous twelve months, he quoted a recent attempt to release 215,000 men from Government departments and from industry for military service, which had resulted in the calling up of exactly *one man*! Lord Derby, Secretary of State for War, commented:

'. . . it seems clear that, practically, the Army is now provided with men only after all other needs of the Nation have been cared for. Unless this policy is changed, the strength of the Army will continue rapidly to diminish, and, so far as military operations are concerned, our chances of winning the war will be correspondingly reduced.

'. . . the [Army] Council believe that no completely satisfactory solution of the question of Man-Power will be obtained until it is found possible to adopt a system of general liability to National Service, as suggested by the Military Members in their Memorandum of November 28th last.'[13]

Wully left Haig in no doubt as to the prospect. On May 26th he wrote:

'Lord Derby and I had a long talk with the Prime Minister last night on the subject and as an indication of what the position is I may say that the Prime Minister told us that he was afraid the time had now arrived when we must face the fact that we could not expect to get any large number of men in the future but only scraps. He said this because of the large demands for ship-building, food production, and labour unrest, and I am afraid that there is no getting away from the fact that there is great unrest in this country as a result partly of the Russian revolution. There have been some bad strikes recently and there is still much discontent. An announcement even appeared in some of the newspapers yesterday with regard to the calling together of a committee of workmen and soldier delegates to consider the political situation. This shows the way the wind is apt to blow.'

Wully was not exaggerating. The summer of 1917 was almost as critical a period for Britain as for the other belligerents. Deep into its third year, the war seemed no nearer an end than in 1914. The country was in an uncertain temper. The daily diet of casualty lists, sacrifices, and privations had depleted the reserves of resilience and determination, and there was an actual shortage of food. Daylight air raids on London, though puny by Second War standards, caused quite disproportionate alarm. Strikes were a symptom of war weariness and social unrest, and the example of Russia presented a mixed horizon of hopes and horrors. All this—quite apart from the inherent intractability of the problem—was an added deterrent to settling the manpower question in the way that Wully wanted. Labour, Lloyd George told him, would not stand any further compulsion. Wully disagreed. He was not unsympathetic. He was accustomed to talking to the Trades Unions. As the son of a village postman he knew well what working men and their families had to put up with, and he was keenly aware that the Military Service Acts were working unjustly.

'The majority of "Labour" was quite as determined to see the war through, and to accept the sacrifices which that entailed, as was the majority of any other part of the nation. What "Labour" did not want was a continuance of the system which opened the door to log-rolling and corruption as to who should be sent to the front and who should be kept back. Under the existing system young men employed in munition factories, in agriculture, on the railways, remained safely at home, some of them receiving wages of £15 to £20 a week, while older men from the same factory, farm, or station, were sent into the trenches on a mere pittance. Possibly the latter class were released from their work because their employers deemed them to be less efficient, but they were not likely to believe that they were, and so long as the selection was left to the judgment of an individual, however capable and impartial he might be, a sense of unfair discrimination was bound to prevail. The simplest and fairest plan was to make all and sundry alike liable to serve, and then, within the limits of the number allotted, use for the fighting line the youngest first.

'Mr Lloyd George became Prime Minister at a time when the people were ready to give their political leaders full liberty of action, and he enjoyed the further advantage of having the experience of the past two years to guide him as to what was required and what could be done. So far as man-power was concerned, he made poor use of these opportunities, and under his management the situation became not better but worse.'[14]

The fact was that the tribunals were too lenient, and the protected occupations too defensive and entrenched, to let anyone go unless compelled to do so. When plans were made to withdraw men from certain industries, strikes broke out, and the plans came to nothing. The Government was not as yet prepared to exert outright compulsion for the reasons given, but also because Lloyd George revolted emotionally against the demands of the Westerners—and here was an effective means of blocking them.

Wully wanted half-a-million men by July, but he never got them. Although the BEF reached its peak in manpower in the summer of 1917,[15] it went into battle in Flanders under-strength.[16] It took at least three months to train a man for war in France,[17] and so Third Ypres was fought by veterans and by men recruited at the end of 1916 and in the early part of 1917. The loss of a quarter of a million men at Ypres was never made good, hence the Army was on the decline from the moment that the battle started. It was the extent of that decline that Wully feared most, its effect upon British fighting power, and so upon the prospects of winning the war. It was the main reason for a critical conversation between Wully and Haig at GHQ on June 9th, for Haig had made quite clear his inflexible determination to see his plans through. On May 28th he wrote:

'Your letter of 26th May in which you tell me that the Prime Minister has stated that "we could not expect to get any large number of men in the future but only scraps" is very serious reading.

'I presume the General Staff will point out clearly to the Government what the effect of such a decision is likely to be. It would be well also to indicate what the results of our present operations might have reasonably been had our Divisions here been maintained at full strength. Briefly the offensive on the Arras front could have been maintained at full pressure, at the same time as the attack in the North. And in my opinion the Enemy would undoubtedly have been forced to withdraw to the line of the Meuse!

'As to what the effect of the curtailment of drafts in the future may be, (as foreshadowed in your letter) it is difficult to estimate, until we know what is meant by "only scraps". There seems little doubt however that victory on the Western Front means victory everywhere and a lasting peace! And I have further no doubt that the British Army in France is capable of doing it, given adequate *drafts* and *guns*.

'Another conclusion seems also clear to me, and that is that the Germans can no longer attack England by means of a landing on her coasts. Consequently the time has now arrived for sending every available trained man to reinforce the Divisions now in France.

'For the last two years most of us soldiers have realised that Great Britain must take the necessary steps to win the war by herself, because our French Allies had already shown that they lacked both the moral qualities and the means for gaining the victory. It is thus sad to see the British Govt failing at the XIIth hour!'[18]

*   *   *

Early in June Wully went over to France to see Foch, his opposite number in Paris, visit First Army and look up his son Brian, then serving on XI Corps staff. The battle of Messines started on June 7th and on the 9th Wully saw Haig. Their meeting was briefly recorded in Haig's Diary as follows:

'I had a long talk with Robertson. He wished me to realise the difficult situation in which the country would be if I carried out large and costly attacks without full co-operation by the French. When Autumn came round, Britain would then be without an Army! On the other hand it is possible that Austria would make peace, if harrassed enough. Would it not be a good plan, therefore, to support Italy with guns? I did not agree. Altogether I thought Robertson's views unsound. I told him that I thought the German was now nearly at his last resources, and that there was only *one sound* plan to follow, viz., *without delay* to

1. Send to France every possible man.
2.   ,,   ,,   ,,   aeroplane.
3.   ,,   ,,   ,,   gun.' [19]

This puts Wully in a poor light, as if he was vacillating or trying to run out on Haig at the last moment. It is so completely out of character that the Diary entry must be re-examined in the light of wider knowledge of events and of deeper understanding of Wully. The key point is that Haig made the mistake of assuming that Wully was as convinced as he was about *all* aspects of Third Ypres. He was not. Wully's position has been carefully explained. Strategically he was in favour of the offensive, but not if it was to be fought without French help, and not if the tactics employed meant gaining a few miles of territory at disproportionate cost. He had no say in Haig's detailed plans, but was all the more determined—as a colleague and not as an opponent—to discuss all the implications with him. This he did, and perforce played the part of devil's advocate.

The discussion was a long one, and on the 10th (Sunday) it was renewed after church with Kiggell (Haig's Chief of Staff) also present. Haig noted:

'A night's reflection and Duncan's [the chaplain's] words of thanksgiving for our recent victory [at Messines] seemed to have a good effect on him. He was less pessimistic and seemed to realise that the German Army was in reduced circumstances.' [20]

Haig was deceiving himself. Wully had no illusions about the German Army, and not many about the French. It was incumbent on him to voice his objections, and persuade Haig to acknowledge some of the dangers which the latter, driven on by a single overriding idea, was too ready to overlook. Thus in the appreciation which he forwarded to the War Office on June 12th, Haig stated his aims in more cautious terms:

'Given sufficient force, provided no great transfer of German troops is made in time from east to west, it is probable that the Belgian coast could be cleared this summer, and the defeats on the German troops entailed in doing so might quite possibly lead to their collapse.

'Without sufficient force I shall not attempt to clear the coast and my efforts will be restricted to gaining such victories as are within reach, thereby improving my positions for the winter and opening up possibilities for further operations hereafter if and when necessary means are provided.'[21]

For Wully the discussions of June 9th and 10th had been both a duty and a necessity, in order to clear the air. Thereafter, he swallowed his reservations and made up his mind to back Haig's plans before the War Policy Committee and the War Cabinet, without whose sanction the offensive could not start. It is possible, in the light of after events, to say that Wully made the wrong decision: that Third Ypres should never have been fought in the way it was, or for that matter fought at all. If so—and that is a subject on which the last word has not yet been said—it is only right to emphasise that Wully's decision was made, not by default, but as a deliberate act, reached after a full consideration of facts and probabilities available at the time. It was also prompted by a strong sense of loyalty to Haig, as the tried commander in whom all the soldiers believed, and who controlled the most powerful instrument for victory in the war.

Committed though he was, Wully was far from surrendering his own judgment. He hastened at once to check Haig's optimistic assumptions about the German Army, and gave him good advice on how best to argue the case. On June 13th he telegraphed:

'Your appreciation of June 12th arrives very opportunely and I entirely agree with your views and will support them to the utmost of my power. But I cannot possibly agree with some of the statements in the appendix. . . I hope therefore you will agree appendix not being circulated to War Cabinet. . .'[22]

In a letter of the same date, he wrote:

'Don't argue that you can finish the war this year, or that the German is already beaten. Argue that your plan is the best plan—as it is—that no other would even be *safe* let alone decisive, and then leave them to reject your advice and mine. They dare not do that. . .'

Four days later Haig left France for London and appeared for the first time before the War Policy Committee on June 19th. The meeting was held in Lord Curzon's Privy Council office at No. 10 Downing Street. Here Haig displayed his Flanders plan in full: its origin, tactical methods, and strategic objectives, military and naval, immediate and long-range. Owing to the need for secrecy, agreed at the Paris Conference in May, this was the first time that members of the Committee had been confronted with the scheme in all its scope and detail. They were taken aback. So much seemed to depend upon faith, rather than fact, that they found it immensely difficult to assess. If they approved, they might very well be staking everything on the last big effort that the country could afford. The vast sacrifices of the Somme loomed over them. All were desperately aware that this was, perhaps, the most critical decision of the war.

The main discussions took up three days, but conversations continued for the best part of a week, in and out of the office. As anticipated Lloyd George was the chief critic. In fierce exchanges with Wully and Haig, he covered all the old ground and opened up some new. It seemed to him that the BEF was taking on the Germans virtually single-handed. The French role was very uncertain, but even with French help, Allied superiority in men and guns would only be marginal. Nor was this the true Pétain method—limited offensives scattered over a wide front, a blow here and a blow there—but an all-out campaign in a restricted area, where the element of surprise was bound to disappear. The Germans would soon realise what was afoot and rally their entire strength behind powerful defences. Morale at home might not survive another failure. As always the generals were far too optimistic. The nearest strategic objectives were at least twice as far as the furthest advance achieved on the Somme or at Arras. Why should this attack be expected to do so much better? The Prime Minister concluded with his familiar plea—husband reserves, hold the Germans, the strongest enemy, in the west, but concentrate against the Austrians in Italy. Final victory would come with American help in 1918.

In his reply Haig fell back on his belief in the deterioration of the German Army since the Somme, in falling manpower and establishments, and economic shortages due to the blockade. He also thought that the Russian front would hold long enough to prevent the Germans transferring sufficient divisions to the west to upset his attack. The French Army was recovering. It was engaging the Germans in defensive fighting, and would go over to the offensive in due course as promised. His tactics *were* on the Pétain model, for he had planned a step-by-step battle, with a strong strategic purpose, not a limitless offensive. He rejected the Prime Minister's alternative plan, and reiterated his belief in winning the war in the west, 'within reach this year'.

An unexpected ally was Admiral Jellicoe, First Sea Lord, who made the startling statement that unless the Belgian coast was occupied by the winter and the U-Boat bases taken, the war would be lost. Ships were being lost so fast that it was useless to talk about plans for 1918. Jellicoe was violently challenged by the Prime Minister, and with good reason. His statement was inaccurate. Neither Ostend nor Zeebrugge was vital to the U-Boat offensive, which was gradually being mastered by convoys and tactics at sea. Jellicoe, however, stood by what he had said, and made a considerable impression upon members of the Committee.

This was vicarious help of great weight, but it did not turn the scales alone. The best defence of the plan came from Wully, who both spoke and wrote at length, marshalling all the arguments in a sober and reasoned manner, the gist as follows:

France: He supported Haig. He believed that Pétain had got the measure of the troubles in the French Army, which was already taking over part of the British line, and was committed to fighting alongside the British at Ypres. 'Moreover, French disaffection, great or small, was not a good reason for sending British troops to another theatre, since Germany might counter that move by attacking the French in our absence, and under the assumption that the latter were either unfitted or unwilling to fight the consequences might be serious.'

Italy and Austria: 'I further explained, in considerable detail and not for the first time, that Germany could always beat us in concentrating superior force on the Italian front if she so desired. . . As Germany was doubtless quite as anxious to keep Austria in the war as we were to get her out of it, she might be trusted to supply all the help needed. . . Cadorna had not shown any marked ability in the war as yet, and to transfer the main effort to Italy, and so entrust the fate of the war to him, was as serious a step as placing the British armies under the command of Nivelle, which the Ministers now so keenly regretted.' Finally he doubted whether 'a decisive attack on the Isonzo would be allowed to materialise', since a counter-attack from the north would bring it instantly to a standstill. 'Even if this did not happen, and if Trieste were captured, there was no certainty that Austria would ask for peace. . .'

Germany: 'I do not for one moment think that Germany is as yet near the end of her resources either in men or material. I think she may yet take a great deal of beating, and that it is necessary that France should be aggressive as well as ourselves. On the other hand, Germany may be much nearer exhaustion, both on the main fronts and at home, than we imagine, and there are many indications of this. Doubtful situations such as the present one have always arisen in war, and great mistakes have been made by endeavouring to find a way round as soon as the strain begins to be felt. We should be on our guard against this mistake.'

Flanders: A successful offensive here offered concrete strategic advantages, military as described by Haig, naval as emphasised by Jellicoe. Haig's tactics conformed to the required Pétain pattern. 'I deprecate as strongly as anyone our incurring heavy casualties without a corresponding return, but the plan as outlined by the Field-Marshal should secure us against this mistake . . .; we must continue to be aggressive somewhere on our front, and we ought of course to do this in the most promising direction. The plan provides for this, and will enable us to derive a real advantage should the enemy show signs of weakening, while at the same time it permits of our easing off if the situation demands.'

Conclusion: He denied making any 'sure predictions of success' of which the Prime Minister complained. It was a question of doing the best in the circumstances. 'I am therefore in favour of continuing our present plan on the chance of getting a success in the north, not only because of the military situation, but also of the necessity of trying to improve the air and sea situation, and I am consequently averse from diverting any of our resources to Italy.' He added: 'It is a source of deep regret to me that I cannot advise the adoption of the policy so greatly desired by the Prime Minister, for I fully recognise the responsibility which he has to carry. My own responsibility . . . is not small. . .'[23]

For the soldiers the talking was over, though not for the politicians. Hankey recorded:

'All the week the controversy went on, but on Monday (June 25th), after the Committee had adjourned to give Robertson and Haig time to think it over, they adhered to their opinion and Lloyd George felt he could not press his amateur opinions and over-rule them, so he gave in, and Haig was authorised to continue his preparations. The final decision, however, was postponed until after a conference with the French, as Lloyd George declines to agree finally until assured that the French will do their bit by attacking simultaneously.'[24]

*   *   *

The next day, a curious conversation took place. The Prime Minister invited two guests to one of his famous breakfasts at No. 10 Downing Street—Haig and Sir Eric Geddes. Geddes was an extraordinary man, a railway expert whom Haig had appointed Director-General of Transport in France, where he had done great service, he had been transferred to the Admiralty in May 1917, the only man to leap from civilian status to that of General, and then Admiral. The subject of discussion was the Admiralty. They were all agreed as to its inefficiency. The First Lord, Carson, deferred to the sailors, while the First Sea Lord, Jellicoe, had held out till the last minute against convoys and was thoroughly pessimistic about the war at sea, although nothing was said about his recent remarks in support of the Flanders operation. Lloyd George then made the astonishing proposal that Wully should succeed Carson. The matter was seriously debated, though without reaching a conclusion. Haig hastened to the War Office to tell Wully, who turned the idea down flat. In the event Geddes was given the appointment, while Carson was booted upstairs into the War Cabinet. But it is interesting to reflect on what lay behind the proposal. Wully was a powerful personality and an excellent organiser, Lloyd George may have genuinely considered him the best man to overhaul the structure of the Admiralty, and introduce a General Staff system comparable to that which worked so well in the War Office. Or he may have thought that this was a good way of getting him out of the War Office and away from the control of the Army without disgracing him—in other words without sacking him, for at this juncture such a move would still have outraged public opinion and weakened his own position as head of the Government.

*　　　*　　　*

Haig hurried back to France. His plans were already behind schedule and there was no time to be lost. He was anxious to profit from the fine summer weather and launch the great attack while the ground remained dry and hard, so that he might capture at least the tactical objectives east of Ypres before the autumn set in. For him the final consent of the War Cabinet was an academic event. It had to be so. A great operation could not be mounted in a matter of a few days. Preparations had been going forward at least since the previous May, and there were delays enough in France without adding to them from London.

Meanwhile, days turned into weeks, and still no word from Lloyd George. At the end of June Wully had gone over to France to see Foch and Pétain. He was as impressed by the former as depressed by the latter. Pétain, he told Haig, 'talked like a man without a jot of confidence as to the future.'[25] On July 6th he wrote:

'You will remember that you were told to go on with your preparations and that the Prime Minister said he would see the French so as to ascertain whether they really intended to co-operate. He had intended to see them early next week but I think he will not now go much if at all before the 18th. He is more keen than ever on the Italian plan, but I think it will right itself in time, because before long you will be on the point of going off and I cannot conceive that the French will listen to any such proposal as the transfer of major operations to Italy and the practical stoppage of operations on the West Front. The Cabinet have been meeting by themselves on several occasions this week, but eventually they will bump up against me and then there will be trouble. I gather that while the Prime Minister is keen on Italy, Smuts wants to land 150,000 men at Alexandretta (I do not know where he proposes to get them or the ships from), Milner is rather inclined to think that the Balkans will be a good place, while Curzon sticks to our plan. It is pretty difficult doing business under these conditions.'

Ten days later the whole business was at last brought to a head, *without* checking with the French. According to Hankey:

'*July 16th.* In the evening Lloyd George gave a dinner at 10 Downing Street to the War Policy Committee (Curzon, Milner, Smuts and self), Balfour and Carson being also guests. We went over much the same ground as at the last dinner at Curzon's, and the final decision was to allow Haig to begin his offensive, but not to allow it to degenerate into a drawn out, indecisive battle of the "Somme" type. If this happened, it was to be stopped and the plan for an attack on the Italian front would be tried.'[26]

By working flat out for the best part of two days Hankey managed to produce, almost single-handed, the full report of the War Policy Committee for the War Cabinet, who approved it on July 20th. The report was 'sixty pages long and a very complete production, though I say it who shouldn't.'[27]

By this time the battle had become imminent and Wully, well knowing what was involved, was doing all he could to remove obstacles to a final decision. On the 18th he wrote to Haig:

'. . . apparently while all the Members [of the War Cabinet] except the Prime Minister were in favour of accepting our advice they all expressed, so I am told, at different times the fear that you might endeavour to push on further than you were justified pending further artillery preparation, because they have all got in their mind, and correctly so, that the greatest losses sometimes occur in trying to take and hold positions too far in advance. I had a talk with one of the Cabinet on this subject yesterday and impressed upon him that I thought they need have no fear, as it is well understood that the extent of the advance must, roughly speaking, be limited by the assistance of the guns until such times as a real breakthrough occurs. He replied that so long as this step-by-step system of advance was adhered to he would back your plan for all it was worth. I understand that the Prime Minister asked one of the Cabinet when your operations ought to be stopped, if they did not seem likely to achieve complete success—that is, how many losses we ought to incur before stopping. The Cabinet Minister gave a good answer. He said that he could not answer the question merely with reference to losses, and that the time to stop would be when it appeared that our resources were not sufficient to justify a continuance of our effort.'

Haig replied on the 21st, with natural and justified acerbity, that it was 'somewhat startling at this advanced stage of the preparations' to be told that the War Cabinet had still not made up its mind. His letter, however, crossed an official communication from Wully, containing a copy of the conclusions reached by the War Cabinet on July 20th. Wully commented in a covering note:[28]

'I am sending you today a copy of the Draft Conclusions recently reached by the War Cabinet. We had a rough and tumble Meeting yesterday. The fact is that the Prime Minister is still very averse from your offensive and talks as though he is hoping to switch off to Italy within a day or two after you begin. I told him that unless there were very great miscalculations on your part, and unless the first stage proved to be more or less a disastrous failure—which I certainly did not expect it would be—I did not think it would be possible to pronounce a verdict on the success of your operations for several weeks. He seemed to have in mind what the French said last spring when Nivelle told them that he would be able to say in one or two days whether his operations had been successful or not.'

On the next day, July 22nd, Wully went over to France and saw Haig at GHQ. Haig was indignant at the way he had been treated by the War Cabinet, and elaborated on a formal reply which he handed over to Wully. He resented any attempt to tie him down over the detailed progress of the operation, and he ridiculed the delay over the approval. It was his impression that the War Cabinet had no confidence in his plans. If that was so, it added vastly to the burden of his responsibilities as field commander. He wished to know definitely how he stood. As to the Italian plan, he rounded on Wully:

'I urged him to be firmer and play the man; and, if need be, resign, should Lloyd George persist in ordering troops to Italy against the advice of the General Staff.'[29]

Haig had good reason to be angry, and it was natural that he should vent his spleen upon the nearest emissary from the Government he so disliked. In fact, of course, Wully neither represented the Government, nor did he bear responsibility of any kind for its behaviour. He was Haig's best ally, and had fought a hard and wearing battle on his behalf in the staunchest manner. Haig had small conception of this, neither for the first time, nor for the last. The basic trouble derived less from the clash of personalities and ideas, than from the absence of a comprehensive planning organisation, inter-Service and inter-Allied—a fault not tackled till the end of 1917, and not corrected until the war was over.

The final exchange of messages proved no more satisfactory than the earlier. On July 25th the War Cabinet assured Haig of its 'whole-hearted support', but added by way of concession that if the Flanders operation had to be reviewed at any stage, then Haig would be consulted. Haig replied in the sense that, even if the offensive turned out less successful than anticipated, then 'we ought still to persevere in attacking the Germans in France.'[30]

That was how matters stood on the eve of Third Ypres. It represented not an end to controversy but a pause, for the clash was renewed both during and after the campaign. It still continues in retrospect today.

Chief of the Imperial General Staff: August to November 1917

THIRD YPRES was given a grudging and belated send-off by the War Cabinet, but even after the decision had been made, Lloyd George continued—like a man with a grievance—to harp relentlessly upon the alternative Italian plan. He did so at two conferences of the Allies, the first in Paris on July 25th–26th, the second in London on August 7th–8th. Once more he came up against Wully, who prevailed upon both Foch and Cadorna to stand by his firm refusal to contemplate any combined offensive against Austria, at least until after the fighting in Flanders was over and its results assessed: which meant, not before the spring of 1918. As to reinforcing the Italians in case of attack, that was another matter, for it linked up with the future of Russia—a subject of grave concern.

The last Russian offensive had been launched on July 1st and quickly failed. The Germans had counter-attacked with such success that many of the Russian units disintegrated, and the men drifted home. None the less, the eastern front was still in being, and engaged well over 100 enemy divisions. All were agreed, however, that the end could not be far off. Wully had given the matter specific attention as early as May 9th, when he pointed out that the Central Powers might soon be in a position to transfer the bulk of their divisions to the west, a movement limited only by the capacity of the transport system.[1] On July 29th he brought the matter up again, and emphasised the recommendations of a committee of Allied Generals (he among them) which had recently been studying the question in Paris. If Russia did make peace, then the Germans would certainly transfer their main strength to the west, probably to France. In that case it was essential to stand on the defensive in all the secondary theatres, accelerate the arrival of the Americans, and set up a permanent inter-Allied military organisation to deal with the rapid movement of troops from one front to another. In Wully's view the best way to help Russia was to attack the Germans in the west—Third Ypres was shortly about to start—and so relieve pressure in the east.[2]

If it turned out, however, that the Germans switched divisions from Russia to Italy, then it was recognised—by both Wully and Foch—that the Italians would need strengthening by British and French troops, and plans for this contingency had been in hand for many months. On Lloyd George's insistence, however, they were taken to their ultimate stage with Cadorna without further delay. It was a wise decision. The work was completed by the middle of September, some six weeks before the collapse at Caporetto.

But that was not the end of the Italian business. Cadorna was getting ready for another offensive on the Isonzo, the eleventh (August 17th to September 12th). He was short of artillery and munitions, and although he had already received a number of British and French heavy batteries during the summer, he demanded still more. Lloyd George was dead keen to give him what he wanted, if only because it might help the Italians to break the Austrian front on their own, and so achieve the strategic aim he so ardently desired. Wully was as adamant as ever, on the grounds that Third Ypres demanded every gun and every gunner on the western front. Foch, however, weakened. The fact was that he did not believe in the possibility of success in Flanders, or anywhere in France in 1917, and —like Pétain—was hoping to win the war with American help in 1918–19. Following a further urgent call from Cadorna at the end of August, he declared his willingness to send 100 guns to Italy, the weapons to be taken from the French First Army, currently assisting Haig in Flanders. To settle the matter he travelled to London, where he was received on September 4th by an affable Lloyd George and a disgusted Wully and Haig. Under pressure the latter offered to release 50 guns, provided they were replaced before the next phase of the Flanders offensive. Haig then returned to France, and resolved the business by an amicable arrangement with Pétain; but the guns arrived too late to help the Italians on the Isonzo, where— as on several previous occasions—the battle petered out after a promising start, without gaining a decision. Trieste remained Austrian. In sum much counsel was expended upon Italy for an inconclusive result, and at the end of it relations between the Prime Minister and his generals had, if anything, deteriorated still further. Wully was deeply disgruntled. He had told Haig earlier:

'He [Lloyd George] is a real bad 'un. The other members of the War Cabinet seem afraid of him. Milner is a tired, dyspeptic old man. Curzon a gas-bag. Bonar Law equals Bonar Law. Smuts has good instinct but lacks knowledge. On the whole he is best, but they help one very little.'

In the same letter, dated August 9th, he stated roundly:

'Our friends the Allies returned to their respective countries yesterday. The Conference lasted two days. It was of the usual character and resulted in the usual waste of time.'

That was not quite fair, although as Hankey related of the earlier of the two meetings (Paris, on July 25th–26th; London, on August 7th–8th), a great many speeches of great length had been made by representatives of most of the Allies; and it had been hard work to get any real business done.[3] But at least they had cleared the air over some of the outer theatres of war. In the Balkans the Greeks, now united, were beginning to pull their weight in the line; and Lloyd George had insisted on the withdrawal of a second British division from Salonika to Egypt.[4] However, the protests aroused by this very modest step —in an area where the Allies enjoyed enormous superiority— made it unlikely that he could cut the British contingent any further. In the Middle East the situation was not unpromising. Maude was on top in Mesopotamia and had a firm hold on Baghdad. In Egypt, where Allenby had replaced Murray at the end of June, prospects were also brightening again.

*　　*　　*

It will be recalled that by January 1917 Murray had cleared Sinai of the Turks and reached the frontier of Palestine at Rafa. He had done this to ensure the safety of Egypt as a base and centre of communications and, having sent the bulk of his formations elsewhere (mainly to France), had more than fulfilled the task set him by Kitchener and Wully a year earlier. In December 1916 he still had under command four infantry and two cavalry divisions, a force—he told Wully—just adequate to maintain the *status quo*. By then, however, the Government at home was looking round for a resounding victory somewhere, to offset the inconclusive outcome of the Somme and raise national morale. Murray was asked to submit proposals for an advance into Palestine and name his requirements. His answer, briefly, was a request for two more divisions, and a plan for a move along the coast. Shortly afterwards the whole scheme was damped down. Preparations for the Nivelle offensive were getting under way, and every man was needed for France. Murray was told that Palestine would have to wait till the autumn. Meanwhile, so far from receiving any more troops, he would have to send away his best infantry division, the 42nd, and this he did. Wully elaborated in a private letter on the new situation, and indicated that if the war was not won in France during the summer, then he would give Murray his chance later on.

'If the war goes on into next winter it will mean that we have not had any very striking success during the summer. The public will become impatient and we shall have to do something to keep the war alive. . . The autumn and winter are good seasons for you and if we are still fighting then my desire is to give you a really big show and to let you do as much as you can and go as far as you can into Turkish territory.'[5]

Meanwhile, Murray was to build up his force with drafts and units from India and Africa, with the possibility of receiving a cavalry division from France later on. Wully concluded:

'Your operations have hitherto been conducted so successfully and organised in such a good way that I have every hope that you will give the Turk a real good and big shaking next autumn if only I can fit you out with what you need.'[6]

That was clear enough. Nevertheless, Murray explained in subsequent communications, official and private—and he was not contradicted—that he intended to go on acting aggressively, small though his force was (now, a little over three infantry and two cavalry divisions). He was pushing on with the railway and the pipeline and building up his stores, and hoped that the enemy would come out of the desert ahead and attack him. But the Turks did nothing of the kind. They retreated right behind the defensive line Gaza-Beersheba, and it was this move that decided him to go over again to the attack. He advanced various reasons. In his Official Despatch:

'It was to prevent a repetition of these tactics [voluntary withdrawal] and to bring the Turks to fight that I determined to attack the Gaza position as soon as possible, considering that the advantage of thus exerting pressure on the enemy, and possibly taking Gaza by a *coup de main*, would outweigh the risk of making the attack in a waterless country considerably in advance of rail-head.'[7]

In a letter to Wully:

'It is very important that I should occupy the line Gaza-Beersheba as soon as possible so as to raise the Southern Syrians against the Turks and further assist the Arabs in the Hejaz. I am strong enough to do this, and yet at the same time to maintain the full security of Egyptian territory.'[8]

Whatever his reasons—and they all served—it was Murray who took the initiative and he who decided to fight the First Battle of Gaza. He had no idea that his whole future as C-in-C would be affected by the result. In effect he regarded the capture of Gaza more as a natural extension of his move east than as an engagement of critical importance. But the situation was already altering elsewhere. Maude took Baghdad on March 11th, the Russians were showing signs of activity on the borders of Persia, Feisal was holding on in the Hejaz—all aroused the hopes of the War Cabinet, and of Lloyd George in particular who had set his heart on the capture of Jerusalem. Something, but not all, of this was conveyed by Wully in a letter dated March 14th, though it could hardly have been given close consideration by Murray until the battle was over; in any event it could not have altered any of his plans.

Gaza very nearly came off. The battle began early on March 26th in dense fog which led to an unlucky delay. Nevertheless, the advance went well, in intense heat, and by dusk the cavalry had got round the town. Unfortunately the approach of enemy reserves and the shortage of water decided the cavalry commander (Chetwode) to withdraw, prematurely it was judged, when Gaza was on the point of capture. The force commander

(Dobell) also hesitated, and on the next day the Turks could not be dislodged. Murray felt sure that

'Dobell ought to have thrown in the 52nd and 54th [infantry] Divisions in a strong counterstroke [on the 26th], but he was on the spot and judged that to do so before the troops and animals had re-watered was unsound. He was possibly right; I should have attacked.'[9]

Murray correctly delegated the direction of the battle to the men who were fighting it, but he had to bear the responsibility of their mistakes, and he did report the result in over-optimistic terms. The War Cabinet was disappointed and Wully telegraphed an admonition, instructing Murray to try again and then push on deeper into Palestine.[10] Jerusalem was now the objective. Murray was surprised and hurt, but at once set about preparing a second attack, this time of a more deliberate character, but he had to make do with the troops and equipment he already had.

The Second Battle of Gaza was fought April 17th–19th, and met with less success than the First. The Turks had been reinforced and were well dug in, and although they got within a mile or two of the town, the British infantry were unable to take the key of the position, the hill of Ali el Muntar. Casualties mounted, and by the night of April 19th/20th the battle had bogged down. After consultation Murray reluctantly called the attack off, but once again he considered that Dobell had shown a lack of thrust at a critical stage, and he sent him home. But the damage had been done, and Murray's own fate was sealed. Although Wully had staunchly defended him after First Gaza, the War Cabinet now decided to relieve him.

Wully did not oppose the decision, because he felt on balance that it was correct. But he also recognised that Murray had been hard done by, and was privately distressed that he, who had displaced Murray on two previous occasions (as CGS in France and as CIGS), should have to recall him now.[11] But the facts were plain. The strategic situation in the Middle East had tilted yet again. By early May the effects of the March Revolution had made it clear that nothing after all could be expected from the Russians, while it was unlikely that Maude could do very much more in Mesopotamia. This meant that the Turks

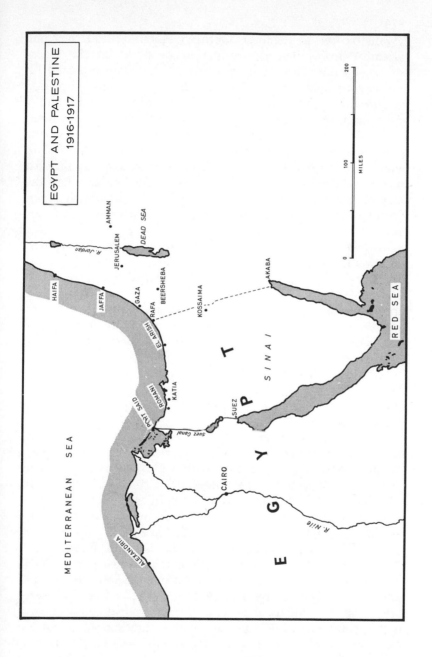

EGYPT AND PALESTINE
1916-1917

MEDITERRANEAN SEA

ALEXANDRIA

PORT SAID

ROMANI

KATIA

EGYPT

CAIRO

R. Nile

SUEZ

Suez Canal

SINAI

EL ARISH

RAFA

KOSSAIMA

BEERSHEBA

GAZA

JAFFA

HAIFA

JERUSALEM

R. Jordan

DEAD SEA

AMMAN

AKABA

RED SEA

0   100   200
MILES

would be free to reinforce southern Palestine, and they had already shown their determination to stand on the Gaza-Beersheba line. After Second Gaza Murray had repeated his earlier statement as to what was needed for a successful invasion of Palestine; namely, five fully-trained and equipped infantry divisions, together with cavalry, and a much larger complement of artillery and supporting arms. He also needed to extend the pipeline and double the railway east from the Delta—all of which would involve eight months of preparation. His forecast was very near the mark. His successor, Allenby, launched the first of his offensives in late October, and then with seven complete infantry divisions, three cavalry divisions, and a six-fold increase of artillery.

Murray was an efficient soldier, who had transformed the situation in Egypt at a very difficult time. Furthermore, he had had to bear the responsibility of several fronts, by contrast with Allenby who was able to concentrate almost all his attention upon Palestine. But it was also true that Allenby was a more imaginative and dynamic commander, and that—for psychological reasons, if for no other—a change was desirable. Murray paid the price of the chances of war. He had made it possible for his successor to succeed—a fact publicly acknowledged by Allenby in 1919—and in all this his career bore a strong resemblance to that of Auchinleck in 1941–2. Both were unlucky commanders.

Allenby, however, was not the first choice to succeed Murray, but Smuts, who had only recently been admitted to the War Cabinet. A strong personality, with wide experience of men and affairs, successful commander in East Africa, above all a 'Colonial' of high repute, Smuts might well have been the very man to take charge of the mixed Empire army in Egypt, fighting a mobile war. But he refused, largely on Wully's advice. The dominant factor was the Russian Revolution. Wully argued that Russian weakness might now prevent the despatch to Egypt of sufficient reinforcements from the west to pull off the big offensive in Palestine at the end of the year. Egypt was a secondary theatre, and the logistical commitment in the whole of the Middle East was staggering. In terms of manpower, three or four men were required to keep a single soldier in the front line, disease caused more casualties than the enemy, while shipping continued as critical as ever. Wully saw no strategic—only political—value in capturing Jerusalem, but he accepted the wisdom of harassing the Turks and encouraging the Arabs, provided it involved no weakening of the west. In the end Allenby proved an excellent choice, and he worked within the terms of Wully's brief. When he arrived in Egypt on June 28th, he took over a growing, but dispirited, army, and instilled new life into it. At the very outset he adopted Murray's appreciation, but he raised Murray's demands, gaining the extra units from Salonika, Africa, and India. He also secured the additional guns and stores. Within a few months he was ready to strike.

*   *   *

Meanwhile, there was no question of attacking the enemy anywhere but in Flanders. However much Lloyd George disliked and discounted it, and however much he tried to divert attention to the war elsewhere, Third Ypres had been in full flood since July 31st, and the course of the war depended upon its outcome.

It is not within the scope of this book to enter into every detail of the fighting, or to argue all the pros and cons, but rather to describe, in outline only, what happened, and to demonstrate how the battle affected the thoughts and decisions of the men in supreme control of the war: principally, of course, to relate the part played by Wully during the three months of its agony.

Third Ypres may be divided into four—the preliminaries, and the three phases of the battle itself: July 31st to August 28th, September 20th to October 12th, and October 22nd to November 10th. The preliminaries had begun with the battle of Messines, fought by Second Army (Plumer), and already described: a classical limited offensive, which aimed at and succeeded in straightening out the salient south of Ypres; but it was not exploited. The fighting was over by June 14th. Then followed six weeks (of generally fine weather), during which time two more actions were fought, minor in scale, but both highly relevant to the main engagement to come. One was a British attack towards Lens at the end of June which, though it gained a little ground, did not deceive the Germans into thinking it was anything but a feint. The other was a German attack on July 10th–11th, which succeeded in wiping out an important part of the bridgehead over the River Yser at Nieuport. This was a serious reverse for the British, since the area was essential to the coastal attack to be launched by the Fourth Army (Rawlinson). Haig decided to disregard it, and in the end the coastal operation was abandoned, as the main Ypres offensive never made sufficient ground.

It was now getting on well into July and one delay succeeded another, almost all for technical reasons over the mounting of the attack by the Fifth Army (Gough) and the French First Army (Anthoine). Nevertheless, air fighting began in earnest on July 11th and the artillery bombardment on July 16th. The latter continued unabated for fifteen days, of unprecedented weight and fury, expending $4\frac{1}{2}$ million shells. The effects, though shattering enough, were not wholly satisfactory. Many of the German strong-points (especially the concrete forts or 'pill-boxes') survived, while the bulk of the enemy units were held back for the purposes of counter-attack. Furthermore, the ground was so badly torn up that it constituted a serious obstacle to the advance, notably of the tanks, and when it rained (as it soon did) the craters filled with water and became lethal to everybody. Finally, the Germans were now fully warned of the imminence of the attack, the preparations for which they had long observed.

The assault started early on July 31st. The original plan had been for a step-by-step advance, concentrating on the ridge which ran like a dog-leg east and north-east of Ypres, commanding all the country on either side. Secure here, the rest of the advance in the plain to the north should go forward with comparative ease. Gough, however, considered it too deliberate. He wanted to thrust right through to the village of Passchendaele near the far end of the ridge as quickly as possible, while keeping pace to the north: in other words he envisaged not a step-by-step but an all-out attack, aiming at a break-through, this to be followed by exploitation with cavalry and a rush to the ports. Haig did not dissuade him: partly because he agreed with the aim, partly because he underestimated German resistance and thought he could break it down by sheer weight, partly because the victory at Messines had—in his opinion—

wasted much of its effect through failure to exploit, and partly because he feared the rain. However, Davidson, Haig's DMO, criticised Gough's plan for what it was, a repetition (in more scientific form) of the tactics employed on the opening day of the Somme, and a reversal of the method that had so recently been agreed. He said that Gough was expecting far too much far too quickly at such an early stage. After the enemy had been worn down by a series of set-piece attacks and his reserves drawn in, then might come the chance to break through and exploit— but not before. Davidson, however, was not supported, even Plumer advised against him, while Gough maintained in after years that *his* plan merely conformed to Haig's wishes.

However that may be, Gough prevailed, and on July 31st the offensive was opened by four French divisions on the left and nine British divisions on the right. It started quite well, making ground everywhere except on the extreme right, where II Corps was held up, after barely a mile, on the commanding ridge in front of Gheluvelt. This was the key position: a wooded, broken territory, cunningly defended by concealed machine-gun posts and strong-points, and well supported by artillery further back. It proved a holocaust for the tanks. Had this been a step-by-step battle, then a halt would have been called at about 9.30 am—on that first day—when the initial impetus had run out. The troops would have been relieved, and preparations begun for a new and deliberate assault 48 hours later. Instead, the offensive was continued almost at once and went on all day without result. II Corps made no further impression, while the Germans recovered a little ground by counter-attacks in the plain. Worst of all it began to rain, and proceeded to deluge for three days. The battleground became a waste of water and mud, a veritable swamp in which men were swallowed up and drowned if they ventured off the plank causeways. Further fighting became impossible and the battle was stopped. By this time the British had lost over 30,000 in killed and wounded (about half the casualties of the first day of the Somme), for a maximum gain of two miles, without seizing command of the critical ridge.

The rain stopped on August 4th, but the weather refused to improve, and on the evening of the 8th it poured again. Haig,

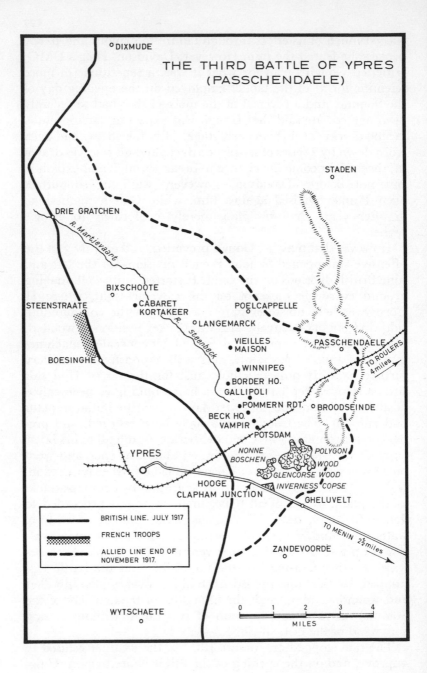

THE THIRD BATTLE OF YPRES
(PASSCHENDAELE)

DIXMUDE

STADEN

DRIE GRATCHEN

R. Martjevaant

BIXSCHOOTE

STEENSTRAATE

CABARET KORTAKEER

POELCAPPELLE

R. Steenbeck

LANGEMARCK

PASSCHENDAELE

BOESINGHE

VIEILLES MAISON

TO ROULERS 4 miles

WINNIPEG

BORDER HO. GALLIPOLI

POMMERN RDT.

BROODSEINDE

BECK HO. VAMPIR

POTSDAM

NONNE BOSCHEN

POLYGON WOOD

YPRES

GLENCORSE WOOD

INVERNESS COPSE

HOOGE CLAPHAM JUNCTION

GHELUVELT

TO MENIN 2½ miles

BRITISH LINE. JULY 1917

FRENCH TROOPS

ALLIED LINE END OF NOVEMBER 1917.

ZANDEVOORDE

WYTSCHAETE

0   1   2   3   4
MILES

however, waited patiently, he had no intention of giving up, while Kiggell told Wully on the morning of the 8th:

'The ground is drying and unless the weather turns wet again we should be able to get a move on soon.'

On the 10th a second unsuccessful attempt was made on Gheluvelt, and on the 16th, when the ground was comparatively dry, a big effort at a break-through round Langemarck in the centre came to nothing. On the 22nd Gheluvelt was repeated and failed, and on the 24th an important feature in this area (Inverness Copse) was lost.

On August 25th Haig decided to hand the whole battle over to Plumer and the Second Army. There was no question now but to revert to step-by-step tactics, and for this Plumer needed three weeks to prepare. The first phase of Third Ypres was over, and it had proved a great disappointment. The British had used up no less than fourteen of the twenty-two divisions put into the line during the course of the month, losing over 60,000 men. By contrast Anthoine's four divisions had suffered remarkably little and had made as good progress as anywhere else in the line. This was an important stage in the recovery of French morale, improved still further by the first of Pétain's promised attacks at Verdun on August 20th–26th, an undoubted success conducted on the limited lines approved. At Lens, too, the Canadians carried out a diversionary action in the second half of the month, which went well. But these visible victories were generally achieved outside the Ypres area, where the hellish conditions engendered as much despair as the accumulation of casualties and the obvious failure to get on. August 1917 was, in its way, as black a month for the British Army as August 1918 was to be for the German.

Haig held on. He assumed—on insufficient evidence at the time—that the Germans had suffered much more than the Allies and were near to breaking. That was not true, though they had suffered very heavily. Out of thirty-seven divisions employed, twenty-three had had to be withdrawn for rest and refit, a larger total than that of the Allies in terms of formations, with almost as large a casualty list. Furthermore, they had been compelled to draw upon divisions from other parts of the western front, which meant that any idea of attacking the

French had to be shelved. Thus, one of Haig's aims had already been partially achieved, but the full achievement could only be assessed after the end of the campaign in November.

* * *

Few of these compensations, however, were realised at the time, certainly not in London where by mid-August the success of the offensive was already in doubt. Hankey recorded on August 15th:

'I had a short talk with the Prime Minister and Robert Cecil. I impressed strongly on the former that he ought to investigate the question of the Flanders offensive, which seems to be rather hung up, with a view to the possible adoption of the alternative Italian plan before Cadorna had started. I found him unresponsive, though he sent for Robertson in order to instruct him to report on Haig's next objective. In this connection it must be noted that Robertson is going to France tomorrow. The P.M. is obviously puzzled, as his predecessor was, how far the Government is justified in interfering with a military operation.'[12]

For the moment Lloyd George held his hand. He had always detested the Flanders plan, and now he suspected that his worst fears were being realised. Third Ypres was getting nowhere, and was floundering in water, mud, and blood. His first chance came at the end of the month, when Cadorna repeated his request for heavy guns and other help, in order to sustain the Isonzo offensive. Wully was urgently sent for.

'*August 29th.* Robertson and Maurice arrived about 11.0 am and an agreement was reached that a telegram should be sent to the British Ambassador in Rome . . . warning him that we could only assist at the expense of an abandonment of the Flanders offensive; that this would be trumpeted by the Germans as a defeat to our arms; that we could even consider facing this, if we were assured that a really great victory could be won with our aid on the Italian front; but that we knew by experience the optimism of generals, and we should therefore require a convincing appreciation. Robertson . . . on the previous day had dissented strongly from the whole idea, and I am certain that he only agreed to this telegram because he was sure that the Italians could not convince us. Maurice, with whom I had a talk, was also strongly opposed. He told me that Haig, and still more Kiggell, his Chief of Staff, still believed we could clear the Flanders coast—his reason being that there only remained five German divisions that had not passed through the mill, and that the reserves with which they were filled up were the poorest material. I am bound to say that I could not share this optimism.'[13]

The meeting, with its frustrating and all too familiar exchanges, was enlivened by an amusing incident at luncheon.

'In order to put Robertson in a good temper Riddell had ordered an apple suet pudding, of which Maurice had said he was very fond. When Robertson saw it he expressed the greatest delight; he had two large helpings and frequently commented on its excellence. Of course we all pretended it was a chance. . .'[14]

But the sequel was Foch's visit to London on September 4th to press for the release of 100 French guns for Cadorna, and the attendance of Haig at that meeting at which he emphasised the overriding need to continue the battle in Flanders. Haig got his way, and by a majority the War Cabinet gave its approval to the next phase, due to start on September 20th. Although he won his point about the guns, the Prime Minister was still unable to convince his colleagues about Third Ypres. He did not relax his efforts, however, and watched impatiently for the next opportunity.

For Wully, too, August had been a most miserable month. His was a detestable position. The problems were almost insoluble, but he had to grapple with them, somehow, day after day. His staff watched his struggles with increasing concern, so much so that Whigham, DCIGS, felt impelled to write privately to Haig, telling him of the mounting pressure against Wully and of the devoted way he was championing Haig's plans; also that he was virtually alone and badly in need of encouragement. This did elicit a response. On August 13th Haig wrote Wully a long letter, setting out his views, and ending:

'Please accept my hearty thanks for the way you supported the sound policy at the recent Conference and my heartfelt wishes for your continued success.'

But he could not refrain from inserting:

'The only point I am not in accord with you on is the desirability of issuing such pessimistic estimates from your Intelligence Branch. They do, I feel sure, much harm and cause many in authority to take a pessimistic outlook, when a contrary view, based on equally good information, would go far to help the nation on to victory. Personally I feel we have every reason to be optimistic. . .'[15]

But Haig was deceiving himself. Macdonogh was a sounder and more realistic Director of Intelligence than Charteris, as Wully had tried to impress upon him earlier in the summer. Moreover, British resources of manpower could not be blinked any more than the German. On August 17th Wully wrote:

'I am having a meeting with A-G's people tomorrow to see if we can scrape you up any more drafts than those we have already in view, and you can depend upon our sending you every man we can. . .

'But I suggest it is equally necessary that your Staff should *immediately* take steps to scrape up all the men they can in France. . .

'I repeat that all that we can do at home will be done. In this connexion I would like to disabuse you of the idea which seems to prevail in France, namely, that a lot of men who might be sent out are kept at home. I have just been through the classification of the men in Home Service Divisions and brigades, and I find there are less than 8000 'A1' men. (This is exclusive of the 67th Division which as you know is being drawn upon.) . . . I may say that the Home Service divisions and brigades are now largely made up of 18-year old boys. . .'

Soon afterwards Wully told Repington that

'Though the Germans were putting in their boys of 18, he did not wish us to put in ours of 18 years 8 months, as some people wished. He would wait till they were 19, and he judged by his own boy who was still only a boy.'[16]

Haig was already busy combing out all the men he could find in France, but he had to tell his Army Commanders on August 21st that the BEF would probably be 100,000 men under establishment by the end of October. The most productive source of manpower lay outside the Army altogether: in Ireland, still beyond the conscription law; in the protected trades which Lloyd George refused to touch on the grounds that all were vital to the war effort; and in extending the age for military service. These were measures of a kind that only the extreme emergency of March 1918 could enforce. Meanwhile, Wully simply butted his head against a brick wall. Repington told him that

'the War Office and Derby would soon be attacked on the subject of men. I said that I knew that the General Staff had warned the War Cabinet time after time and no later than Saturday last, but this had been going on for ten months, and the question was why the Army Council did not insist.'[17]

But the Army Council *had* insisted—to no effect. The fact was that the matter had long passed out of the hands of the Army and rested entirely with the War Cabinet. Reluctance to settle this issue, for whatever reason, was essentially one more facet of the dispute over strategy.

As to Flanders, Wully was becoming deeply perturbed. He told Repington that 'there was nothing for us but to go on, Haig thought he was killing a lot of Germans.'[18] He hoped it was true, for there was no other visible sign of success. So far he had not questioned Haig's methods. Tactics were the business of the field commander, strategy was his. Thus, he had backed Third Ypres in terms of strategy to the Government, but he had also argued—on Haig's assurance—that the battle would be conducted economically on limited lines, step-by-step. That had been falsified already, as we have seen, though GHQ insisted that rain had been the real trouble—in other words that all August had been a false start. True or not, it was cold comfort as an argument, especially at the onset of autumn; and it rendered the tactical outlook very bleak indeed. As Wully commented:

'Of course the difficulty is the ground in Flanders. . . A year ago we thought that victory lay in having a large amount of heavy artillery. We have got a large amount now, but the enemy's machine-guns are still a difficulty not yet surmounted. Our hope is, I gather, that the artillery will knock out the hostile machine-guns, but unfortunately this entails the entire destruction of the surface of the ground and renders it almost impassable, especially in Flanders. We would therefore seem to be confronted with the problem that unless we use a great deal of artillery fire we cannot get on, and if we do use it the ground is destroyed. . . For this the tanks seem to offer the best prospect, but goodness knows if they will furnish a sufficient answer.'[19]

As it happened the next phase of the offensive began remarkably well.

*   *   *

The second phase of Third Ypres opened on September 20th and closed on October 12th; it consisted of five separate battles. The ground had dried out since August and the first three, fought in continuing good weather, were almost completely successful. The last two, fought after the rain had come down again, failed.

Plumer's methods resembled those he had employed at Messines, characterised by an overwhelming impact of force upon a very limited frontage. He doubled the concentration of artillery, notably of heavy pieces, and used it to knock out strong-points and gun positions, and to break up enemy counter-attacks. He also laid a thick protective barrage, 1000 yards deep, ahead of his infantry, and trained them intensively to deal with the German system of elastic defence. Great exertions were demanded of the gunners, engineers, and supporting services to maintain the advance, and staff planning was of a high order.

It worked. On September 20th the Second Army got well forward on the Gheluvelt plateau, and beat off all counter-attacks, the Fifth Army conforming on the left. On September 26th Polygon Wood was taken and most of Zonnebeke. On October 4th the line was pushed forward again to Broodseinde, Gravenstafel, and Poelcapelle. An overall advance of 2–3 miles had been made in a fortnight: with the result that the preliminary objective—Passchendaele village and the tip of the ridge running north to Staden—were now only a few thousand yards off. The spire of Passchendaele church was visible from several parts of the line. Here then at last was the commanding position so long desired, and its propinquity revived all Haig's hopes for a break-out. How near, too, were the Germans to collapse? They had certainly suffered very heavy casualties. Haig could not restrain his optimism, and once again he moved up his cavalry and his tanks in readiness for the pursuit. All depended on the weather.

But the rain that had begun so fitfully on October 3rd now set in in earnest. It soon converted the battlefield into a sea of mud, repeating the conditions of August. But this time it was too late in the year for the ground to dry out, even had there been another prolonged relief from the wet, while the continual shelling had irretrievably wrecked many of the watercourses and whole acres of land drains. On October 7th both Plumer and Gough said they preferred to stop. It was clear to them, and soon even to Charteris, that all hopes of bursting into the heart of Belgium had gone. The grand design could not now possibly be fulfilled. But Haig felt that they were so near to success that they must go on, at least to secure part of the objective as a winter line. The Army Commanders deferred, but more out of loyalty than conviction. Haig had other reasons for going on, too, the very same that had been advanced earlier in the year in support of the campaign, and which in his view were as valid and vital as ever: namely, that only by holding fast to the initiative would it be possible to keep our principal allies in the field, and to destroy the resistance of the German Army itself, which—he was still convinced—would soon reach breaking-point.

So reasoning, Haig gave orders for two more attacks, on October 9th and 12th. Both failed, or gained so little ground at such great cost that they amounted to failure. Only then was the offensive stopped, though not for long, as Haig had no intention of halting in Flanders yet.

By this time, however, Wully was deeply concerned about the action he should take. He disagreed categorically with Haig —as he always had done—over the resources and resisting power of the German Army, and he saw few prospects for further fighting in Flanders. Should he not, therefore, intervene to stop the offensive for good and all? He commented later:

'. . . wishing to satisfy me that GHQ were right, Sir Douglas Haig . . . asked me to interview his Army commanders and ascertain for myself whether they did not agree with him. That, of course, I could not well do, and he then invited me to meet them at a conference which he was about to hold on the matter. Whatever these commanders may have thought they certainly did not in the discussion which took place express an opinion contrary to his, or give any indication that they entertained one. Haig and his Army Commanders being better judges of the enemy's condition than I could claim to be, I was not prepared to carry my doubts to the extent of opposing him, and of therefore obstructing the application of that little extra pressure upon the enemy which experience has so often shown may convert an inconclusive battle into a decisive victory.'[20]

It was an old dilemma and a desperately difficult decision to take, but a sad outcome none the less. There is little doubt that, in contrast to the conversations of June 9th–10th—when he felt justified in swallowing his objections—Wully allowed himself on this occasion to be persuaded against his instincts and inner convictions. In talking to him about it after the War, Spears recorded:

'My impression was that he regretted having followed the orthodox course and thought he should have devised a means of forming an independent judgment.'[21]

What he could not do, and what he should have felt free to do, was to talk the whole thing over with the Prime Minister. But that was impossible. Relations with Lloyd George were such that they prevented any possibility of unbiassed judgment. Both Wully and Maurice were hag-ridden by the constant fear that if they failed to support Haig, then the Prime Minister would step in, and profit from the situation to launch some far-fetched enterprise and let the Western front go hang: in their view, the surest way to destroy the Army and lose the war.

*　　*　　*

On September 24th Wully had written to Haig:

'The Prime Minister has been away during the last fortnight and his mind has consequently been very active. I have had to knock out a scheme for operations in the Aden hinterland involving the employment of not less than a division. I have also had to destroy one for landing ten divisions at Alexandretta all of which would have had to come from you. Further, I have had to fight against sending more divisions to Mesopotamia. Generally, all round, I have been quite successful, although the expenditure of energy which ought otherwise to be employed has been a little greater than usual. The whole Cabinet are very anxious to give the Turk as hard a knock as possible this winter; they have heard he is very sick of the whole business and they think if we gave him a hard knock and at the same time treated him liberally, at the expense of Russia who has let us down so badly, it might be possible to arrange matters with him.'

The reference to Russia had been given point by recent events. Early in September the Germans captured Riga, and Kornilov, the Russian C-in-C, attempted a *coup d'état* that failed. Kerensky's Government was tottering and within a few weeks it collapsed altogether. A second Revolution took place, and by November 7th all was over (October 28th by the old-style calendar). Lenin and the Bolshevik party seized power and decided to end Russian participation in the war. An armistice was arranged in December, but a definitive treaty was not agreed—after difficult and disastrous negotiations for the Russians—until March 1918. So far as the Western Allies were concerned, however, Russia had been written off by the end of September, and on the 25th she formed one of the principal subjects of discussion at the conference held at Boulogne between Lloyd George and Painlevé, together with their military advisers, Wully and Foch. Neither Haig nor Pétain was present.

What would be the consequences of Russian defection? Was there anything in the latest German peace enquiries (nothing, it transpired)? What were the prospects in Flanders? Could the heavy guns come back from Italy now that Cadorna had gone over to the defensive? How much had the French Army recovered and when would Pétain put in his promised attack at Fort Malmaison on the Chemin des Dames (not until October 23rd)? Satisfactory answers were hard to find, for the war was in a nebulous and confused condition. The plainest issue derived from the latest French request that the BEF take over more line.

This was less of a bombshell than might appear. The possibility had been anticipated ever since the French Army troubles early in the summer, and was in part a direct consequence of them. Since every *poilu* was now entitled to ten days' leave every four months as of right, it meant that a considerable proportion of the French Army was permanently absent from the front. In addition, the Army as a whole was contracting in size through lack of drafts. Lastly, the French emphasised that they held a far longer frontage than the British, and had borne all the worst of the fighting for the first two years. It was time that the BEF relieved them. The War Cabinet acknowledged the force of the appeal, if not all the reasoning. Since the BEF, for example, was engaging a relatively higher proportion of enemy divisions in active operations, and fighting them hard, mere length of frontage was irrelevant. However, aware of French sacrifices and sensibilities, the War Cabinet had no wish to act ungenerously, and accepted the principle of extension. Wully announced this to the conference, but he at once made it clear that nothing could be done until after Third Ypres was over; it should form, in fact, part of the planning for 1918. Details would be left to Haig and Pétain to settle between them.

The French, however, were not content to let matters rest there, but pressed continuously over the next three months or so for positive action. Agreement was complicated by the despatch of five British and six French divisions to Italy after the débâcle at Caporetto at the end of October, and by British commitments at Cambrai at the end of November. In the end the French First Army was taken out of the line at Ypres, while the British Fourth Army (relieved on the coast by the French) was transferred south, and by the end of January 1918 had extended the British front by 30 miles, down as far as Barisis, east of Noyon.

More important—to this account—than all the moves that led up to the extension, were some of its effects. It hastened the formation of the Supreme War Council—to be described shortly—and soured the good relations between Wully and Haig. It is indeed arguable that their alliance began to break down over this, and that it contributed materially to Wully's isolation and dismissal in February 1918.

Although Haig was not present at the Boulogne Conference, he was visited by Wully and Lloyd George immediately afterwards and, according to Hankey, told of what had taken place.

'. . . Lloyd George told Haig of the Boulogne agreement. Haig was immersed in the Flanders offensive which he was personally directing and intended to continue all the autumn. He did not there and then refuse to carry out the Boulogne decision, but he made no secret of his view that it was inconsistent with the plans he was pursuing, and that no action should be taken until the plans for 1918 had been decided.'[22]

Haig reported the incident differently. In his Diary for October 3rd:

'A great bombshell arrived in the shape of a letter from the CIGS stating that the British Government had "approved in principle" of the British Army in France taking over more line from the French, and details are to be arranged by General Pétain and myself. This was settled at a Conference at Boulogne on September 25th at which I was not present. Nor did either L. George or Robertson tell me of this decision at our interview. All the P.M. said was that "Painlevé was anxious that the British should take over more line." And Robertson rode the high horse and said that it was high time for the British now to call the tune, and not play second fiddle to the French, etc, etc, and all this when shortly before he must have quietly acquiesced at the Conference in Painlevé's demands! R. comes badly out of this, in my opinion, especially as *it was definitely stated (with the War Cabinet's approval) that no discussion re operations on the Western front would be held with the French without my being present.*'[23]

The two accounts are not wholly incompatible. Haig may or may not have been told verbally of the decision, but he was certainly not consulted about it beforehand. It was not long before Wully heard of his displeasure.

'I gather from Lord R. Cecil that you are perhaps a little disappointed with me in the way I have stood up for correct principles, but you must let me do my job in my own way. I have never yet given in on important matters and never shall. In any case, whatever happens, you and I must stand solid together. I know we are both trying to do so.'[24]

This was certainly no time to fall out for the Prime Minister was piling on pressure every day. Wully and Haig needed each other more than ever.

Following Boulogne Haig had been asked to submit his views about future policy, taking into account Russia's disappearance from the war. This he did on October 8th. He took the opportunity, not only to reiterate his firm belief in Western strategy and the continuation of Third Ypres, but to reject the latest French demand and insist that every Ally look after its own defence, above all to refrain from calling on the British, whose Army was the only one engaging the Germans in serious battle. However Haig may be criticised for the way he conducted Third Ypres, he never wavered in his aim, and at this moment his single-minded persistence stood Wully in great stead. Indeed, already worried about Flanders, Wully was now beginning to have doubts about the consequences of Russian peace moves upon the chances of winning the war in the west.

'As regards the collapse of Russia I enclose some rough notes recently prepared for me with which I generally concur. They may be useful to you.

'The view taken, and quite naturally, by certain people here is that the collapse of Russia would make our task very much harder, and no doubt it would. Germany has some 90 divisions on the Russian front while Austria has between 30 and 40. . . Of the 90 German divisions some would no doubt have to stay in and about Russia for a long time to come, but the withdrawal to the West Front during the winter of even 30 divisions would make a considerable difference. . .

'My views are known to you. They have always been "defensive" in all theatres but the West. But the difficulty is to *prove* the wisdom of this now that Russia is out. I confess I stick to it more because I see nothing better, and because my instinct prompts me to stick to it, than to any convincing argument by which I can support it. Germany may be much nearer the end of her staying power than available evidence shows, but on the other hand France and Italy are not much to depend upon, and America will require a long time. Further, it is argued that stagnation will destroy the Nation's determination. It is not an easy business to see through the problem when present resources of both sides and hostile gains are considered.'[25]

Haig's Memorandum arrived just when Wully needed it most.

'Your memorandum is splendid. . .

'He [Lloyd George] is out for my blood very much these days. Milner, Carson, Curzon, Cecil, Balfour, have each in turn expressly spoken to me separately about his intolerable conduct during the last week or two and have said they are behind us. Since then he has got my Future Policy Paper and your Memo. A Cabinet is now sitting. He will be furious and probably matters will come to a head. I rather hope so. I am sick of this d—d life.

'I can't help thinking he has got Painlevé and Co. here in his rushing way so as to carry me off my feet. But I have big feet! The great thing is to keep on good firm tactical ground. This is difficult for he is a skilful tactician but I shall manage him.'[26]

Matters had indeed come to a head. Lloyd George had known only too well what Wully and Haig would say in their

Papers, and he had no intention of giving in this time. The alternative—or rather the solution to the whole problem of strategic planning and advice—was in outline already in his mind: namely, 'some central body to control the operations of all the Allies',[27] but he did not yet see how to bring it about. On this occasion he adopted another expedient, and it very nearly induced Wully to resign there and then, and several members of the War Cabinet as well. Claiming that he was merely following a precedent set by Asquith at the outset of the war, he by-passed the CIGS altogether and sought military advice elsewhere: from Lord French (C-in-C Home Forces) and Henry Wilson (GOC Eastern Command), both known to be critics of current military policy, and French an embittered one. Hankey recorded:

'*October 10th.* . . The Prime Minister saw Robertson in the afternoon, but the interview was unsatisfactory. At 7.20 pm Curzon called on me and told me that Derby had told him that Robertson had just offered his resignation. Derby had, in order to gain time, refused to accept it that night, and had asked Robertson to dinner. Curzon had then explained to Derby . . . that there was no lack of confidence in Robertson; that the War Cabinet was merely following Asquith's precedent in August 1914 in calling a War Council before taking a great decision; and that it was like calling an independent medical opinion. Curzon then went on to tell me that, if the Prime Minister drove out Robertson, Robert Cecil, Balfour, Derby, Carson, and he himself, probably, would leave the Government, which would then break up.

'*October 11th.* Before the War Cabinet I walked round St. James's Park with Lloyd George and Philip Kerr. I repeated Curzon's warning in very straight terms and he (Ll.G.) took the hint very quickly. . .'[28]

As for Wully—before finally deciding to resign, he sent Whigham over to France post-haste to tell Haig what had happened and ask his advice. Haig replied on October 11th:

'Whigham has told me the story. It is most terrible to think that the CIGS shd be thus worried in the midst of his great task—and you have my fullest sympathy.

'My advice is as follows:

'To continue in your appointment but if your advice is not accepted to at once resign.

'It is most desirable in my opinion however that a protest shd be handed to the P.M. giving full reason why it is undesirable for the Govt. to call in other mil. advisers now that the Imperial Genl Staff is in existence.

'Every good wish and good luck in your difficult task.'[29]

Wully accepted the advice and waited to see what French and Wilson would produce. It was still touch and go, but had its comic side, as the delivery of the Reports involved a complicated game of 'hunt the slipper'. Instead of going direct to Wully or the War Cabinet, they were handed on October 20th to Hankey, two copies of each Report. This was fortunate, for they

'confirmed my worst anticipations. They both recommended a central council, including a staff of generals in Paris, to be independent of the national General Staffs. This alone is enough to drive Robertson into resignation. They both condemned the continuance of the Flanders offensive next year, which is the course that Robertson and Haig recommend. In addition French's report hit out hard at Robertson and Haig, whose views were challenged in principle and detail.'[30]

Hankey passed the Reports to Derby, and also showed them 'unofficially' to Lloyd George and Milner, and there the matter stuck. On October 24th, however, French agreed to tone down some of his comments, and Hankey and Wilson helped him revise his Report. Hankey then took the papers to Wully, who would read them and pass them on to the War Cabinet with his comments in the ordinary way. The affair then suddenly fizzled out. Wully took all French's cracks in good part (20 out of 26 pages still devoted to this), and found that neither adviser was in favour of a campaign outside France. Both preferred to stand on the defensive, await the Americans, and under the new central directing body attempt a final solution in 1918 or 1919. Wully commented:

'But neither officer explained the dangers which attached to a waiting policy. As I pointed out to the War Cabinet, if by some miracle we could smoothly pass over the next eighteen months, and in 1919 resume the war under present conditions, plus the reinforcement in France of a million well-trained American troops, there would be no question as to which was the best policy to adopt. But unfortunately we could not perform miracles, and therefore had to consider whether the Entente might not, despite American assistance, be weaker, and not stronger, in 1919 than in 1918.'[31]

Finally, Lloyd George offered Wully an olive branch. He agreed

'not to decide either for or against a big offensive next year owing to the uncertainty of the position in Italy and Russia, but to be prepared for either.'

Furthermore

'. . . according to Robertson as reported by Derby, he had promised to try and get London as the *habitat* of the inter-ally Council of War which reconciled Robertson to it. Robertson also seemed to think that he and Haig could meet French's criticism. Derby was much relieved and so was I. . .'[32]

Barely had this skirmish been broken off, when a series of events erupted which hastened the main engagement between Wully and the Prime Minister and gave the latter an advantage that he never yielded. All were battles—the last phase at Ypres (October 22nd–November 10th), the rout of the Italians at Caporetto (October 25th–November 10th), Allenby's victory at Gaza-Beersheba (October 31st) leading to the capture of Jerusalem (December 11th), and the first battle of Cambrai (November 20th–December 4th)—and all, both victories and defeats, contributed in various ways to Wully's discomfiture.

*　　*　　*

The final agony at Ypres was now at hand. While United Kingdom and Anzac troops had borne the brunt of the first two phases, it was now the turn of the Canadians, transferred from the Lens-Vimy area to the Second Army in front of Passchendaele itself. Although the weather relented a little about the middle of the month, the ground was as saturated as ever and the swamps remained. At intervals further rain added to the misery and the mud. Physical endurance and morale had already been stretched to the limit, and conditions were so bad as to make it almost impossible to prepare for the battle, let alone fight it. Making roads, moving guns and stores, even getting rations up to the men, called for superhuman effort, and all under harassing bombardment from enemy aircraft and artillery. Yet the effort was made, and the attacks went in on October 22nd and 26th and November 6th and 10th, each grinding forward a few yards until, finally, the remains of the village of Passchendaele were taken and a portion of the ridge beyond. But the minimum winter line was never reached, and of course all hopes of a break-through had long since disappeared. On November 20th Haig called off all further attacks, and at long last Third Ypres was at an end.

The total cost was appalling and, at first sight, criminally expensive in terms of results, a quarter of a million casualties for an average gain of four miles, and an incalculable burden of physical and mental suffering which has never been forgotten. Passchendaele, above all the last phase, is still a synonym for the ultimate of horror, and unnecessary horror at that. Moreover, measured territorially, none of Haig's aims was achieved: no break-through, no drive to the ports, not even the full occupation of the ridge. But a closer assessment is neither so simple nor so damning. Indeed, no one has said the last word yet, perhaps for the very reason that, while the positive advantages of Third Ypres undoubtedly existed and were of the greatest importance, they are impossible to prove.

Let us look at two only: as they related to the Germans and the French.

So far as can be ascertained the Germans suffered almost as many casualties as the British, including prisoners; and judging by their own first-hand accounts they endured just as much horror. Haig, of course, claimed that the German Army was as good as done for. That was patently not true. By the end of the year divisions were flowing back from Russia, sufficient to make good the damage of 1917 and accumulate a formidable striking force for the spring of 1918. But, by their own admission, the destruction of so many of their best formations in Flanders, and their losses of trained and seasoned men, contributed directly to their failure to win the war outright in the following March and April. Third Ypres was partly responsible for that.

As for the French, it is true that Haig advanced paradoxical arguments. At first he said he would fight in Flanders only if the French played their part; then that he had to do so to save them from being attacked. The validity of both propositions has been denied, but they did not in practice cancel each other out. The French did fight both in Flanders and elsewhere, though later than promised and on a comparatively small scale—but they fought, and with success. The fact that only a few of their formations were committed and that these did well, does not alter the other fact that the bulk of their Army remained inactive and in an uncertain state. Pétain repeatedly besought Haig to attack, lest the Germans turn on him and profit from his weakness. If they had, there might well have been a disaster of the size of Caporetto. Haig recorded pessimism from Pétain on this score as late as September 19th.[33] It was certainly a strong contributory reason to his prolonging Third Ypres, though not the only one. Finally, the very fact that the French insisted at Boulogne and afterwards that the BEF take over part of their line was an indication, if not of weakness, at least of declining strength.

The end of Third Ypres brought Wully neither comfort nor credit in the eyes of the Prime Minister, who held him responsible equally with Haig for its disappointing outcome. Moreover, Wully was the whipping-boy always to hand. Unhappily the battle that followed brought no relief either, despite its brilliant start. In the Third Army area (Byng) little fighting had been going on since the Arras offensive of the previous spring. The downland round Cambrai was dry and comparatively untouched, but the German defences—part of the Hindenburg Line—were well sited, wired, and gunned. They, too, would doubtless have stood proof against the customary form of attack. In the early morning of November 20th, however, over 300 British tanks moved suddenly out of the mist against them in a mass assault and took the defenders by surprise. The tanks crushed the wire, dropped fascines of brushwood into the trenches, crossed them and rolled on, infantry following. But the tanks were not the only surprise. Instead of a preliminary bombardment lasting several days, there was none. Instead of a creeping barrage accurately registered, fierce covering fire was put down ahead of the tanks when the assault was loosed, adequately ranged by survey. Thus the ground was not pulverised into destruction, nor were the defenders warned. The advance went wonderfully well. With one exception in the centre, it breached the defences on a six-mile front, and then got through every line but the last. By that time, however, all the tanks had been used up and the crews exhausted, the infantry could not get on without them, the cavalry as usual were too vulnerable to exploit. The Germans rushed up their reserves and the battle became static. Cambrai failed by a short head, and the attackers found themselves shut up in a dangerous salient. A few days later, on the 30th, the counter-attack came in and broke through in the south, collapsing the flank and gaining ground beyond the original British start-line. In the north the defence held, but Haig decided to pull back part of the way to straighten the line. Losses were about equal on both sides, some 45,000 (including prisoners), but for the British it was a great disappointment, not so much on account of what they had lost, but of what they had failed to gain. A bold experiment had misfired, but the lessons would be well applied in the second battle of Cambrai in August of next year. The repercussions of First Cambrai were felt far beyond Third Army. The news was badly handled. The victory was trumpeted at once, but the defeat only grudgingly let out. The public was confused and disappointed, and an enquiry was set up to find out what had happened and apportion blame. Lloyd George castigated Haig and later tried to use the battle as an excuse to get rid of him. Thanks to Derby his manœuvre failed, but through Derby he did succeed in getting rid of Charteris, who had long misled Haig as to the real resources of the enemy and had been the chief instigator of his extraordinary optimism about German weakness. Other officers at GHQ lost their jobs too, including Kiggell, the CGS; and Gough was violently attacked.

For Wully the bitterest irony of all arose out of the one unequivocal British success, at a time when the Allies were suffering a succession of checks and defeats. It will be recalled that, since the end of June, Allenby had been getting ready to do what Murray had twice failed to bring off in the spring—capture Gaza and invade Palestine in earnest. By the autumn he had improved his stores and communications and enlarged his force to three cavalry and seven infantry divisions, with a considerable increase in artillery. It was a far stronger army than that of the Turks opposing him, though he did not seem to realise it. On being told, however, early in October that the

War Cabinet expected him to get as far as Jerusalem and Jaffa, he took fright and sent in an exorbitant demand for reinforcements, due, it appeared, to exaggerated reports of Turkish strength.[34] His demand, naturally enough, was refused; and at the end of the month he attacked with what he had. His success was immediate. He broke through the Turkish defences between Gaza and Beersheba, captured both these towns, and drove north. Early in December he took Jerusalem, thus fulfilling the Prime Minister's dearest wish. Indeed, the capture of the Holy City acted not only as a set-off to disappointments elsewhere, but was a moral stimulus out of all proportion to its strategic value. No matter, Wully was as pleased as anyone about it; but he did not budge from the view he had always held, namely that Palestine was a sideshow and should not be allowed to detract from the main struggle in the west. Therefore it was unwise to become too deeply committed against the Turks, however intoxicating the success.[35] He felt precisely the same about Maude's successes in Mesopotamia. Lloyd George, however, saw only sinister meaning in this attitude. He considered that Allenby's exorbitant demands in October had been instigated by Wully, solely to stifle the Palestine offensive for fear it should halt the flow of drafts to France. Further, he made it the substance of his accusation when, in December, he tried to persuade the Secretary of State for War to get rid of both Wully and Haig, the latter for having mishandled Cambrai. Derby, however, defended them both with skill and success, so that Lloyd George dropped these particular lines of attack. It is hardly necessary to point out that Palestine and Cambrai were but skirmishes in a larger, more embittered campaign: that of the Prime Minister against his generals.

*   *   *

As the autumn advanced, the struggle at the top grew ever tauter and more intense, with Lloyd George striking here, threatening there, seeking to switch every event to his advantage. Caporetto, though a dreadful disaster for the Allies, fell right into his lap. The facts need only be summarised.

The Italians had halted their last attack on the Isonzo in the middle of September and gone over to the defensive. Cadorna, long fearful of an assault by the Germans, was convinced that—

in view of what was happening in Russia—he had not long to wait. He was right. A German Army HQ arrived and half a dozen German divisions, most of them from the east. These troops formed the spearhead of an offensive launched on October 24th at the northern end of the Isonzo front. The weather was bad, the bombardment sudden and short, and the defenders tired and dispirited. On the 25th the enemy broke right through, and in the next few days the Italians retreated pell-mell some seventy miles to the line of the River Piave. There they stood. The Germans and Austrians were unable to maintain their momentum. French and British divisions were arriving, Diaz replaced Cadorna, and by November 10th the worst was over. But the Italians had lost nearly 300,000 prisoners, and all that great loop of territory which lies between Venice, the Alps, and the Isonzo.

For the British, Caporetto could hardly have come at a more awkward moment. The last phase at Ypres was just starting, and the BEF was compelled to release two divisions at once (three more followed), a serious inroad into its diminishing strength. But there was no alternative. Plans had recently been completed against this very contingency, and Wully had no choice but to instruct Haig accordingly. Haig was put out. It could only mean one thing—the end of his hopes in Flanders.

'I am doing my best to comply with your demands on this Army to supply a Field Force for Italy.

'. . . I have not sufficient information on which to base a definite opinion, but it is obvious that your plan at once surrenders the initiative which we enjoy here. And not only are we conforming to the Enemy's dictation in going to Italy, but on arrival there, our Divisions will run grave danger of getting involved in a disaster through becoming attached to an already demoralised Allied Army.'[36]

Wully knew all the objections by heart, but there was nothing for it, and he had already left for Italy himself, reaching Cadorna's HQ on October 31st.

'I found him at Treviso, Udine, his previous headquarters, having been occupied by the enemy two days before. Having discussed matters with him, and observed the condition of the retreating troops, I telegraphed my report to the War Cabinet, and then pro-

17. The visit of Henry Wilson, CIGS, and Winston Churchill, Secretary of State for War, to Wully when he was C-in-C, British Army of the Rhine in 1919. Wilson is on Churchill's immediate right

18. Wully speaking to Foch at Cologne Station in 1919

19. Unveiling the War Memorial
at Witley in Surrey

20. Receiving a key to unlock the War Memorial gates
in the city of Lincoln in 1922

ceeded to Rome in order to see the Italian War Minister before returning to London.'[37]

Wully's dry note concealed powerful emotions. With memories of Mons as clear as yesterday in his mind, he watched the eddies of this new retreat. One comment summed up all he thought and felt. On hearing of the fall of Cividale, he had grunted with sour force—'Shittydale'.

Back in London Lloyd George was at full stretch. Hankey reported:

'Ll.G. and I recalled with satisfaction the Memorandum . . . prepared for the Rome Conference last January, insisting on a *defensive*, if not an offensive, plan for Allied co-operation on the Italian Front, which had eventually resulted in arrangements for Allied reinforcements being made. Ll.G. of course is furious. The Germans have struck at the weak link, just as he himself wanted to do on (almost) the very same spot—a plan which the General Staff rejected with contempt.'[38]

But it was an ill wind—and during the next few days everything raced forward towards the setting-up of the Supreme War Council (as it came to be called) and its *advisory* General Staff, that 'central directing body' which had been fermenting in Lloyd George's mind. On October 30th the proposal was considered by the War Cabinet, and later that day the French representatives arrived in London to join in the discussion. On the next day Maurice (in the absence of his chief) was asked to draft a constitution, while Hankey got busy with plans for the secretariat. On November 2nd the scheme was approved by the War Cabinet, and Henry Wilson was appointed British Military Representative. Foch was nominated for France. On the 3rd the Government party travelled to Paris where, on the 4th, they had further talks with the French, and also advised Pershing (American C-in-C) and Haig of what was afoot. Then they took train for Italy for the conference at Rapallo on November 6th and 7th.

*　　*　　*

Meanwhile, Wully had been summoned from Rome where, he told Haig, 'the P.M. has wired me a new idea every day'.[39] His summons was the first hard news he had had of the new plan. He did not like it, nor did he care for the manner in which he had been apprised of it. He came to Rapallo in a deeply suspicious frame of mind, and his suspicions were immediately confirmed. In his view Lloyd George had taken advantage of his absence to rush things through, and he blamed Derby for letting him get away with it. He anticipated another bitter struggle with the Prime Minister and wrote wearily, 'I daresay I can make it more or less all right'.[40] He was soon disabused. As Hankey explained to him first thing on the morning of November 6th, it was impossible to stop the Supreme War Council. The War Cabinet was absolutely committed to the idea, and that was that. Why kick against it? Hankey did, however, coat the pill by exposing his own original doubts of the practicability of the scheme, although these were fast disappearing and would shortly vanish altogether. But he made no impression upon Wully who 'made no secret of his objections to the scheme, and I deduced from his manner that he was half inclined to chuck the appointment of CIGS.'[41] However, the day passed peaceably enough, with the conference concentrating on the Italian situation. It was on November 7th that the storm burst. The subject was the Supreme War Council, its definition and initiation, and Wully signified his disapproval by walking ostentatiously out of the room. On the way out he asked Hankey to record his action in the minutes, and this was done.

Why did Wully react so violently and, it might be said, so unreasonably against what was in principle a sound idea?

The answer turns on this very point. Wully did not dispute the principle—if he had done, then it would be correct to write him off at once as a hidebound isolationist—but he deeply distrusted the motive and the practice. What had happened?

Unified direction of the war was not, of course, a new idea. The value of it was self-evident, and there had been several attempts to bring it about. As early as October 1915 Lord Selborne (then a member of the Cabinet) had proposed an Allied Council sitting in Paris, or alternatively meeting twice a week, once at Calais, once at Dover. The Council had never sat or met at all. At that time the war was going very ill, with *inter alia* the Dardanelles dying on its feet and the Salonika force charging into the Balkans. Wully, still CGS in France, had watched with horror the total lack of strategic planning and Allied co-ordination at the top. He was called upon for advice, and sent in two Memoranda—one to the War Office, one to the Cabinet[42]—in each of which he proposed a plan, the restoration of the General Staff machinery, and proper co-operation with the French. His words added impetus to the next step, a suggestion for a 'Joint Standing Committee to co-ordinate the action of the Allies in regard to the war', to consist of Ministers and technical advisers. Nothing, however, came of this either. Instead, intermittent conferences were called, as the occasion seemed to demand, to settle immediate problems. There was no permanent integrated planning in the accepted sense.[43]

On the other hand, after Wully became CIGS and Haig C-in-C, BEF, at the end of 1915, there was a marked improvement in liaison with the French. The two men hit it off with Joffre, and although the latter had a weakness for Salonika, all three were primarily Westerners. Moreover, the military meetings, with Joffre in the chair, exerted international authority. Although Russia was inadequately represented, members discussed operations on all the fronts, and Joffre came to be regarded virtually as C-in-C in the west. This was due partly to French preponderance on land in Europe (outside Russia), and partly to Joffre's personal influence, which cemented everyone together. In this respect he stood alone, above all the other Allied leaders, political as well as military. The failures of 1916 were due only in part to the absence of proper planning machinery: more to the general inadequacy of preparation before the war, the lack of a powerful and trained British Army comparable to the French and the fact that it was thrown into battle before it was ready, and the necessity to evolve weapons and techniques suited to siege warfare, notably the right use of artillery and tanks. Notwithstanding, the initiative was firmly grasped in the west, and the German Army in France thrown on the defensive.

After Joffre resigned and Lloyd George succeeded Asquith in December 1916, unified direction actually declined. No one replaced Joffre, though Lloyd George—by sheer dynamism and persistence—took up the reins in his own way. He insisted on more frequent meetings between the Allies, politicians and generals together, and infused them with energy and ideas. He had a large view of the war. Unfortunately his methods often vitiated the good in his aims. He intrigued too readily, and he got up against his own generals by undermining their authority. His mishandling of the Nivelle affair was a notorious example of this. Single command in the field was sound sense, but both Lloyd George and Nivelle behaved in a stupid and shameful manner. The Calais business stank in the nostrils of Wully and Haig, and it prejudiced them against repeating the experiment in practically any form. It created a most unfortunate precedent. A great pity, for in two other instances the principle had worked quite well in a small way: Gouraud and Hamilton at the Dardanelles, Milne and Sarrail in the Balkans; but these were local arrangements on the periphery of the war. Neither led to any victories. In any event, the larger principle of Allied co-operation and central direction had, by May 1917, been retarded through the worsening of relations between political and military leaders, both in France and in England. Moreover, French preponderance on land had sharply declined.

And yet May 1917 was the critical month: the very moment when a joint organisation for planning and control, inter-Service and inter-Allied, was most needed.

Western strategy had been given full rein for two years: ever since the French offensives of 1915, then the British effort on the Somme in 1916, and now the inconclusive battles of Arras and the Aisne in April–May 1917. At the end of it all, the Germans, though certainly depleted, were still in possession of an important part of France and strongly entrenched in the Hindenburg Line. It was high time for a searching review before further commitment. Such a review, to have any value, should only have been undertaken by a joint organisation of the kind described, with all the facts and all the authority at its command. It could then have arrived at a comprehensive assessment of strategy, including political and economic factors, taking into account the stalemate in the west, the alternatives in Italy and elsewhere, the impact of the Russian Revolution, the morale of the French Army, the U-Boat offensive, and much else. As a result it might, or it might not, have authorised Third Ypres. If it had done so, it would only have been after an impartial examination of strategic objectives in Belgium, naval claims about the Channel ports, the ground and climate in

Flanders, French co-operation and the timing of other offensives, and the real state of the German Army and German resources. Had that happened, then at least Third Ypres would have been launched on the basis of the best advice available and of a general decision. The outcome of the battle might have been no different, but in that case the cost would have been reckoned as the price paid for an *agreed* operation, and its constructive results properly appreciated.

This, of course, is the judgment of hindsight, but it is no less valid on that account.

What actually happened was that Third Ypres was fought almost—it might be said—in default of a decision: due mainly to the drive and convictions of Haig, backed after initial doubts by Wully, but in the teeth of opposition by Lloyd George and of reluctance on the part of most of the War Cabinet. The French were critical too, though they were more concerned that the British should fight somewhere in France, rather than not at all. The rights and wrongs of the battle itself, and the fact that it belonged to a long-standing strategic plan, devised in agreement with Joffre, are not relevant to the point that no such step should ever have been taken without unity of opinion at the top, or at least a very heavy majority in favour. It follows that much of the opprobrium generated by Third Ypres, and which fell almost entirely upon the shoulders of Wully and Haig, was also irrelevant. They may well have been right, if not all through, at least in making the attempt. Criticism should be directed less against individuals than against the system of control, or lack of it, and which in turn operated against a background of enmities, misunderstandings, and sheer inexperience of war on a world scale. For that, all the individuals concerned must bear their part of the blame.

So it turned out that almost every event of 1917 served to intensify the suspicion between Wully and Lloyd George. It reached the point where neither was able to see the good in anything that the other said or did. Each sought an ulterior motive. For example, Lloyd George, as we have seen, saw nothing but evasion in Wully's reluctance to let Allenby go beyond Jerusalem, a plot in short to save soldiers for the west, regardless of strategic advantages in the east. On the other hand, Wully, mindful of Calais and Nivelle, regarded the Supreme War

Council merely as a device of the Prime Minister's to get round the War Office and get rid of him. There was an element of truth in both, but the truth itself was larger than any personal motive or method employed.

*   *   *

The idea of a common authority was revived during the late summer of 1917, a period of acute anxiety arising out of the demoralisation of the French and Russian Armies and of the depression over Ypres. In particular the Paris Conference of July 25th–26th, overcrowded with delegates, proved so nearly abortive that it filled most of the leaders with despair. Massive meetings of this kind were futile. Wully shrugged his shoulders with disgust and went back to his desk, determined more than ever to back Haig to win the war in the west. Others, no less disgusted, began to think in terms of some kind of directing organisation, small but effective, to pull the whole Allied effort together.

Smuts was one of these, and his thoughts were crystallised by a talk with Henry Wilson, currently unemployed, but who managed, nevertheless, to remain in circulation.[44] Wilson contended

'that there ought to be a body composed of three soldiers, English, French, and Italian, with suitable staffs and full knowledge, who would be empowered to draw up plans of attack and defence along the whole line from Nieuport to Egypt.'[45]

Soon afterwards Wilson heard that Lloyd George was thinking of compelling Wully to submit all his plans to a committee of three generals, including Lord French and Wilson himself. Wilson soon disabused French of this fatuity, but outlined his own idea instead. French was taken with it, and so was Lloyd George, when the three met on August 23rd. The Prime Minister promised Wilson the post of British representative and told him to go and preach the gospel to other members of the War Cabinet, which he did.

Lloyd George could not have been taken entirely by surprise, for he had already heard of similar proposals from France. Painlevé had sounded him and Milner about an inter-Allied staff in Paris, with Foch at its head, but was told that the idea—

though attractive—was premature, and that British opinion needed time to come round to it. Even so, by the end of August, the general conception of a directing body had been bruited about, and Hankey only just prevented the Prime Minister from telling the whole story in a letter to President Wilson on August 30th.[46] The matter required further thought. Besides which, neither Wully nor Haig had been told, nor were they given any inkling of a private conversation between Painlevé and Lloyd George at Boulogne on September 25th, when it was finally agreed between the two men to go ahead with the plan at the first opportunity.

Wully, however, was not entirely in the dark. At his meeting in Paris on July 25th–26th with Foch, Cadorna, and Pershing, to consider what should be done in the event of Russia falling out of the war, the suggestion was made of 'a permanent inter-Allied military organisation, which would study and prepare the rapid movements of troops from one theatre to another.'[47] Wully did not vote against the idea, though suspicious and unsympathetic. He told Haig:

'As you can imagine I would have nothing to do with an Allied Staff, and I have heard since that the French Ministers are very sick in consequence. You know the meaning of this Allied Staff without my explanation. But of course I could not refuse to work out arrangements with them to support Italy in case of need and this will eventually be done. . .

'. . . as the French keep rubbing in that it is necessary to have a Central Staff at Paris, I can see Lloyd George in the future wanting to agree to some such organisation so as to put the matter in French hands, and to take it out of mine. . .'[48]

Thus it was not technical co-operation that Wully objected to—that was indispensable—but the wider implications of strategic control. Haig agreed with him.

'. . . in any case the idea of organising an Allied Staff in Paris is quite unsound, even if a really good French Staff Officer were in existence.'[49]

August and September passed without an overt move, but on October 10th the Prime Minister set the trap. He told Wully of his intention to consult Lord French and Henry Wilson on strategy, and on the 11th the War Cabinet formally invited them to submit their reports. They did so by devious means, as has been described, towards the end of the month. It was, of course, a device for airing the plan for a Supreme War Council, and it worked. It nearly caused Wully to walk out there and then, a move which would have pleased the Prime Minister very much, as it would have enabled him to kill two birds with one stone—securing both the plan and Wully's resignation without further ado. But he underestimated Wully's strength, and the support he commanded among members of the War Cabinet, not to mention the Army and the country at large. Curzon gave a clear warning that, if Wully went, he and several others would leave the Government too. Lloyd George, however, was deflected only for a moment, his goal was well in sight. On October 14th Hankey recorded:

'The P.M., Balfour, Smuts, Franklin Bouillon, Foch and I had an informal conference in the library in the morning. The P.M. horrified me by raising the question of an inter-allied War Council *and permanent General Staff* in Paris. Of course Franklin Bouillon and Foch leaped at it. I had no time to warn the P.M. that in Robertson's present hurt, bruised and suspicious frame of mind he will see in it merely a proposal further to upset his authority and may resign. When I warned him of this afterwards he was astonished, and hardly credited it! . .'[50]

Ten days later Caporetto started, and thereafter it was a straight sprint to Rapallo.

*   *   *

The Supreme War Council was formally constituted on November 7th and took its first decision on that day. The general aim of the Council was to 'watch over the general conduct of the war', but in view of the uncertainty over Russia it concerned itself particularly with the fronts where the three Western Allies were engaged. The Council was composed of the Prime Minister and one other Minister of the Government of each of the Great Powers. Their job was to take counsel and recommend action for decision by the Governments concerned. Likewise, in strictly military matters, the various General Staffs and Commanders remained responsible to their own Governments as before, but they were under obligation to submit their plans to the Council for comment and co-ordination.

For this purpose, Permanent Military Representatives were appointed to act as 'technical advisers' to the Council. These officers, together with their staffs, were to be stationed at Versailles—where the Council would also normally meet every month—and were empowered to receive 'all the proposals, information, and documents relating to the conduct of the war.'[51] It was clear, then, that although the Supreme War Council (including the PMRs) was in principle only an advisory body, in practice it would have very considerable power and be in a position to direct the war.

Wully had no objection to the Supreme War Council as such, namely as a permanent institution for inter-Allied consultation.

'The establishment of the Council filled a much-felt want, for it enabled ministers to meet regularly, helped to secure co-ordination of national policies, the proceedings could be properly recorded by the permanent secretariat, and in many ways it furthered the methodical despatch of business.'[52]

But here was the crux—

'But it should be noted that, although the object of setting up the Council was to ensure the better co-ordination of *military* action, the members of the Council were ministers, and therefore it was a political and not a military body. Consequently, it did nothing to improve the system of *military* command, while in one respect it struck deeply at the root principle of all military organisation, in that the "technical advisers" were empowered to advise the Council, i.e. their ministers, independently of their General Staffs.

'It is the right of a government to select its own professional advisers and to change them as often as it pleases, but it ought not to appoint independent advisers in addition, for such a proceeding must produce divided responsibility, delay, friction, and confusion.'[53]

This was the cardinal point at issue, and the reason for the appointment of Henry Wilson. If Lloyd George gave in on this, it would defeat the whole scheme to by-pass Wully, indeed wreck—for him—one of the main objects of the Supreme War Council. The struggle was on. The Army Council took up the cudgels at once.

'. . . they pointed out to the War Cabinet that by Letters Patent they exercised the powers and authority of a Commander-in-Chief in regard to all questions connected with the Military Forces. They therefore assumed that the "technical advice" given by the British military representative to the Supreme War Council would be given on their behalf, and that he would, like all other military officers, receive his instruction from them. The War Cabinet replied that they did not question that he was subject to their jurisdiction, but they counted on the good will of the Council in making a success of the new scheme, and they wished it to be understood that the military representative would have "unfettered discretion as to the advice he offers".'[54]

The orthodox solution lay in the fusion of the two posts of CIGS and PMR, so that one man held them both; but that was impossible. Lloyd George would not accept Wully in such a capacity, nor was he as yet strong enough to replace him with Henry Wilson. In any event that would have made nonsense of the independence of the technical adviser. So a compromise was reached whereby Wully was permitted to attend the meetings of the Supreme War Council in company with Henry Wilson. For the time being, therefore, the difficulty was patched over by a system of dual counsellors; but like all patches it soon worked loose.

No such difficulties, however, were permitted with the appointment of the other PMRs, despite Lloyd George's protests. In all three cases—France, Italy, and USA—the Chiefs of Staff sent subordinates, if they did not attend themselves. In the case of France Lloyd George had his way at first, insisting that Foch relinquish his duties at the French War Office. But he met his match when Clemenceau replaced Painlevé as Prime Minister in the middle of November, and the arrangement was cancelled. By sending Weygand to Versailles, Foch made sure of hearing his own voice fully and faithfully reproduced.

Finally, there was yet another possibility for co-ordinating military action—the appointment of an Allied Commander-in-Chief. The idea had been at the back of Painlevé's mind when he first approached Lloyd George, and he wanted Foch to have the job after serving a preliminary term as Allied Chief of Staff. But there were obvious difficulties—*inter alia*, the selection of the right man, and the fact that if the Allied Ministers were not agreed on strategic policy, how could a single general impose agreement on them. Lloyd George was in any event opposed to the proposal. Speaking in the House of Commons on November 19th he said that such an appointment 'would produce real friction, and might really produce not merely friction between the armies, but friction between the nations and Governments.' He, too, had not forgotten Nivelle. The real solution lay in joint consultation by the Chiefs of Staffs, under the authority of the Heads of Governments, and for an Allied Commander-in-Chief in the field to carry out the strategic policy agreed. But that had to wait until the next German war.

Meanwhile, history took an ironical turn. Foch did indeed become Allied Commander-in-Chief, not at the instance of the Supreme War Council, but at the personal request of Haig, who called upon him to direct the diverging movements of British and French troops after the German onslaught of March 1918. Pétain had prophesied earlier that an Allied C-in-C was only possible among Allies where one Army was the dominant partner.[55] The French and British had been roughly equal since early 1917, hence their disunity when their commanders disagreed. Thus it required a desperate emergency to secure unified command in March 1918, just as the disaster of Caporetto had been necessary to secure a system of joint consultation six months earlier.

*　　　*　　　*

November was a volcanic month for the Prime Minister, who was determined to ensure the acceptance of Rapallo at the earliest opportunity. On the 11th he saw Clemenceau, the future French Prime Minister, in Paris to secure his support. On the 12th he delivered a forceful, scorching speech in a plea for unity: forceful because he marshalled his arguments with power and passion; scorching because he made it clear that he attributed the disappointments of 1917 and the poor prospects for 1918, after three years of war, to the incompetence of the generals. His speech made a great impression in London as well as in Paris. On the 13th he reported to the War Cabinet, and on the 14th he addressed the House of Commons. Five days later, after a crucial debate, Parliament approved his actions; and he was able to announce the backing of President Wilson as well. On November 30th the Supreme War Council assembled at Versailles and, under the direction of Clemenceau, set up a framework of committees for the study of technical and specialised questions. On December 1st it held its second formal session and proceeded at once to a general review of the war. Although the Russians had dropped out, the presence of the Americans ensured as full and effective a representation as could be expected, and imparted impetus to their own participation in the hostilities. Lloyd George's triumph was complete. It was a remarkable example of war-winning drive and will power. Within a month he had translated the whole plan into action and, seen apart from the baser motives and animosities, it constituted a fine act of statesmanship.

Meanwhile, the war went on—with varying fortune. In Italy, Foch, Cadorna, and Henry Wilson had been deputed to find out what was happening and recommend action. But the front was already being stabilised, the enemy drive was almost exhausted, so that by the middle of November the Italian Army (with British and French troops coming up) had re-established itself on the line of the River Piave. In Palestine, Allenby had won Third Gaza and was driving towards Jerusalem. In the Balkans, Sarrail was being replaced by Guillaumat, one of Clemenceau's first decisions, and although the Balkan stalemate would not be broken for another nine months, the new C-in-C, by his tact and efficiency, renewed hope on what had at one time seemed a hopeless front. In Russia, the Bolsheviks had seized power, and it was only a question of time before she formally withdrew from the war. In practice she was already out of it, and by the end of the year the Germans were switching troops fast from east to west. In Flanders, the last attack had been made on Passchendaele Ridge. The conditions there, and the transfer of five British divisions from France to Italy, made it impossible to prolong an offensive that had already gone on too long. On November 20th Cambrai was launched with its initial exhilarating success, but by early December the German counter-attack had wiped out the advance and converted a near-victory into a near-defeat.

Like Wully, Haig was enduring a period of twilight. He had come nowhere near to achieving his original aims in Flanders, and such visible success as he had achieved had only been won at great visible cost. Cambrai was a terrible disappointment.

He had lost five divisions to Italy where, instead of helping him to win the war in France, they could only hope to stop a retreat, and on a front where no decisive victory could be expected. He was desperately short of men, with little prospect—so far as he or Wully could see—of adequate replacements; and now he was being asked to extend his line as well. As to Rapallo, though not directly involved, he did not care for what he heard, but was inclined to be philosophical about it. He wrote to Wully on November 12th:

'The adoption of the Scheme having apparently been decided on by superior authority, there is nothing to be gained by a statement of my views on that aspect of the problem. I fear, however, that it will prove very difficult to work satisfactorily.

'. . . Governments may not confirm the plans agreed on by this War Council, or they may not all act loyally on their agreements. Nor will the representatives necessarily be very competent to pass judgment on strategical plans and to form strategical opinions. They will of course have the assistance of the new military machinery which is to be created, and it is with the working of this that you and I will be mainly concerned no doubt.

'The procedure to be adopted in this working seems to me very important if the possibilities of friction are to be minimised.

'I presume all my plans, reports, etc., will be submitted to you and to you only, and that the instructions of the British Government will come to me through you. Any other system would, in my opinion, be highly unsatisfactory if not entirely unworkable.

'I also presume that I shall have no direct official liaison with the military representatives of the Supreme War Council and that these representatives, or their agents, will not be empowered to visit my Army or subordinate Commanders, or troops, to discuss action past or future. If they are to be so empowered the situation would certainly be very difficult and likely to become impossible. It would be almost equivalent to charging the military representatives of the Supreme War Council with many of the functions of the Commander-in-Chief.

'As regards your own position, and that of our own War Cabinet, the relations between you and it, between it and the Supreme War Council, and between the latter (and the military representatives on it) and yourself, it is evident that very careful organisation will be required if utter confusion is not to result. But that is not a matter for me to offer opinions on.

'The object of ensuring common plans and coordination in executing them is of course admirable, and I think that as the Government has apparently decided on this Scheme, all we can do is try and work it until and unless we find that it is not possible to do so.

'If it were still possible however to prevent this Supreme War Council from coming into existence, I think it would be greatly to the interest of Gt Britain to do so.'[56]

Such was the position at the end of November 1917.

Chief of the Imperial General Staff: December 1917 to February 1918

By early December the turbulent events of the autumn were cascading together, like mountain tributaries, into a common stream. Third Ypres, Caporetto, and Cambrai had run their course, the drive to Jerusalem was nearly over, the Supreme War Council had been firmly founded, and its members were getting down to positive planning. A general flow was forming —though still undecided in direction, and many obstacles remained in mid-stream. Which way was the war going?

On November 19th Wully had advised the War Cabinet against standing on the defensive in 1918. Morale as well as strategy was involved.

'. . . if it would pay us to wait for the Americans and to defer our main effort till 1919, it would equally well pay the enemy to deprive us of the opportunity and try to get a decision in 1918. He would, if the Entente were visibly on the defensive, be able to deal with us as and when he wished; our Armies would deteriorate in efficiency; and the spirit of the nations, not excluding our own, would suffer. With nothing to fear from England, France becoming weaker both in numbers and determination, Russia and Italy probably going out of the war altogether, to say nothing of the smaller members of the Entente, the Germans would find a combination of circumstances which would not fail to render them perfectly complacent.

'*The conclusion that I arrive at is that the Campaign of 1919 may never come*, and in any case we shall next year inevitably have to bear the chief brunt of the war. It is upon us that the burden of supporting the weaker Allies will mainly rest. . .'[1]

If Russia made peace, he concluded, then the Germans would be able to attack in the west; in which case the best Allied plan was to hold grimly to the initiative and, by spoiling attacks, forestall and disrupt enemy preparations. If, however, Russia stayed in the war, then the Allies should make ready to launch a big offensive in the spring and aim at 'a definite decision in 1918'. That meant economising on every front except France, sending every available ship to bring over American troops, and getting to grips—at this eleventh hour—with the problem of manpower. The British Army was already 100,000 under strength. Half a million more men were needed by April 1918 to make good winter wastage and meet the demands of the year ahead. If that was settled—and only the War Cabinet could settle it—serious planning could begin at once. But time was short.[2]

Lloyd George was no more impressed by this advice than on previous occasions. Moreover, it had been written on the very day of his triumph in the House of Commons, November 19th, when his plans for the Supreme War Council were approved. He found it convenient, therefore, to refer the whole matter—with one exception—to the new body, although no answer could be expected from the 'technical advisers' for several precious weeks. The exception was manpower, and after continued pressure by Wully, Haig, Derby, and the Army Council itself, he set up a Cabinet Committee to go into the subject, first meeting on December 10th.

The meeting was long overdue. The Army authorities had never ceased to warn the Government, and whatever the rights and wrongs of their case in the past, it carried full force now. By any calculation Haig was short of men in France, and it was becoming clearer every day that the Allies would have to meet a massive German assault in the spring. The Committee, however, maintained that its duty was to consider manpower in relation to the war effort as a whole, and to safeguard the staying power of the Allies until the Americans could swing the scales. Meantime, Britain was bearing the main burden: on sea, in the air, in finance, shipbuilding, coal, munitions, and other industry, and was also making great strides in the production of timber and food. All this had to be taken into account and co-ordinated with the requirements of the Army. It was a question of priorities. No Service or department was prepared to make a voluntary cut in its personnel, indeed most were asking for more. Only the War Cabinet could decide, and enforce that decision. It was now that the bad relations between Lloyd George and his generals bore such bitter fruit. For the Prime Minister it was the same old story as before. He had been hearing it for at least two years: namely, a plea for more and yet more men to sustain and be slaughtered in hopeless battles in France, each of which had been portrayed to him—so he contended—in over-optimistic terms. How did Haig reconcile his confident statements before and during Passchendaele, and his supposition that the German Army was at the end of its tether, with his and Wully's present demand for 600,000 Category A (physically fit) men, 320,000 men of lower categories, and 240,000 18-year-olds for Home Defence? Lloyd George was determined not to yield again and referred the matter to the Ministry of National Service, which had taken over most of the recruiting machinery and disputed the War Office figures. In the end the Ministry could only offer about one sixth of the Category A men, and about one third and one half of the others—though the men were found quickly enough when the Germans nearly broke through three months later.[3]

Finally, the Committee, which had no soldier on it except Smuts, drew up the following list of priorities:

Navy and RAF (in process of formation as a separate Service).
Shipbuilding, tanks and aeroplane production.
Food and timber.
Army—by inference in fourth place, though not specifically listed there.

The Committee further explained that:

(1) Since the fighting in 1918 was likely to be defensive, losses would tend to be less.

(2) In reckoning 'wastage', the Committee relied upon the French method, which allowed for a lower casualty rate.

(3) The number of infantry battalions per division should be reduced from 12 to 9, and new divisions formed out of the surplus in order to create a larger mobile reserve.

(4) Cuts should be made in cavalry and home defence formations.

The Army Council disagreed in almost every particular, and pointed out that:

(1) Defensive fighting could well be more expensive than offensive. At Verdun, for example, the French (the defenders) had lost more heavily than the Germans. It all depended on the intensity of the battle.

(2) They did not know how the French reckoned casualties, but suspected that *every* soldier returning to service in a division was credited against the casualty rate. The British only took account of the men going back into the fighting line, hence the two methods were not comparable.

(3) Reducing the number of infantry battalions would not correct the shortage of personnel in the artillery and other arms. New divisions could not be created out of infantry alone, nor would such a move correct the shortage of infantry in the divisions so deprived.

(4) Cuts in cavalry and Home Defence formations had already been agreed. But Wully commented: 'The general result was to leave four divisions for home defence and to set free about 40,000 mostly belonging to categories below A1 for employment in France.'

(5) A number of active divisions would none the less have to be broken up in order to keep the remainder up to strength.[4]

The Army Council closed with a solemn warning as to the risks that were being run, in view of German preparations for attack. It was imperilling the BEF and endangering the very possibility of winning the war. Grave and prophetic words— but all to no avail. The War Cabinet stood by its decision, and likewise refused to cut down commitments in distant theatres, or divert the drafts going out to them. The reduction of infantry was duly carried out, but only in UK divisions in France, not in Dominion formations or in any others stationed abroad. The reorganisation—a highly complicated business—was completed just before the German attack in March, but as anticipated it did not make possible any addition to the general reserve.

*   *   *

Even before the manpower discussions began, the strategic situation had visibly deteriorated. On December 3rd hostilities ceased between Russia and Germany, and on the 15th an armistice was signed. The Germans were now transferring divisions from east to west at the rate of 2–3 per week, and had been doing so since early November. The first of the two alternatives, proposed by Wully in his Memorandum of November 19th, had therefore materialised. Russia was out of the war for good, which meant that the Germans would now concentrate on seizing the initiative in the west. In view of the manpower situation, nothing could stop them, and on December 3rd Haig

21. Wully with one of his grandchildren

22. 'A determined rather than skilful player'

23. Lloyd George, third from right, with Asquith, centre, after the war

had already warned his Army Commanders that they 'must be prepared to meet a strong and hostile offensive'.[5]

Unfortunately Lloyd George remained unconvinced. At its meeting on December 1st the Supreme War Council had instructed the PMRs to prepare a series of appreciations (duly rendered as Joint Notes during December and January), but had decided to postpone its next session for two months. Until then, therefore, there was no authority capable of persuading the Prime Minister to change his mind. Meanwhile, the capture of Jerusalem on December 11th proved too much for his impetuous spirit. He demanded to know at once how far Allenby could go. How soon could he occupy the whole of Palestine, and what did he need to push on to Aleppo, 350 miles to the north, to cut the railway to Mesopotamia? Allenby fortunately returned a cautious reply. Winter rains, railway construction, and all the other hazards of build-up were against him. He might reach the line Nazareth-Haifa by the following June or July. To take Aleppo, however, he required another eight to ten divisions (16–18 in all besides mounted troops), and large consignments of munitions and engineering material as well: all of which would strain the shipping situation to the utmost. In a confirmatory Memorandum Wully advised that, while Allenby should be allowed to exploit his success (particularly in the Hejaz) with what he had, the larger proposal be written off.

'The vital point to remember is that the conquest of Palestine requires men and material which can be provided only at the expense of the Western Front, and I would submit that the War Cabinet should, before deciding to extend the Palestine campaign, consider carefully the probability of the enemy attempting to force a decision on the Western Front, including Italy, early in 1918, and the possibility of his succeeding in doing so, if we do not concentrate our resources there.'[6]

But Lloyd George would not listen. Once again the matter was taken out of Wully's hands, and referred to the Supreme War Council at its next meeting at the end of January. And there—on the advice of the PMRs—it was duly decided to prosecute the Palestine campaign after all, a decision that impelled Wully to make a formal protest in open conference, in direct opposition to his own Prime Minister, and in the presence of all the other delegates. He did so utterly out of conviction, but it was a serious discourtesy, of course, and gave Lloyd George an additional excuse for getting rid of him a fortnight later. Soon afterwards Smuts was sent out to see Allenby and make final preparations, but the campaign was anticipated by the German offensive in France, and in the end Palestine had to be denuded of troops in order to bolster up the west. Wully was proved right after all, but it was small comfort to him—or anyone else—by then.

The year ended with a move towards peace, an offer put out by the Germans, at Russian request, on Christmas Day on the basis of 'no annexations, no indemnities'. Wully was asked, among others, for his advice. It was not easy to give, if only because any prospect of peace after more than three years of murderous warfare was morally difficult to reject. He opened his reply by enquiring into the motives behind the offer. The Germans were not likely to throw up the sponge at this stage, operating as they did from a position of strength. Secure in the east, they clearly hoped to weaken the Western Allies by propaganda, while keeping themselves intact. Were they not, in fact, only seeking a truce? If it failed, then they would have a good excuse to persuade their own people to go on fighting. If it succeeded, then they could husband their resources for a second, more conclusive, war later. Wully emphasised that, in refusing to treat, the Allies would have to face the stark and simple issue as to whether they could outlast the enemy. It meant realising that Germany was in a position to launch a powerful offensive in the west, before the Americans could redress the balance of strength; that the offensive might go off at any time after the middle of February, with a feint or two before the main attack, almost certainly in France, and probably south of Arras (Wully was right). In that case, reserves must be ready, cool heads kept, and every effort made to accelerate the arrival and build-up of American troops. By so enduring, 'we may hope to get eventually a favourable peace.'

Wully concluded with this warning:

'I venture to think that up to the present the people of this country have not been called upon for such sacrifices as they are capable of and are willing to make, once they realise that what they are fighting for is not mere territorial aggrandisement but their very lives and Imperial existence. . . The two main essentials to enable us to endure are shipping and men, and to provide both in adequate quantities will call for much greater sacrifices than any we have yet made. Without adequate ships and without adequate men—that is, all the men who can possibly be made available—to fight on land I do not think that we can hope to obtain a favourable peace. Therefore, if these ships and men cannot be produced, I can only advise the War Cabinet that, militarily, there seems to be no alternative but to accept peace on Germany's terms, and these I fear would, sooner or later, be disastrous to the British Empire.'[7]

Wully wrote this on December 29th, before knowing the Cabinet decision on manpower, and so had to express himself in general terms. But although there was no doubt of where his sentiments lay, the War Cabinet seemed shaken and undecided, and presented him a few days later with a questionnaire of extraordinary childishness. Three of the four questions boiled down to this: Can we win the war? If so, how?

By this time Wully had seen a draft of the Manpower Report and knew the worst. But he had already given an adequate answer, and was only able to repeat himself in different words. He added that, if the Army was to come fourth in the priority list, a decline in strength was inevitable. It would lose 25% of its infantry and be unable to sustain the existing total of divisions in France and Italy, even at the reduced establishment; and that left out of account the higher rate of loss anticipated by the War Office in view of the hard fighting ahead. But he declared:

'. . . we can win if we will but determine to do so, and if we act accordingly. We cannot expect to win without making the greatest possible effort, and enduring a far greater strain than any which we have yet felt.'[8]

Shortly afterwards Lloyd George made a public statement of war aims, and on January 8th President Wilson published his famous Fourteen Points. Rejection soon followed from spokesmen of the Central Powers, and peace was put off until the bitter end, nearly a year later. While no one had expected anything of these peace manœuvres, Wully, and others of like opinion, had continued to hope that the War Cabinet would modify its attitude to manpower. But they hoped in vain. 1918, therefore, began badly. While the soldiers had no illusions about what lay ahead, their confidence was undermined by the knowledge that the War Cabinet was neither prepared to back them, nor even knew its own mind. As Wully put it:

'Mr Lloyd George's attitude at this period was difficult to understand. He continued to dally with the manpower question; persisted with the desire to undertake extensive operations in Palestine, in disregard of the daily increasing danger on the main front in France; and yet he appeared to doubt our ability to bring the enemy to terms.'[9]

Moreover, the prospects took yet another turn for the worse, when Haig attended a War Cabinet meeting on January 7th. He was asked whether, if he were German C-in-C, he would venture an all-out offensive on the Western Front. Never good at expressing himself clearly in speech, Haig was hampered on this occasion by two considerations: his own statements about the deterioration of the German Army in the latter part of 1917; and his real doubt as to whether the Germans would risk an attack of such a size as—assuming it was held—would invite their own destruction afterwards. He therefore advanced a cautious negative reply, although he fully believed that the next few months would be the critical ones. Unfortunately the impression he gave was seized upon by Lloyd George to indicate that he expected *no* German attack in France, and therefore that the large drafts demanded by the War Office would not be needed after all. Unwittingly Haig had let the War Cabinet out of an embarrassing difficulty. After the meeting both Wully and Derby explained to him the damage he had done. He found it hard to believe, nevertheless he agreed to put the matter right by letter at once, and by word of mouth when he saw the Prime Minister next on January 9th. Wully wrote to him that night:

'For a long time past they [the War Cabinet] have been trying to persuade me to say that the Germans may not attack this year. Unfortunately you gave as your opinion this morning that they would not do so, and I noticed, as Lord Derby also did, that they jumped at the statement. . .

'The long and short of it is that the Cabinet think that by giving us 100,000 men this year in place of the 600,000 we have asked for, you will be able to hold your own. Personally I think that it is doubtful. My belief is that the Germans will make the heaviest attack possible this year. . .

'I did not think it necessary to say anything to you before the meeting on the subject of men as I felt you would not fail to rub that in. Curzon's questions were intended to give you the opportunity. Of course you do not quite understand these fellows as well as I do.

'Derby is very anxious, and so am I, that you should write the paper they referred to. It may be very short. You do not know the factors. But you do know you must be kept up to strength, and you wont be unless we get far more men.'[10]

Haig duly sent the note, in an attempt to correct the false impression he had made, and repeated the substance of it at his interview on the 9th. But all to no purpose. Lloyd George simply brushed Haig aside, asking what was the value of a man's opinion, when he said one thing one day, and the opposite the next.

*   *   *

Since, clearly, there was no longer any hope of getting the extra drafts for the BEF, Wully now turned to the one remaining source of reinforcement and reserve—the Americans. However, he was to be disappointed. Although the USA had entered the war in April 1917, it had had virtually to start from scratch as a fighting power, and barely five divisions had arrived in France before the end of the year. It was hoped to bring over ten more by June 1918, a total of fifteen (out of 45 to be raised in all), but only a small proportion was expected to be battleworthy by then. By that time, however, the Germans were fully expected to have let loose their great assault. Reports of massive concentration and preparation were already coming in, indicating that the attack would certainly be made in France (not Italy, as once seemed possible) and that it would not be long in coming. By June, in fact, all might be over. If the Americans were to help in time, more of them would have to be got over much more quickly.

All this had been foreseen, and in December 1917 the US Government had been asked to consider letting the men come over in individual units (rather than in fully-equipped divisions) for incorporation into Allied formations, and to postpone the creation of a homogeneous American Army until later. Wully talked the matter over with Pershing, the American C-in-C, on January 9th and 10th, and put up a proposal that 150 battalions of infantry be sent over ahead of all other troops. The British

Government was prepared to make special transport arrangements, and the men could arrive within three to four months. They would first be taken into British brigades, but in due course be reassigned to groupings of their own.

'For some reason I could not convince the General of the seriousness of the position. He seemed to think that I was exaggerating the imminence and possible consequences of the attack which threatened, and he shrewdly observed that it was difficult to reconcile my request for assistance in defence of the Western Front with Mr Lloyd George's desire to act offensively in Palestine. There was, unfortunately, no answer to that argument. . .'[11]

On January 19th further pressure was brought upon Pershing by Pétain and Haig and, after reference to Washington, the whole matter was thrashed out again on January 24th at a conference at Compiègne between the three Commanders-in-Chief, sitting together with Wully and Foch. On Wully's proposal the discussion revolved round the general question of Allied defence of the Western Front. After outlining their arrangements for mutual support, Pétain and Haig pointed out that—with their contingents continually losing strength—they were unable either to act offensively or find anything but local reserves for defence. As Wully said, the real reserve was the American Army. They did agree, however, to try to bring back the British and French divisions from Italy, although Foch refused to discuss a similar proposal in regard to the Balkans.

Pershing then made his contribution. He would soon have a corps of four divisions ready to fight, and he now hoped to have eighteen in France, or on the way there, by July. But, although he was willing for some of the units to train with the British, he rejected any idea of incorporation, or of having his men serve in any formation or under any flag but their own. Considerations of national honour, political expediency, and technical efficiency prevented him from saying anything else. Wully commented:

'. . . General Pershing is looking older and rather tired, and I doubt if he yet has an intelligent and considered view of the nature of his task, or how to set about it.

'My general impression is that America's power to help us win the war—that is to help us defeat the Germans in battle—is a very weak reed to lean upon at present, and will continue to be so for a very long time to come unless she follows up her words with actions more practical and energetic than any she has yet taken.'[12]

*   *   *

Meanwhile, preparations were going forward for the third session of the Supreme War Council on January 30th. The Council, it will be recalled, had not met since December 1st; but since that date the PMRs[13] had been busy investigating various aspects of strategy, and issuing a series of Joint Notes embodying their conclusions. Two of these Notes, Nos 12 and 14, issued on January 21st and 23rd respectively, were of direct concern to Wully. Not only did they bear upon the immediate situation but, in certain important elements, ran counter to his own opinion and advice. They heralded, in fact, the last trial of strength between the two British military advisers, himself and Henry Wilson, a contest shortly to be played out. In the meantime Wully worked hard to offset Versailles by continuing the conferences (such as that of January 24th) between Allied Commanders and Chiefs of Staff. As he told Haig on January 12th:

'The Versailles people are doubtless doing their best, but they cannot help being a probable source of mischief unless we responsible people have made up our minds on all points *beforehand* and are in accord with the French.

'I am therefore suggesting to Foch that you, Pétain, Pershing, Foch, and myself, should have a talk before the Versailles Conference. We can then all get at Pershing and ascertain what he is doing and hopes to do, while Foch and I can also hear what you and Pétain are proposing to do and so be in a position to get done what you want done without the interference of the young men at Versailles.

'The latter have been very busy with war games which is their panacea for everything. I suggested to them on Thursday that there was not much doubt as to what the enemy can do and may do, but there is a good deal of difficulty in providing the means we need to defeat the enemy, and that is the direction in which they should put their energies chiefly.'[14]

In Joint Note No. 12 the military position of the Allies was reviewed, and the German threat in the west acknowledged. Emphasis was laid on the need to safeguard the Western Front, all the way from the Channel to the Adriatic, and to treat it as a single strategic responsibility. It was considered that the Germans could be held in France, providing that the British and French Armies were maintained at their existing strength; that they were reinforced by the Americans at the rate of two divisions per month; and that communications, defences, and war equipment of various categories were improved. In Italy a number of defensive measures were also recommended, but no increase of troops. No other front was deemed worthy of special action, with one exception—Turkey. In the opinion of the PMRs, the defeat of Turkey would not only affect the war as a whole, but possibly revive pro-Allied resistance in the east. They did not, however, offer any practical advice as to the means of prosecuting an offensive against her. In general, they held that there was little prospect of winning the war before 1919, by which time it was hoped that the Germans would be exhausted and the Americans deployed in full force.

Wully lost no time in pointing out to the War Cabinet the fallacies of this Note. Briefly, that it was impossible to keep the British and French Armies up to strength owing to the manpower position, about which repeated warnings had been given; that the rate of American reinforcement was totally unrealistic; and that—in the absence of more positive steps—the safety of the Western Front would remain in doubt. Hence, any major diversion against Turkey was out of the question. Not only would it weaken the west, but it would put an intolerable strain upon shipping and other resources, without guaranteeing the success hoped for.[15] In his view, moreover, no account had been taken of dealing decisively with the Germans in France, once their spring offensive had been stopped, and thus of finishing the war in 1918.

Joint Note No. 14 recommended the creation of a General Reserve, both in Italy and in France.

The subject matter of both these Notes was referred for discussion to, and constituted the main business of, the forthcoming meeting of the Supreme War Council at Versailles on January 30th. The stage was set, both for the public play without and for the private play within.

*　　*　　*

The Council conferred for four days. It was attended by the

political and military chiefs of the four main Allied nations, Britain being represented by Lloyd George, Milner, Wilson, Haig, and Wully. The indefatigable Hankey was in charge of the Secretariat. After preliminary discussions with Pershing, members pitched straight into the vexed question of the Western Front. All the familiar ground was covered again, Pétain and Haig concentrating on the contraction of their Armies, and calling for an acceleration of American help. Lloyd George soon rebelled against these arguments and demanded more positive statistics, regarding combat strengths, reserves, and casualties. When these were produced on the 31st, the Prime Minister found himself at a disadvantage, for—to Foch, at any rate—they seemed to show that the British were capable of a still greater effort.[16] Lloyd George, however, replied with a spirited apologia of the British contribution to the war, and succeeded in deflecting the matter. Clemenceau then took the floor. As a Westerner he distrusted the proposal to attack Turkey, and maintained that only in the east could the drafts be found to fill up the declining divisions in the west. His was a classical exposition of Western policy, and provoked an answer no less authoritative or acute. Lloyd George reminded the company of the high costs and meagre results of Western offensives to date; he doubted, in fact, whether it was possible to drive the Germans out of France, where the front was too strong for either side to break through. It would be far better to follow the German example and do to Turkey what Germany had already done to Serbia and Roumania. Moreover, the Turkish campaign would take place in an area—the Middle East—where great successes had already been obtained and where large resources already existed for further effort.

The discussion went on. On the morning of February 1st, however, the Council accepted Joint Note No. 12, on the condition that no action would take place in Palestine for two months, and that the British would do nothing to weaken the BEF. Before passing this Resolution, Clemenceau turned to Wully and asked him for his opinion. As already recorded, he got the reply he hoped for. But it was not the reply that mattered so much on this occasion, for most knew what Wully thought of the Turkish plan, as the fact that he spoke out against his own Prime Minister in open Council. Afterwards, in apologising to Lloyd George, he justified his action on the general grounds that had he not done so, the other delegates might have assumed his compliance. Specifically he had in mind the example of Lord Fisher who, as First Sea Lord in 1915, had refrained from criticising the Dardanelles operation, though privately and professionally he was against it.

'The Palestine and Dardanelles cases taken together furnish an instructive example of the dilemma in which a naval or military adviser may find himself when Ministers are bent on forcing through plans of operations of their own, knowing that the professionals do not approve of them. If the adviser, believing a plan to be bad, remains silent, as Lord Fisher did at the War Council when the Dardanelles project was being discussed, the result may be disaster and he will be blamed for not having pointed out the danger. If he protests, as I did at Versailles, his relations with Ministers may become impossible, as mine did, and he may still fail to prevent the objectionable plan from being carried out, in which case the result may again be disaster, as happened on the Western Front in March, 1918.'[17]

Wully had no doubt in his own mind, but that he had done right. Furthermore:

'My experience is, that if officers act in this manner, it will be seldom that Ministers will either wish or dare to override their opinion. They may for reasons of policy, quite properly negative proposals which their professional advisers put forward, but that is quite a different thing from insisting upon the execution of military operations which those advisers pronounce to be militarily unsound.'[18]

Lloyd George, however, was the exception, and he was deeply incensed. He told Wully that

'as I had already acquainted him with the General Staff's views, there was no necessity to repeat them before the Council. This, I may observe, was quite a different attitude from the one he had taken up when giving evidence before the Dardanelles Commission a year or so earlier. He then agreed with the Commissioners that if naval and military advisers present at Ministerial Councils did not express dissent, it was legitimate to assume that they agreed with what was being done.'[19]

*   *   *

The Supreme War Council considered Joint Note No. 14

(*re.* a General Reserve) on the afternoon of February 1st. As with No. 12, much preliminary sounding and sparring had already taken place. On January 30th, for example, Wully had submitted a Memorandum to the Prime Minister, in which he clearly defined the various functions of reserves in war, both tactical and strategic, and set out his own views on the present case. He gave contemporary illustrations: the use by Germany of a reserve of six divisions to defeat the Italians at Caporetto, and of eleven by the Allies to help stop the enemy on the River Piave. In France, the immediate problem related to defence. Pétain and Haig had their own reserves in readiness, and a plan for mutual support. Was that enough? Wully thought not.

'It may happen that one Commander-in-Chief may be heavily attacked and in need of help, while the other may be quite correctly anticipating an equally heavy attack to follow later, and in this case he may not feel himself in a position to give his colleague the help asked for. In such circumstances both the British and the French Commanders-in-Chief might feel themselves bound both by their duty to their Governments and to their troops, to take a local rather than a general view of the situation.'

This was a remarkably accurate forecast of what happened after March 21st, when the danger arose of Haig and Pétain retiring in different directions, and of the Germans getting in between them. In such a case, Wully suggested, the solution lay in the existence of a 'superior authority' to

'form a correct appreciation of the general situation on the whole front; and be in a position to issue such instructions to the Commanders-in-Chief as would best ensure the success of the operations as a whole.'

What form should this 'superior authority' take? A Generalissimo? Lloyd George had already spoken against the idea, and for once Wully agreed with him.

'Political, military, and moral difficulties seem to me insuperable. It is part of our Constitution that Ministers must be responsible to Parliament for all the actions of the Executive, and I cannot see that under our system of Parliamentary Government it would be possible for, say, a French Officer to be in complete command of a British army of about two million men. As a matter of hard fact he could not possibly be in complete command because he could not be given powers of promotion or discipline, and without these powers his authority would be limited and unsatisfactory. Whatever powers it might be decided to give him, in spite of constitutional and legal objections, a British Commander-in-Chief would not hesitate, I think, to refuse to obey the orders of the Generalissimo, if in his judgment they were such as his troops ought not to carry out. There are also the feelings of the troops to be considered. If there were any great outstanding General whom everybody would be willing to follow, then perhaps some working arrangement could be made to have a Generalissimo, but there is no one man who could satisfy the various countries and troops concerned.'

Wully then advanced his own solution.

'In my opinion the duty of the High Command must be exercised . . . jointly by the Chiefs of the British and French General Staffs. . . This would be following the German example. . . They have no one Commander-in-Chief on the West Front . . . the Chief of the German General Staff merely gives such general instructions as are necessary to ensure mutual assistance and co-operation. . . The Commanders of the different sectors . . . do the remainder. What we want is not a new machinery but an improvement in, and more definite recognition of, the existing machinery. No doubt the present system might be made much more efficient by establishing closer and more constant relation between the different Staffs, and this should be done.'

After discussing ways in which the other Allied Chiefs of Staff might fit in to this proposal, Wully concluded:

'The advice I submit to you is . . . that the High Command . . . must necessarily be exercised by the Chiefs of the General Staff, the responsible and authoritative advisers and executive officers of the Governments. Recognise and settle this point and the question of reserves will then settle itself.'[20]

Foch fell in with Wully's proposal, which was laid before the Supreme War Council on February 1st. It did not find favour, however. The Italians had objections, and it was also pointed out that—with his HQ in London—Wully could not always be available in an emergency. Apart from this, of course, Lloyd George had not the slightest intention of letting Wully regain— and indeed improve—the position he had held before the creation of the Supreme War Council, together with its 'technical advisers'. An alternative suggestion to vest control of the reserves in the PMRs (as representative of the Council, the ultimate authority) was also turned down. Foch could not allow Weygand (his subordinate) such scope, nor obviously could Wully give it to Wilson (not his subordinate). Indeed, Wully saw at once that, if he gave way on this, he would be yielding a vital principle and his own position into the bargain. Hitherto the PMRs had acted solely as *advisers*, and although he violently disputed the idea that the British Government receive advice from two independent sources—the PMR and the CIGS —he had got round the difficulty more or less by attending Council meetings himself. Now, however, it was proposed to give the PMRs *executive* authority. That raised even larger issues. Deeply troubled, he sent a new note to the Prime Minister after the meeting on February 1st.

'No British officer in France, who is not a Member of the Army Council and in direct touch with that body, can have the necessary information as to the state of the troops, the supply, munition and medical situation and other questions essential to the effective control of military operations. On these questions I feel that both the Secretary of State for War and the Army Council should be consulted, as they affect vitally the principles of command and administration of our troops in the field.

'There are also constitutional questions to be considered. . . I do not quite see how a British Commander-in-Chief can be made, constitutionally, to obey the orders of an Allied body, or indeed of anyone except the Army Council and the Secretary of State for War —a Minister of the Crown. If the CIGS were made a Member of the Versailles body, as is proposed in the case of General Foch, this difficulty could be more easily surmounted perhaps.'[21]

He then restated his plan for control by the British and French Chiefs of Staff (in association with the other Allies), and added:

'When the British Chief of the General Staff cannot be present he will be represented by a British General Officer.'

In short, by a subordinate. This met the objection raised against his original proposal, and was indeed the right answer, but it made no impression upon Lloyd George. Wully also pointed out that, should Foch be brought in as President of the PMRs Committee (as had been scouted), then he would gradually assume the position of Generalissimo, an idea already rejected.

Wully's words had no effect. Though refused in its first form, the alternative proposal was fast gaining ground, and on the next day—with one important amendment—it secured approval. Hankey related that, at breakfast on February 2nd, he, Lloyd George, Milner, and Henry Wilson discussed it together.

'Eventually they decided that the reserves should be under the control of a committee consisting of the British [Wilson], Italian [Cadorna] and United States [Bliss] Permanent Military Representatives with Foch in the chair. [Weygand was excluded.] Having with some difficulty persuaded the Italians to accept it, Ll.G., in a speech of great skill, announced it to the Council, bringing tears to the eyes of Foch, Clemenceau and even Orlando. Foch was so much moved that he could make no reply.'22

Hankey added:

'Pershing, in accepting the scheme, expressed regret that Robertson, for whom he had formed a high regard, could not be included in the new committee.'

What Wully felt was not recorded, but his bitterness can be guessed, for this was the ultimate development that he had foreseen from the first and the show-down that Lloyd George had long schemed for. While he sat there, silent and stolid, it was resolved that the new committee—to be known as the Executive War Board—should in effect be awarded many of the powers of an Inter-Allied High Command: namely, that it should determine the strength and composition of a General Reserve for the French, Italian, and Balkan fronts; decide the areas of concentration, movement, and employment; and—by way of a supplementary resolution, an afterthought, in fact—transmit orders direct to the Armies concerned. This was the critical factor. As Wully pointed out, the Board now had all the powers hitherto reserved only to the Chiefs of Staff and Ministers of War: in short, a rival authority to the constitutional arrangements of the countries concerned. This was something he could never accept.

Meanwhile, the new Board set to work, and in the following few months endeavoured to carry out its commission. How and why it failed is not the concern of this book. It is enough to state that, although 30 divisions were nominally allotted to the General Reserve (10 British, 13 French, 7 Italian), not one was yielded by Haig or Pétain, though six were offered by Diaz (Cadorna's successor). In practice no General Reserve was formed at all. All that happened was that Foch, on his own initiative, succeeded in having one British division transferred from Italy to France. Otherwise, all the reinforcements and reserves that had to be rushed up after March 21st continued to be controlled by the Chiefs of Staff, the Commanders-in-Chief, and by Foch when he became Generalissimo.

* * *

It is not proposed to discuss any of the other subjects debated by the Supreme War Council—for example, the extension of the British line in France, or Henry Wilson's erroneous forecast of the coming German offensive—but rather to show how the creation of the Executive War Board led to Wully's dismissal in the middle of February, and to relate the crowded incidents of those two weeks.

Hitherto this chapter has by design stuck closely to the sequence of events which culminated in the decision of February 2nd: in other words, all that Lloyd George did to get his own way, by holding back on commitments in France, by reservations on manpower, and by turning to the PMRs—first for alternative advice, and then for alternative authority. True, the Executive War Board had something to recommend it—as an idea for an embryonic form of Inter-Allied High Command—but in application it had none. In the form it took it was no more than a typical Lloyd George device, in which idealism got confused with intrigue. There was no justification whatever in setting up one system to compete with another, in order principally to by-pass one man, whom he as Prime Minister had the right to replace at any time. The fact was, of course, that, so far, Lloyd George had not felt strong enough to force this issue and win out against political opposition and public outcry; but now the prospect seemed far brighter.

Naturally the story concerns far more than a succession of cold facts and arguments over a system of command. The whole atmosphere surrounding Wully and Lloyd George was charged with tension and personal animus, which permeated every contact and exchange. It had been so for a very long time, so that by February 2nd the personal, as well as the public, relationship between the two men was at flash point. The animus was not generated solely by technical disagreements. There were other sources of friction, at first sight surprising in that—as mentioned earlier—both Wully and Lloyd George were self-made men of humble origin, and might therefore have had a good deal in common. But it was not so. Indeed, Lloyd George got on better with Haig, the pillar of social and military Establishment, than with Wully, whose start and way up in life had been as hard as his own. Everything was outweighed by other, mainly temperamental, differences. In race, the mercurial Celt stood opposite to the deliberate Saxon (Scottish forebears notwithstanding), and a frontier lay between. In speech the Prime Minister was Merlin indeed, and relied upon the spoken word to cast spells both upon his hearers and upon himself. It cut no ice with Wully, who found talking difficult at any time, and listening a bore if the speaker was not direct or short. He himself spoke bluntly and to the point, with earthy humour, just as he had done as a NCO. He was incapable of 'wrapping' anything up in speech, and probably thought it immoral to do so. A colleague related how at a War Cabinet meeting:

'Wully read out a crystal clear statement of the situation and of the imminent danger in France, and enumerated the measures needed to meet it. The statesmen then made set speeches and Wully whispered to his neighbour [a visitor]: "Here, you have to listen to this rot just once; I have to listen to it every week." At the end Lloyd George asked him if, having now heard the advantages of fighting elsewhere than in France, he had not changed his mind. To which Wully replied by reading out his original statement once more, word for word.'[23]

Not tactful, and behaviour certainly not calculated to appeal to the Prime Minister, who was as vulnerable to charm as he was skilful in exerting it. Lloyd George could often overcome an enemy by wit and warmth. Wully just grunted. It did not make things easy.

Wully once remarked:

'The discussion of questions of policy and political matters generally leads to no practical result nor benefit of any kind to the soldier, nor is it his business.'[24] (See page 334–7).

He wrote this in 1910, when Commandant of the Staff College, as a comment upon an essay submitted by a promising young student, Lieut A. P. Wavell, of The Black Watch. He did not, of course, appreciate the prophetic purport of his words, as they were to apply both to his and to Wavell's subsequent careers. Politics did, however, become their business inasmuch as the jobs they held brought them both into the sphere of Government and into close contact with politicians. The disagreements between Wully and Lloyd George in the First War had a striking parallel with those between Wavell and Churchill in the Second, and in both cases it might well be said that their experiences led 'to no practical result' (other than their own removal), and certainly brought them 'no benefit of any kind' as soldiers.

With Wully the political contretemps was fiercer and more involved, and at one time seemed to threaten the very future of the Government. Lloyd George feared the consequences of dismissing both him and Haig, and was convinced that by the end of 1917 'the generals' were planning to take control and run the war themselves. That was nonsense. But it was quite true that Wully and Haig had powerful friends, including many who opposed Lloyd George in Parliament, and who considered that 'the generals' were being unduly handicapped in the performance of their duties. Whereas Lloyd George had the backing of his own section of the Liberal Party, the Socialists, and the strong support of Bonar Law, Milner, and the bulk of the Conservatives, he was distrusted—and often actively opposed—by all the Liberals behind Asquith ('the Squiffites'), the right-wing Tories, and even by certain members of the War Cabinet, such as Curzon and Carson. And he had many enemies outside Parliament. It was these groups and individuals who used Wully (and, to a less extent, Haig) as the focus of their opposition during 1917 and early 1918.

Wully did not meddle with politics in any crude sense. The fact that Lloyd George was a natural Radical, and Wully a natural Tory, is irrelevant. Wully did not want to become a politician, and he publicly stated on many occasions that government was the business of MPs and Ministers, never of Service or other technical advisers. At the same time he did not hesitate to speak out on controversial subjects—on manpower,

One of the provisions of the treaty with Austria after 1866 was directed to ensuring the neutrality of Austria & goodwill of Austria in a possible war between Prussia & France. Bismarck & Prince ... (I've forgotten his name, the Bavarian Minister) worked unceasingly to educate German Public Opinion, to a war with France, between 1866 & 1870, as well as to introduce a military system into Bavaria similar to the Prussian system.

I have now read nearly 14 pages, and can find nothing confirming or modifying the strategical & tactical lessons of the 4 Campaigns mentioned. What on earth has the paragraph here marked got to do with either strategy or tactics?

W.M.M.

TRANSCRIPT

Comment by CR (Lt-Col. Charles Ross, member of the Directing Staff).

One of the provisions of the treaty with Austria after 1866 was directed to ensuring the neutrality and goodwill of Austria in a possible war between Prussia and France. Bismark & Prince ... (I've forgotten his name, the Bavarian Minister) worked unceasingly to educate German Public Opinion, to a war with France, between 1866 and 1870, as well as to introduce a military system into Bavaria similar to the Prussian system.

Comment by WRR (Major-General Sir William Robertson, Commandant of the Staff College).

'I have now read nearly 14 pages, and can find nothing confirming or modifying the *strategical* and *tactical* lessons of the 4 campaigns mentioned. What on earth has the paragraph here marked got to do with either strategy or tactics?'   WRR

EXTRACT from the military history paper written by Lieutenant A. P. Wavell (later Field-Marshal Earl Wavell) in response to the examination question couched as follows:

'How far are the strategical and tactical lessons drawn from the campaigns of 1815, 1862, 1866 and 1870 confirmed or modified by the experience of the recent wars in South Africa and Manchuria?'

favourable circumstances, as regards alliances etc. Meanwhile the plan of campaign is developed and perfected (Moltke's Projects). A good plan requires good intelligence which must be obtained in peace.

Thus the preparation falls under 3 heads :-

(a) Preparation of the Policy;

(b) Preparation of the Instrument;

(c) Preparation of the Plan.

But there is one part not illustrated by Prussia, which is the first and most important for nations with a democratic form of Government. That is Preparation of Public Opinion. Bismarck prepared for and brought on the wars of 1866 and 1870 against the wishes of the people, who did not understand his aims. But the necessity, where the Government is popular, of first convincing the people that preparation is necessary is the hardest task of all + precludes secrecy. Napoleon III, dependent for his throne on the popular will, did not dare attempt it. A popular form of Government is unfavourable to preparation for war.

yes.

Defects in the Instrument must be corrected by the experience of self and others. Thus Prussia corrected her mobilization after 1864, and reorganised the artillery arm after 1866. As regards weapons, the progress of modern science must be watched to secure an advantage or at least equality. Thus with a breechloader the Austrians might have won at Nachod and given Benedek another 24 hours to decide on a plan. But the Prussians won in 1870 with an inferior rifle for which however the superiority of their artillery compensated.

I congratulate you on this
admirable piece of work.
But there are many points which
you have overlooked — as regards
the preparation of a theatre of hostilities,
a vital part of preparation for war.
This is not only a question of secret service,
but a knowledge of the country, the
supplies usually available, the roads
nature of the communications, the
provision of interpreters, guides, maps.
The relation of the army to the friendly,
neutral, or perhaps, hostile, inhabitants.
Think of the work the Japanese put in in
Korea & Manchuria before a shot was fired.
Think of the administration of Korea that
they were obliged to take over, and the
number of officials employed in it.
Nothing of this sort can be attempted
until a national policy has been
evolved.
Still, I repeat, that I regard this
as an admirable piece of work

CR.

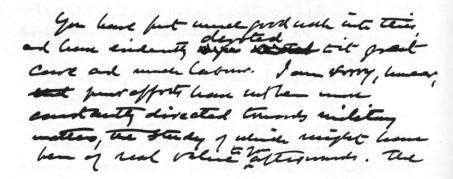

You have put much good work into this,
and have evidently devoted to it great
care and much labour. I am sorry, however,
that your efforts have not been more
constantly directed towards military
matters, the study of which might have
been of real value to you afterwards. The

discussion of questions of policy and political matters generally leads to no practical result not benefit of any kind to the soldier, nor is it his business.

WRR

25/10

TRANSCRIPT

Comment by CR

'I congratulate you on this admirable piece of work. But there are many points which you have overlooked—as regards the preparation of a theatre of hostilities, a vital part of preparation for war. This is not only a question of secret service, but a knowledge of the country, the supplies usually available, the nature of the communications, the provision of interpreters, guides, maps, the relation of the army to the friendly, neutral, or perhaps, hostile, inhabitants. Think of the work the Japanese put in in Korea and Manchuria before a shot was fired. Think of the administration of Korea that they were obliged to take over, and the number of officials employed in it. Nothing of this sort can be attempted until a national policy has been evolved.

Still, I repeat, that I regard this as an admirable piece of work.' CR.

Comment by WRR

'You have put much good work into this, and have evidently devoted to it great care and labour. I am sorry, however, your efforts have not been more constantly directed towards military matters, the study of which might have been of real value to you afterwards. The discussions of questions of policy and political matters generally leads to no practical result, nor benefit of any kind to the soldier, nor is it his business.'

WRR   July 25th 1910.

for instance, or the functions of the Supreme War Council—not only to members of the War Cabinet but to others too. He was not giving away secrets, for these were matters of common discussion, but he did solicit support where he could. He lobbied, in fact. Hankey recorded on November 15th 1917:

'I lunched with the Asquiths, having Ll.G.'s consent. . . Asquith, while talking of the Italian situation, let the cat slip out of the bag, mentioning that he had seen Robertson that morning. I have no doubt that Robertson is intriguing like the deuce. Last night House [President Wilson's representative] let slip that Robertson was coming to see him this morning. His private secretary, thinking I was on Robertson's staff, came in to say that Bliss particularly wanted Robertson to repeat to House what he had said to him. Why does Robertson cut the War Cabinet and see House and the Leader of the Opposition? Was it in order to intrigue against the Council [Supreme War Council]? . .'[25]

Was this really so surprising or blameworthy? It would never have happened had Wully not been driven to it, for by the autumn of 1917 his position as chief military adviser to the Government was being constantly circumvented by his own Prime Minister in all the ways described. This was the lesson learned by Winston Churchill and applied by him in the Second World War. When Churchill lost confidence in his Chief of Staff (e.g. Dill) or in a field commander (e.g. Wavell) he sacked him and found him another job. But when he disagreed with an official adviser in whom he yet retained confidence (e.g. Alanbrooke), however violent the clash of opinion, he gave way. In such circumstances he never overrode technical advice, or undermined the man who gave it.

All one can say about Wully, perhaps, is that he should have left the War Office before he did, through dismissal or resignation. He did not resign because, in his fervent opinion, it was in the best interests of the Army that he should stay; and there were many who agreed with him. His was not an enviable position, far from it. Esher, who was generally critical of Wully at this time, wrote to Haig:

'Robertson is having the wind knocked out of him. It reminds me of poor old K [Kitchener], sitting crumpled up in his room at York House. Luckily for him *he* lies peacefully under the quiet northern seas.

'No such luck for Robertson. These fellows will beat him black and blue, until he has not a breath in his body.'[26]

*   *   *

One of Lloyd George's loudest complaints against 'the generals' derived from the attitude of the Press, generally antagonistic to the Government. Certain papers were, by reason of policy, consistently hostile; such as the *Westminster Gazette*, edited by J. A. Spender, which supported Asquith; or the *Morning Post*, edited by H. A. Gwynne, organ of right-wing Conservatism. But the toughest opponent, and the most formidable figure in Fleet Street, was Alfred Harmsworth, Lord Northcliffe, proprietor of *The Times*, *Daily Mail*, and other newspapers. It was Northcliffe who had pounced on a report by Repington, *The Times* military correspondent, to mount a massive attack on Kitchener for the shells shortage in May 1915, an act which influenced the reconstruction of the Asquith Government, bringing in Lloyd George as head of the new Ministry of Munitions. Later, he conducted another violent campaign which preceded and contributed to the fall of Asquith as Prime Minister at the end of 1916. He also attacked Lloyd George, when Secretary of State for War, for interfering with strategy; and his general line of 'hands off the Army' was, of course, popular with 'the generals'. Wully, unwisely perhaps, once replied to a message of his in the following terms:

'It is very hard work trying to win this war. The Boche gives me no trouble compared with what I meet in London. So any help you can give me will be of Imperial value.'[27]

Northcliffe was a wayward, dangerous man and his power went to his head. He talked openly of making and breaking Governments, not only the British. But Lloyd George was astute enough to divert his energies for a time, by persuading him to take over the direction of the British War Mission in the USA during the summer of 1917. Northcliffe proved a great success in America, and returned in November well satisfied with what he had done and pleased with the Prime Minister, who rewarded him with a viscounty. Thereafter, although he soon found new causes for quarrels, Northcliffe caused *The Times* and the *Daily Mail* to alter their attitude, so that by the end of 1917 the balance of Press support had swung towards the Government.

Northcliffe's action undoubtedly encouraged Lloyd George to intensify his campaign against Wully and Haig, so that in December he attempted an outright assault. On the 11th he asked Lord Derby to dismiss them both, on the immediate grounds that Wully had caused Allenby to put in exaggerated demands for reinforcements in Palestine, while Haig—having failed disastrously over Third Ypres—had further mismanaged the first Battle of Cambrai. Derby defended them both in a firm and well-reasoned letter, and made it clear that if they went, he would go too. He met Lloyd George part of the way, however, by getting rid of some of Haig's staff officers.[28]

In January 1918 Lloyd George tried again by offering Derby the post of Ambassador in Paris, with a view to appointing a more amenable Secretary of State for War. But again Derby resisted with skill and success, and linked his own career with the retention of both Wully and Haig in their existing posts.

A third attempt by the Prime Minister to rid himself of one or both of 'the generals' followed a few days later, in connection with a Press article by Repington.

Repington was an able military journalist, with any number of contacts in the right places, not only the War Office. Although no friend of Haig, who disliked Press men on principle, he got on well with Wully and certain members of his staff, and was undoubtedly a 'generals' man'. He was fully aware of all the points of contention between the Army and the Government. Soon after *The Times* began to take its new line, he fell out with Northcliffe and the editor (Dawson), and finally resigned on January 16th 1918. He then transferred to the *Morning Post*, and on the 24th published a highly critical article on the subject of manpower. Lloyd George told Derby that he proposed to charge the General Staff with communicating official secrets to the Press. Derby replied that the charge would not stand:

'. . . in the face of his [Repington's] statements that many official persons, civil as well as military, have communicated with him from time to time on the subject of man power, and that no Cabinet paper has been given to him by any soldier, I don't see how we can single out the General Staff as the source of his information.'[29]

Derby went on to point out that Repington's figures and statements were inaccurate—the product of good guessing more than anything else; moreover, that the Manpower Report had been widely circulated, and that it would lead them nowhere to threaten all who had received it with 'dire pains and penalties'. A further accusation by Lloyd George that Repington's article had encouraged the Turks to stay in the war also came to nothing. Derby remarked that the *Daily Mail* was doing just as much damage by attacking the War Office—as it then was—and that only the Director of Public Prosecutions could decide whether there was ground for legal action in either case.

Once more Derby had won the day, but his success was only temporary. It was only a question of time before some new assault was launched, and an opportunity soon presented itself at the third session of the Supreme War Council, January 30th to February 2nd, as already described.

*   *   *

The full magnitude of the decision on February 2nd to set up the Executive War Board to control the General Reserve was not immediately apparent. That it would cause constitutional complications was, however, generally realised, and Haig immediately asked, 'By what channel am I to receive orders from this new body?'[30] Lloyd George replied to the effect that orders would be issued by the members of the body nominated by the Supreme War Council. This clarified nothing, and Haig asked that the exact position be defined on paper. In practice he was not unduly worried, since he did not see where the Executive War Board would get the troops from to form a General Reserve. He wrote to his wife on February 5th:

'Anyway don't let the Versailles Conference trouble you—the machinery there is so big and clumsy it will take some time before it can work fast enough to trouble me.'

In the same letter Haig criticised Wully.

'I, like you, am sorry for Robertson, but then it seems to me (and I can write it to you privately) that he has not resolutely adhered to the policy of "concentration on the Western Front"—He has *said* that this is his policy, but has allowed all kinds of resources to be diverted to distant theatres at the bidding of his political masters. So I think he ought to have made a firm stand before.'[31]

This was manifestly untrue and unfair, and it boded ill for Wully who was now to need all the support of all his friends. He did not yet fully realise that Lloyd George had forced him into an impossible position, but he was soon to find out.

Nothing happened for a few days. All were concerned with attempts at translating the resolution of the Supreme War Council into practical action. On February 7th, however, the inertia was broken; and so it is proposed to tell the rest of the story, as it unfolded, day by day.

February 7th

Wully wrote to Haig:

'It would help me if you could *incidentally* drop a line to Derby and say what you think about the Reserve question, so far as concerns the proposal that the Executive Committee should issue orders to you on this subject—thus constituting two authorities from which orders will issue—Versailles and London. I ask this because LG states that you are quite agreeable and in fact [have] accepted it. This is what I hear. The solution is, put me on the Versailles Committee, then all is well, I think.'[32]

Derby wrote to Haig in a similar vein: namely, that the Prime Minister had assured him of Haig's acceptance. Was that really true? Lloyd George was determined to get rid of Wully. If he succeeded, should he (Derby) resign too? The Prime Minister wanted a private talk with Haig. Would he please come over?

On this date Wully also told Lloyd George he was having to go to Eastbourne for a few days, on doctor's orders, to recuperate from the effects of a heavy cold. It was a most unfortunate absence. He returned precipitately on the 11th, having been warned (probably by Maurice) that events were going against him.

February 8th

Haig telegraphed Derby, saying he would arrive in London on the 9th, and adding that although he considered a General Reserve correct, he disagreed with the system set up to control it.

February 9th

Haig arrived at Victoria Station at 3.30 pm and was met by Derby, who drove him by a roundabout route to Downing Street. On the way he was told that the War Cabinet had decided the previous day to replace Wully as CIGS, and that the post in future would revert in status to that prevailing before the Kitchener-Robertson Bargain. The Secretary of State for War would regain full responsibility for the War Office, but the CIGS would continue to be regarded as the 'supreme military adviser' to the Government. On the other hand, the PMR at Versailles was to become a member of the Army Council, with the grade of a Deputy CIGS, retaining full powers to issue orders in respect of the General Reserve.

At Downing Street Haig told Lloyd George that the PMRs had been given inflated powers, able to commit the British Government regardless of his (or anyone else's) advice. This was going much too far. No one could give him (Haig) orders except the Army Council or a senior Field-Marshal. He preferred Wully's proposal whereby the latter and Foch—the two Chiefs of Staff—should issue orders jointly in regard to the Reserve. To everyone's surprise Lloyd George protested agreement and announced his intention of sending Wully to Versailles and of making Henry Wilson CIGS.

'This came as a pleasant surprise to Derby, who evidently was much exercised in his mind as to how to get out of his present difficulty with Robertson. The latter had lately become most difficult to deal with and lost his temper quickly, he told me.'[33]

The draft instruction was thereupon amended, though in such a way as to confirm the contradictory nature of the duties of the PMR. While retaining full freedom in the matter of advice, he was yet to consult with and report to the CIGS, who in turn would advise the Cabinet. Such was the conclusion agreed to. Apart from warning the Prime Minister about the distrust of Henry Wilson by the Army, and apart from refusing the suggestion that he himself should become 'Generalissimo of all the British Forces', Haig had nothing more to say.

However regarded, the new dispensation was detrimental to Wully at all points. Whether he stayed on as CIGS, with reduced powers, or accepted the post of PMR, he was bound to be side-tracked by the Prime Minister, who was now free to throw his weight upon whichever side Wully was *not* on. It was an ingenious and totally successful manœuvre. That night Milner telephoned to Henry Wilson to come at once to London.

February 10th (Sunday)

Henry Wilson arrived in London and saw Milner, who told him what had happened. In his Diary he noted:

'Lloyd George had three plans, namely: 1, send Robertson to York and replace him by Plumer; 2, send Robertson to York and replace him by Haig, replacing Haig by Plumer; 3, send Robertson to Versailles and bring me here as CIGS. After tremendous discussion and vacillation he had now decided on 3, and had sent an emissary to Robertson, who is in the country for a few days, to offer either Versailles or a Command. This is pushing about with a vengeance. Milner said that he was sure Lloyd George now meant to carry this out, so that I really am afraid that I may find myself CIGS within the next few days.

'If, however, Robertson refuses Versailles, then Milner and I agreed that he should put in someone junior to me, and let me have a directing voice in Versailles if I was CIGS. The whole thing is rather muddlesome.'[34]

This last admission revealed—if any revelation was needed— the very nakedness of the manœuvre. That the PMR should be independent of and co-equal with the CIGS was a duality which could never work, whoever held either job. The CIGS had either to be his own PMR, or at least his superior, just as Foch was to Weygand. As it was, the British were the only exception to this rule.

February 11th

The amended War Cabinet instruction was shown by Derby to both Wilson and Wully, now back in London. Wully was not surprised at the decision to remove him from the War Office, for his inability to see eye-to-eye with the Prime Minister was fundamental.

'Further, Lord Derby had already told me in the course of conversation that the Prime Minister could not "get on" with me. After that there was nothing more to be said, and I said nothing except to ask when it was desired that I should hand over my duties to my successor.'[35]

Versailles, however, was another matter. Wully was adamant in his refusal on the familiar grounds that a dual authority for the direction of the war was an impossibility. He said it all again to Haig, when the latter came to see him at the War Office later in the morning. Haig disagreed and told him that:

'. . . as the British member of the Versailles Committee, he was in the position of "Generalissimo" and further, that this was no time for anyone to question where his services were to be given. It was his *duty* to go to Versailles or anywhere else if the Government wished it. I am afraid that in the back of his mind he resents Henry Wilson replacing him in London, and means to embarrass the Government to the utmost of his power.'[36]

Haig then saw the King and urged him to insist on Wully going to Versailles.

Meanwhile, two further communications passed between Wully and Derby.

In the first Wully restated his position with admirable firmness and clarity. Whoever held the job of CIGS should also be PMR.

'The General Staff Officer, who is to give orders regarding the reserves . . . must be in constant and direct touch with the various departments of the War Office—the Great Headquarters of the Imperial Military Forces—and be directly served by, and in close touch with, the Intelligence Branch of the General Staff. Only the CIGS, residing normally at the War Office, can be in this position. . .'[37]

Moreover, he saw no difficulty in one man combining the two jobs.

This was the point that Derby fastened on in his reply.

'When the Committee at Versailles was purely advisory it might have been done, though even then I do not think it would have been advisable. Now that it is executive I think it is absolutely impossible. CIGS living in London cannot possibly give a decision, delay in the giving of which might be fatal in France.'[38]

He besought Wully to think it over again.

February 12th

Lloyd George was now, by turn, in a difficulty. He did not feel well, and knew that only Milner really backed him if it came to the worst. Other members of the War Cabinet had agreed to replace Wully as CIGS, but they did not wish him to disappear altogether. Rumours were flying about, and in a difficult debate in the House of Commons Asquith put some awkward questions. He asked particularly for an assurance that neither Wully nor Haig stood in any danger of being displaced. Lloyd George managed to side-step this questioning, but the future of the Government was at stake, and the Squiffites scented a return to power.

February 13th

Hankey reported a new complication.

'Lloyd George told me that he had come to the conclusion that he could not sack Robertson, who was willing to stay on as CIGS with reduced powers. Northcliffe's attack on Robertson had, he said, made it impossible for him to get rid of him, as all the world would say that it was done at Northcliffe's dictation.'[39]

However, Derby now offered a way out, with Wully remaining where he was at the War Office.

'I suggest that the position between General Robertson and Sir Henry Wilson should be practically the same as between General Foch and General Weygand. . . That would mean that Sir William Robertson would be our Representative on the Executive Committee, but that when not possible for him to be there, and if sudden decisions had to be arrived at, General Wilson should be authorised, as an Army Councillor, to take decisions in the Army Council's name.'[40]

Wully conceded this, for he had himself made a similar suggestion earlier on.

'There need be no difficulty in the CIGS being represented on the Executive body, in his absence, by a Deputy who would keep him fully informed of the work of the Executive, warn him when his presence was required, and act for him in case of necessity.'[41]

The War Cabinet would not agree, however. Lloyd George could not possibly do so, for it would have allowed Wully—

albeit diminished in status vis-à-vis the Secretary of State for War—to remain the real master of the field.

February 14th

Wully appeared personally before the War Cabinet and, in a long statement, reviewed the whole position—without avail. For his part, he refused steadfastly either to become PMR, or to remain CIGS so long as an independent PMR sat at Versailles. Moreover, he questioned whether, in any event, he should stay on as 'supreme military adviser', since his advice was being rejected on a point of cardinal importance. Later in the day he reiterated his refusal to Balfour in a picturesque phrase, to the effect that an objectionable object in the middle of the table was equally objectionable from whichever end of the table you looked at it. That was his final word, and it was also the turning point of the drama. The War Cabinet promptly offered the post of CIGS to Plumer, leaving Wilson as PMR. Derby wrote to Wully:

'I am afraid that I must at last take your "No" as being a final decision, but I need not tell you with what deep regret I do so. . .

'I admire extremely the courage which prompts you to adhere to your decision. . .

'After hearing your statement this morning, the Cabinet were quite unanimous in holding to the conditions laid down. . . The Cabinet have decided to offer your post to Sir Henry Plumer, on the same conditions as those offered to you, and, in the event of his accepting, I am authorised to offer you the Command in Italy. . .'[42]

February 15th

The drama was not quite done, however. Plumer telegraphed his refusal, and in so doing threw the War Cabinet into a very awkward predicament.

'The position was very critical for the Government, as two great generals had refused the post of CIGS on the ground of objection to the Government's Versailles policy, and if they could not find a distinguished officer to fill the bill they were faced with resignation or defeat.'[43]

However, as Hankey anticipated, Lloyd George—always at his best in a tight corner—rose to the occasion.

'Sure enough it was so. He declared he was better than he had been for months. As the result of our talk he decided that Wilson should become CIGS, and if Derby resigned . . . Milner should become Secretary of State for war.'[44]

Meanwhile, Derby had been telegraphing the latest situation to Haig, and had asked him to come over to London once again. Haig consented and said that, in his opinion, the best solution was still the Foch-Weygand arrangement. Wully, too, got in touch with Haig. His letter showed him to be calm, clear —and resigned to his fate.

'Notwithstanding what you said, it seemed to me to be fundamentally bad and dangerous for you to receive orders from two authorities, Versailles and London, and impossible for anyone but the CIGS to give orders about Reserves any more than about anything else. . . I could not possibly accept a system as CIGS which I had already condemned as dangerous, and said so. It would have been disgraceful. I may have acted wrongly, but I do not think so. . . The whole thing is, in fact, a plot to get me away from here. . . I would have been a useless fool at Versailles, with Wilson here as CIGS, who could always have scotched me. . . It was best to be firm and act according to conviction.'[45]

February 16th

Lloyd George reported to the King. It was now a simple issue—Wully or himself. If His Majesty insisted on retaining his Chief of Staff, then he—the Prime Minister—would have to resign. Although the King was as loyal to Wully as ever, he could not possibly force a constitutional issue of this kind and override Lloyd George. The matter was a foregone conclusion. That afternoon the Government announced Wully's resignation and Wilson's appointment in his place, and—we are told— the Prime Minister retired to his home to sing his favourite hymns.

Wully first heard of his 'resignation' in the Press.

'Strictly speaking, this was not correct. I had not resigned for I was not in a position to do so, having been told on the 11th that I was to leave the War Office.'[46]

But it was an academic point. The battle was over, and he had lost it. No member of the War Cabinet resigned on his account, though Curzon came near to doing so. As to the attitude of others, only two call for comment—Haig, who had now arrived in London, and Derby who met him, just as he had done a few days earlier. Wully sent Haig a little note, making an appointment for the following day. It is significant that this was the first, and perhaps the last, time, that he ever addressed him by his Christian name: 'My dear Douglas'. It was a penetrating personal reminder of Haig's aloofness and of Wully's extraordinary deference towards him. Now, however, at the point of departure, relaxed and resigned about the future, Wully looked back at the man to whom he had given unswerving, uninterrupted loyalty, without which Haig would certainly have foundered before now. Wully counted upon a complementary act of solidarity: in short, that Haig should give in *his* resignation. But Haig did nothing of the kind.

February 17th (Sunday)

Haig saw Wully at 9.30 am. He told him that now the constitutional objection had been met by making the PMR a member of the Army Council, there was no legal ground upon which he could make a stand. His consent to the dual system of control by PMR and CIGS was not required, though he did not approve of it, nor indeed of the Executive War Board itself. But that was as far as he could go. Later in the morning he accompanied Derby to the Prime Minister's house at Walton Heath, and repeated the substance of his statement. He would abide by the decision of the War Cabinet, and that was that.

In Beaverbrook's words:

'What a relief for the Prime Minister! And yet what bitter disappointment! Relief because by retaining Haig, the measure of his peril in the House of Commons was lessened; disappointment because, in his heart, Lloyd George had hoped to make a clean sweep of his military advisers. To him, therefore, the outcome was a mixed blessing.
'What was the reason for Haig's unexpected submission?'[47]

One reason may have been political. Haig realised that Lloyd George was bound to win over Parliament in the end. He had already defeated Wully and weathered the King's disapproval on that account. If Haig resigned, then Lloyd

George would almost certainly appeal to the electorate—and who was there to succeed him? Asquith? Bonar Law? No others, certainly. But neither of these men had Lloyd George's dynamism and drive which, despite all his drawbacks, were essential to carrying the country through to victory. The country knew it, and Haig knew it. Anyway, as a soldier, he had no wish to dabble overtly in politics.

There was another, more important, reason: Haig's conviction that only he could command in France. Like Lloyd George he had had his failures, and he had been in the saddle a long time. Nevertheless, the Army was as devoted to him and had as much faith in his leadership as ever. No one could take his place. Moreover, now that a great battle was nearing, his departure would have been a great psychological disaster. He was to justify this judgment in the months that followed, when he both sustained the BEF in defeat and rallied it to counter-offensive and final victory in an unbelievably short time afterwards. As he had told the Prime Minister a few days earlier, 'he knew every detail of the situation, and it would not be fair to the Army to suddenly appoint a new Commander in such a grave emergency.'[48] He was right. However ungrateful and self-interested he may have seemed to Wully—and to Derby—Haig's coolness and calculation served the situation best.

As to Derby, he got the worst of every world. Haig left him stranded like 'a whale on a sandbank'[49] and derided him into the bargain.

'Derby is a very weak-minded fellow I am afraid, and, like the feather pillow, bears the marks of the last person who has sat on him! I hear he is called in London "genial Judas"!'[50]

Wully, too, thought he had not been 'quite straight', while his colleagues in the Government, the Prime Minister above all, had little real respect for him. And yet Derby had done well by his friends. He was far stronger than he seemed, and shrewd too. He had defended Wully and Haig manfully for months on end, and since early December had warded off at least three direct assaults by the Prime Minister. He deserved their gratitude, not their kicks. Unfortunately he now proceeded to spoil everything by bad tactics. Having threatened all along to resign if anything was done to break up the partnership of

Wully and Haig, he teetered and tottered at the very moment when he should have taken the plunge. True, he was in torture as to where his duty lay. But by going around and asking everyone—the King included—whether he should resign or not, he only made himself ridiculous. Eventually he did stay, but by that time everyone was laughing at him. He might well have saved himself all the trouble, for within a month he was shunted off as Ambassador to Paris, while Lloyd George sent Milner to the War Office in his place.

Little remains to be told.

On February 19th Lloyd George disposed of the whole episode, with his accustomed skill, in the House of Commons. Esher commented:

'Human nature being what it is, Wully is well-nigh forgotten already.

'The opposition benches made perfunctory speeches, and shed crocodile phrases over his departure. . .'[51]

Hankey had tea with the Prime Minister afterwards.

'He was in great spirits, and walked up and down imitating Wully's heavy walk. He is gone, and Henry Wilson reigns in his stead.'[52]

Yes, Wully's tremendous tenure of power was over, and there was no recall. Nor was his immediate fate very kind. Italy? India? Ireland? The Command of an Army in France? All were suggested, but he got none of these things, only the Eastern Command which he himself had given Henry Wilson the previous summer, and which the latter had left for Versailles. It was a sad come-down, and Wully—for the moment— was naturally very bitter. But the bitterness passed. He was faintly amused when Henry Wilson solved the CIGS–PMR relationship by having Rawlinson (his successor at Versailles) replaced at the end of March by a comparatively junior officer, to whom he could give orders without a qualm. Thus the CIGS came out on top after all, as Wully had always said he would have to. By then, of course, the Prime Minister had no need to by-pass his chief military adviser.

As to the future—though past the peak of his career, Wully still had several years of service ahead. As to the past—that was a story that could wait for the telling.

Reverberations, and the Maurice Case

ALTHOUGH, in the end, no one 'in the know' had been surprised at Wully's going, least of all himself, the news came as a
great shock to the rest of the country. It created a *furore* in the
Press, especially as Wully had told reporters that he had not
resigned, and when the real reasons for his dismissal came out
in the House shortly afterwards. It provided fresh ammunition
for all the correspondents and leader writers, who had been
battling away for months over Government policy and the
higher direction of the war. Indeed, the Press had never left the
subject alone since August 1914, though with the important
difference, already mentioned. For, whereas in the past editors
had been generally critical of the Government, Northcliffe's
recent change of heart had swung an important group of
papers, if not actually over to the side of the Prime Minister,
at least away from that of 'the generals'. Moreover, since
Repington had left *The Times* early in 1918, a new campaign
had opened, and battle had been joined as between the anti-
Government view expressed by him in the *Morning Post*, and the
anti-War Office view expressed by Lovat Fraser in the *Daily
Mail*. It was in connection with this campaign, it will be
recalled, that Derby had managed to dissuade Lloyd George
from taking his critics to the courts.

On February 11th, however, in the very middle of the final
controversy over Wully, Repington had challenged the Government on three vital and relevant issues—the dual system of
strategic control by Versailles and the War Office, the proposal
to launch a campaign against Turkey, and the failure to keep
the Army up to strength. Repington did not mince his words,
and stated *inter alia* that most people had ceased to trust the
Prime Minister. Clearly, on this occasion, his article went far
further than good guesswork, and owed its precise information
—if not its inspiration—to friends in the right places. Maurice
was suspected as being the principal source. Lloyd George
hesitated no longer, and on February 16th—the very day that

Wully's dismissal was announced—Gwynne and Repington appeared at Bow Street, charged with having contravened Regulation 18 of the Defence of the Realm Act, in that the article in question had revealed the supposed plans and conduct of military operations on the Western Front. Repington recorded 'no such crowd at Bow Street since Crippen',[1] a crowd that included a number of friends and interested persons, such as Lady Robertson, Maurice himself, and Macdonogh. It was, in fact, a *cause célèbre*, for everyone was aware of the true issues at stake.

The case took up two days, prosecution on the 16th, defence (after adjournment) on the 21st, when counsel made a strong plea on the lines that all that Repington had written had in substance already appeared in enemy newspapers. The magistrate, however, decided against the defendants, and fined them £100 each plus costs. Nevertheless, the latter chose to regard the conviction as indicating a technical breach only, and as a virtual justification of their action in attacking the Government. Afterwards Maurice commiserated with Repington, and told him that he had been ordered not to talk to him about the war; while Repington himself dined out on Wully's supposed remark that the two of them 'could no more afford to be seen together just now than we could afford to be seen walking down Regent Street with a whore.'[2] By that time, however, Wully had left the War Office, Lloyd George had won the debate in the House of Commons, and the immediate conflict was over. Even so it was not the end. A second clash was to follow three months later, involving not Wully but Maurice, though essentially it was all part of the same struggle waged by both.

A truer test of public feeling, and of the immense respect and affection that Wully inspired, was the shoal of letters that he received from a remarkable variety of correspondents within a few days of his dismissal. In each case the message was much the same: one of sorrow, sympathy, gratitude for his achievements, often laced with a biting comment about his opponents.

Stamfordham wrote personally and on behalf of the King, who was deeply distressed, and who insisted that Wully and his wife stay on at York House. Curzon communicated spidery and flowery phrases, Carson simpler ones, while many other Ministers, MPs, and public persons wrote in after their fashion.

From the Navy came a feeling note from Jellicoe, himself a recent casualty at the Admiralty. From the Army in France and other fronts flowed a multitude of messages, mostly from men who had served at one time or another under Wully's orders. From the War Office, where he had passed round personal notes of farewell, he received letters from subordinates of every grade, officers who had known him both as a taxing taskmaster and as a most lovable man. Finally, there were the messages from an extraordinary galaxy of friends and strangers: from Lady Roberts (widow of the old Field-Marshal), former students of the Staff College, an old comrade of the 16th Lancers, two Bishops, 'Sabretache' of the *Tatler*, a Mr Potter who had addressed a concourse at Tower Hill and recorded a resolution of protest, and a Patriot who told him, 'The Country and its thanks are behind you. So Cheero and go on and prosper like the great Britisher you are, and take no notice of Word Mongers and Amateur Strategists.' A Mother besought him, 'Go to Versailles and make all safe for England'; while an anonymous fanatic (anti-Semite, this time) sent him a poem on a postcard that would have done credit to Joseph Goebbels or Julius Streicher. Entitled 'The Hidden Hand', it began:

> *Who* are the Pacifists? *Lets* look at their noses
> *Are* they tiptilted like petals of Roses?
> Or like sausages do they hang down at the ends?
> Then they are *Jews*, they are *Jews*, they are *JEWS*, my friends![3]

*   *   *

At 4.40 am on March 21st the Germans launched their long-awaited offensive in France, and for the time being all else paled into insignificance beside the new emergency. The blow was even more devastating than had been feared. The enemy had amassed a vast preponderance of men and material—71 divisions against 26, 2500 guns against less than 1000—and assailed the British Third (Byng) and Fifth (Gough) Armies on a front lying roughly between the rivers Scarpe and Oise, west of Cambrai and St Quentin. The Fifth Army bore the brunt and was overwhelmed, and by April 5th (when the attack finally came to a stop) a huge new salient had been carved out, at its deepest some 40 miles, reaching almost to the gates of Amiens. Much of it comprised the former battlefield of the

Somme and of the area devastated by the Germans in their retirement to the Hindenburg Line. On either side of it, the line had had to be swung back: by the French who formed a flank on the south, and by the Third Army which held grimly on to the hinge near Arras in the north.

At one moment acute danger arose lest the enemy penetrate between the Allies. Pétain talked despondently of retiring SW to cover Paris, a move certain to open a gap between his left and Haig's right, and seemed to assume that Haig would retire north to cover the Channel ports. Haig had no such intention, insisted at all costs on keeping the line intact, and pleaded for French support. He was at his very best, displaying admirable determination and resource. It was largely due to his initiative that, at a meeting at Doullens on March 26th, Foch was authorised to co-ordinate the movements of both Allied Armies, and a little later was given the formal appointment of Allied Commander-in-Chief in France. Thus, after three and a half years of warfare, unified command was secured at last. As so often happens in history, it needed a dire emergency to bring it about, and almost came too late. On the other hand, in contrast to the Nivelle proposal in 1917, the result this time came quickly and willingly and by consent. Moreover, it safeguarded the rights and responsibilities of both Haig and Pétain, and it made Foch answerable to *both* Governments, not only his own. At one stroke, therefore, it went far towards solving the problem of strategic planning and control of reserves, and it enabled Foch so to co-ordinate Allied strength as, not only to save the front in the west, but to help bring the war to a successful conclusion before the end of the year.

It is not necessary to follow the full course of the German offensive, which loosed one blow after another at different points of the line all through the spring and early summer of 1918. Each enjoyed initial success, but each petered out in the end. Likewise there is no need to describe the Allied counter-strokes, which beat the Germans back and drove them to defeat in November. All this is related elsewhere. Of concern here only is the impact of the first German assault upon the attitude and actions of the British Government. In a word, the German success in March compelled the War Cabinet to authorise— indeed extend—those very measures which Wully had been urging upon it in the months preceding his dismissal: the release of drafts and reserves at home,[4] the transfer of troops from other theatres to France, and the call-up of more men for the Army from industry, agriculture, and other occupations. There was no holding back now.

'So urgent was the need for men now seen to be that on the opening day of the new session, April 9th, the Prime Minister moved the first reading of a new Manpower Bill, and all other Government business was set aside until the Bill was finally passed. By it the military age was raised to fifty and in some cases to fifty-five years. . . Tribunals were to be reconstituted, and the rights of appeal to be limited . . . the Military Service Acts were to extend to Ireland [though never enforced]. . . The Bill passed through all its stages and became law within ten days of its introduction. . . These measures were estimated to produce 350,000 Category A men and 170,000 of lower categories within the next three months—a very different estimate from that made by the Cabinet Committee a few weeks before. . .'[5]

Altogether, thanks to new legislation and other drastic action, over 540,000 men were sent to France between March 21st and August 31st, and another 100,000 collected from the other fronts. On bare statistics, therefore, the War Cabinet was clearly guilty of starving the BEF of men before the German offensive. The men were found quick enough when they had to be. The crux of the conflict between the Government and the Army resided in the *right use* of manpower. Lloyd George, in particular, mindful of Third Ypres and other battles, was convinced that the Western Front was over-insured, and that neither side would break through the other's defences. He was not, therefore, at heart apprehensive of any new attack the Germans might mount, however many divisions they brought back from Russia, but he did fear that if he released more men for France, Haig would fritter them away in a new Passchendaele. Both he and the War Cabinet looked to the Americans to make good declining Allied strength in France (hence the high priority awarded to the Navy and to shipbuilding), and he of course always believed in knocking out Germany's allies as a preliminary to final victory.

In the event Lloyd George was proved utterly wrong in his assessment of the Western Front early in 1918. The BEF was over-extended and dangerously depleted and—quite apart from the defence preparations and the tactical handling of the battle itself, which is another subject—it was running far too great a risk to *count* upon stopping such a massive build-up of German offensive power without proportionate reinforcements, and simply because, hitherto, in trench warfare defence had always beaten attack. This was more than just an error of judgment. As earlier related, Lloyd George had been given specific and repeated warnings by Wully, his chief military adviser, and he had chosen to disregard them as much on emotional as on rational grounds. The fact that Haig had been less specific and had been compromised by his over-optimism about the German Army at the end of 1917, should not have affected the issue. The fact was that Lloyd George *wanted* no more Western strategy, whatever the realities. In consequence history must charge him with a large part of the responsibility for the débâcle of March–April 1918. A second, related, charge is connected with his attempt to shift the blame on to Haig and falsify certain facts, when confronted with them by Maurice early in May. That story will now be told.

* * *

After Wully left the War Office, Maurice had no wish to retain his job as DMO. The two men had cemented a remarkable partnership, and as Wully's closest adviser and loyal friend, Maurice clearly had no love for Henry Wilson, the new CIGS. In any event he was long overdue for a command. Arrangements therefore were soon made to find him a successor, and it was agreed that the new DMO should take over in the middle of April. After that, Maurice would take leave before reporting for duty in France early in May. He had every hope of being given a division.

The first fortnight of April was an extremely busy and anxious time, and Maurice hardly had a moment to raise his head. A mass of new work had been thrown on the Directorate by the German offensive, and all this had to be concerted with the task of tidying up and handing over. It is not surprising, therefore, that he missed reading the Prime Minister's speech on the new Manpower Bill in the House of Commons on April 9th, in which it was stated that the 'Army in France was considerably stronger on the 1st January 1918 than on 1st January 1917.'[6] Two days later the new DMO (Radcliffe) arrived at the War Office, and on April 14th Maurice left for a four-day duty visit to France. It was not until then that he became aware of Lloyd George's statement and of the fierce wave of resentment it had aroused in the BEF, battered but not broken by the German assault, on the grounds that it tended 'to throw the whole responsibility for failure unfairly upon Haig, at a time when he required all the support, both moral and physical, which the Government could give him.'[7] As a result he promised everyone he talked to, at GHQ and elsewhere, that he would go into the matter directly he got back to England.

He was not, however, the first to take action. Returning to London late on April 17th, he spent the whole of the next day formally handing over to Radcliffe, and was not able actually to procure a copy of Hansard until the 20th. Meanwhile, on April 18th (Maurice's handing-over day) the Prime Minister had been asked by Sir Godfrey Baring in the House of Commons to justify his statement of April 9th. This was the core of the whole drama, although hidden at the time from Maurice who, busy with Radcliffe, was told neither of the question nor of the answer; in fact he knew nothing of them until the 'Maurice Debate' of May 9th.

Baring's question cannot have been unexpected, but it caused disquiet. Lloyd George, always rather free with facts and figures in his speeches,[8] had presumably based his earlier statement on the strength returns issued by the Adjutant-General of the BEF on February 4th 1918, summarised on page 359.

These statistics clearly showed that the Prime Minister had been correct, but only in regard to the *gross* totals (fighting, administrative, and non-combatant troops), 1918 exceeding 1917 by over 300,000. In regard to the *nett* totals (fighting troops only), however, they showed a decrease of over 70,000, chiefly in the infantry ($-69,934$). This was Maurice's point when, in due course, he asserted that only the gross total had gone up, mainly due to the influx of a large number of

Fighting troops	Jan. 8th 1917	Jan. 5th 1918	Difference
Cavalry	42,569	32,809	
R.A.	249,308	280,604	
R.E. Field Units ⎫		50,472	
„ Tunnelling ⎭	124,276	12,108	
Infantry (incl. cyclists)	735,681	665,747	
M.G. Corps	37,260	46,850	
Tanks	3,574	9,316	
Total fighting troops*	1,192,668	1,097,906	− 99,762
Transportation	Nil	72,065	
Lines of Communication	275,900	388,900	
Total Strength (incl. a number of non-combatant and labour units not quoted above)	1,646,600	1,949,000	+ 302,400

*Note. The 1917 total of fighting troops has to be reduced by 24,202 Railway, Inland Water Transport, and other R.E. personnel transferred to Transportation by 1918. Thus the comparative totals should read 1,168,466 and 1,097,906 respectively, and the difference − 70,560.[9]

unarmed British and Chinese labourers.[10] He added that not only had the nett total gone down as between the two dates, but that between January 1st and March 21st it had declined yet further, for that was the period in which Haig had had to disband well over 100 infantry battalions, owing to lack of drafts.[11]

Such a conclusion should, of course, have come out in the answer given to Baring on April 18th, but by an extraordinary chain of events it did not. When Baring's question came up, material for an answer was urgently demanded from the Military Operations Directorate by Macpherson, Under-Secretary of State for War, who was to reply for the Prime Minister. The figures were worked out and a note sent over at once by the officer deputising for Maurice and Radcliffe, both —it will be recalled—deeply engaged in the business of handing over. Note in hand, Macpherson thereupon gave Baring his answer: namely, that the *combatant* strength of the British Army in France was greater on January 1st 1918 than on January 1st 1917; further, that if labour and other non-combatant units were included, the increase was more marked.[12]

The critical adjective was, of course, *combatant* or *fighting*, and the Prime Minister was to ring confusing changes on it later, in the Maurice Debate of May 9th. But on this occasion there was no need to confuse, for the note justified his original statement in every respect.

But—and this was the marrow of it—*the note was wrong*. Prepared in a hurry, a mistake had been made, whereby the British Army in Italy had been lumped in with the British Army in France, and certain labour units added to both totals. The figures sent over were: 1,253,000 for January 1917, and 1,298,000 for January 1918.[13]

However, the mistake was soon discovered, and a correction despatched the same day, the fact also being reported both to Kerr (PPS to the Prime Minister) and to Macpherson.

From evidence which only appeared years later, it seems likely that the corrected return never reached the Prime Minister at all, and that he was never told of its existence by Kerr, Macpherson, or anyone else. Amazing to relate, the corrected return was only discovered at some unspecified date by J. T. Davies and Miss Frances Stevenson, both members of Lloyd George's personal secretarial staff. An account of the discovery is given in the diary of Miss Stevenson (later, Countess Lloyd George), entry dated October 5th 1934, and published by Lord Beaverbrook in *Men and Power, 1917–1918* in 1956. It runs as follows:

'Have been reading up the events connected with the Maurice Debate in order to help Ll.G. with this Chapter in Vol. V [of the *War Memoirs*], and am uneasy in my mind about an incident which occurred at the time and which is known only to J. T. Davies and myself. Ll.G. obtained from the W.O. the figures which he used in his statement of April 9th in the House of Commons on the subject of man-power. These figures were afterwards stated by Gen. Maurice to be inaccurate.

'I was in J. T. Davies' room a few days after the statement, and J.T. was sorting out red dispatch boxes to be returned to the Departments. As was his wont, he looked in them before locking them up and sending them out to the Messengers. Pulling out a W.O. box, he found in it, to his great astonishment, a paper from the D.M.O. containing modifications and corrections of the first figures they had sent, and by some mischance this box had remained unopened. J.T. and I examined it in dismay and then J.T. put it in the fire, remarking, "Only you and I, Frances, know of the existence of this paper."

'There is no doubt that this is what Maurice had in mind when he accused L.G. of mis-statement. But the amazing thing was that *the document was never fixed upon*. How was it that the matter was never clinched, and Maurice or someone never actually said: "The figures supplied by us were so and so"? They argued round and over the point, but never did one of them put any finger on it. . .'[14]

All this is anticipating events, but it is necessary to answer Miss Stevenson's query—so far as any final answer can ever be given—in order to hold the thread of the story. Maurice was formally succeeded as DMO by Radcliffe on Monday April 22nd, but had handed over to him—as noted—on the previous Thursday, the 18th, the day of the Baring affair. He then took a week's leave and decided upon a certain course of action, which led to his discharge from the Army after the debate in the House of Commons on May 9th. From that date onwards (when he learned of the Baring question and answer for the first time), and possibly even from April 22nd, he had no access to War Office documents and could do nothing to prove that the Prime Minister was, wittingly or otherwise, guilty of mis-statement. It was not until 1922 that he was able, thanks to the Duke of Northumberland (who had been acting as GSO1 of MO3 in April 1918), to obtain proof of the correction sent over on April 18th; but he never knew, of course, that it had not reached the Prime Minister and that Davies had destroyed it. Nevertheless, he had obtained a vital clue, and on the strength of it he wrote to Lloyd George on July 15th 1922 and asked him to put matters right. The latter, however (always, it may be assumed, ignorant of the correction), merely replied that 'what he said in 1918, he said in good faith upon the information supplied to him', and left it at that.[15] Maurice then published a pamphlet, *Intrigues of the War*, giving his side of the story, but it was not until the publication of Beaverbrook's book in 1956 that the missing clue came to light.

To return to the chronological sequence of events.

Maurice was on leave in the country for the whole of the week beginning April 22nd. He had taken with him the appropriate copy of Hansard and, in fulfillment of his promise to the men he had talked to in France, he made a detailed study of Lloyd George's speech of April 9th. In it he found two statements calling for objection. One referred to the comparative strengths of the BEF as at January 1st 1917 and January 1st 1918. The other referred to the number of white (as distinct from Indian) troops in the Middle East: the implication being, either that they were insufficient to constitute a worthwhile reinforcement for the BEF, or that the Turkish front was too critical to allow of their being moved.

While so engaged, Maurice read a further report, this time of statements made in the House of Commons on April 23rd by Bonar Law, to the effect that the recent extension of the British front in France (down to Barisis in the Fifth Army area, within the general location of the German attack) had not been forced on Wully and Haig, either by the War Cabinet or by the Supreme War Council, but had been solely a military decision agreed between the British and French.[16]

Here, in Maurice's opinion, were three Government pronouncements, not only untrue in themselves, but calculated to throw upon Haig all the responsibility for the recent disasters in France. 'Simultaneously', he wrote afterwards, 'I learned that a scheme for removing Haig from the supreme command in France was rapidly coming to a head.'[17] What this scheme was he did not say, but that he was justified in concluding that the Prime Minister wished and had long been planning so to act there is no doubt. Ample evidence could be found in the latter's treatment of Haig all through 1917, and specifically (as we now know) in his communications with Derby in December, when he made a determined bid to get rid of both Haig and Wully. Moreover, the dismissal of Gough (commander of the Fifth Army), insisted upon by Lloyd George despite Haig's objections, was yet another pointer. Haig sensed the position keenly himself, when he wrote to Derby on April 6th:

'But, as I have more than once said to you and to others of the Government, the moment they feel that they would prefer someone else to command in France, I am prepared to place my resignation in your hands.'[18]

By the end of the week, Maurice had made up his mind as to what he should do. Summarised, this was his view.

Thanks to his previous position as DMO, he possessed unique

knowledge of all the facts and pressures, political and military. It was clear to him that by almost all his actions since becoming Prime Minister in December 1916, Lloyd George had demonstrated his intense hostility to Western strategy and thus to the two men—Wully and Haig—who had counselled it and directed it. Unable in 1917 to replace either of them or break their partnership, he had conducted a campaign of attrition against them and against the national interest, and had finally succeeded, first in by-passing Wully, and then in disposing of him. It was now Haig's turn. But to get rid of Haig at this crisis of affairs was not only morally indefensible, but would invite utter disaster and loss of the war. The morale of the BEF was already suffering under the campaign working up against him. If he went, collapse might follow, for no one could replace him as commander in France, and no one possessed the confidence of the troops as he did.

'I was concerned to prevent what appeared to me to be action fatal to our cause. I believed the moral strength which the justice of our cause gave us was our chief asset, and that we should impair and even destroy altogether that moral strength if the Government, after refusing throughout the latter half of 1917 to take the steps which the soldiers had urged upon them to meet the German attack, threw the blame for the March disaster upon the soldiers, and then removed Haig. I believed that a public challenge would have the effect of making known to the whole Cabinet the facts as to the strength of our armies in France and in the East, and would stop the attacks upon Haig.'[19]

Maurice was well aware of what might happen to himself. He was about to commit an act of great moral courage and extreme indiscipline.

'I knew that I was sacrificing a career of some promise and giving up my means of livelihood, but I believed that I was acting rightly, and that if I was right I would not suffer materially.'[20]

His own integrity, and the tradition of selflessness and social conscience inherited from his family, above all from his grandfather, Frederick Denison Maurice, the great Christian Socialist, left him no other course once his mind had been made up.

364

'I had no political motive. . . I had made up my mind that I must act alone, as I could not brief anyone without disclosing confidential information, which I would not do. I therefore communicated with no one even remotely connected with the Press, and the only person in any way connected with politics whom I consulted was Lord Salisbury, to whom I told only what I had heard in France.'[21]

On April 30th, the day after his return to London, he wrote to Henry Wilson, CIGS, 'calling his attention to the incorrect statements of Ministers and to their effect in France.'[22]

Receiving no reply, he waited until May 5th before writing the letter that was to burst like a bombshell in the columns of the Press on May 7th. He could afford to wait no longer, for he was due to report for duty in France on May 10th, and he was determined to 'face the music' at home. On this point, however, he displayed a truly paradoxical sense of honour, amounting to outright eccentricity. Having posted the letter, he then deliberately departed once more for the country, leaving his family to cope with the horde of callers and reporters, who were to besiege his house in Kensington Park Gardens, and never got off the telephone. His purpose was, not to deflect the rumpus from himself—for that was why he acted before returning to duty—but, by getting away from the people who would press him with questions, to avoid any possible charge of political involvement. He also had the odd thought that his letter was as far as he ought to go.

'It would have been easy for me to go to the House of Commons and coach those who were ready to attack Ministers. I stayed in the country.'[23]

It was a foolish mistake. He left the field wide open to his adversaries, and Lloyd George was not the sort of adversary to refuse even the slimmest chance of manœuvre. As it turned out, Maurice's absence from London on May 9th, during the critical debate in Parliament, allowed the Prime Minister full scope, since no one who spoke for the Opposition had any real grasp of all the facts and factors involved. And yet everything was in character, too. From the very start, Maurice had a strong presentiment that, whatever the outcome, he would have to pay the penalty, hence the fatalism of his attitude. It was in this sense that he addressed a moving message to his children before he left London for the second time. With it he enclosed a copy of the letter which appeared in the Press on May 7th. It was published in full by *The Times* and the *Morning Post*, and copied by the other newspapers.

'Sir

My attention has been called to answers given in the House of Commons on April 23rd by Mr Bonar Law to questions put by Mr G. Lambert, Colonel Burn, and Mr Pringle as to the extension of the British front in France (Hansard, vol 105, No. 34, p. 815). These answers contain certain misstatements which in sum give a totally misleading impression of what occurred. This is not the place to enter into a discussion as to all the facts, but Hansard's report concludes:

"Mr Pringle—Was this matter entered into at the Versailles War Council at any time?"

"Mr Bonar Law—This particular matter was not dealt with at all by the Versailles War Council."

I was at Versailles when the question was decided by the Supreme War Council to whom it had been referred.

This is the latest of a series of misstatements which have been made recently in the House of Commons by the present Government.

On April 9th the Prime Minister said:

"What was the position at the beginning of the battle? Notwithstanding the heavy casualties in 1917 the Army in France was considerably stronger on the 1st January 1918 than on the 1st January 1917." (Hansard, vol 104, No. 24, p. 1328)

That statement implies that Sir Douglas Haig's fighting strength was greater on the eve of the great battle which began on March 21st and that it had not been diminished.

That is not correct.

Again in the same speech the Prime Minister said:

"In Mesopotamia there is only one white division at all, and in Egypt and Palestine there are only three white divisions, the rest are either Indians or mixed with a very small proportion of British troops in these divisions—I am referring to the infantry divisions." (Ibid p. 1327).

That is not correct.

Now, Sir, this letter is not the result of a military conspiracy. It has been seen by no soldier. I am by descent and conviction as sincere a democrat as the Prime Minister, and the last thing I want is to see the government of our country in the hands of soldiers.

My reasons for taking the very grave step of writing this letter are that the statements quoted above are known to a large number of soldiers to be incorrect, and this knowledge is breeding such distrust of the Government as can only end in impairing the splendid *moral* of our troops at a time when everything possible should be done to raise it.

I have therefore decided, fully realising the consequences to myself, that my duty as a citizen must override my duty as a soldier, and I ask you to publish this letter in the hope that Parliament will see fit to order an investigation into the statements I have made.

I am, Sir,

Yours faithfully,

F. MAURICE

MAJOR-GENERAL'[24]

20 Kensington Park Gardens
  May 6, 1918.

*   *   *

Any estimate that Maurice may have allowed himself of the impact of his letter was far exceeded in reality. Its appearance on May 7th produced a major news sensation and a first-class political crisis. The Press lined up once again, as it had before over Wully's dismissal, and as it had intermittently for months over the direction of the war. This time, however, the atmosphere was intensified by the disasters in France; and leader writers—even in moderate newspapers—were predominantly critical of the War Cabinet. Opposition papers, such as the *Westminster Gazette* and the *Morning Post*, were violently hostile and made it quite clear that the Government, or at least the Prime Minister, should go. Maurice's letter had merely put the official seal on a situation that had long been known outside Parliament, and all agreed that the present administration would stand or fall by the way it replied to Maurice's accusations.

That, too, was the opinion of Lloyd George himself and of most of his colleagues in the Cabinet. They were also aware that Maurice had shaken the faith of many of their supporters. Bonar Law was greatly upset. An upright, Puritanical character, he had virtually been called a liar, and he wished to vindicate himself before an impartial tribunal. Lloyd George, more resilient and less scrupulous, felt sure that this was an attack organised by the military, and that it would be a duel to the

THE TRUTH.

TO THE EDITOR OF THE MORNING POST.

SIR,—My attention has been called to answers given in the House of Commons on April 23rd by Mr. Bonar Law to questions put by Mr. G. Lambert, Colonel Burn, and Mr. Pringle as to the extension of the British front in France (Hansard, vol. 105, No. 34, p. 815). These answers contain certain misstatements which in sum give a totally misleading impression of what occurred. This is not the place to enter into a discussion as to all the facts, but Hansard's report of the incident concludes:

Mr. Pringle—Was this matter entered into at the Versailles War Council at any time?

Mr. Bonar Law—This particular matter was not dealt with at all by the Versailles War Council.

I was at Versailles when the question was decided by the Supreme War Council, to whom it had been referred.

This is the latest of a series of misstatements which have been made recently in the House of Commons by the present Government.

On April 9th, the Prime Minister said:

"What was the position at the beginning of the battle? Notwithstanding the heavy casualties in 1917 the Army in France was considerably stronger on the 1st January, 1918, than on the 1st January, 1917." (Hansard, vol. 104, No. 24, p. 1328.)

That statement implies that Sir Douglas Haig's fighting strength on the eve of the great battle which began on March 21st had not been diminished.

That is not correct.

Again in the same speech the Prime Minister said:

"In Mesopotamia there is only one white division at all, and in Egypt and in Palestine there are only three white divisions, the rest are either Indians or mixed with a very small proportion of British troops in those divisions—I am referring to the infantry divisions." (Ibid, p. 1327.)

That is not correct.

Now, Sir, this letter is not the result of a military conspiracy. It has been seen by no soldier. I am by descent and conviction as sincere a democrat as the Prime Minister, and the last thing I desire is to see the government of our country in the hands of soldiers.

My reasons for taking the very grave step of writing this letter are that the statements quoted above are known by a large number of soldiers to be incorrect, and this knowledge is breeding such distrust of the Government as can only end in impairing the splendid *moral* of our troops at a time when everything possible should be done to raise it.

I have, therefore, decided, fully realising the consequences to myself, that my duty as a citizen must override my duty as a soldier, and I ask you to publish this letter in the hope that Parliament may see fit to order an investigation into the statements I have made.

I am, Sir,

Yours faithfully,

F. MAURICE,

MAJOR-GENERAL.

20, Kensington Park-gardens,

May 6, 1918.

death. Either he would win and thereafter have his way over the war, or he would lose and be succeeded by a junta of generals. As always he was at his very best in a tight corner. His fighting instincts had been aroused, and he made very careful and thorough preparations with his friends.

There was not long to wait.

On April 7th Asquith declared his intention of asking for a complete investigation by a Select Committee of the House of Commons. The Government countered with a proposal to invite two judges to conduct an enquiry. This offer was refused by Asquith, and was then withdrawn altogether on Churchill's advice. The latter made the point that 'no Government ought to put up a set of judges to say whether they are liars or not.'[25] A debate was then fixed for May 9th. Such then was the scene as the curtain went up on the last act, and already the Government had gained an advantage. Asquith had been unwise to reject the Government's offer, for it would have subjected Ministerial words and actions to a cool judicial scrutiny, unaffected by political passions; and that would have done the administration no good at all, whatever the final verdict. On the other hand, in Parliament the Opposition was divided, and neither Asquith nor Carson was able to bring the Squiffites and the Right-Wing Conservatives together. Moreover, no Opposition speaker knew the real facts, and since Lloyd George was determined to thrash the whole matter out in debate and burst the boil for ever—in short to treat the motion as a Vote of Censure—the Opposition was doubly at a disadvantage. Finally, Maurice himself was nowhere to be found; he was certainly not on hand to help out at the House of Commons.

The debate went the Government's way almost from the first. Asquith opened with a wordy, long-winded garble, packed with parentheses, in which he confined himself to discussing the form of the proposed enquiry. He hardly mentioned Maurice or his letter at all. It was rather like a commanding officer inspecting his men's buttons, rather than their weapons, before they all went over the top.

Then Lloyd George got up, and pitched straight into it. In no time he held the House in his hand, thanks to an inspired mixture of truth and near-truth, all purveyed with matchless verve and rhetoric.

First, he made much of the point that Maurice had never called his attention to any inaccuracy in his speech of April 9th. There had been plenty of opportunity to do so before Maurice left the War Office. Instead, the matter had been saved up for a Press attack. Was that fair?

(As we know, owing to extreme pressure of work, Maurice had never read the speech of April 9th at the time, and did not even hear of its contents until he went to France on April 14th. There was no reason why he should have read it. Ministers made speeches every day, and although a statement in this one was based on statistics, provided in the ordinary course of duty by his department, they had not been specially asked for; nor had the material been devilled in any way by him or his officers. As to nailing its inaccuracy, this he did, together with the two other statements, in his letter to Wilson on April 30th.)

Secondly, he dealt with the strength returns of the BEF. There is no need to retell the tale, but Lloyd George was on sure ground here. After trying to confuse the House by challenging the definition of combatant and non-combatant, he merely reasserted that his original statement had been based on and substantiated by the official figures. As to the answer given by Macpherson to Baring on April 18th, he produced the actual note sent over by the MO Directorate, and waved it in the air.

'*Mr George Lambert:* Is it initialled?
The Prime Minister: It is initialled by his deputy! (Laughter) My right hon. friend is going to draw that distinction, is he? That shows what sort of impartiality you get! This is the note etc etc.'[26]

(As related, the full story only came to light some 38 years later.)

Thirdly, he dealt with the Army in the Middle East. There was no dispute about the single British division in Mesopotamia. As to the three said to be in Egypt, this statement had been made at a Cabinet meeting, and afterwards sent to Maurice for checking. The latter had telephoned 'no comments'.

(In early April 1918 Allenby had an Army of eight infantry and three mounted divisions, composed of British and Indian troops in the approximate proportion of 6:1. Orders, however, had already been given for the transfer to France of a large part of this force: two complete divisions, plus 44 battalions and certain other units. Lloyd George protested that he was not aware of the proposed move at the time he spoke. It may therefore have been a genuine misunderstanding. But—in the context of the speech—it seems likely that he quoted the smaller total in order to reinforce the impression he wished to convey: namely, that there were no troops to spare on that front.)

Fourthly, he dealt with the allegation that the BEF had had to extend its line in France on the orders of the Supreme War Council, and against the advice of Wully and Haig. He denied it flatly. The extension had been completed by agreement between Haig and Pétain *before* the relevant meeting of the Supreme War Council on February 1st. It had originally been put forward, as a surprise request, by M. Painlevé at the Boulogne Conference in September 1917. Neither he (Lloyd George) nor Wully had been prepared for it, though they guessed it might come up some time in view of French Army difficulties that summer. Wully had dealt with the matter himself and expressed the greatest reserve. While yielding in principle, he had refused to commit himself to any firm date or length of line; in any event nothing was possible till the Third Battle of Ypres was over and plans agreed for 1918. Later Clemenceau had brought the matter up again, exerted pressure, and asked for a decision from the Supreme War Council. By that time, however, Haig and Pétain had agreed on a modified plan, and the British had duly taken over as far as Barisis. Lloyd George added shrewdly that no difficulty would have arisen between the Allies on this point, had there been unity of command, as now prevailed under Foch.

(All this was substantially correct. But Haig, who had not been present at Boulogne, had always taken exception to the plan and to the way it was conveyed to him. In his view a vital decision affecting the BEF had been made in his absence and for this he blamed Wully as much as the Prime Minister. In the end he bowed to *force majeure*. Although, therefore, it was technically true to say that the extension had come solely out of a *military* agreement, the full explanation was that Haig had been compelled, against his better judgment, to fall in with a *political* demand. Maurice had phrased this charge inaptly, for the operative influence was certainly *not* the Supreme War Council, which had only met after all was over.)

At this point there was little doubt that the Prime Minister had gained the day. But, successful as he was, even he could not have captured a hardened House, had he not been able to quote Maurice's own statistics against him. That was the turning point. Lloyd George then ended his speech with a homily upon Maurice's indiscipline, and called upon Members to rally behind the Government in its efforts to deal with the German offensive and overcome the worst crisis of the war.

'I really beg and implore, for our common country, the fate of which is in the balance now and in the next few weeks, that there should be an end of this sniping.'[27]

After that, everything was an anticlimax, and no speech that followed cut any ice at all. The House then divided, and the Government defeated the Opposition by 293 to 106.

The Maurice Debate had two important results. One affected Lloyd George and the Liberals. The other affected Maurice and Haig.

In the first place it ensured Lloyd George's authority as Prime Minister for the rest of the war, and enabled him to win the next election (the Coupon Election of December 1918), and personally to stay in power until 1922. It also decided the fate of the Liberals. Many of those who had voted with Asquith on May 9th lost their seats at the end of the year, and the division between the two halves of the party proved so disastrous that Liberalism all but disappeared as a political force within twenty years. The Maurice Debate was the point of permanent cleavage and the start of the decline.

In the second place it led to the immediate end of Maurice's professional career as a soldier. He was retired from the Army on half-pay, and compelled to find other employment. He did so, beginning on May 15th with his appointment as military correspondent of the *Daily Chronicle*. Later he succeeded in making for himself a distinguished academic career; from 1922 to 1933 as Principal of the Working Men's College, which his grandfather had helped to found in 1854; and from 1933 to 1944 as Principal of East London College. He also held the Chair of Military Studies at London University, was a member of the University Senate, honorary fellow of King's College, Cambridge, and recipient of two degrees *honoris causa*. He was also a prolific writer on military history. As if this was not enough, he served the British Legion in high positions. It was characteristic that Maurice refused to allow his dismissal in 1918 to deprive him of further service to the nation; nor did he shroud the remainder of his life in sour recrimination. He never launched a crusade. At the same time he stood firmly by all that he had said and done, and always considered that Lloyd George had use the incorrect return of April 18th to justify his earlier statement of April 9th.

Maurice had no lack of champions. Indeed, the majority of Army officers, and of many others in the Services and public life, continued always to believe in him as a man who had sacrificed himself for the truth. In their eyes he was a martyr, a victim of guile, and guilty of nothing but irregular and unlucky tactics. Haig also sympathised, but deprecated Maurice's action on the grounds that no soldier should meddle in politics, whatever the emergency. For his part, Maurice believed to his dying day that his letter had saved Haig, and that Lloyd George had been on the point of getting rid of him, as he had already got rid of Wully. It was fortunate indeed that Haig was not removed from his command. His determination, skill, and cool head saved a series of bad situations, all during the German offensive from March till July. After that he progressively strengthened his own position, as the BEF launched one successful attack after another, making the major contribution to the whole Allied offensive under Foch.

The dismissal of Maurice was the logical aftermath of the dismissal of Wully. Whereas Wully had made his final stand upon his refusal to accept the Executive War Board (of the Supreme War Council) as a rival authority to the CIGS and the Army Council in matters concerning the British Army, Maurice had taken issue over Government statements concerning the BEF and the implied attempt to shift the blame for March 1918 upon Haig. But, in both cases, the underlying reason was the same; namely, the struggle between the Prime Minister and his military colleagues over strategy and the conduct of the war.

Full of Days, Riches and Honour

ALL during the early months of 1918, after his dismissal, Wully was a spectator of events, a watcher in the wings at Eastern Command. It was a hateful position. It galled him to see all his warnings about the BEF coming true, and it was agonising to follow the destruction of the Fifth Army without being able, any longer, to lend help from a position of power. He was not entirely out of touch, however, so long as Maurice remained at the War Office. Moreover, there was an intermittent stream of suggestions, mostly unofficial, as to ways in which he might return to full and active participation in the war. One such message reached him from Maurice himself, when the latter was paying his historic visit to the BEF April 14th–17th.

'The situation is grave but not desperate. The real gravity lies in the steady exhaustion of our army, which is of course what the Germans are aiming at. . . I had a long talk with Lawrence (CGS) last night and he told me that Sir Douglas has asked that you should come out. I knew that the King had pressed that you should be sent and that Haig had been asked to take you. Haig's suggestion is that you should come out as 2nd in command. It may appear to you that this is only a nominal position without any definite functions and you may not feel inclined to take it. I am convinced however that your presence would have great effect both in the Army and at GHQ. . .'[1]

Wully replied:

'I am ready to help, but its no use *pretending* to help. I must have a definite status. I dont like the term "2nd in command", though perhaps something on the lines of Lords K [Kitchener] and Bobs [Roberts] in S. Africa might help. But I dont think anyone can help unless Ministerial control and hourly interference is rigorously suppressed. . . I practically left W.O. on this point, and I'd like to get it put right when next I get into harness. . .'[2]

Shortly afterwards the Maurice case blew up, with rumours that Maurice was merely acting as agent to a group of eminent plotters, Wully among them, who were planning to upset the

Government. This, of course, was just what Lloyd George had expected. But it was quite untrue. Maurice had acted entirely alone and, whatever his feelings about Maurice's action and his friendship for the man himself, Wully had no call to be involved when in fact he had had nothing to do with it. He therefore told Lord Milner, successor to Derby as Secretary of State for War:

'During the past week a story has been persistently circulated in a certain section of the London Press—the same section which suddenly and simultaneously attacked me early in the year—insinuating that Mr Asquith, Lord Jellicoe, General Trenchard and myself met recently at a special dinner or in conference—before the Maurice letter—and conspired together to upset or cause trouble to the Government. I wish to say that so far as I am personally concerned this story is an absolute fabrication.'[3]

Milner forwarded this letter, with a favourable comment, to the Prime Minister, and this may have had some bearing on the fact that no objection was offered to Wully's appointment soon after as C-in-C, Home Forces, in succession to Lord French. Although not a war command, yet this was a post of great importance and responsibility, and Wully held it for eleven months, until May 1919. It revived all his interest and energy, and he threw himself into the work. Travelling for the most part in a special train, he visited each regional Command and every military station from Cromarty to Plymouth within six months. He was genuinely and humanly concerned, as much for the conditions of service as for the efficiency of the coast defences, and paid attention alike to hospitals, labour and administrative units, women in uniform, and port garrisons: the latter always liable to surprise test at some unearthly hour of the morning. He showed great interest in the anti-aircraft defences of London—now reasonably efficient after some bad experiences with German raiders earlier in the war—and he made some prescient remarks about air power in future wars.

'Modern war being largely a matter of war against economic life, it has turned more and more towards the enemy's home country, and the old principle of making war only against armies and navies has been consigned to the background. Raids on non-military places and people may be regarded as barbaric . . . but they are bound to play a prominent part in the next contest, and on a far more extensive scale than in the Great War. A new weapon . . . will always open up new paths for itself, and in the case of the aeroplane can be followed within a few minutes of the declaration of war—if not before. . . In the next war the enemy's radius of action will doubtless be much increased, as well as the number and destructive power of his aeroplanes, and, in the air as on land and sea, our best form of defence will lie in the ability to attack.'[4]

Indeed, although cautious towards the introduction of tanks in 1916, his was not a closed mind to inventions. On the contrary, he was remarkably aware of the possibilities of new weapons (and their antidotes), and of the necessity for scientific research in war as in peace.

Soon after the war ended in November 1918, trouble arose over demobilisation and the general return to civilian life. The demobilisation scheme was being badly worked, and it was not until Churchill succeeded Milner at the War Office early in 1919 that a more equitable scheme was adopted, and one which told the soldiers where they stood. Wully handled a difficult, at times even ugly, situation in Home Forces with firmness and understanding. He was well aware of the worries of the men, especially the middle-aged husbands, who were anxious about employment, their families, and the fidelity of their wives. He took an active part, too, in revising the rates of officers' pay and allowances.

In April 1919 Wully handed over Home Forces to Haig, and took up the last job of his military career as C-in-C, British Army of the Rhine, and Military Governor, in succession to Plumer. As at Home Forces, he stayed in this post for eleven months, and likewise found it full of interest and—at times—of anxiety; certainly it was no sinecure. He had to face two difficulties: the occupation of enemy territory, and all the social and political problems attached to that; also the maintenance of his own troops in efficiency and good heart, despite the constant drain by demobilisation and the natural desire of everyone to give up soldiering and go home.

As regards the Germans, he took the line of interfering as little as possible in civil affairs, and only did so when internal disputes seemed likely to affect public services or to demand the intervention of his troops.

'The procedure I laid down was that all disputes likely to lead to a strike must in the first instance be submitted to a German 'court of conciliation', in which both sides were represented; if no agreement was reached the case was submitted to a British court of arbitration, whose decision was final and binding. . . It should be added that when a strike did occur no picketing was allowed; protection was always afforded to those men who wished to work; every consideration was given to the point of view of workmen, who, by our intervention, frequently obtained the terms they demanded; and anyone who did not abide by our decision, whether employer or employee, was liable to be dealt with as an offender. . .'[5]

Although the British zone of occupation, like the rest of the country, was short of food and other necessities, and subject to separatist outbreaks or other movements of violence by Left and Right, Wully had remarkably little trouble.

As regards the British soldiers he found that, in addition to the general dislocation of a diminishing and rapidly reconstructing army, there was a chronic shortage of commanding officers and cooks, both persons essential to the welfare of any unit. He took the simplest and most effective line. While badgering the War Office, he also explained the situation to the men, through extensive inspections, told them the cause of their troubles and what was being done to surmount them. He also got everyone down to hard training. By then, a large proportion of the troops were young soldiers, who had never been in action and hardly knew how to fire a rifle. It was vital that they be welded into an effective force, since the Allied Armies had to be prepared for an advance deeper into the country, with the strong possibility of irregular warfare, should the Germans refuse to sign the Peace Treaty. On June 17th units began their concentrations for an advance east, but on June 28th the Versailles Treaty was duly signed, and the emergency evaporated. Although ratification was not completed until January 1920, demobilisation and reductions continued, so that in March 1920 Wully was finally instructed to hand over his command to a more junior officer. By then he had not only brought his troops through a period of doubt and dislocation, but had fully upheld the dignity of his command, rendering and receiving visits from a large company of Royalty and Heads of State, from brother commanders in the Allied Armies—notably from Foch,

Allied C-in-C—and from a delegation of the Army Council headed by Churchill and Henry Wilson. It was fitting that, in Germany itself, Wully should enjoy many of the visible honours due to a man who had done so much towards winning the war. It is also notable to record that, eighteen years later, his son was to hold exactly the same position as commander of the British Army of Occupation and Military Governor of the British Zone.

One honour he was not permitted to enjoy was attendance at the peace celebrations, held in London on July 19th 1919. As he recorded pointedly, he was not invited. Lloyd George was not a generous opponent. Likewise when the list of war honours and rewards was published, Wully found himself well down the list with a baronetcy and a sum of £10,000. Haig got an earldom and £100,000, French and Allenby £50,000 each, most of the Army Commanders (not Gough) £30,000 each. Wilson, Birdwood, and Trenchard received the same as Wully. Moreover, the monetary awards, substantial though they all were, and altogether questionable by today's standards, were considerably lessened in value by the fact that only the income was available; the capital could not be touched. It was Churchill, however, who made the most satisfying amends. Thanks to him Wully received promotion to Field-Marshal soon after his return from Germany, filling the vacancy[6] created by the death of Sir Evelyn Wood, an officer whom—remarkably enough— Wully had served for a short time, many years before, as a junior NCO. No soldier in the British Army, actually or metaphorically, carried his baton in his knapsack—either in Wully's day or before it. The proposition was unthinkable, for the difficulties were insuperable—socially and financially as well as militarily. Wully was the first man ever to break through the barrier. He created a record, one which has never been equalled since, it may be added, in precisely similar terms, though under present conditions of service any man can rise from the bottom to the top in the British Army, and need fear no barriers. But Wully was the first regular ranker so to rise, and his achievement must be measured accordingly. *C'est le premier pas qui coûte.*

When the time came for him to leave Germany, Wully found the partings very painful. There were so many loyal friends, who insisted on making his departure an occasion of signal honour, a few travelling with him all the way to the pier at Calais to see him off. Some—like Beddington—had studied under him at Camberley and served him during the war or since. To the very end they found him the same: a man of the highest standards, tremendous application and force of character, yet always human and humorous. Very little escaped him and no one ever got the better of him in the Army. Beddington related how, at Cologne, one of his duties was to produce a political summary of the German newspapers, the report to be on Wully's breakfast table every morning before 9.0 am. Never good at getting up early, Beddington came to rely more and more on the abilities of his clerk, who normally took down his dictation. In the end the clerk took to composing a couple of alternative summaries himself, one of which Beddington would usually adopt and sign.

'Not long after I gave up Intelligence I was out with Wully one day in his car, and for something to say I told him of this naughtiness on my part. His comment was—with a broad grin—"My boy, I have at times puzzled over those summaries, for I was convinced that a better brain than yours had put them together." '[7]

On his return to England, Wully found that he had to make an abrupt adjustment. The anticlimax began at Victoria Station itself.

'Here there was no guard of honour, no official greeting of any kind, and having secured a broken-down taxi I drove off to my residence in Eccleston Square, and thereupon joined the long list of unemployed soldiers on half-pay.'[8]

A further disappointment awaited him when the Irish Command, which he had hoped for, went to someone else, and he realised that after 42 years service his career in the Army had finally come to an end. Soon afterwards, however, the promotion to Field-Marshal was announced, while other honours continued to come his way. He was already Colonel of the Royal Scots Greys, the regiment in which one of his grandsons and the husband of a granddaughter would serve in later years; and when he vacated the position in 1925, he became Colonel of the 3rd Dragoon Guards, the regiment he had joined when first commissioned, and therefore a matter of great pride and satisfaction. In addition he assumed the Colonelcy of the

Royal Horse Guards (The Blues), which carried with it the dignity of Gold Stick and member of the Royal Household. This was a formal strengthening of the informal friendship which had long existed between Wully and Mildred and the King and Queen, and which was kept going by occasional meetings and private dinners at Buckingham Palace. Wully was also awarded honorary degrees at Oxford and Cambridge, and was in great demand on a host of public occasions—dedicating war memorials (he performed this duty at his old village of Welbourn in 1920), presenting colours, laying foundation stones, making speeches, and all the rest. Such is the accustomed pattern of the life of a great public servant on retirement, and no one would have been surprised had Wully been content to leave matters there. But he was not.

For a year, 1921–22, he rested on his laurels. He had a bout of illness and reaction, and was happy enough to build up his strength and energy, and cultivate his friends. He and Mildred were popular guests at country house parties, and it was here that, once again, he began to display his extraordinary force of will and power of application. Never in the past having had the time or means to pursue sport, he now (at the age of 61) decided to begin doing so. He took up golf (at which he made himself into a determined rather than a skilful player), fishing, and shooting. In the latter case, by taking lessons and listening carefully to his coach and loader, he turned himself from a poor shot into a very fair performer with a 12-bore, and became a familiar figure at shooting parties.

He was not content, however, to pass all his time in this manner, and in 1922 he set off on a new and remarkably successful career in business, and one which filled the rest of his life with much interest and striking material success. When he came back from Cologne, he only had about £600 free capital, his life savings, as distinct from the Treasury Grant of £10,000, which was capital held in trust. He had no other means other than his pay as a Field-Marshal. Thanks to his many friends and contacts, he was soon invited to join a number of important Boards, one appointment leading to another as his colleagues came to appreciate his excellent judgment, shrewd and practical views, and his refusal to push himself forward in any way. Among his first directorships were those of British Dyestuffs, the

Palestine Corporation, and the London General Omnibus Company, where he exerted much influence for the welfare of the men—as some remember to this day. However, the position which gave him most to do, and brought him the greatest financial reward, was that of Chairman of the Brewers' Trustees, an association for representing the collective views of the industry. By saving money on his fees and by investing it wisely, he quickly amassed a small private fortune, so that after he died in 1933 his estate was valued for probate at over £49,000; and this leaves out of account substantial sums which he had previously given to members of his family, and certain annuities purchased for a brother and two sisters. All this was a remarkable tribute to his business acumen. The fact was that, like many successful professional and business men, his abilities were such as to take him to the top, whatever he did.

And there were other blessings: a supremely contented family life, and the pleasure of seeing his two daughters and elder son happily married, with the latter making good headway in his career in the Army. One grief, however, hit him and Mildred very hard—the sadness of seeing their younger son, John, grow up a difficult, nervous boy, with indifferent health, and totally unable to find a niche for himself at school or among his companions. He was near death at least once during the war, and finally succumbed to pneumonia in 1928 at the age of 18. As is so often the case, the parents had a special love for their youngest and for him, a wayward son, who had always confused and often exasperated them. After John's death, Wully became depressed—he felt perhaps he had never understood the boy, and so had failed to give him the right kind of help—and he retreated into himself.

At this, as at other times, he was sustained by his religion. The heritage from his mother had been complete. For the whole of his life he was a devout, though undemonstrative Anglican. He rarely missed Communion on Sunday, and always fasted beforehand. Stories, too, were current of the lengths to which he would go to attend a service or find a church in the most difficult circumstances. His faith expressed itself in other ways as well: notably in the amount of time he devoted, during his retirement, to speaking and writing against war. Though a soldier all his life, and active in the greatest emergency in the history of the Empire, there was nothing inconsistent in his disowning war as an instrument of policy. He had been sickened by the casualties, by the cruelty, and by the waste of life and wealth, and he spoke from the heart—out of humanity —not, as some critics have implied, out of disappointment at being dismissed from his post before the war ended.

'We shall never know precisely how much it cost. In direct outlay the figure is probably 40,000 million pounds, in indirect cost it may be estimated at 30,000 millions, a total of 70,000 million pounds. The loss of life was 10 million men and boys—largely boys; and, more than that, over 20 million men were wounded, and many maimed for life.'

As to the next war

'. . . the horrors which may be suffered by the civil population through air attacks and new chemical substances seem almost to be without limit.'[9]

But he was no out-and-out Pacifist. He condemned 'unpractical pleas for disarmament', and said that efforts should be directed towards removing causes of friction, and checking ambitious policies of self-aggrandisement.

Even so, Wully's principal writings were about war, not peace. Leaving on one side the articles he wrote for various newspapers, mainly comments on manœuvres and current military developments, he produced two books: *From Private to Field-Marshal*, published by Constable in 1921, and *Soldiers and Statesmen, 1914–1918*, published in two volumes by Cassell in 1926. The first was his autobiography, dedicated to the memory of his mother, a clear, unemotional account of his remarkable life, touched with dry humour. It is full of interest, though over-weighted here and there with lengthy extracts from letters and memoranda, which the ordinary reader would prefer to skip—none the less, it is a valuable account. The second was, and remains today, a fine collection of historical studies, an invaluable record of some of the principal events and problems of the war as they appeared to those conducting it on the British side. The book is not easy to read, as it is essentially a collection of staff appreciations, and therefore of chief interest to the historian or specialist. But it is comprehensive, meaty and balanced, and carries an added authority by virtue of the authorship—written as it was by a man intimately involved, and in a position of power. No historian of the First World War can afford to neglect it. These books alone are sufficient to extinguish any impression that Wully was illiterate, or that he remained as rude and uncultivated as his origin was humble. In fact he was a man of remarkably wide mental accomplishments —author, business executive, and chief staff officer of the British Army—a trio that anyone with, say, an aristocratic or academic upbringing would have been proud to achieve.

Edmonds recorded that early in 1933 he and Wully walked round St James's Park together, talking over old times. 'He seemed a bit wheezy in the chest, but was otherwise well. He said that his one regret was that he had never had a command in the field to show what he could do. "I could have thrown in a bit of strategy," he added.' Edmonds replied that, considering all he had done and deserved, he should rest content; moreover, he had brought off the impossible in an exclusive service, in which the relics of the feudal system still lingered.'[10]

A few Saturdays later, on February 11th, he played 18 holes of golf, and went to bed that night, tired, but otherwise in normal health. The next day he woke up none the worse, called for his morning tea—'Where's the damn tea?' he is supposed to have said—and fell dead of a thrombosis. He was 73.

The dénouement was as unexpected as his death. There was no military funeral, at his own request. After burial at Brookwood Cemetery, a memorial service was held on February 16th at Westminster Abbey, which all attended in plain clothes. All the notabilities or their representatives were there, and such contemporaries as had survived. Lloyd George came in person. It was soon over. The service was as simple and unpretentious as the man who had begun life in 1860 as Will Robertson, and ended it in 1933 as Field-Marshal Sir William Robert Robertson, Bart, GCB, GCMG, GCVO, DSO, DCL, LLD.

Appendix 1

General Headquarters,
British Army in the Field in France.
5th December, 1915.

Dear Lord Kitchener,

You were kind enough yesterday to express your willingness to receive some observations of mine regarding the conduct of the war, with special reference to the status and duties of the Chief of the Imperial General Staff.

For a long time past I have given careful and anxious consideration to this question. Both the history of past wars and our experience in the present war show that certain conditions are normally essential to the successful conduct of military operations though there have it is true, been isolated instances of commanders of genius who have triumphed in the absence of these conditions.

These conditions are:—

I. That there should be a supreme directing authority whose function is to formulate policy, decide on the theatres in which military operations are to be conducted, and determine the relative importance of those theatres.

This authority must also exercise a general supervision over the conduct of the war, and must select the men who are to execute the policy on which it has decided. Its constitution must be such that it is able to come to quick decisions, and therefore as regards the conduct of the war it must be absolute. The War Council should be capable of performing the functions of this supreme authority, provided it is relieved of responsibility to the Cabinet as a whole as regards the conduct of military operations, and that it has real executive power and is not merely an Advisory Committee.

The War Council will frequently find itself in a position similar to that of a Commander in the Field—that is, it will have to come to a decision when the situation is very obscure, when information is very deficient, and when the wishes and the powers of our Allies are uncertain. Whatever these difficulties may be, if and when a decision is required it must be made. If it is deferred success cannot be expected; the commander concerned will have a grossly unfair burden placed upon him, and in fact the absence of a decision may be little less than criminal because of the loss of life which may be entailed.

II. In order that the War Council may be able to come to timely decisions on the questions with which it has to deal, it is essential that it should receive *all* advice on matters concerning military operations through one authoritative channel only. With us that channel must be the Chief of the Imperial General Staff. It is his function, so far as regards military operations, to present to the War Council his reasoned opinion as to the Military Effect of the policy which they propose, and as to the means of putting this approved policy into execution. The War Council are then free to accept or reject the reasoned advice so offered.

Advice regarding Military Operations emanating from members of the Cabinet, or of the War Council in their individual capacity, or from any other individual, should be sifted, examined and presented if necessary with reasoned conclusions, to the War Council by the Chief of the Imperial General Staff before it is accepted by the War Council.

III. All orders for the military operations required to put into execution the policy approved by the War Council should be issued and signed by the Chief of the Imperial General Staff, under the authority of the Secretary of State for War, *not* under that of the Army Council. Similarly, all communications from General Officers Commanding regarding military operations should be addressed to the Chief of the Imperial General Staff. In fact, the same procedure is required in London as obtains in the Field—the War Council being in the position of Commander-in-Chief of the whole of the Imperial Land Forces, and, with the War Office Staff, constituting the Great General Head Quarters of the Empire.

IV. The adoption of the system by which communications regarding military operations are issued and received by the C.I.G.S. will greatly expedite the despatch of business and will help to preserve greater secrecy than now prevails.

Instances have occurred in the war of the contents of the most important documents becoming public property within a few days. Than this nothing could be more harmful to the conduct of the War. It would be for the C.I.G.S. to give orders as to the reproduction and distribution of these communications, and he would of course be responsible for seeing that the S of S for War and the War Council receive at all times full information of all that they should know.

V. The Chief of the Imperial General Staff must be free to devote his entire time to the duties above indicated, and have sufficient leisure to think quietly out the many difficult problems which are continually arising, and also to keep himself thoroughly fit in mind and body. He must therefore be relieved as far as possible of War Office routine duties. To do this the Assistant Chief of the Imperial General Staff should become a Deputy Chief of the Imperial General Staff with authority to represent, as and when necessary, the Chief of the Imperial General Staff in all Army Council business.

VI. The number of General Officers Commanding with which the Chief of the Imperial General Staff should deal should not exceed the number which experience shows to be possible—about half-a-dozen. For this, it is necessary that a General Officer Commanding-in-Chief should be appointed to the command of the Home Forces or those in Great Britain, as may be deemed best, his position being exactly similar to, say, that of the General Officer Commanding-in-Chief in France, except that the present system of administration need not be disturbed. He would also be responsible for Home Defence, the troops for this purpose being allocated, of course, under instructions issued by the C.I.G.S. as in all other cases—vide para (III).

I need not go more fully into my reasons for the above proposals, as I am sure they will be obvious to you.

It is of paramount importance in war that there should be a definite plan of operations, and that that plan should be carried out with promptness and decision. It is impossible that this should be so if the War Council is itself compelled to listen to conflicting advice, and to decide between the merits of rival experts. It is equally impossible that this should be so if the War Council has to submit its plans for the conduct of the war to the approval of the whole Cabinet. The War Council is now conducting military operations in a number of separate theatres of war and has control of large reserves which may be thrown into one theatre or another. France has no reserves left, therefore the decision as to the future conduct of the war by the Western Allies rests in great measure with the War Council. It is vital then that it should possess the machinery both to come to timely decisions, and to have its decisions executed.

My proposals seem to necessitate some modification of the Orders in Council which lay down the constitution of the Army Council and the duties of the Chief of the Imperial General Staff. If that is so those orders should be amended for the period of the war. They were never intended, I suppose, to meet a situation such as now exists, and they certainly do not meet it.

I hope you will not think that I have any desire to make a bargain for myself, but I feel strongly that I cannot serve the War Council, and my King and Country as Chief of the Imperial General Staff unless the above conditions are fulfilled. It is my conviction that the system by which the war has been conducted hitherto has been such as to make victory very difficult indeed, if not impossible. Having no faith in it I could not do justice to it, and therefore if my proposals cannot be accepted you would be better advised to select an officer who sees in the existing system a possible means of bringing this war to a successful conclusion.

I hope, however, that the proposals may not be considered unacceptable, and that they will be adopted whoever may fill the post of Chief of the Imperial General Staff. If the appointment were offered to me, I should have to make a few slight alterations in the General Staff organization at the War Office, and would wish to replace 2 or 3 officers by officers from this country.

I need not trouble you with these alterations except to say that:—

The Directorate of Home Defence and part of the Training Directorate would be handed over to the Staff of the General Officer Commanding-in-Chief Home Forces as his Staff. The remaining part of the Training Directorate would be placed in the Staff Duties Directorate.

One of these two Directors could be abolished.

The D.M.O. Branch would be divided into the two Directorates of "Operations" and "Intelligence".

The Chief of the Imperial General Staff would then have to deal with—Deputy C.I.G.S.; Director of Operations; and Director of Intelligence. The Director of Staff Duties would be under the Deputy C.I.G.S.

I enclose a duplicate copy of this letter which I hope you will send to the Prime Minister, should it ever be contemplated to offer me the appointment of Chief of the Imperial General Staff.

Believe me
Yours sincerely.
W. R. ROBERTSON.

Appendix 2

Dictated

Private

16th January 1917.

My dear Wigram

We have finished with General Nivelle to-day. The chief object of his mission was to get Haig to take over more front, finish taking it over by 15th February, and then for a big and decisive attack to be started. It is the old story with the French. Before an attack they have always wished us to take over more front and at the same time put up a good fight, and of course it is not easy to do both. I was not so much concerned with taking over the front as I was with the proposed early date, because it has always been understood between the Allies that the best thing to be done is for them to attack simultaneously, otherwise of course the enemy would be free to deal with one of us at a time. Nivelle is however biassed by his last success at Verdun and bases everything upon it. As a matter of fact he did no more at Verdun than has been done elsewhere beyond taking a few more prisoners in somewhat less time. He did not get through, and as usual he was pulled up as soon as the enemy's reserves got to work. The same thing has happened on every other occasion and the difficulty has always been to bring up fresh troops in order to deal with the enemy reinforcements. Nivelle appears to be very optimistic. That is a very desirable thing but at the same time it is a pity that he talks so confidently in public.

We had a long sitting yesterday and at 5 pm Haig and myself were sent away and the War Cabinet took on the matter themselves and considered how much line Haig should take over and when the attack should be made. This morning we two met them again and they told us that the extension of front should be made. As regards the date it transpired this morning that Nivelle really had no new proposal to make, but only wished to be *ready* by the 15th February in case it was then necessary to attack in order to relieve the situation elsewhere. He said he would be quite satisfied if he could attack by the end of March. We had always contemplated getting on the move not later than the 1st May so there is really very little difference between his plan and the plan we had previously worked out in consultation with Joffre. Therefore, apart from wasting two days in unnecessary talking, nothing has been achieved except that Haig has to take over a little more front than he had hoped.

He had already agreed to take about half of what he was asked whereas he now has to take the whole. In return for that we hope to be able to send him two divisions additional to those previously promised. He has now got 57. We hope to send him three more T.F. divisions by the end of February; one from Egypt; and the Portuguese division. This will give him 62 in all. To help him in taking over the balance of the new front we hope as I have said to send him two more, and this will complete all we have except those composed of Home Service men. Strange to say the Prime Minister has always been a great opponent to making an attack before all the Allies are ready. He has constantly laid great stress upon this and has in fact thrown a good deal of cold water upon any attack being made on the West front. But Nivelle, like Sarrail, seems to have impressed him and he was all for attacking on the 15th February until we more or less convinced him that that would not do. As it now stands the attack will really be made when Haig and Nivelle are ready and that will not be before April.

Yours sincerely,
W. R. Robertson.

Notes

Where a source, published or unpublished, is quoted more than once, the full title is given in the first instance only, afterwards in short. Otherwise, the following abbreviations have been used:

Robertson (1): *From Private to Field-Marshal*. Constable 1921.
Robertson (2): *Soldiers and Statesmen, 1914–1918*. Cassell 1926.
Beaverbrook (1): *Politicians and the War, 1914–1916*. Oldbourne 1960.
Beaverbrook (2): *Men and Power, 1917–1918*. Hutchinson 1956.
The great majority of quotations from Haig's Diary are taken from the text, which appeared in *The Private Papers of Douglas Haig, 1914–1919*, edited by Robert Blake. Eyre and Spottiswoode 1952.
See also *Sources and Selective Book List*, pp. 406–7.

Chapter 1
1. *The Brudenells of Deene*, by Joan Wake, p. 459. Cassell 1953.
2. Robertson Papers. His parents proposed at one moment to try and buy him out of the Army, but were dissuaded by Col. Wardlaw Ramsay, Mrs Leslie-Melville's brother.
3. Robertson (1), p. 1.

Chapter 2
1. Robertson (1), pp. 2–3.
2. Out of ten companies in each battalion, six were usually sent abroad, and four kept at home to form a miniature reserve.
3. Purchase did not apply to the Artillery and Engineers, known as the 'scientific corps'. The Infantry and Cavalry were the only 'purchase corps'.
4. See *The Reason Why* by Cecil Woodham Smith, pp. 21–5. Constable 1953.
5. Virtually every post in the Government service was open to purchase.
6. This was the period fixed in 1847. Before that it had been for life.
7. *Camp and Barrack-Room or The British Army As It Is*, by a late Staff Sergeant of the 13th Light Infantry. Chapman and Hall 1846.
8. Even so, soldiers were better fed than most poor people outside the Army, especially in regard to meat.

9. Robertson (1), p. 5.
10. *Canteens in the British Army*, by John Fortescue, p. 19. CUP 1928. I have drawn upon this book and upon various articles on Barracks, listed in the Book List, for the substance of these paragraphs.
11. Robertson (1), pp. 15–16.
12. Ibid, p. 16.

Chapter 3

1. Robertson (1), p. 3.
2. Robertson Papers.
3. Robertson (1), p. 5.
4. Ibid, p. 6.
5. See *Through the Ranks to a Commission*, by J. E. Acland-Troyte. Macmillan 1881.
6. Selected from an odd collection including History, Geography, Algebra, Plane Trigonometry, Elementary Mechanics, Mensuration, Practical Geometry, Fortification, Drawing, Surveying, Chemistry, and one Modern Language (European or Oriental).
7. *Days That Are Gone*, by B. de Sales la Terriere, pp. 110–11. Hutchinson 1924.
8. Robertson Papers.
9. Ibid.
10. Robertson (1), p. 36.
11. Ibid, p. 42.
12. Robertson Papers.
13. Robertson (1), pp. 76–7.
14. Ibid, p. 79.
15. Ibid.

Chapter 4

1. Le Marchant had hoped to set up a college offering instruction to boys, cadets, and NCOs, as well as to officers, but this was turned down. Meanwhile, the Royal Military College was officially established, and plans made to house both Departments on Bagshot Heath. Building was slow, however. The Junior Department did not move from Great Marlow until 1812, the Senior from High Wycombe (after a second temporary home at Farnham) until 1820. Separate accommodation was provided in 1862.
2. Lord Panmure, in a speech in the House of Commons on June 5th 1856.
3. Although a few prominent officers passed through the Staff College at this time, most graduates were glorified surveyors—

clearly not the object of staff training, although it does explain why so many educated soldiers were Royal Engineers right up to the end of the century.

4. *The Staff and the Staff College*, by A. R. Godwin-Austen, p. 163. Constable 1927.
5. Dawkins Committee 1901, Elgin Commission 1903, Esher Committee 1904.
6. There was also a Mobilisation Division, which had started as a sub-division of Intelligence.
7. *A Guardsman's Memories*, by Major-General Lord Edward Gleichen, p.142. Blackwood 1932.
8. Ibid.
9. Ibid, p. 176.
10. *Secret and Confidential*, by Brigadier-General W. H-H. Waters, pp. 244–5. Murray 1926.
11. Robertson (1), p. 129.
12. Ibid, p. 130.
13. Ibid, p. 131.
14. They were really 'mobilisation centres with storehouses for the assembly of military equipment', intended for the Volunteers.
15. The Kaiser was a grandson of Queen Victoria.
16. Robertson Papers.
17. Ibid.
18. Good as the plans were, the French never knew if the BEF was really coming, nor did the British properly know the French plan of campaign: hence many of the disasters of 1914. See Robertson (2), Vol. 1, Chapter 1, and *Douglas Haig, The Educated Soldier*, by John Terraine, pp. 62–3, Hutchinson 1963.
19. Information supplied by Lt-Col. W. R. V. Isaac.

Chapter 5

1. Another son, John, was born in 1909.
2. Wilson commanded IV Corps in France for most of 1916.
3. *An Autobiography*, by Viscount Haldane, p. 187. Hodder and Stoughton 1929.
4. *The Development of the British Army, 1899–1914*, by Colonel John K. Dunlop, p. 29. Methuen 1938. Much of this section is derived from my reading of this book.
5. *Memories of Forty-Eight Years Service*, by General Sir Horace Smith-Dorrien, p. 360. Murray 1925.
6. Robertson (1), p. 184. Wully was Commandant of the Staff College at the time, while George had ascended the throne the year before.

7. Godwin-Austen, p. 242.
8. Ibid, p. 256.
9. Robertson (1), p. 175.
10. Ibid, pp. 176–7.
11. Ibid, p. 181.
12. Brigadier Sir Edward Beddington.
13. Beddington Memoir.
14. Edmonds Papers.
15. See *Mutiny at the Curragh*, by A. P. Ryan, Macmillan 1956, and *The Unknown Prime Minister*, by Robert Blake, Eyre and Spottiswoode 1955.
16. Robertson (1), p. 193.
17. Ibid, p. 194
18. Brigadier Sir Edward Beddington.
19. Beddington Memoir.

Chapter 6
1. Beddington Memoir.
2. Until the early 19th century, it was customary for the Master-General of Ordnance to have a seat in the Cabinet.
3. Robertson (1), p. 202.
4. Ibid, pp. 202–3.
5. Ibid, p. 204.
6. Ibid, pp. 204–5.
7. Ibid, p. 209.
8. Ibid, p. 212.
9. Ibid, pp. 208–9.
10. Ibid, pp. 210–11.
11. Ibid, p. 215.
12. Robertson Papers.
13. Ibid.
14. Ibid.
15. Ibid.
16. Wilson's Diary, as quoted on p. 202 of Vol I of *Field-Marshal Sir Henry Wilson*, by Major-General Sir C. E. Callwell. Cassell 1927.
17. Robertson (1), p. 218.
18. Hankey was then acting as Secretary to the War Council. See his *The Supreme Command, 1914–1918*, Vol I, Chapter XXIII *et seq.* Allen and Unwin 1961.
19. Lord Beaverbrook maintained that the Government fell, not owing to the shells row, but to the quarrel between Churchill and Lord Fisher at the Admiralty. See Beaverbrook (1), pp. 94–7.

20. Robertson (1), p. 228.
21. *Prelude to Victory*, by Major-General Sir E. L. Spears, pp. 35–6. Cape 1939.
22. Robertson (1), p. 221.
23. Robertson Papers.
24. Ibid.
25. Colonel Lord Malise Graham, then acting as ADC to Lieut-General Sir C. Fergusson, commanding II Corps.
26. The following comment appears in the *Official History, 1915*, Vol II, p. viii.

    'Of the many mistakes made in the war, most of them part of the price of unreadiness, Lord Kitchener's use of the remaining Regular troops after the departure of the original BEF to form first the 7th and 8th and later the 27th, 28th and 29th Divisions, instead of employing their officers and other ranks to train and leaven the New Army, was probably the most expensive. The difficulties of organising new divisions were further increased by the failure to take advantage of the experience and the machinery of the Territorial Associations in expanding the military forces, and by employing high class Territorial battalions, full of potential officers, as fighting units.

    'Sir John French too, in view of the critical situation in France, repeatedly refused in 1914 to part with a single officer or man to assist in training troops at home. These short-sighted views not only led to terrible delays but prevented the proper training of the new units. The British new divisions were really not ready for the field until 1st July 1916 and even then were very uneven.'
27. Robertson Papers.
28. Hankey, Vol I, p. 339.
29. Robertson Papers.
30. All the extracts quoted are from letters in the Robertson Papers.
31. Letter from Haig to Robertson, dated September 16th 1915. Haig Papers.
32. Haig's Diary for March 17th 1915. *The Private Papers of Douglas Haig, 1914–1919*, edited by Robert Blake, p. 88. Eyre and Spottiswoode 1952.
33. Ibid for October 9th 1915. Blake, p. 107.
34. Edmonds recorded that Wully told him after the war: 'The whole trouble at Loos arose from the determination of the Commander-in-Chief to order—if not to lead—forward the three reserve divisions himself, in order personally to administer the *coup de grâce*. He wanted to be able to write in his Despatch,

"At this moment I ordered (led) forward my reserves." '
Edmonds Papers.

35. Robertson (2), Vol I, pp. 160–3, and Memorandum in Robertson Papers.
36. Murray Papers.
37. Haig's Diary for October 17th 1915. Blake, pp. 108–9.
38. Under date October 2nd and October 9th 1915. Robertson Papers.
39. Haig's Diary for October 17th 1915. Blake, p. 108.
40. Ibid for October 24th 1915. Blake, p. 109.
41. Ibid for November 14th 1915. Blake, p. 113.
42. Letter from Robertson to Haig, dated November 15th 1915. Robertson Papers.
43. Printed for the Committee of Imperial Defence, under date November 8th 1915.
44. Robertson Papers.
45. Robertson (1), p. 237.
46. Robertson Papers.
47. Kitchener's hand-written letter is in the Robertson Papers. Illustrated on pp. 140–1.
48. Robertson (1), p. 238.
49. Ibid, pp. 238–9.
50. Robertson Papers.

Chapter 7

1. Robertson (1), pp. 249–50.
2. Ibid, p. 250.
3. His promotion to General was made substantive in June 1916.
4. Beaverbrook (1), p. 197.
5. *The Memoirs of Lord Ismay*, pp. 166–7. Heinemann 1960, and the Viking Press, USA.
6. *Defence by Committee*, by F. A. Johnson, p. 161. OUP 1960.
7. Ibid, p. 162.
8. Beaverbrook (1), p. 197.
9. Johnson, p. 158.
10. Ibid, p. 158.
11. Robertson (2), Vol I, pp. 182–3.
12. Hankey, Vol II, p. 544.
13. Ibid, p. 446.
14. Ibid, p. 445.
15. Ibid, p. 446.
16. *The First World War, 1914–18.* Personal Experiences of Lt-Col. C. à Court Repington, Vol I, p. 182. Cassell 1920.
17. Ibid, p. 410.

18. Brian Robertson is, of course, a highly distinguished man in his own right. After serving in the First World War, he remained in the Army for nearly sixteen years following the Armistice in November 1918: in India (mostly on the NW Frontier) 1920–5, at the Staff College, Camberley, 1926–7, at the War Office 1928–31, and as a member of the UK Delegation to the Disarmament Conference at Geneva, 1932–3. In 1934 he retired with the substantive rank of Major. He then went into business and became Chairman and Managing Director of Dunlop South Africa Ltd in 1935. In 1940 he joined the Union Defence Force as a Lt-Colonel, and was then seconded to the joint British/South African Staff under General Alan Cunningham, taking part in the campaign leading to the capture of Addis Abbaba. In 1941, as a Brigadier, he transferred to the staff of the Eighth Army and became its chief administrative officer under successive GOCs. In 1943 he served General Alexander in Italy in a similar capacity and followed him to Allied Force HQ. In 1945 he was appointed Deputy Military Governor, Germany, becoming C-in-C and Military Governor two years later, and High Commissioner 1949–50. From 1950–3 he was C-in-C Middle East Land Forces and negotiated the evacuation of the Suez Base with Nasser. Retiring a second time from the Army, this time with the rank of General, he served as Chairman of the British Transport Commission 1953–61. In 1933 he succeeded to the baronetcy awarded to his father. In 1961 he was created Lord Robertson of Oakridge.

19. Robertson (1), p. 270.

20. Much of this information has been extracted from the Murray Papers: in particular, from the Despatches, Correspondence, and Technical Reports.

21. Robertson (1), p. 277.

22. Memorandum dated December 27th 1915. Robertson Papers.

23. Memorandum dated March 21st 1916. Robertson Papers.

24. Robertson (1), p. 264.

25. See the *Official History, 1916*, Vol I, p. 27.

26. Letter from Robertson to Haig, dated April 26th 1916. Robertson Papers.

27. Printed in the *Official History, 1916*, as Appendix 4 to Vol I.

28. Hankey, Vol II, p. 495.

29. Haig's Diary for April 14th 1916. Blake, pp. 137–8.

30. *Official History, 1916*. Vol I, p. 25.

31. Letter from Robertson to Haig, dated March 5th 1916. Robertson Papers.

32. Information and quotation in this paragraph taken mainly from the Robertson–Haig correspondence and Haig's Diary, as edited by Blake.

33. Letter from Lord Esher to Robertson, dated June 27th 1916. Robertson Papers.

34. In round figures: British 400,000; French 200,000; German 600,000. See the *Official History, 1916*, Vol II, pp. xv–xvi.

35. The Brusilov offensive also contributed to the relaxation of German pressure on Verdun.

36. Lloyd George became Secretary of State for War on July 7th 1916.

37. Robertson Papers.

38. Ibid.

39. Dated June 26th 1916. Robertson Papers.

40. Diary entry dated August 3rd 1916. Report dated August 1st. Blake, pp. 157–8.

41. Letter from Robertson to Haig, dated August 1st 1916. Robertson Papers.

42. Letter from Haig to Robertson, dated August 9th 1916. Haig Papers.

43. *Journals and Letters of Reginald Viscount Esher*, Vol IV, pp. 45–6. Nicholson and Watson 1938.

44. Haig's Diary for September 15th 1916. Blake, p. 167.

45. Letter from Robertson to Haig, dated September 25th 1916. Robertson Papers.

46. Letter from Haig to Robertson, dated September 28th 1916. Blake, p. 168.

47. Robertson Papers.

48. Repington, Vol I, pp. 358–9.

49. Letter from Robertson to Asquith, dated November 13th 1916. Robertson Papers. Asquith received the letter during the conference in Paris and persuaded Lloyd George that Wully should stay. When the Russian conference eventually took place in February 1917, Britain was represented by Milner and Henry Wilson.

50. Hankey, Vol II, pp. 558–9.

51. See, for example, Beaverbrook (1), p. 328 *et seq*; Hankey, Vol II, pp. 562–70; and the memoirs of other leading men concerned.

52. Robertson (2), Vol II, p. 304.

53. Letter from Robertson to Haig, dated December 10th 1916. Robertson Papers.

54. Memorandum dated October 26th 1916. Robertson Papers.

55. Robertson (2), Vol II, p. 304. The Memorandum referred to is in the Robertson Papers.

56. Letter from Robertson to Haig, dated November 30th 1916. Robertson Papers.
57. See, for example, the letter from Esher to Haig dated November 28th 1916, and several others written by Esher to both Haig and Robertson. Haig and Robertson Papers.
58. Hansard for December 19th 1916.
59. Esher, Vol IV, p. 55.

Chapter 8

1. Letter from Robertson to Esher, dated August 9th 1916. Robertson Papers.
2. Letter from Esher to Haig, dated September 2nd 1916. Haig Papers.
3. Memorandum dated November 24th 1916. Robertson Papers.
4. Hankey, Vol II, p. 607.
5. Letter from Robertson to Wigram, dated January 12th 1917. Robertson Papers.
6. Ibid.
7. Ibid.
8. Ibid.
9. Haig's Diary for December 20th 1916. Blake, p. 187.
10. Dated October 26th 1916.
11. Submitted by Robertson as CIGS on December 1st 1916. See the *Official History, 1917*, Vol I, p. 21, and Robertson (2), p. 193 and p. 243.
12. Printed in the *Official History, 1917*, as Appendix 5 to Vol I.
13. Ibid, Appendix 7.
14. *Prelude to Victory* by Major-General Sir E. L. Spears Bt, p. 40. Cape 1939.
15. Ibid, pp. 43–6. For Robertson's part in this and the Calais Conference I have generally followed Spears' account, since the author was closely involved in the Nivelle affair, and had the opportunity of discussing it in detail with Robertson later. I have also referred to Robertson (2), to Robertson's correspondence with men such as Wigram (see particularly his letter of January 16th 1917, printed here as Appendix 2), to the Haig Papers, and other authoritative sources, e.g. Hankey, Blake, Duff Cooper, etc.
16. Printed in the *Official History, 1917*, as Appendix 8 to Vol I.
17. Letter from Robertson to Haig, dated February 14th 1917. Robertson Papers.
18. Spears, p. 133.

19. Bertrand de Sauvigny's Despatch of February 16th 1917, printed in translation as Appendix IX in Spears.
20. Spears, p. 134.
21. Ibid, p. 143. On p. 135 Spears wrote: 'Lucas, utterly devoted to his chief, was known as "The Monument". He often looked harried, and no wonder, but his frequent preoccupations did not detract from his powers as a keen observer and cryptic recorder of the minor eccentricities of the great!'
22. Ibid, p. 144.
23. Ibid, p. 146.
24. Hankey, Vol II, p. 616.
25. Ibid.
26. Spears, pp. 150–1.
27. Ibid, p. 151.
28. Ibid, pp. 183–4.
29. Ibid, pp. 194–5.
30. Letter from Robertson to Nivelle, dated March 13th 1917, printed in Spears as Appendix XXII.
31. Letter from Robertson to Haig, dated April 10th 1917. Robertson Papers.
32. Letter from Robertson to Haig, dated April 14th 1917. Robertson Papers.
33. Robertson (2), Vol II, pp. 228–9.
34. Letter from Robertson to Haig, dated April 20th 1917. Robertson Papers.
35. Haig Papers.
36. Blake, p. 221.
37. Robertson Papers.
38. Haig's Diary for April 30th 1917. Blake, p. 222.
39. Haig's Diary for May 1st 1917. Blake, p. 223.
40. Callwell, Vol I, p. 325.
41. Ibid, p. 340.

Chapter 9

1. Haig's Diary for May 4th 1917. Blake, pp. 227–8.
2. Letter from Esher to Haig, dated May 8th 1917. Haig Papers.
3. This account follows, in summarised form, that given in the *Official History, 1917*, Vol II, pp. 22–8.
4. Author's italics. Robertson Papers.
5. See p. 274.
6. Hankey, Vol II, pp. 672–3.
7. Robertson commented: 'The procedure followed by this Committee was, I think, unique in the annals of military history,

and it reminded one more of the Law Courts than a Council Chamber. Instead of being received as a military chief, the accuracy of whose views, so far as they were military, were not in dispute, I was made to feel like a witness for the defence under cross-examination, the Prime Minister appearing in the dual capacity of counsel for the prosecution and judge.' Robertson (2), Vol II, footnote to p. 242.

8. A remark attributed to Winston Churchill.
9. Repington, Vol I, p. 514.
10. Callwell, Vol I, p. 359.
11. Repington, Vol I, p. 571.
12. Memorandum submitted by the Adjutant-General to the Army Council regarding *The Position and Prospects of Recruiting*, dated May 31st 1917. Robertson Papers.
13. Covering note to the above Memorandum, when submitted to the War Cabinet, dated June 7th 1917. Robertson Papers.
14. Robertson (2), Vol I, pp. 306–7.
15. Ibid, p. 313.
16. On August 8th 1917, the Secretary of State for War forwarded to the War Cabinet a note from the Adjutant-General containing the following statement: 'The British Infantry in France is some 40,000 under strength, not counting drafts under orders today, while some 30,000 lower categories on demand for Transportation, RAMC, and Labour, are not at present forthcoming,' Robertson Papers.
17. Robertson (2), Vol I, p. 299.
18. Blake, pp. 233–4.
19. Haig's Diary for June 9th 1917. Blake, p. 236.
20. Ibid for June 10th 1917. Blake, p. 237.
21. Ibid for June 12th 1917. Blake, p. 238.
22. Blake, p. 239. The appendix, written by Charteris, reviewed the reserves of German manpower and concluded that they had fallen very low. Following Macdonogh's brief, Wully had already advised the War Cabinet on May 9th in the opposite sense, mainly on the grounds that the Germans would be likely to strengthen the west at the expense of the east, following the Russian collapse. He was right, although the Germans did not transfer any large number of divisions from east to west until late in the year: viz., eight in July, five in September, four in October, ten in November, and after that forty (plus eight from Italy) in four and a half months, in time for the spring offensive of 1918. See the *Official History, 1917*, Vol II, footnote on p. 96.

23. Extracts and summary mainly from Robertson (2), Vol II, pp. 240–7, and from the *Note by the CIGS*, dated June 23rd 1917. Robertson Papers.
24. Hankey, Vol II, p. 683.
25. Letter from Robertson to Haig, dated June 30th 1917. Robertson Papers.
26. Hankey, Vol II, p. 683.
27. Ibid.
28. Dated July 21st 1917.
29. Haig's Diary for July 22nd 1917. Blake, p. 246.
30. *Official History, 1917*, Vol II, p. 106.

Chapter 10

1. Memorandum of May 9th 1917, entitled *Military Effect of Russia seceding from the Entente*. Robertson Papers.
2. Memorandum of July 29th 1917, entitled *The Present Military Situation in Russia and its Effect on Our Future*. Robertson Papers.
3. Hankey, Vol II, p. 687.
4. The 60th Division left Salonika for Egypt in July, the 10th Division followed in September.
5. Letter from Robertson to Murray dated January 31st 1917. Murray Papers.
6. Ibid.
7. Murray's Fourth Despatch dated June 28th 1917. Murray Papers.
8. Letter from Murray to Robertson dated March 11th 1917. Murray Papers.
9. Letter from Murray to Robertson dated April 3rd 1917. Murray Papers.
10. Telegram dated April 2nd 1917. Murray Papers.
11. Robertson had also succeeded, though not displaced, Murray as CGS to Smith-Dorrien at Aldershot in 1907.
12. Hankey, Vol II, p. 693.
13. Ibid, p. 694.
14. Ibid, p. 695.
15. Robertson Papers.
16. Repington, Vol II, p. 29.
17. Ibid, pp. 29–30.
18. Ibid, pp. 30–31.
19. Letter from Robertson to Haig, dated September 15th 1917. Robertson Papers.
20. Robertson (2), Vol II, p. 262.
21. Spears, p. 342.

22. Hankey, Vol II, p. 748.
23. Blake, p. 256.
24. Letter from Robertson to Haig, dated October 9th 1917. Blake, p. 259.
25. Letter from Robertson to Haig, dated September 27th 1917. Robertson Papers.
26. Letter from Robertson to Haig, dated October 9th 1917. Blake, p. 259. Haig's Memorandum of October 8th, Blake, p. 258.
27. Hankey, Vol II, p. 711.
28. Ibid, pp. 712–13.
29. Robertson Papers.
30. Hankey, Vol II, p. 715.
31. Robertson (2), Vol II, pp. 259–60.
32. Hankey, Vol II, p. 716.
33. Haig's Diary for September 19th 1917. Blake, p. 255.
34. Allenby asked for thirteen extra divisions—seven at the front, and six others to act as replacements to worn-out formations.
35. Memoranda dated October 9th and November 15th 1917. Robertson Papers.
36. Letter from Haig to Robertson, dated October 28th 1917. Robertson Papers.
37. Robertson (1), p. 313.
38. Hankey, Vol II, pp. 717–18.
39. Letter from Robertson to Haig, dated November 4th 1917. Robertson Papers.
40. Ibid.
41. Hankey, Vol II, p. 720.
42. Memoranda dated October 31st and November 8th 1915 respectively. Robertson Papers.
43. In a Memorandum dated February 12th 1916, Robertson went so far as to urge the War Committee to take the initiative in diplomacy, suggesting the detachment of Turkey and Bulgaria from the Central Powers, the wooing of Holland, and activities in Scandinavia and the USA. He wanted a common Entente policy, diplomatic as well as military. His efforts were not welcomed by the Foreign Office. Robertson Papers.
44. Wilson became GOC Eastern Command as from September 1st 1917, with HQ in London.
45. Callwell, Vol II, p. 7.
46. Hankey, Vol II, p. 695.
47. Ibid, p. 689.
48. Letter from Robertson to Haig, dated August 8th 1917. Blake, p. 251.

49. Letter from Haig to Robertson, dated August 13th 1917. Robertson Papers.
50. Hankey, Vol. II, pp. 713–14.
51. Ibid, pp. 722–3.
52. Robertson (1), p. 328.
53. Ibid.
54. Robertson (2), Vol I, p. 216.
55. Haig's Diary for November 1st 1917. Blake, p. 262.
56. Robertson Papers.

Chapter 11

1. Author's italics. Robertson Papers.
2. Memorandum of November 19th 1917. Robertson Papers.
3. 100,000 Category A, 100,000 lower categories, 120,000 18-year-olds for Home Defence. Category A was the vital one.
4. Information summarised from Robertson (2), Vol II, pp. 317–20, and various Memoranda.
5. *Official History, 1918*, Vol I, p. 37.
6. Memorandum of December 26th 1917. Robertson Papers.
7. Memorandum of December 29th 1917. Robertson Papers.
8. Memorandum of January 3rd 1918. Robertson Papers.
9. Robertson (2), Vol II, p. 281.
10. Letter from Robertson to Haig, dated January 7th 1918. Robertson Papers.
11. Robertson (2), Vol II, p. 329.
12. Memorandum of January 12th 1918. Robertson Papers.
13. Wilson, Cadorna, Bliss, Weygand.
14. Robertson Papers.
15. Memorandum of January 25th 1918.
16. Since Lloyd George had requested advice over the method of calculating 'wastage' (see pp. 315–16), Foch was privy to a good deal of inside information on the subject of British manpower.
17. Robertson (2), Vol II, p. 288.
18. Ibid, p. 289.
19. Ibid, pp. 287–8.
20. Robertson Papers.
21. Memorandum of February 1st 1918. Robertson Papers.
22. Hankey, Vol II, pp. 769–70.
23. Edmonds Papers. General Horne was the visitor.
24. See pp. 334–7. Wavell's essay with Ross's and Robertson's comments upon it are in the possession of the Staff College, Camberley.
25. Hankey, Vol II, p. 728.

26. Letter from Esher to Haig, dated December 2nd 1917. Haig Papers.
27. Letter from Robertson to Northcliffe, dated October 11th 1916. Printed in *Northcliffe* by Reginald Pound and Geoffrey Harmsworth. Cassell 1959.
28. Beaverbrook (2), pp. 186–91.
29. Ibid, pp. 376–7.
30. Haig's Diary for February 2nd 1918. Blake, p. 282.
31. Blake, pp. 282–3.
32. Robertson Papers.
33. Haig's Diary for February 9th 1918. Blake, p. 284.
34. Callwell, Vol II, p. 58.
35. Robertson (1), p. 335.
36. Haig's Diary for February 11th 1918. Blake, p. 284.
37. Robertson Papers.
38. Ibid.
39. Hankey, Vol II, p. 777.
40. Memorandum by Derby to the War Cabinet of February 13th 1918. Robertson Papers.
41. Memorandum by Robertson to Derby of February 13th 1918. Robertson Papers. See also p. 345.
42. Letter from Derby to Robertson, dated February 14th 1918. Robertson Papers.
43. Hankey, Vol II, p. 778.
44. Ibid.
45. Letter from Robertson to Haig, dated February 15th 1918. Robertson Papers.
46. Robertson (1), p. 336.
47. Beaverbrook (2), p. 210.
48. Haig's Diary for February 9th 1918. Blake, p. 284.
49. Beaverbrook (2), p. 211.
50. Haig's Diary for January 14th 1918. Blake, p. 279.
51. Letter from Esher to Haig, dated February 19th 1918. Haig Papers.
52. Hankey, Vol II, p. 779.

Chapter 12

1. Repington, Vol II, p. 231.
2. Ibid, p. 234.
3. Robertson Papers.
4. At the beginning of 1918 there were nearly 1½ million men in the Army stationed in the UK. Robertson's inability materially

to reduce this number (an Army Council, not a General Staff responsibility) is discussed in Robertson (1), pp. 342–4.

5. Robertson (2), Vol I, p. 332.

6. Hansard 1918, Vol 104, Col 1337.

7. *Intrigues of the War*, by Major General Sir Frederick Maurice and the Marquis of Crewe, p. 34. *Westminster Gazette*, 1922.

8. Hankey, Vol II, pp. 798–9.

9. *Official History, 1918*, Vol I, Appendix 7.

10. In his pamphlet, *Intrigues of the War*, published in 1922, Maurice quoted different gross totals at slightly different dates— 1,299,000 at January 1st 1917, 1,570,000 at January 1st 1918— the dates being chosen no doubt to correspond more nearly to those given by the Prime Minister in his speech of April 9th. It has not been possible to equate Maurice's figures precisely with those supplied by the Adjutant-General of the BEF shown on page 359, or those relating to the labourers. But, while differing in detail, they both pointed to the same conclusion: namely, that as between January 1917 and January 1918, the nett or fighting strength of the BEF went down, while the gross strength went up. The *Official History* (Appendix 7, referred to in Note 9 above) states that the gross increase was accounted for by wounded and sick, by a large rise in labour units, and by a small rise in Transportation due to the formation of that service in mid-1917.

11. See page 316.

12. Hansard 1918, Vol 105, Col 563.

13. Authority as for Note 9.

14. This extract appears on pp. 262–3 of Beaverbrook (2). As to the date on which J. T. Davies and Miss Stevenson discovered the corrected return, the matter was discussed in correspondence in *The Spectator*, issues dated November 16th and 23rd, and December 7th 1956. Countess Lloyd George denied that the discovery had been made after May 9th, although the entry in her diary gives the opposite impression. Moreover, as Miss Nancy Maurice pointed out, it was unlikely that an official dispatch box would remain unopened and unreturned for not less than three weeks, viz. from April 18th until some date after May 9th.

15. *Intrigues of the War*, pp. 37–42. It is very hard to understand why no one in the MO Directorate 'spoke up' before 1922.

16. Hansard 1918, Vol 105, Cols 851–2.

17. *Intrigues of the War*, p. 34.

18. Blake, p. 301.

19. *Intrigues of the War*, p. 35.
20. Ibid.
21. Ibid, p. 34.
22. Ibid.
23. Ibid, p. 35.
24. See p. 367.
25. Letter from Churchill to Beaverbrook, dated November 27th 1926, and quoted in Beaverbrook (2), p. 382.
26. Hansard 1918, Vol 105, Cols 2360–1.
27. Ibid, Col 2373.

Chapter 13
 1. Letter from Maurice to Robertson, dated April 16th 1918. Robertson Papers.
 2. Letter from Robertson to Maurice, dated April 17th 1918. Robertson Papers.
 3. Letter from Robertson to Milner, dated May 17th 1918. Lloyd George Papers, quoted in Beaverbrook (2), p. 251.
 4. Robertson (1), p. 351.
 5. Ibid, p. 362.
 6. Until 1945 the establishment of Field-Marshals was limited to eight, two of them from the Indian Army.
 7. Beddington Memoir.
 8. Robertson (1), p. 377.
 9. Robertson Papers.
10. Edmonds Papers.

Sources and Selective Book List

The Beddington Memoir
The Edmonds Papers
The Haig Papers
The Murray Papers
The Robertson Papers
Hansard

BEFORE 1914

An Autobiography, by Viscount Haldane. Hodder and Stoughton 1929.

A Guardsman's Memories, by Major-General Lord Edward Gleichen. Blackwood 1932.

Army School Regulations. HMSO 1882.

Army Transport and the English Constitution, by Ruperť C. Jarvis. *Journal of Transport History*, Vol II, No 2. November 1955.

Camp and Barrack-Room or The British Army As It Is, by a late Staff Sergeant of the 13th Light Infantry. Chapman and Hall 1846.

Canteens in the British Army, by John Fortescue. CUP 1928.

Days That Are Gone, by Colonel B. de Sales la Terriere. Hutchinson 1924.

Life of Major-General Sir John Ardagh, by his wife. Murray 1909.

Life in the Ranks of the British Army. Official Pamphlet, *c.* 1880.

Lord Cardwell at the War Office, by General Sir Robert Biddulph. Murray 1904.

Memories of Forty-Eight Years Service, by General Sir Horace Smith-Dorrien. Murray 1925.

Secret and Confidential, by Brigadier-General W. H-H. Waters. Murray 1926.

The Brudenells of Deene, by Joan Wake. Cassell 1953.

The Cannock Chase Manœuvres of 1873, by M. J. Wise. *Army Quarterly* July 1954.

The Development of the British Army, 1899–1914, by Colonel John K. Dunlop. Methuen 1938.

The Predecessors of the RASC, by Lt-Col. C. H. Masse. Gale and Polden 1948.

The Reason Why, by Cecil Woodham Smith. Constable 1953.

The Staff and the Staff College, by A. R. Godwin-Austen. Constable 1927.

1914 AND AFTER

Brasshat, by Basil Collier. Secker and Warburg 1961.

Douglas Haig, The Educated Soldier by John Terraine. Hutchinson 1963.

Field-Marshal Sir Henry Wilson, by Major-General Sir C. E. Callwell. Cassell 1927.

Haig, by Duff Cooper. Faber 1935.

Intrigues of the War, by Major-General Sir Frederick Maurice and the Marquis of Crewe. *Westminster Gazette* 1922.

Journals and Letters of Reginald Viscount Esher. Nicholson and Watson 1938.

Kitchener, by Philip Magnus. Murray 1958.

Men and Power, 1917–1918, by Lord Beaverbrook. Hutchinson 1956.

Mons, by John Terraine. Batsford 1960.

Mutiny at the Curragh, by A. P. Ryan. Macmillan 1956.

Northcliffe, by Reginald Pound and Geoffrey Harmsworth. Cassell 1959.

Politicians and the War, 1914–1916, by Lord Beaverbrook. Oldbourne 1960.

Prelude to Victory, by Major-General Sir E. L. Spears. Cape 1939.

Soldiers and Statesmen, 1914–1918, by Field-Marshal Sir William Robertson. Cassell 1926.

The First World War, 1914–1918. Personal Experiences of Lt-Col. C. à Court Repington. Cassell 1920.

The First World War, by Cyril Falls. Longmans 1960.

The Memoirs of Lord Ismay. Heinemann 1960.

The Official History of the War, 1914–1918, France and Belgium, by Brigadier-General Sir James E. Edmonds. HMSO.

The Private Papers of Douglas Haig, 1914–1919, edited by Robert Blake. Eyre and Spottiswoode 1952.

The Supreme Command, 1914–18, by Lord Hankey. Allen and Unwin 1961.

The Unknown Prime Minister, by Robert Blake. Eyre and Spottiswoode 1955.

The World Crisis, by W. S. Churchill. Revised edition published by Odhams.

Through the Fog of War, by Liddell Hart. Faber 1938.

War Memoirs of David Lloyd George, Nicholson and Watson 1933–6.

GENERAL

Defence by Committee, by F. A. Johnson. OUP 1960.

From Private to Field-Marshal, by Field-Marshal Sir William Robertson. Constable 1921.

Sir William Robertson, by G. A. Leask. Cassell 1917.

The Military Staff, Its History and Development, by J. D. Hittle. Military Service Publishing Company, USA, 1949.

Index

This Index is divided into:

REGIONS (Africa, America, Europe, India, Middle East), subdivided into COUNTRIES, each with dependent subjects (Government, Army, Chief Places, Campaigns, Battles, etc.)

SUPREME WAR COUNCIL

PERSONALITIES

Note: Only the principal references are recorded
Figures in italics refer to illustrations in the text

REGIONS